S0-BFA-418

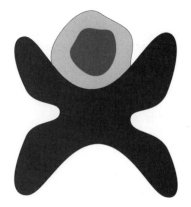

BC Car-Free

Exploring Southwestern British Columbia *Without* a Car

Volumn 1

Vancouver & the Lower Mainland
Vancouver Island & the Gulf Islands
The Sunshine Coast
Stein Valley & Manning Park

By Brian Grover

Copyright ©2001 Brian Grover
All rights reserved. No part of this book may be reproduced in any form by any means without the written permission of the publisher, except by a reviewer, who may quote passages in a review.

Canadian Cataloging In Publication Data
Grover, Brian James 1955-
BC Car-Free: Exploring Southwestern British Columbia *Without* a Car.

ISBN 0-9688018-0-3

1. Outdoor Recreation — British Columbia — Guidebooks
2. Public Transportation — British Columbia — Guidebooks
3. Hiking — British Columbia — Guidebooks
4. Kayaking — British Columbia — Guidebooks
5. Cycling — British Columbia — Guidebooks
6. Whale Watching — British Columbia — Guidebooks
7. River Rafting — British Columbia — Guidebooks
8. Horseback Riding — British Columbia — Guidebooks
9. Cave Exploring — British Columbia — Guidebooks
10. Canoeing — British Columbia — Guidebooks

Published by:

Whisky-Jack Communications
702-1075 Jervis Street
Vancouver, B.C.
V6E 2C2
phone/fax (604) 685-6285
brian@whisky-jack.com
www.whisky-jack.com

Acknowledgements:

Graphics: All sketches used in this book were drawn by Manami Kimura who has published a Vancouver guidebook entitled *Binbo Hima Ari (Vancouver City Edition)* for students and other visitors from Japan. She has also translated *BC Car-Free* into Japanese, publishing the guidebook online as *Binbo Hima Ari (Vancouver Outdoor Edition.)* Advertisers interested in reaching this captive market should visit www.hima-ari.com/adsales.htm. Kimura, a freelance writer, translator, illustrator and web designer, can be reached at mami@hima-ari.com.

Photography: Unless otherwise noted all photos used in this book were taken by the author. Since full colour reproduction throughout would have resulted in a prohibitively expensive publication the original colour Kodachrome or Ektachrome slides were scanned in black and white. To view colour originals go to www.whisky-jack.com and download, gratis, the BC Car-Free Screensaver.

Layout & Design are the fault of the author.

Printing & Binding: Transcontinental Printing (Canada) Ltd

Contents

Map Legend

Amenities

- Campground
- Hut; Shelter
- Toilets
- Water
- Fires Permitted
- Picnic Area
- Covered Picnic Area
- Showers
- Lodge; Hotel; B & B
- Coin Laundry
- RV Camping
- Pay Phone
- Groceries
- Medical Attention
- Police
- Recycling
- Info Centre
- Restaurant
- Coffee Shop
- Ice Cream Parlour
- Pub
- Liquor Store
- Art Studio; Gallery
- Service Station

Natural Features

- Petroglyph; Pictograph
- Wildlife Viewing
- Tower or Platform
- Whale Tours or Habitat
- Deer
- Bears
- Eagles
- Owls
- Viewpoint/Photo Op
- Geological Anomaly

Maritime Features

- Marina; Yacht Basin
- Anchorage
- Dock
- Boat Launch
- Boat Rentals
- Rowing
- Lighthouse
- Hot Spring

Transportation

- Transit
- Bus Station or Stop
- Train Station
- Airport or Float

Recreation

- Hiking
- Steep or Talus
- Rock Climbing
- Cycle Shop or Route
- Mountain Biking
- Horseback Riding
- Stream Ford
- Golf Course
- Tennis Courts
- Roller Blading

Water Recreation

- Swimming; Beach
- Scuba
- Wind Surfing
- Surfing
- Diving
- Kayak Route/Shop
- Canoe Route/Shop
- Rafting Route/Shop
- Fishing or Charters

- Car Rental; Taxi
- Ferry
- 4 Wheel Drive Access

Other Map Symbols

- Mine
- Pier
- Church
- School
- Public Building
- Hostel

- Court; Bank
- Industrial Complex
- Beacon
- Traffic Signal
- Snow or Ice Field
- Significant Tree

- Peak
- Rolling Stones
- ---------------- Hiking Trail
- ———— Main Road; Highway
- ———— Secondary Road
- ———— Side Road

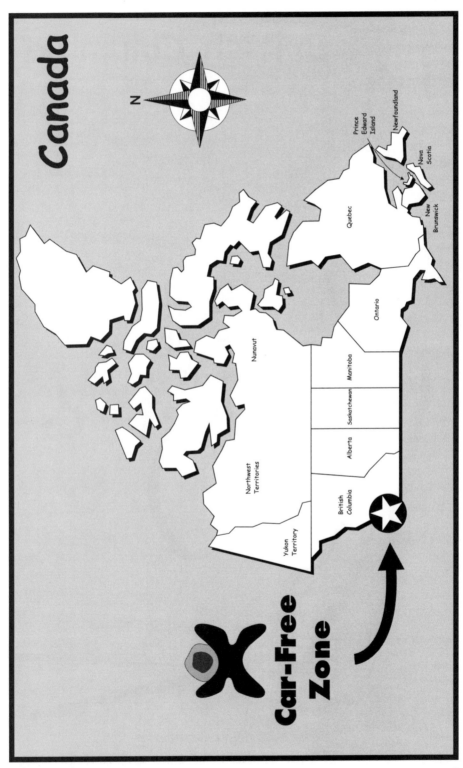

Canada

N

Newfoundland

Prince
Edward
Island

Nova
Scotia

New
Brunswick

Quebec

Ontario

Nunavut

Manitoba

Saskatchewan

Alberta

Northwest
Territories

British
Columbia

Yukon
Territory

Car-Free
Zone

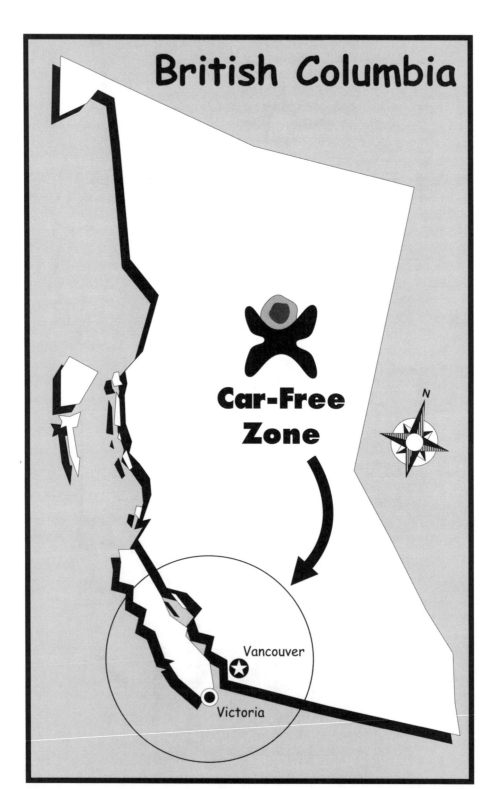

British Columbia

Car-Free Zone

Vancouver

Victoria

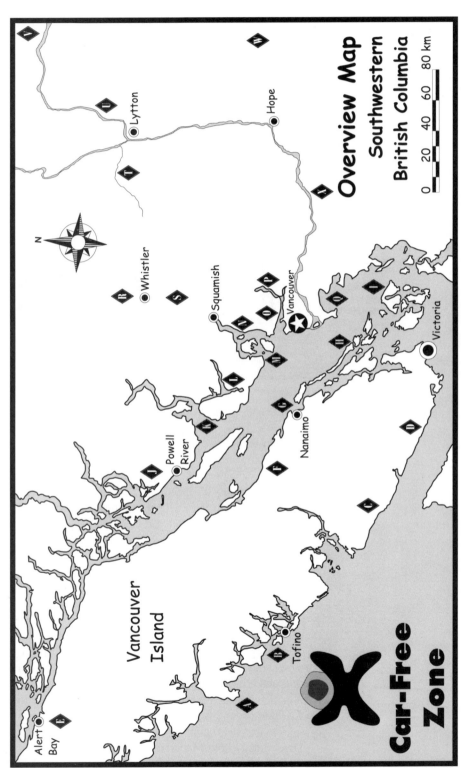

Overview Map
Southwestern
British Columbia

0   20   40   60   80 km

N

Car-Free
Zone

Vancouver
Island

Alert Bay

Tofino

Powell River

Nanaimo

Whistler

Squamish

Vancouver

Victoria

Lytton

Hope

Introduction

After returning from several years living in Japan and France I suddenly realized how dependent I had become on

Totem Town
Gazing ever-seaward, one of the most recent totems to preside over Alert Bay's historic cemetery depicts a wonky-eyed halibut, personified. Whether intent on whale watching, salmon fishing or just looking for a charming backwater Cormorant Island is sure to please. Shutter bugs will find limitless photo ops in the tiny community of Alert Bay.

Nikon F
200 mm Nikkor lens
Kodachrome 200 film

public transportation. Prior to globetrotting I had always owned a car. I also realized how woefully inadequate the transportation alternatives are in Vancouver. Of course a bicycle is fine for running most errands around town. The problem was when I tried to resume my outback-bent life-style. In Japan many trailheads are easily reached by train or bus. In fact, rail companies publish impressive booklets detailing hiking trails and other recreational opportunities along their lines. By contrast, the underlying assumption here in western Canada, is that everybody has a car. When I contacted Maverick Coachlines to find out what kinds of activities were accessible along their routes, a staff member declared that they were not a public transportation company. At BC Rail the reception was icy, as if invaders from a far-flung galaxy were wasting the 1-800 service.

Very few guidebooks even pay lip service to public trans-portation. Even in those situations where heading out on one bus and returning by another one makes perfect sense, most guidebook authors will tell their readers to arrange to have a car left at both ends of the trail instead. Clearly some changes to the traditional mind set are in order.

Determined to avoid the headaches and expense of own-ing a car, I set out to find out just what could be undertaken without one. This book, then, is the fruit that effort.

We live in a time where owning a car is an expense many people just do not want to contend with. More and more people—especially the enlightened young —are choosing, for financial, environmental or lifestyle reasons, to forego the dinosaur. I, for example, can work one day less a week, without a car to support. I have 52 three-day weekends every year!

Yet as a society we routinely oppose the establishment of intelligent public transit alternatives in our neighbourhoods, preferring to send noxious, chronic lung-disease-causing fumes to our neighbours up the Fraser Valley than to make the transition to communal modes of getting around. We complain about road rage, gridlock, crowded highways, unused commuter lanes and then we dash out to buy bigger, better, faster sports-utility vehicles. More than half a million cars hit the tarmac daily in the Lower Mainland. That's more than one car per household. On any statutory holiday expect the local news crews to be out eliciting inevitable comments from travellers stuck in ferry line-ups. Such trite tirades are rendered moot if we consider that every one of those stalled at ferry terminals would have boarded in a timely fashion had they left their dogma at home in the garage. Unlike most of the rest of the world, we are stuck in a time warp dating back to the 1950s.

This book is dedicated to and written for those who do not want to sit around complaining about the high cost of gasoline or auto insurance at dinner parties, do not want to spend their Thursday afternoons getting a brake job, who dislike parking fines, speeding tickets and tow trucks with equal acrimony.

Put another way, for every $100 Canadians spent on retail purchases in 1999, $35 of that was spent on their cars, $8 on home furnishings and electronics, $10 on clothing and $20 on food. Obviously getting rid of the dinosaur can be economically liberating.

Finally this book is a message. There is a growing constituency which believes we already have enough pavement, we just need to start using it better.

Information

When I first started this project of course I did a literature search and was startled to find that many guidebook authors, encouraged by their publishers no doubt, purposefully tried to include as little information as possible. Their motivation was not laziness *per se*, but rather a desire to extend the shelf life of their books. After all a completely empty book would never go out of date. Here is an illuminating quote from one of these books:

> "Descano Bay is the Gabriola terminus for ferries from downtown Nanaimo; schedules are available on BC ferries, or at the Infocentre in Nanaimo. Check telephone directories or inquire at local outlets for information on the air transportation and water taxis to the island, and taxis and bicycle rentals on Gabriola."

Gems like this are sprinkled throughout this particular book which is by no means atypical. The reason we purchase a guidebook is so we can have just that kind of information at our fingertips in advance without riffling through telephone directories or contacting local outlets. While not very useful for the reader such an approach makes great sense to both publisher and author since the book will not require updating very often.

BC Car-Free will require frequent updating. In fact I have no doubt that some parts of the book will be out-of-date by the time it rolls off the press. Phone numbers change, businesses fail, prices go steadily up. But the point of creating this book is to provide a kind of one-stop shopping for information so readers can quickly make plans, get an idea of how much their trip is going to cost, develop a clear picture of the kind of services which will be available, phone ahead for reservations and jump on the bus.

To keep the book as fresh as possible I have created a message board at my internet site. Using the logbook, readers will be able leave a message mentioning which parts are out of date or inaccurate, update phone numbers, prices and so on which may have changed and add information which I may have missed or dismissed. Readers should habitually refer to this site, **www.whisky-jack.com/postings_frm.htm**, before following this book into the hinterland.

The other cardinal sin many guide book writers fall heir to is what I called the turn-left-at-the-next-sword-fern syndrome. Too often writers over-describe the route creating not a clear picture but confusion in the reader's mind. The truth of the matter is most people use a guide book to get to the trailhead and then just follow the dotted line. Nobody looks for the next sword fern from which to turn left. I must admit that I'm somewhat guilty of this sin too but I have tried to minimize this tendancy. I give you everything you need to get to the trailhead and quickly walk you through a route which suited me at the time. When it comes to multi-day backpacking or kayaking or canoeing trips then it becomes necessary to make decisions about route, camping and so on that fit your schedule.

Starting Point

This book assumes that you will be starting your backcountry trip from downtown Vancouver. Of course your personal situation may vary somewhat but transportation routes as described emanate from the downtown core.

Accommodations

Budget accommodation options such as tenting, hostelling, travellers inns and so on have been included in the information table following each section when available. Likewise, accommodation networks or hotlines have also been included but individual B & Bs, hotels and the like have only been included where the establishment may have something of additional interest to the recreating public such as kayak or bicycle rentals, horseback riding or whale watching tours.

An exhaustive survey of available accommodations is in itself a book and that book is readily available free of charge at tourist information centres throughout British Columbia. At the Vancouver Travel Infocentre ask for the *British Columbia Accommodation Guide* by name. Being expensive, the *Accommodation Guide* is kept behind the counter and given out only to those who ask for it. While you are at it ask for the *Outdoor & Adventure Guide* which lists outdoor recreation opportunities throughout the province. The *Road Map and Parks Guide* used to be free, then the price popped up

to a nominal loonie. Governments know a good thing when they see it however and soon enough the price inflated again. The information is good and certainly well worth the current price of $3 even though the paper used is cheap and tears easily. Besides roads, the maps contain detailed information about provincial parks.

Gnarly Giant
The world's oldest yellow cedar. Gunpowder was being invented by the Chinese and Charlemagne was being crowned Holy Roman Emperor at about the same time as this cypress set down roots atop what we now call Cypress Provincial Park.

Nikon F
28 mm Nikkor lens
Tri-X Pan 400 ISO film

Out-of-towners can call 1-800-663-6000 from anywhere in North America to have these guides sent to them. From the Lower Mainland area call (604) 663-6000. From overseas direct dial (250) 387-1642. Those in the United Kingdom can call (0891) 715-000 or FAX (0171) 389-1149 while Germans should call 06181-45178 or Fax 06181-497558.

Reservations are allowed in some but not all campgrounds operated by BC Parks. To make reservations call 1-800-689-9025 unless calling from the Lower Mainland. Vancouverites should dial (604) 689-9025 instead or try the internet at *www.discovercamping.com*. The reservation service is available from March 1 to September 15 each year and bookings can be made up to 3 months in advance. Non-reservation enquiries can be directed at BC Parks staff in Victoria at (250) 387-4550.

To book B & B accommodations anywhere in the province contact:

Western Canada Bed and Breakfast Innkeepers Association; (604) 255-9199; P.O. Box 74534, 2803 West 4th Ave., Vancouver, B.C.

Visitors to Vancouver may find a bed to snuggle into from amongst the following budget-priced accommodations. Keep in mind that some downtown eastside "hostels" are in operation mainly to allow the owners to keep their lucrative pub licenses in compliance with BC's draconian liquor laws.

Hostelling International - Vancouver Downtown
1114 Burnaby Street, Vancouver BC V6E 1P1; 1-888-203-4302; (604) 684-4565 Fax: (604) 684-4540; van-downtown@hihostels.bc.ca

YWCA of Vancouver
733 Beatty Street, Vancouver, BC, Canada V6B 2M4; 1-800-663-1424; (604) 895-5830; Fax (604) 681-2550; hotel@ywcavan.org

Hostelling International - Vancouver Jericho Beach
1515 Discovery Street, Vancouver BC V6R 4K5; 1-888-203-4303; (604) 224-3208 Fax: (604) 224-4852; van-jericho@hihostels.bc.ca. Though inconveniently situated, the hostel operates a shuttle service to downtown Vancouver

Vincent's Backpackers Hostel
927 Main Street, Vancouver, BC V6A 2V3 (604) 682-2441 Close to SkyTrain.

New Backpackers Hostel 347 West Pender Street, Vancouver BC (604) 688-0112

Harbourfront Hostel 209 Heatley Ave, Vancouver, B.C. (604) 254-0733; (604) 435-0447 FAX Close to Chinatown, Gastown and SkyTrain; Pick up at airport, train or bus depot.

Welcome Hostel 406 Union Street, Vancouver, B.C. V6A 2B2 Phone/Fax (604) 251-8050; Pager: (604) 735-3183

Dale's Hospitality Home 5535 Marine Drive, West Vancouver, BC V7W 2R4, (604) 921-6628; 5 minutes from Horseshoe Bay ferry.

Monika's Hospitality Home 6196 Elm Street, Vancouver, B.C. V6N 1B1 ph/fax: (604) 261- 7824 Guest house catering to international students.

Rose Anne's Hospitality Home 6160 Canun Place, Richmond, BC V7C 2N2 (604) 274-1038; 10 minutes

Graffiti Tree
In 1993 MD and LG scraped bark off nearly 50% of the circumference of this subalpine ancient to scribble some charmed runes. What deep insight moved them to such an effort? "To hope is to recognize the possibility," they wrote, a trite cliché that probably killed the tree.

Nikon F
28 mm Nikkor lens
Ektachrome 100 ISO film.

from airport by bus.

Globetrotters Inn 170 West Esplanade, North Vancouver, BC V7M 1A3; (604) 988-2082; fax (604) 988-4386

Paul's Guest House 345 West 14th Ave., Vancouver, BC V5Y 1X3 (604) 872-4753

The Cambie International Hostel 300 Cambie St., Vancouver, BC;
(604)684-6466; (604)687-5618 FAX; Doubles and dorms; Free hot breakfast

Global Village Backpackers 1018 Granville St, Vancouver, BC; (604) 682-8226; (604) 682-8240 FAX; Four beds per room.

Maps

The maps in this book contained a wealth of information about services, routes and points of interest but are far too small for including detailed topographical information as well. The main branch of the **Vancouver Public Library** at the corner of Robson and Homer Streets has an excellent if somewhat disorganized collection of maps and maritime charts on the sixth floor.

For each trip I have included the name and number of the appropriate topographical map or nautical chart which you are advised to rely on in the field. To quickly access other titles in the Geological Survey of Canada 1:50,000 series of topographical maps ask the librarian for a copy of the *Canadian Gazette* which cross references place names throughout the nation with map number.

Library patrons can use a gigantic map photocopier for two bucks a pop. Full-colour maps are nice if you can afford them but for sports like cycle touring or back-packing they tend to be too bulky and heavy. Photocopies on the other hand use thinner paper and can be quickly cut down to size. Some people like to laminate their maps with clear Mac-Tac vinyl or purchase fancy map covers but I usually just use the largest zip lock bag I can find to protect them. No matter what you do they just get soggy anyway here on the coast.

International Travel Maps & Books at 345 West Broadway [(604) 879-3621] or downtown at 552 Seymour [(604) 687-3320] has government topographic maps and charts as well as a selection of waterproof, tear proof recreation maps printed on plas-tic. Find them on the net at *www.itmb.com*.

Metric

Measurements in this book are entirely in metric. I have made no attempt to cater to those still stuck in a time warp with the archaic English measurement system. The following may help however translate some of the most common measurements for you.

- Two and a half [2.54 actually] centimetres will get you an inch but if given an inch you'll probably be inclined to take 1.6 km.
- A metre is about 3 feet [3.2 to be exact.]
- A kilometre is very roughly half a mile or precisely: km x .62 = mile
- To convert Celsius on the fly double it and add 30. If hiking with a Dick Tracy watch complete with built-in super computer try this: 9/5 x Celsius + 32 = Fahrenheit.
- Two wrongs don't make a right but 2 pounds do make a kilogram, nearly. 2.2 does a better job.
- If you drink a litre of water from a stagnant pond then you will be up by a US quart but very, very sick.

Water

All the guide books tell you to boil, filter and chemically treat all water and I will too just to cover my butt in the event of liability issues. I always disregard this good

advice, drinking directly from the stream, and thus far have never been sick. If you choose to enjoy the taste of unadulterated stream water too then you did so of your own volition. If the water made you sick then it's your fault and not the fault of this book or the bear which crapped upstream.

Whatever your choice is get your water from clear run-

Mystery Photo
This is the very last side bar I have to write before putting this project to bed and I can't for the life of me remember when I took this photo. The grey matter seems to have become soft and spongy and steadfastly refuses to divulge the whereabouts of this scene. Needless to say it's driving me crazy. Recognize that peak? Drop into my website at *www.whisky-jack.com* to jog my memory with your best guess. The winner gets to feel smug for upwards of thirty seconds while I get my side bar and get my sanity back.

Nikon F
50 mm Nikkor lens
Tri-X Pan 400 ISO film

ning brooks not from lakes or ponds. Water from snow pack is better than water from glaciers. The latter contains too much clay. Carry lots of water, at least 40 litres, whenever kayaking as good water can be surprisingly hard to find on the *wet* coast of Canada. A green algae bloom in tide pools or wet patches trickling across a beach does not mean something horrible died in the water. It just means the water is brackish. Freshwater will be found upstream.

If your source of water is at a popular camping spot then go upstream away from the camp to get your drinking water. Take great pains to clean yourself and your dishes or clothing well away from the bank of any water body or the water will become polluted. Leftover food does not belong in the water. If fires are allowed and it is safe to do so, burn it. Try to avoid using soaps or detergents but when you must only use the biodegradable kind available from outdoor stores.

Red Tide

Warm weather causes toxic plankton to bloom all over the coast of British Columbia whether a month has an "R" in it or not. If you are not absolutely sure that the shellfish you are about to eat is safe then don't eat it. Bivalve molluscs like oysters, clams and mussels are all susceptible to red tide. Butter clams are the very worst, retaining toxins for long periods of time. Cooking does not alter the toxicity of these filter feeders in any way.

If you are going to an area where shellfish harvesting might be possible then make it a habit to call the federal government's **Red Tide Hotline [604-666-2828]** for an up-to-date report on shellfish harvesting in the area. As with most government services this one too is needlessly confusing. You must know the number of the "management area" you're going to be in but of course this number is not available over the telephone. It is available on the Internet but is incredibly difficult to find with a search engine. You can find it by going to **www.pac.dfo-mpo.gc.ca/ops/fm/areas/ areamap.htm.** Of course, the actual red tide closures are not posted at the department of fisheries Internet site. You have to go back to the phone and work your way through the seemingly endless layers of the voice messaging system. Where appropriate, I have included Fisheries Management Area numbers in the information table following each activity description.

Fishing Licenses

Licenses are required for fishing in fresh or saltwater, crabbing, or shellfish harvesting. In downtown Vancouver fishing licenses can be purchased at **The Bay** department-store, sports section (on the corner of Granville and Georgia) or at the **Army and Navy** department store in the combat zone between Gastown and Chinatown. Outside of the city most sporting goods shops sell licenses. Proceeds go towards management of Canada's fisheries resources. The fines for fishing without a license, over-harvesting or disregarding size limits are very hefty and most Canadians support even more egregious enforcement.

Tides and Currents

Tidal charts can be purchased at most marinas or sporting goods shops. The main branch of the **Vancouver Public Library Science Section** has copies behind the desk, just ask the librarian.

An even better solution is to download Ed Wallner's excellent if somewhat prehistoric DOS-based tide and current program. I have posted a copy of the shareware program called *Tides* on my website at *www.whisky-jack.com/tides.htm.* Included are supplementary data for the British Columbia coast that was compiled by Paul Getman of Coal Harbour, BC from data constants published by the Canadian Hydrographic Service. Though primitive graphing capabilities are included in *Tides*, try printing the data to file then loading it into a spreadsheet graphing module to create an easy to read curve for kayaking, fishing or just hanging around the "salt chuck." Practical use in the field has shown *Tides* to be extremely accurate with far more tidal stations than found in government-published tidal charts. The download size is just 219 KB. Wasn't DOS wonderful?

A new, freeware, or rather careware, Windows-based tide and current prediction program became available at the cusp of the new millennium. Also called *Tides*, the program, written by Washington state math and sailing nut Paul Lutus, looks good and

appears to work well though I have yet to put my life on the line with it. Because it is careware, you have to be nice to people if you want to use it. In addition to the tide stations included in the Windows-flavoured *Tides,* a huge, import-able database of additional data sets for the BC coast is also included. For me at least, generating then exporting data to

Sudden Surprise
The sun peeks out again, sheepishly, after delivering a surprise black squall. Never underestimate what the weather can deliver. This time, while kayaking in Desolation Sound, just ten minutes warning was enough time to set up the tent and stow the gear before the wall of water hit. Station Island in the distance is the tidal midpoint of Georgia Strait.

Nikon F
135 mm Nikkor lens
Kodachrome 64 ISO film

MS Excel seems to produce a more usable tide graph. A link to the author's website is included from my own. Download size: 1.3 MB.

Night Sky

Also on my website [*www.whisky-jack.com/meteor.htm*] you'll find a list of upcoming astronomical phenomena that could make sleeping under the stars an extra delight. While satellites and space junk whiz by overhead on any night of the year, other phenomena such as meteor showers, lunar and solar eclipses follow a predictable pattern. Keep in mind that by planning your trip around the new moon you can ensure that the sky is dark enough to fully appreciate what the heavens have to offer.

Outdoor Equipment

By far the best place in Vancouver to buy new outdoor equipment is the member-owned **Mountain Equipment Co-op** [130 West Broadway.] Staff are extremely well-informed, prices are very fair and quality is excellent. Lifetime memberships cost a mere $5. Stores like the Army and Navy or 3

Lording It Over Overlord
The view doesn't get any better from up on top of Panorama Ridge. Overlord Glacier dominates the background.

Nikon F
28 mm Nikkor lens
Kodachrome 64 ISO film

Vets only sell outdoor trash that can cause real problems in the field. As a bonus, staff at the latter one will yell at you if you walk into the store with a knapsack.

MEC also has a gigantic notice board for those interested in picking up their equipment second hand. **The Buy & Sell** classified ad newspaper, also available online at *www.buysell.com*, is another good source of bargains as well. For many newbies the outdoor lifestyle becomes a consumer experience. They buy all the name brand gear, head out into the outback, despise it, then, after a hiatus of several years, sell off their equipment at garage sale prices. Look for these guys.

Renting is always a possibility but it does tend to be expensive, especially if you intend to take up the great outdoors as a lifestyle. Rental shops seem to find it difficult to survive in Vancouver. About the only one that seems to be able to make it in the local market is associated with the outdoor club at the University of British Columbia. Though inconveniently situated for most of us [6000 Student Union Boulevard, UBC; 604-822-1684] **UBC Outdoor Equipment Rentals** nonetheless has the goods if you need them.

Co-operative Auto Network

BC Car-Free provides enough information to keep you tramping, splashing, clomping and whizzing about the province for several years at least. Public transportation however is still in its infancy in BC and many more outdoor delights cannot be readily reached without a car. In Vancouver there exists a middle ground between outright car ownership and high-priced car rentals. The Co-operative Auto Network was formed to empower members to make a positive environmental choice without sacrificing mobility. Based on a European model, CAN is a car sharing co-op. Much like in a credit union, members purchase shares in the co-op and have access to more than 30 cars strategically placed around the lower mainland. CAN also has vehicles in Nanaimo and Tofino on Vancouver Island and members can access vehicles belonging to a similar co-op in Victoria.

The share price of $500 is hefty but refundable. A nominal membership fee of $20 includes a credit check and all applicants must provide verification of their safe driving record. Rentals cost just $15 per day or $1.50 per hour, whichever is less, plus a kilometre charge of between 15 to 30 cents per kilometre depending on monthly usage. The mileage charge includes the price of gasoline. There is a monthly charge of $10 for administration. This fee also varies depending on usage.

Just like a rental car company members can call, book a car, truck or minivan then go pick it up. Depending on where you reside, the nearest car may be just a block or two away. Vancouver's West End and Kitsilano areas in particular are well-covered.

The Co-operative Auto Network is located at #209-470 Granville Street in Vancouver. Call for details at (604) 685-1393. Find them online at *www.cooperativeauto.ne*t.

Outdoor Clubs

New in town? Looking to widen your circle and expand your horizons? Joining an outdoor club could be the answer. Clubs catering to a wide range of interests, abilities and ages exist though tracking down just the right one could be a bit tough on your own. Fortunately organizations exist to keep track of the comings and goings of the various local clubs

Outdoor Recreation Council of BC; An umbrella organization for every imaginable outdoor sport in the province. Check the listings below for information on mainstream activities. To find clubs devoted to other more specialized activities such as fishing, snowmobiling, orienteering and so on contact ORC directly. 334-1367 West Broadway; Vancouver, BC; V6H 4A9; (604) 737-3058; FAX (604) 737-3666; www.orcbc.bc.ca; orc@intergate.bc.ca

Federation of Mountain Clubs of BC; Hiking Club Information; 47 West Broadway; Vancouver, BC; (604) 878-7007; FAX (604) 876-7047; fmcbc@mountainclubs.bc.ca; www.mountainclubs.bc.ca

Cycling BC; Cycling Club Information; 332-1367 West Broadway; Vancouver, BC V6H 4A9; (604) 737-3034; FAX (604) 738-7175; office@cycling.bc.ca; www.cycling.bc.ca

Horse Council of BC; Horse Riding Club Information; 2669 Deacon Street; Abbotsford, BC V2T 6H3; (604)504-0245; 1-800-345-8055; FAX (604) 504-0248; hcbc@uniserve.com; www.horsecouncilbc.com

Federation of BC Naturalists; Birding and Wildlife Watching Information; 425-1367 West Broadway; Vancouver, BC V6H 4A9; (604) 737-3057; (604) 738-7175; fbcn@intergate.bc.ca; members.xoom.com/fbcn

BC Speleological Federation; Caving Club Information; PO Box 8124; Station Central Post Office; Victoria, BC V8W 3R8; (250) 923-1311; FAX (250) 923-6211; dps@istar.ca

Sea Kayak Association of BC; Kayak Club Information; PO Box 751 Postal Station A; Vancouver, BC V6C 2N6; (604) 228-1450; gramon@dowco.com

Recreational Canoeing Association of BC; Canoeing Club Information; 4782 Fernglen Drive; Burnaby, BC V5G 3V7; (604) 437-1140; rcabc@bc.sympatico.ca; www3.bc.sympatico.ca/canoebc

Advertising Opportunity

BC Car-Free has been published in Japanese as well as English. Called *Binbo Hima Ari: Vancouver Outdoor Edition*, the Japanese version is published, free of charge, on the Internet. Companies eager to reach the 250,000 Japanese visitors who pass through Western Canada each year are invited to help support this venture through advertising sponsorship. Outdoor equipment retailers, B & B or resort owners and eco-tourism companies specializing in such activities as river rafting, whale watching, sea kayaking, fishing or backpacking will find this to be an ideal opportunity to target this lucrative market segment.
Check Japanese edition out at *www.hima-ari.com/outdoor/outdoor.htm.*

Day Hiking

More people get into trouble when day hiking than backpacking, kayaking or any other activity. People head out with the intention of doing a quick hike then returning to the city. They travel light but by doing so find themselves ill-equipped to handle emergency situations when they arise. When it comes to hiking it seems that a Visa card is the one thing that you *can* leave home without. The following is a list of essentials which no hiker should ever forget.

Checklist

☐ **Flashlight with fresh batteries.** Can be used as a signal at night as well as a source of light.

☐ **Whistle.** A whistle can be used to contact rescuers or other hikers across a distant valley even in thick forest cover. Three whistle blasts or three of anything for that matter, including shotgun blasts, signal fires or logs in a triangular pattern, is an international distress signal.

☐ **Waterproof matches AND lighter.** A lighter is useless when wet. Keep matches and lighter in a waterproof film container.

☐ **Firestarter or candle** can be very helpful getting the fires started during inclement weather. Usually small, dry twigs can be found close to the trunk of small trees. Ostensibly rotten red cedar logs often contain dry, pitch impregnated wood just under the moss and decay. Use a pocketknife to shave thin strips of wood which can be used as firestarter.

☐ **Pocketknife.** The uses are manifold.

☐ A **large orange plastic bag** can be used as a waterproof sleeping bag and signal flag.

☐ **Water and food**. A selection of granola bars, energy bars and the like will go a long way towards reducing the misery of a couple nights in the bush.

☐ **Extra clothes** including a wool sweater, long pants but not jeans, waterproof shell with hood or hat. Wool stays warm when wet. Cotton including denim robs the body of heat when wet. Breathable fabrics like gortex are far superior to just a plastic or nylon windbreaker and are priced accordingly. Hypothermia is the enemy.

☐ **First aid kit** *and* **first aid course**, not in that order.

☐ **Compass, topographical map** and the skills to use them.

☐ **Common sense.**

Lighthouse Park

Level: Easy; A Variety of Short Trails
Elevation: Negligible   **Season**: Year Round

Burning Bright
Beams on high for 90 years, the Point Atkinson Lighthouse still cuts a dashing figure in the dark, guiding mariners safely into Canada's busiest port.

Nikon F
135 mm Nikkor lens
Kodachrome 64 ISO film

Access: Take the **#250 Horseshoe Bay** bus as far as aptly named Beacon Lane. [For details on **Getting to Horseshoe Bay** see page 320] Outbound buses from Vancouver, should pass a fire station and small shopping plaza on the right side of the road just before the Lighthouse Park site. If new to the area ask the driver to call out the stop. Do not take the **#257 Horseshoe Bay Express** bus.

Lighthouse Park is not a hike in the strictest sense. Rather it is a network of short, interconnected forest paths that provide enough hiking to last for hours. Getting there is easy and takes just 40 minutes on a good day. After getting off the bus carefully cross busy Marine Drive and follow the lane down to the end. Before plunging into the forest on one of the many trails grab a brochure entitled "Self-Guiding Trail" at the information signboard. Produced by the District of West Vancouver, this unpretentious pamphlet provides an excellent introduction to coastal rainforest flora. The trail it documents starts just beyond the gate and leads down to Starboat Cove. Included are seven points of interest for would-be naturalists.

The centerpiece of the park is, of course, the Point Atkinson Lighthouse. This structure was built in 1912 though the park dates to 1881 when the Government of Canada set aside 73 hectares of forest to act as a dark backdrop to the original tower. The light and foghorn are still important navigational aids for mariners plying the coastal waters around Vancouver.

Out of the practical concerns for illumination the government inadvertently set aside

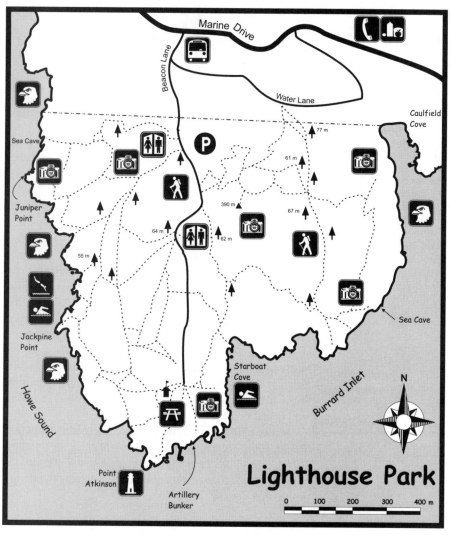

the lower mainland's largest single collection of ancient trees. While the entire North Shore was being systematically denuded at the beginning of the 20th century, the lofty ancients of Lighthouse Park continued to thrive relatively unmolested as they had for century upon century. Randy Stoltmann in his definitive *Hiking Guide to the Big Trees of*

Snapshot

Photographing ancient big trees can be a challenge. This subject is usually too big to fit in a frame and too dark or contrasty for a decent available-light exposure. If equipped with a flash or a stray patch of sunlight avails itself try using your hiking partners for juxtaposition. Move in for a head-and-shoulders shot, contrasting the smooth skin of the human subjects with the rough and ragged bark of the tree.

Douglas fir has the most dramatically fissured bark on the west coast. When the tree is situated in more open terrain lay down near the base of the tree and shoot up. To add human subjects have them bend over, peering down into the field of view to avoid the old "gigantic nostrils" shot. With a wide-angle the perspective of the tree will soar away into infinity while the texture of the bark in the foreground should remain crystal clear. Expect some distortion of your human subjects. The shot right was taken at Gator Gardens in Alert Bay, the dark swamp water acting as a mirror capturing both the stunted skunk cabbage and the ancient cedar snags soaring overhead.

Nikon F
28 mm Nikkor lens
Kodachrome 200 ISO film

Southwestern British Columbia has identified a dozen notable groves or single trees, primarily Douglas fir, in the park. Most extend well over 60 metres high and some boast bark that is more than 30 cm thick.

Near the water's edge look for bald eagles and their nests in the 400-year-old Douglas fir and cedar trees. These ancient evergreens provide the perfect vantage for bald eagles with an eye for salmon supper.

While exploring this tiny rain forest jewel you'll encounter high rocky bluffs overlooking the sea. On one of these basalt outcroppings you'll notice a large cement bunker with rusty doors. This former gun emplacement was built during World War II in preparation for the Japanese attack which never came. Though of little strategic importance now, the bluffs of Lighthouse Park provide a panorama extending from Lion's Gate Bridge and Stanley Park to the east through Spanish Banks and Point Grey to the south and on to Bowen Island in the west.

Just one fifth the size of Vancouver's world-renowned Stanley Park, Lighthouse Park is an ideal place for a picnic, a stroll or just a quiet moment to breathe in the salt air.

Return to Vancouver by retracing your steps in the opposite direction. 🐾

Capilano Canyon

Level: Moderate   **Distance:** 5.9 km   **Time:** 3 hours

Elevation: 120 m   **Season:** Year Round   **Map:** Unnecessary

Access: From downtown Vancouver during peak hours Monday through Saturday hop on the **#246 Lonsdale Quay via Highland** bus at any of the stops along West Georgia Street. Stay on the bus until the corner of Capilano Road and Woods Drive in North Vancouver. Do not get off at the corner of Capilano Road and Marine Drive. The driver will usually call out the best place to transfer to the **#236 Grouse Mountain** bus. Capilano Heights Chinese Resturant on the right side is your cue to get off the #236 at the corner of Clements Road. Cleveland Dam is directly across the street.

During non-peak hours the #246 bus does not service downtown Vancouver. Take the **#240 15th Street** bus to the corner of Marine Drive and Capilano Road instead where you can catch the **#246 Lonsdale Quay via Highland** bus up Capilano Road. Transfer to the #236 as above.

For an alternate route take **SeaBus** to Lonsdale Quay in North Vancouver and board the **#236 Grouse Mountain** bus. No transfers will be necessary to reach the trailhead described above.

There's Capilano Canyon, the cheesy tourist trap with the suspension bridge, and then there's Capilano Canyon as the locals know it. Many locals prefer walking or running the length of the river, exploring the gorge, the surrounding rain forest and the boulder bars further downstream.

This hike starts at Cleveland Dam and follows the river downstream to its mouth. For a better workout undertake the route as described in reverse.

The top of Cleveland Dam is directly across the road from the bus stop. Acrophobics especially have got to check out the spillway. Built in 1954, the dam has created 5.6 kilometre-long Capilano Lake. The reservoir now supplies 40 per cent of the Lower Mainland's drinking water. Logging in the watershed, and the resulting erosion, is often blamed for Vancouver's cloudy water.

Doubling back, on the east to side of the dam, you'll find a staircase leading down to a viewpoint offering excellent views of the spillway and the gorge below. Continue downstream on Palisades Trail to the salmon hatchery where a saga unfolds from midsummer to fall every year. [See page 249.]

As Randy Stoltmann points out in his fabulously original book *"Hiking Guide to the Big Trees of Southwestern BC,"* the parking lot of the hatchery holds natural treasures too including one of the biggest Douglas firs in the lower mainland. This one weighs in at 5.7 metres around and 77 metres tall. At the edge of the canyon in front of the tour bus turnaround a record-sized Pacific yew will also be found. In fact, four out of the province's five biggest yews are in Capilano Regional Park. Incidentally, yew, which is generally small and uncommon, contains a powerful anticancer agent called taxol. Though hitherto considered a junk species by the forest industry the Pacific yew is now considered a threatened one in some circles. Efforts to synthesize this late-stage treatment for ovarian, breast and a variety of other cancers have thus far proved unsuccessful adding further pressure to this slow-growing conifer. Taxol is rendered from the bark of the Pacific yew with three century-old trees required to extract a single treatment.

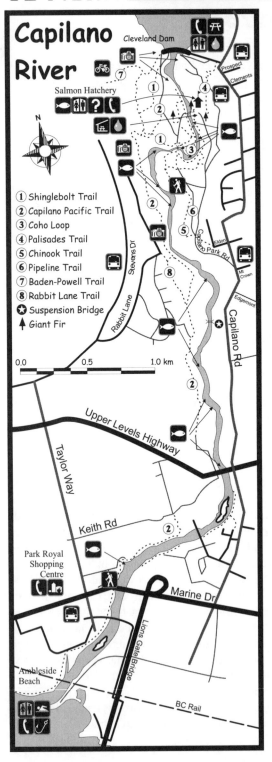

Capilano River

Cleveland Dam

Salmon Hatchery

1. Shinglebolt Trail
2. Capilano Pacific Trail
3. Coho Loop
4. Palisades Trail
5. Chinook Trail
6. Pipeline Trail
7. Baden-Powell Trail
8. Rabbit Lane Trail
⭐ Suspension Bridge
🔺 Giant Fir

0.0   0.5   1.0 km

Prospect
Clements
Stevens Dr
Capilano Park Rd
Eldon
Mt Crown
Edgemont
Capilano Rd
Rabbit Lane
Upper Levels Highway
Taylor Way
Keith Rd
Park Royal Shopping Centre
Marine Dr
Lions Gate Bridge
Ambleside Beach
BC Rail

Cross the bridge just below the hatchery and turn right. A brief walk leads upstream to the Second Canyon Viewpoint while a side trail will reveal two ancient firs. A few steps further on the aptly-named Grandpa Capilano boasts a 2.4 metre girth. Imagine, this 61 metre monster was just a sprout when Columbus was blundering into the New World half a millennium ago.

Next retrace your steps downstream following Coho Loop as far as the pipe-bridge for another great look at the canyon. Our route remains on the west side however so begin climbing Shinglebolt Trail until you reach Capilano Pacific Trail. There will be no need to change trails from this point forward. Capilano Pacific will soon take you to a viewpoint of the lower canyon, past the barbed wire enclosure of Capilano Suspension Bridge and on to Keith Road for a 20-minute detour under the Upper Levels Highway. Turn left on Village Walk #3 to regain the trail at the river's edge. After passing under the bridge at Marine Drive you can amble down to Ambleside Park where the Capilano River empties into Burrard Inlet. A sure sign that the salmon are running is the mob of fisherman silhouetted against the sewage treatment plant below the railroad tracks. Alternately, walk west to Park Royal Shopping Centre to pick up a bus bound for downtown. From the south side of Marine Drive the #250 Vancouver bus or any bus with the numbers #251 #252 #253 or #254 during peak hours will do the job. 🐾

Blisters & Footcare

by Steve Grover

Boots have to fit well. When buying new boots try on several brands, looking for a fit that is comfortable and appropriate for the type of hiking intended. Feel inside for thick seams or irregularities that will rub against your foot.

If boots are too loose or too tight they will cause problems as your foot moves or swells during the hike. Boots should be big enough to accommodate an insole and two pairs of socks.

A steep uphill grade will cause heel movement in the boot while a downhill grade will cause pressure on the toes. Both actions can cause blisters.

Good hiking boots will have a locking cleat by the ankle to allow for tight lacing in one part of the boot and flexibility in the other. For uphills the upper part should be tight. The toe end of bootlaces should be tight to prevent slippage on downgrades.

New boots have to be broken in before you start a big trip. Wear them about town for progressively longer periods each day until they feel comfortable for the whole day. Starting a major hike with brand new boots could ruin not only your trip, but that of your companions.

Sock It To 'Em

Socks should be clean and dry. Sand or debris in socks will rub against the foot causing blisters. Wet socks make skin soft and prone to blisters. Hikers should wear a clean pair of socks every day on the trail. That means either bringing enough to last on long trips or washing and drying socks every few days. Inner socks should be ultra-thin and made of polypropolene, a fabric which wicks moisture away from the feet. Outer socks should be moderately thick and be made of wool which insulates even when wet.

At the end of a day's hiking it is a good idea to don a pair of light camp shoes to give feet a rest and boots a chance to dry out.

Blisters can be prevented by protecting tender spots or pressure points with *Dr. Scholl's Moleskin*, slippery adhesive tape or adhesive foam padding. Application of tincture of benzoin (Friar's Balsam) to the skin will ensure that adhesive protection will not work loose even under wet conditions. Loose or bunched up coverings can add to problems.

When a hot spot or blister has already formed, Friar's Balsam or adhesive protection should not come into direct contact with the damaged skin. Rather the blister should be allowed to poke through a "doughnut" cut in moleskin to alleviate pressure. Once enough layers are built up, the doughnut hole should be covered with adhesive or a final layer of moleskin for protection.

Prevention The Key

Water blisters, once formed, should not be drained as they will then be open sores susceptible to infection. If blisters break the area must be kept clean and the sterile dressing covering the wound must be changed daily.

Once a blister forms, treatment and protection of the dressing becomes more complicated. Prevention should always be the goal.

Bowen Island

Access: For details on getting to Bowen Island see **Getting to Horseshoe Bay** on page 320. Ferry schedule information is located in the side-bar to the left. In addition to hourly service by BC Ferries, Bowen Island is also serviced by water taxi. Call Cormorant Marine at (604) 947 - 2243 or (604) 250 - 2630. For those who are in a hurry to relax contact Bowen Taxi at (604) 947-0000.

Visiting Bowen Island is always a treat. This funky little community on the edge of West Vancouver is not a suburb nor is it a rural backwater like many of the Gulf Islands. Just 3,000 full time residents call this 5260-hectare rock home. In addition to kayaking opportunities which are detailed on page 262, Bowen Island offers three pleasant hikes. All start from the ferry terminal and all are accessible most of the year.

If lucky, you'll miss a ferry or two after the hike and — *shucks!* — have to do some carbo-loading in the Bowen Island Neighbourhood Pub [(604) 947-2782.] Cappuccino, ice cream and the usual post-hike rewards are also available from the cluster of shops just above the ferry landing.

Bowen Island

Bowen Island (Snug Cove) to
West Vancouver (Horseshoe Bay)
Crossing Time: 20 minutes

Leave Bowen Island	Leave Horseshoe Bay
5:45 am[2]	6:05 am
6:35 am	7:00 am
7:35 am	8:00 am[1]
8:30 am[1]	8:55 am[3]
9:25 am	9:50 am
10:50 am	11:15 am
11:40 am	12:05 pm
12:30 pm	2:30 pm
3:00 pm[2]	3:30 pm
3:55 pm[3]	4:25 pm
4:50 pm	5:25 pm
5:50 pm	6:25 pm
7:20 pm	7:45 pm
8:10 pm	8:35 pm
9:00 pm	9:25 pm
9:45 pm	

[1] Daily except Sundays.
[2] Daily except Sundays & Holidays.
[3] Wednesday sailings will be replaced by Dangerous Cargo sailings. No passengers.

Dorman Point Trail

Level: Easy
Time: $1\frac{1}{2}$ hr
Map: 92 G/6

Distance: 4 km
Elevation Change: 50 m
Season: Year Round

Aim for the Snug Cove Picnic Area at the head of the bay upon reaching shore. Access is just up Government Road on the left, behind a number of small shops. Dorman Point Trail continues past the picnic tables leading steeply up to a rocky bluff just 2 km away. Whytecliffe Park directly across on the mainland and the University Endowment Lands in the distance should be visible when weather conditions allow.

Return the same way you came or take Robinson Road and Dorman Road to add some variation to the walk. 🐾

Killarney Lake

Level: Easy   **Distance:** 8 km   **Time:** 2½ hr

Elevation Change: Negligible   **Map:** 92 G/6   **Season:** Year Round

After disembarking from the ferry go straight up Government Road to Gardena Drive on the right. The historic Union Steamship Company Store here, dating from 1924, now houses government offices. The mock Tudor structure was once the centre-piece of a private resort boasting campgrounds, 180 cottages and a dance pavilion capable of accommodating more than 800 revellers. The concept of "camping" has certainly changed since the "good old days."

The entrance to Crippen Regional Park is just beyond the store. Follow Maple Trail, to the left of the park entrance, but first you may wish to explore the Lagoon or the Causeway. The latter provides picture-perfect views of the mountains above Howe Sound on clear day.

After a few minutes Maple Trail will merge into the Hatchery Trail from which both Bridal Veil Falls and a complex network of fish ladders can be seen. Look for spawning coho salmon in the creek every October and November.

Cross Millers Landing Road to continue through forest along the Hatchery Trail or turn right, following the road a couple hundred metres to find the start of the Killarney Creek Trail. Trails are well-marked throughout Crippen Regional Park. The Hatchery Trail is less direct, following the course of Terminal Creek past a huge, hollowed-out cedar snag before intersecting Meadow Trail. A left then leads to tiny Terminal Creek Hatchery itself while a right leads past an equestrian corral, through an open field dominated by thistles to meet up with Killarney Creek Trail beyond.

Take a left onto Killarney Creek Trail and continue through a stand of towering alder. Soon the trail will split but it matters little which branch you take. This explanation will take the counter-clockwise route around Killarney Lake. Both the Hatchery Trail and Killarney Lake Loop Trail are closed to mountain bike and equestrian users due to the fragile nature of the terrain.

Originally dammed to create a catch-basin for drinking water, marshy Killarney Lake now provides significant habitat for a variety of waterfowl, lesser creatures and their predators. Much of the foreshore is blanketed with lily pads. Watch for tiny insect-chomping sundew plants at the edge of the bog as well.

About 1½ km into the loop you'll find a small viewpoint overlooking some swampy sections of the shore. Half a kilometre onward is a boardwalk at the head of the lake: halfway point of the 4-km loop and the perfect place for lunch.

Back in the forest, you'll encounter another boardwalk and a viewpoint before reaching the dam and picnic area at the end of the trail. You can return to the ferry the way you came or follow Mount Gardner Road directly downhill [left from the lake] to complete the circuit. 🐾

Mount Gardner Trail

Level: Challenging

Time: 6.5 hr

Map: 92 G/6

Distance: 17 km

Elevation Change: 756 m

Season: Year Round

Bowen Island Bus

Trip Time: 23 minutes

Leave Ferry Dock	Leave Bluewater
5:40 am	5:13 am
6:30 am	6:03 am
7:30 am	7:03 am
8:25 am	7:58 am
3:50 pm	8:48 am
4:45 pm	4:17 pm
5:45 pm	5:17 pm
6:45 pm	6:17 pm

$1 on Bowen Island only. Usual TransLink fares apply beyond the island.

The easiest way to reach the trailhead to Mount Gardner is go straight up Government Road from the ferry dock turning right onto Mount Gardner Road near the Bowen Island Community School. Continue past the recycling depot to the Killarney Lake Picnic Area. A more attractive but roundabout route would be to follow the previous hike as far as the picnic area at the outfall of Killarney Lake.

From the dam either stay on the road or follow the lakeside in a clockwise direction to where a gravel bar allows unimpeded access to the lakeshore. Cross the bridge here and look for a trail leading left, away from the lake. Upon reaching Mount Gardner Road turn right and walk as far as the next road on the left. The paved road changes names at this point with Mount Gardner Road continuing uphill as a gravel road. If hiking in a hurry or on a mountain bike stay with the secondary road to reach the summit in record time.

For a more pleasant hiking experience however, climb Mount Gardner Road for 20 minutes or so to just beyond the gate which blocks public vehicle access. A short distance further on, clearly-marked Skid Trail leads off to the left dropping down at first to a creek crossing then up again. The route is decidedly up for the next half-hour before branching into two trails. The right fork leads back to Mount Gardner access road while the left fork, now called Short Cut, stays with the forest. Take the short cut, bearing left when you reach Mount Gardner South Trail. As you might expect the access road lies to the right. Forty minutes further on bear right and continue climbing through the steep switchbacks of the Old Trail. Head first to the 756-metre South Peak, just to say you did it, then cut over to North Peak for a panorama overlooking Howe Sound. The lower North Peak is topped with a microwave transmission site.

Return via Mount Gardner North Trail for more views of Keats Island and the Sechelt Peninsula beyond it. To avoid retracing your steps descend the mountain over either the Bluewater Trail or Bowen Bay Trail. A rudimentary bus service operates hourly during morning and evening rush hours Monday to Friday. If able to reach Bowen Bay Road between 4 and 6 pm plan on the flagging down the bus. Expect the bus across the road from the foot of Bowen Bay

Trail at about 20 minutes after the hour. Get a transfer as it is usable throughout the TransLink system of the Lower Mainland. 🐾

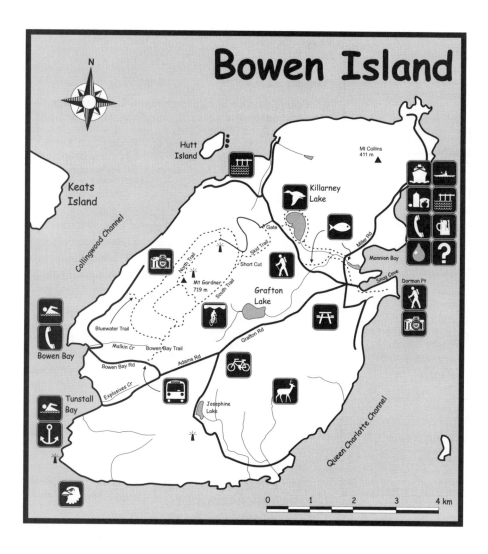

Gambier Island

Gambier Lake

Level: Moderate

Time: 6 hr

Season: Year Round

Distance: 15 km

Elevation: 475 m

Map: 92 G/6 & 92 G/11

Access: Take the bus to Horseshoe Bay [See Page 320] and catch the ferry to Langdale [See Page 333] on the Sunshine Coast. Crossing time is 40 minutes. As you step off the loading ramp of the Langdale ferry you'll find the foot passenger ferry to New Brighton immediately on your right. Since this ferry services both Gambier Island and Keats Island make sure you get on the correct sailing.

Gambier Island Ferry

Crossing time 10 ~25 minutes. Some sailings stop at Keats Island before arriving at destination. Holiday Mondays follow Sunday schedule.

Leave Langdale		Leave New Brighton	
Time	Day	Time	Day
7:30 AM	Daily	7:55 AM	Daily
8:10 AM	Daily	8:40 AM	Daily
9:50 AM	Daily	10:00 AM	Daily
10:10 AM	Daily	10:20 AM	M-F
11:45 AM	Daily	11:55 AM	Daily
12:10 PM	Daily	12:20 PM	Daily
3:00 PM	M-Sa	3:10 PM	M-Sa
3:50 PM	Su	4:00 PM	Su
4:20 PM	M-Sa	4:30 PM	M-Sa
6:00 PM	Daily	6:10 PM	Daily
6:20 PM	Daily	6:30 PM	Daily

Alternate Transportation to Keats Island

Gibson's Water Taxi (250) 886-0226
Cell: 240-4109
Located in Gibsons

Gambier Water Taxi (250) 886-8321
Cell: 740-1133
Located in Gibsons

Cormorant Marine (604) 250-2630
Located in Horseshoe Bay Regularly scheduled service to Gambier Island

Mercury Launch & Tug (604) 921-7451
Located in Horseshoe Bay Regularly scheduled service to Eastbourne

Gambierians are a straightforward lot and the naming conventions on the sparsely populated island certainly substantiate that. From the Gambier Island General Store take the left fork and begin climbing the dusty road. Within a few minutes pass by an old farm called plainly, "The Farm" where presumably farmers do — what else? — farming. The next two kilometres continue upwards through a new subdivision that is gradually being sold off and developed. The road levels out just before reaching an intersection where a hand-painted sign, partly obscured by a stand of young alders, indicates with typical economy of expression that "Lake" lies along the left fork. Simply put, from The Ferry follow The Road past The Store and The Farm to The Lake. There may be little need for adjectives when you only have one of everything.

The oiled road soon gives way to a rougher forest access road that plunges down through a cool, dark forest of mature second growth that is most welcome on a hot day. Moss and mushrooms flourish everywhere in the deep forest gloom, scenery befitting an Emily Carr epiphany. At the next intersection stay left as well and note the dark green marker high on a tree. This is the colour of the day and following these infrequent signs will lead you safely to your destination.

Suddenly the forest opens up as your pass across the top of an old clear-cut. Note Mount Elphinstone in the distance and the single giant Douglas fir that dominates the view here. As the sign succinctly says Sir Douglas was given an undercut, what loggers use to aim a tree when they fall it, in 1894. For some reason however this tree then received a reprieve and the wedge-shaped cut-out was stuffed back into the gash. Over the ensuing century the wound healed though a pitchy scar can be clearly discerned even today. Likely the tree was left behind as a seed tree, one of the earliest "silva-cultural" techniques practised in the province.

From the logging clear-cut the road drops down past

The Kindest Cut
Venerable Sir Douglas towers above everything en route to Gambier Lake including, it seems, the sun. The lord of the forest received a gash then a reprieve from the bite of the cross-cut saw.

Nikon F
28 mm Nikkor lens
Kodachrome 64 ISO film.

another left fork to the bridge across Mannion Creek. The next road to the right is marked with all sorts of orange and blue ribbons and spray paint and can be safely ignored. Just beyond it another well-marked though unnamed right turn leads on to Mount Liddell and Gambier Lake. If running out of steam go straight for one kilometre instead, descending steeply to reach the saltwater at Andys Bay.

The route to Gambier Lake follows a deteriorating logging road to one further intersection. The left fork extends on to Mount Liddell but hang a right instead and rise to the headwaters of Mannion Creek before dropping down to The Lake itself.

If more interested in scenic vistas than forest understory follow the left fork instead and climb past tiny Muskeg Lake working northwards around the base of Mount Liddell before doubling back up to the summit. The ascent to 993 metres is more than compensated for by the view overlooking the mountains of both the Sechelt Peninsula and the Sea to Sky corridor to the east. 🐾

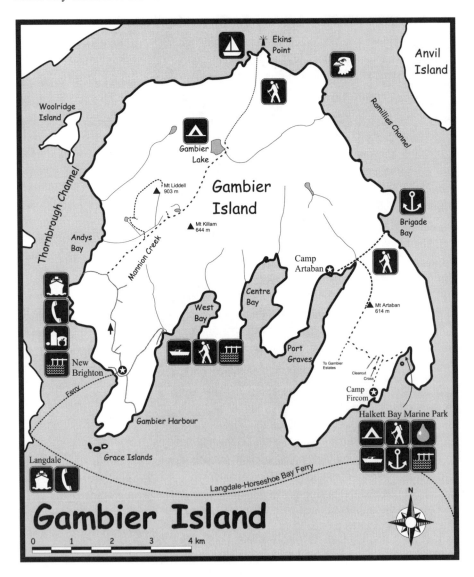

Ekins Point

Anvil Island

Woolridge Island

Ramillies Channel

Gambier Lake

Mt Liddell 903 m

Gambier Island

Thornbrough Channel

Andys Bay

Mt Killam 644 m

Brigade Bay

Mannion Creek

Camp Artaban

Centre Bay

West Bay

Mt Artaban 614 m

Port Graves

To Gambier Estates

Clearcut Cross

New Brighton

Camp Fircom

Gambier Harbour

Halkett Bay Marine Park

Langdale

Grace Islands

Langdale-Horseshoe Bay Ferry

N

Gambier Island

0   1   2   3   4 km

West Bay Amble

Level: Easy

Time: 1½ hr

Season: Year Round

Distance: 4 km r/t

Elevation: 50 m

Map: 92 G/6

Access: As above or, to avoid retracing your steps, contact Cormorant Marine water taxi [(604) 250-

Think globally, buy locally. Gambier Island Store has a sandwich and a porch swing with your name on it.

Nikon F
28 mm Nikkor lens
Kodachrome 64 ISO film.

2630] in Horseshoe Bay to find out if any trips are planned directly to West Bay. Though scheduling is sporadic and custom trips prohibitively expensive it may be possible to piggyback on another previously scheduled outing for just $15 or so. From West Bay just follow the directions below in reverse, returning via ferry from New Brighton and Langdale.

A boat ride or two, a pleasant rural stroll, and lunch at a charming country store are the highlights of this low-key day trip. From the government wharf in New Brighton climb the hill past the pay phone, staying with the right fork when you reach the Gambier Island General Store [(604) 886-3838.] Soon enough the road levels out, taking you past old homesteads and newer recreational properties as it winds through mixed forest of maple, hemlock and fir. Chest-high glades of sword fern burning with backlight offer plenty of opportunities for the photographically-inclined. Continue straight at the only other intersection en route to reach the long pier at West Bay. Or turn right and take a side trip to Gambier Harbour, adding 6 km to your day. Return to the general store for a gourmet sandwich before heading back to the city. Later in the summer picking blackberries along the foreshore is a good way to kill time while waiting for the ferry. 🐾

Buntzen Lake

Access: For details on **Getting to Buntzen Lake** see page 334.

Devil's Club

No, not a place where off-duty satanists hang out. Devil's club is a member of the ginseng family and as such is said to have curative powers for several afflictions. Commonly associated with the word "ouch!" this thorny understory shrub can otherwise be identified by large limp, maple-shaped leaves and a cluster of red berries . In coastal British Columbia devil's club was traditionally used to provide relief from arthritis and rheumatism. As a wilderness food source, young stems of the devil's club can be cooked as greens while the roots can be peeled, rinsed and chewed raw. Devil's club bark was once mixed with various kinds of berries and boiled to make purplish dye for native basketry.

Illustration by Manami Kimura

Buntzen Lake, on the far side of Burrard Inlet, has been an important source of hydroelectric power for the Lower Mainland since 1903. More than a source of power though, Buntzen Lake Reservoir is the centrepiece of a host of recreational activities attracting more than half a million visitors each year. Trout fishing, canoeing, swimming, picnicking, horseback riding, mountain biking and hiking are all popular pursuits in the park.

If trout fishing is your objective Buntzen Lake is well-fished but is well-stocked too. In cooperation with the BC Fish and Wildlife Branch, BC Hydro raises and releases 15-20,000 catchable trout each year. Non-*aficionados* will be pleased to note that the Anmore General Store at the entrance to the park sells worms, and fishing licenses as well as a limited selection of fishing tackle.

Canoes, kayaks and mountain bikes can be rented from the store as well. Drop in to the store to take care of the paperwork and pick up life jackets, paddles and so on. For those who arrive by bus, staff at the store will shuttle you down to South Beach where your boats are waiting.

South Beach, adjacent to the main parking area, is the hub of the more sedate forms of recreation. For that reason South Beach is often as crowded as the city streets left behind on a hot summer day.

Hiking and mountain biking trails radiate from the main picnic site. Hikers will be pleased to note that trails in the vicinity are numerous, offering a variety of hiking experiences for all levels of fitness. At the easy end of the scale Buntzen Lake offers everything from a simple lakeside stroll to longer rambles over fairly even terrain. Hard core hikers won't be disappointed either. Trails up to and along the ridges surrounding Buntzen Lake can be challenging and even difficult at times. Among them, the popular group of routes known collectively as the Halvor Lunden Eagle Ridge Trail are treated individually below.

Buntzen Lake Recreation Area closes at dusk. If your group arrived by car be sure you have enough time to complete your hike before the gate is locked. If you arrive by bus keep in mind that the last bus leaves Anmore before 7 pm.

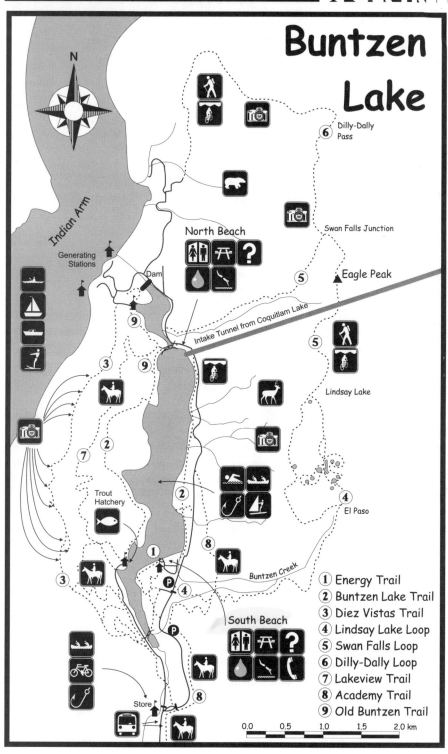

Buntzen Lake

Indian Arm

Generating Stations

Dam

6 Dilly-Dally Pass

Swan Falls Junction

▲ Eagle Peak

5

Intake Tunnel from Coquitlam Lake

North Beach

5

Lindsay Lake

3

9

9

2

7

2

Trout Hatchery

4

El Paso

Buntzen Creek

3

1

8

4

P

P

South Beach

8

Store

1 Energy Trail
2 Buntzen Lake Trail
3 Diez Vistas Trail
4 Lindsay Lake Loop
5 Swan Falls Loop
6 Dilly-Dally Loop
7 Lakeview Trail
8 Academy Trail
9 Old Buntzen Trail

0.0   0.5   1.0   1.5   2.0 km

N

Energy Trail

Level: Easy   **Distance**: 1 km   **Time**: 20 min

Elevation Change: 15 m   **Season**: Year Round   **Map**: 92 G/7

Multiple-Use: Closed to Mountain Bikes and Horses

You won't need much energy to undertake the Energy Trail. Interpretive information on local floral and fauna is the highlight of this pleasant amble. 🐾

Buntzen Lake Trail

Level: Moderate   **Distance**: 8 km   **Time**: 4 hr

Elevation Change: 100 m   **Season**: Year Round   **Map**: 92 G/7

Multiple-Use: Closed to Mountain Bikes and Horses

This well-traveled trail winds around the lakeshore offering many access points for fishermen. Though somewhat long, Buntzen Lake Trail is relatively flat and well-maintained, making it ideal for a family outing. The floating bridge across the slough at the south end of the lake is a great location for bird watching. 🐾

Diez Vistas Trail

Level: Challenging   **Distance**: 7 km   **Time**: 6 hr

Elevation Change: 460 m   **Season**: April - November   **Map**: 92 G/7

Multiple-Use: Closed to Mountain Bikes and Horses

As the name suggests you'll encounter ten viewpoints as you follow this trail along the ridgeline from South Beach to North Beach. On a clear day you'll be rewarded with great views of Indian Arm, Burrard Inlet and Vancouver beyond. The trail is a bit rough in some areas. Return to South Beach via the Powerhouse Road or the Buntzen Lake Trail. Be sure to check out the intake tunnel at North Beach that drops water from neighboring Coquitlam Lake into the Buntzen Reservoir. 🐾

Lindsay Lake Loop

Level: Challenging   **Distance**: 15 km   **Time**: 7 hr

Elevation Change: 1020 m   **Season**: June - October   **Map**: 92 G/7

Multiple-Use: Open to Mountain Bikes and Hikers Only

Popular Lindsay Lake Loop follows Buntzen Creek up to Eagle Ridge and along the ridgeline to Lindsay Lake. As you reach high ground you'll come to a fork in the trail called El Paso. Take the left fork through old-growth forest past five different westward facing viewpoints. At Lindsay Lake the trail loops back following a different route through a sprinkling of mountain tarns. At El Paso once again you'll regain the main route back to the park. 🐾

Swan Falls Loop

Level: Difficult **Distance:** 20 km **Time:** 9 hr
Elevation Change: 1050 m **Season:** July - October **Map:** 92 G/7
Multiple-Use: Open to Mountain Bikes and Hikers Only

This trail is a continuation of the previous one. Instead of looping back at Lindsay Lake, continue northward along the ridge to Eagle Peak. Also known as Mount Beautiful, the summit offers a spectacular panorama in all directions. Beyond the peak the route is somewhat less well-defined, becoming very steep and slippery as it drops back down into the valley bottom at the Swan Falls Junction. This section of trail parallels Trout Creek until it intersects Powerhouse Road just fifteen minutes after reaching Swan Falls itself. If time is a concern Powerhouse Road is the fastest route back to South Beach. Buntzen Lake Trail, though longer, is without a doubt much more scenic.

Dilly Dally Loop

Level: Difficult **Distance:** 25 km **Time:** 11 hr
Elevation Change: 1050 m **Season:** July - October **Map:** 92 G/7
Multiple-Use: Open to Mountain Bikes and Hikers Only

You won't want to dilly dally on the Dilly Dally trail. This route is a continuation of the previous two hikes and is only recommended for the most experienced hikers. Instead of following Trout Creek down to Swan Falls and the valley bottom you'll want to continue along Eagle Ridge to a small prominence locally known as Dilly Dally Peak. After slogging uphill most of the day you'll finally begin losing altitude quickly after passing the peak. Soon the footpath will become an old, overgrown logging road. Needless to say the landscape still bears the scars of unenlightened logging practices. On the plus side however this route provides a number of vantage points overlooking Indian Arm. Croker Lookout in particular offers unimpeded views of the inlet below. Like the previous hike this route will eventually merge into Powerhouse Road which will take you back to South Beach where you started.

Lakeview Trail

Level: Difficult **Distance:** 6 km **Time:** 3 hr
Elevation Change: 150 m **Season:** April - November **Map:** 92 G/7
Multiple-Use: Open to Mountain Bikes, Horses and Hikers

This and the following trails provide a network for horse and bike riders to loop around Buntzen Lake. The Lakeview Trail connects Pumphouse Road to the Old Buntzen Lake Trail following the rugged ridge above Buntzen Lake's western shore.

BC CAR-FREE

Academy Trail

Level: Moderate   **Distance:** 4 km   **Time:** 2 hr

Elevation Change: 100 m   **Season:** April - Nov   **Map:** 92 G/7

Multiple-Use: Open to Mountain Bikes, Horses and Hikers

This equestrian trail provides access to the Park, connecting up with Powerhouse Road about halfway along the eastern shore of Buntzen Lake. 🐾

Old Buntzen Lake Trail

Level: Easy   **Distance:** 1½ km   **Time:** 45 minutes

Elevation Change: 20 m   **Season:** Year Round   **Map:** 92 G/7

Multiple-Use: Open to Mountain Bikes, Horses and Hikers

A short forested route that connects Lakeview Trail with the powerhouse access road in the vicinity of the Buntzen Lake Dam. 🐾

Miscellaneous

Level: Difficult   **Distance:** n/a   **Time:** n/a

Elevation Change: n/a   **Season:** April - Nov   **Map:** 92 G/7

Multiple-Use: Open to Mountain Bikes, Horses and Hikers

Three short, steep trails called Bear Claw, Saddle Ridge, and Horseshoe Trails provide challenging riding for horse and bike riders alike and a shortcut to the Diez Vistas trail for hikers. 🐾

Buntzen Lake Information

Location	Services	Notes
Anmore General Store (604) 469-9928	Bait, tackle and fishing licenses. Canoe rentals $17 per hour; $42 per day. Kayak rentals $25 singles; $30 doubles. Mountain bike rentals $9 per hour; $19 per day.	Shuttle service available. Reservations required.
Alpine Riding Academy 3170 Sunnyside Port Moody, BC (604) 469-1111	Guided horseback riding by the hour. Western and English lessons.	Reservations required. Staff impatient at times.

Lynn Headwaters

Access: From downtown Vancouver hop a **#210 Upper Lynn Valley** bus from Dunsmuir Street next to Burrard Skytrain station. Stay on the bus to the end of the line at the corner of Evelyn & Underwood Streets. Take the short-cut east past two tennis courts and continue half a block to the corner of Dempsey and Lynn Valley Roads. From there you'll see the park entrance to the north. Follow Intake Road for about a kilometre before reaching the park proper.

Those in North or West Vancouver can take the **#228 Lynn Valley** bus from Lonsdale Quay to the corner of Dempsey and Lynn Valley Roads.

Formerly the source of drinking water for the city of North Vancouver, Lynn Headwaters Regional Park was opened to the public when floods damaged water intakes in 1983. Hiking is by far the main attraction here with trails suited to all levels of experience and ability. Be sure to top up your water at the picnic area as most of the water you'll meet up with while hiking has been polluted by people and their dogs. From the picnic area cross the bridge to access the trails of 4,685-hectare Lynn Headwaters Regional Park. An information board here provides hikers with background information on the park, directions, maps, trail conditions and common sense safety information.

Rice Lake

Level: Very Easy   **Distance:** 4 km r/t   **Time:** 2 h

Elevation Change: 25 m   **Map:** 92 G/6   **Season:** Year Round

By far the easiest hike in the area is the pleasant 4 km saunter around Rice Lake. To reach the lake head up the hill to the right of the information board. Follow the directional signs to Rice Lake on the left side of the road. At the dock, pause to ask the trout fishermen about their luck and, out of curiosity, peer into the water along the pilings. Depending on the time of the year you're bound to see countless salamanders. Suspended in the water too, those tiny orange specks are, in reality, a fresh water cousin to the brine shrimp of "sea-monkey" fame. The fresh water variety are called daphnia or water fleas.

Lynn Loop

Level: Easy   **Distance:** 5.7 km r/t   **Time:** 2½ h

Elevation Change: 250 m   **Map:** 92 G/6   **Season:** April to Nov

At 5.7 km, Lynn Loop is slightly longer and a somewhat steeper than the former stroll. In order to avoid climbing the switchback sections at the top end of the trail it is recommended that you complete the trail in a counter-clockwise direction. If so, expect the first half of the hike to wind through a mature, second generation forest while the return trip is more open, following the banks of Lynn Creek. Pause a moment to cool your toes here: but remember your toes and everyone else's have rendered the water undrinkable.

Lynn Loop Trail begins a short distance to the right [south-east] of the bridge. Watch for directional signs on the left of the road towards Rice Lake. The first half of the trail follows the high ground along a bench well above Lynn Creek. The first junction you'll encounter leads up to Lynn Peak. Take the left fork instead for a short distance until you see another side trail veering off to the right. A few minutes along this track leads to a couple of glacial erratics, giant boulders deposited by receding glaciers at the end of the last ice age. Back on the main trail you'll reach a major junction at the 3.1 km mark. Note the massive, upside-down cedar stump here. To return to where you started take the left fork 0.7 km down through a series of steep switchbacks. At the bottom you'll take a left again following Lynn Creek downstream for 1.7 km of easy hiking.

An alternative route continues along the bench land for an additional 2.4 km to the debris chute at the start of the trail to Norvan Falls and on to Grouse Mountain. Though, considerably longer, you'll drop down to Lynn Creek at a much more gradual pace. From the debris chute double back along the Cedars Mill Trail for 2.1 km before re-gaining the Lynn Loop Trail. Altogether, this extension will nearly double your hike to 10.3 km but the going is no more difficult than the shorter option detailed above. 🐾

Norvan Falls

Level: Moderate   **Distance:** 14 km r/t   **Time:** 6 h
Elevation Change: 230 m   **Map:** 92 G/6   **Season:** April to Nov

From the information board take the left fork, following a wide, flat path paralleling the creek. On the left you'll soon notice a stack of old, creosote covered wooden pipes, vestiges of North Vancouver's water supply from the 1920s to 1983. After 1.7 km the trail forks. The easiest and most interesting route lies to the left on the Cedars Mill Trail. In the underbrush to the right of the trail you'll note a miscellany of rusted arti-facts dating to the early days of B.C. logging. These scraps of history are protected so refrain from pocketing a souvenir of your visit.

Except during periods of high water it is possible to catch a glimpse of a giant western red cedar, nearby. A rough trail, adjacent to the old mill site but across Lynn Creek leads steeply up the bank to the foot of a 600 years old conifer measuring 50 metres tall and 4 metres around at the base. Be sure to exercise caution when rock hopping across the waterway. Follow the rough trail back downstream to see other cedar and Douglas fir giants that the loggers overlooked.

At the end of this 2.1 km section the trail opens up on a boulder field, evidence of periodic flooding. Enjoy the sunshine at creek side here as the trail next plunges into the forest darkness following a succession of old logging roads for 2.9 km to the bridge at Norvan Creek. On the way you'll pass by another heap of historic relics. Broken bits of porcelain, a dented tea kettle and old, broken handsaws attest to the forestry opera-tions which began here in the mid-1880s. Check out the massive stumps hereabouts and imagine the backbreaking work that must have been required to saw through one of these giants balanced on a springboard two or more metres above the forest floor. Pic-turesque Norvan Falls will be found 300 metres upstream from the Norvan Creek Bridge. Whether turning back or continuing on to Grouse Mountain plan to stop here for lunch. 🐾

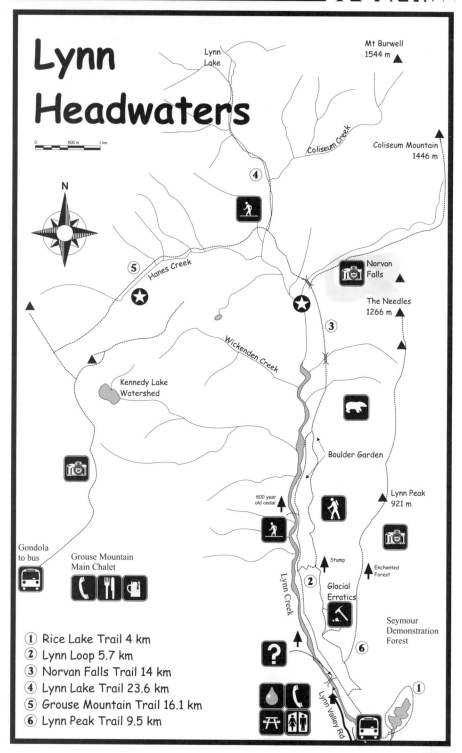

Lynn Headwaters

0   500 m   1 km

N

Lynn Lake

Mt Burwell
1544 m ▲

Coliseum Creek

Coliseum Mountain
1446 m ▲

④

⑤ Hanes Creek

Norvan Falls ▲

The Needles
1266 m ▲

③

Wickenden Creek

Kennedy Lake Watershed

Boulder Garden

Lynn Peak
921 m ▲

600 year old cedar

Gondola to bus

Grouse Mountain Main Chalet

Stump

Enchanted Forest

② Glacial Erratics

Seymour Demonstration Forest

⑥

① Rice Lake Trail 4 km
② Lynn Loop 5.7 km
③ Norvan Falls Trail 14 km
④ Lynn Lake Trail 23.6 km
⑤ Grouse Mountain Trail 16.1 km
⑥ Lynn Peak Trail 9.5 km

Lynn Creek

Lynn Valley Rd

①

Lynn Headwaters and Grouse Mountain

Level: Difficult   **Distance:** 16 km o/w   **Time:** 6 h

Elevation Change: 1122 m   **Map:** 92 G/6   **Season:** May to Nov

The trail to Grouse Mountain continues from where the previous hike left off. Thus far the trail has been relatively flat and well-maintained. The next 1.3 km section continues in much the same vein to the upper reaches of Lynn Creek where it suddenly turns west into the Hanes Valley. A fork to the right follows surveyor-tape markers 3½ km up to Lynn Lake where the creek originates. Expect to going to get much rougher, with the trail often following the creek bed and sometimes disappearing altogether in the underbrush. You'll gain an additional 330 metres of elevation before reaching the lake.

The left fork is no less demanding. Though the trail to Grouse Mountain is well-established, this is a demanding wilderness route with many rough, extremely steep sections. On the way you'll gain an additional 892 metres of elevation. You may encounter heavy snow pack as late as June. During the spring runoff Lynn Creek may be impassable so be prepared to turn back early in the season. After fording the creek you'll be following Hanes Creek up to Crown Pass 4½ km away. Numerous peaks are accessible from the pass while the main route to the left leads down to the Grouse Mountain Skyride an additional 3.6 km away. If hunger and thirst assail you at this point the main chalet has plenty of options to satisfy both. The truly gung ho may be tempted to walk down the Grouse Grind against the current of sweaty trendoids running up. Doing so will add a very steep 2.9 km to your day, saving you $5.

Whether you choose to ride the tram down or hike out you can catch the bus back to Vancouver behind the main office at Grouse Mountain base. The **#236 Lonsdale Quay** bus will take you to the North Vancouver SeaBus terminal from which downtown Vancouver is just a 20-minute boat ride away. Alternately the **#232 Phibbs Exchange** bus will take you to Edgemont Village where you have to transfer to the **#246 Vancouver** or **#246 Park Royal** bus. The latter version is bound for West Vancouver necessitating yet another bus transfer at the corner of Marine Drive and Garden Avenue after the evening rush hour Monday to Saturday and all-day Sunday. With luck you'll meet the connecting **#240 Vancouver** bus for the Lion's Gate Bridge crossing.

For those who may be put off by the elevation gain an alternative would be to undertake the described route in reverse. Gain your elevation by taking the tram up to Grouse Mountain then walking up and over Crown Pass. Hanes Valley will lead you down to Lynn Headwaters Regional Park. 🐾

Lynn Peak

Level: Demanding **Distance:** $9\frac{1}{2}$ km r/t

Time: 4 h **Elevation Change:** 760 m

Season: May to Nov **Map:** Vancouver N 92/G6

For access to Lynn Peak follow the gravel road to the

Deep Dusk
Not easy to see the forest for the trees as these three crowns poke out of the shadows, catching a few final rays of the evening sun.

Nikon F
135 mm Nikkor lens
Kodachrome 64 ISO film.

right from the information board, turning abruptly left on to Lynn Loop Trail after 10 minutes or so. This pleasant forest footpath branches after another 20 minutes. The right fork to 825-metre Lynn Peak is well marked, sloping upwards gently enough at first. Soon however you'll begin mounting a series of switchbacks that zig and zag and zig again for 45 minutes up to a small south-facing break in the trees. Linger not, however, as the best is yet to come. Continue climbing at a more relaxed pace for another 30 minutes and an opening known as the Blimp Lookout reveals views to the east of Mount Seymour. Catch your breath here but save your lunch as a further 30 minutes of climbing will put you on top where you may wish to linger, taking in the panorama encompassing Mount Elsay and Mount Seymour to the east and, on a clear day, Mt. Baker, that massive volcano to the south east in Washington state. When you have had enough of unsurpassed scenery and fresh air retrace your steps back down to the trailhead. 🐾

Mosquito Creek

Level: Easy

Distance: $3\frac{1}{2}$ km

Time: $1\frac{1}{2}$ h

Elev. Change: 200 m

Season: Year Round

Map: See pg 59

Access: The **#246 [Park Royal, Vancouver or Highland]** Bus will connect with the trailhead on Mosquito Creek whether you board at North Vancouver's Lonsdale Quay or at any of the stops along West Georgia in Vancouver. The **#246 Highland** bus only originates in Vancouver Monday through Saturday during peak hours. The **#240 15th Street** bus however follows the same route at any time, necessitating a transfer to the **#246 Highland** on Marine Drive at the foot of Capilano Road in North Vancouver during off-peak hours. Whichever route you take, get off at the corner of Montroyal Boulevard and Glencanyon Drive and walk west, towards the fire hall, crossing the bridge over Mosquito Creek to find the start of the trail.

Cattails

A veritable supermarket on a stick, cattails were once a source of sustenance as well as comfort to Pacific Northwest natives. Young shoots can be eaten as greens in the spring while young flower spikes can be roasted and eaten like cobs of corn. Young roots or rhizomes (underground stems) can be peeled and eaten as is—sashimi-style, hold the wasabi—or dried and pulverized into flour. Early settlers too discovered that cattail pollen could be harvested and added to bread or pancakes. Cattail down or fluff was collected in autumn for use as a wound dressing or for stuffing pillows and bedding. Cattail leaves found use in native basketry.

Illustration by Manami Kimura

For those craving open air, the urban walkway along the banks of Mosquito Creek is a pleasant diversion at any time of the year. The trail follows the creek downhill as far as Evergreen Place where the stream disappears -- *poof!* -- down a giant bathtub drain. Pause a moment to admire the graffiti "tags" which adorn the walls of the overflow chute. The trail continues *sans* waterway through the forest a short distance before it too vanishes, becoming Del Rio Crescent instead. Continue walking southward as Mosquito Creek tumbles out of its subterranean conduit again at busy Queen's Road. After crossing the road you'll find yourself in William Griffin Park. The skateboarders at the skatepark are a marvel to behold, not least because no one bothers to don a helmet. Along the western edge of the trail a new salmon spawning channel is encouraging the return of coho and chum every fall. Beyond William Griffin Park, river and route sneak under the roaring Upper Levels Highway before winding through a thickly forested gully. The trail finally emerges at a grassy field bound by Larson Road and Fell Avenue. Follow the latter two blocks down to Marine Drive and catch the westbound **#240** bus back to Vancouver. 🐾

Mount Fromme

Level: Moderate   **Distance:** 11 km

Time: 5 h   **Map:** 92 G/6 See also pg 59

Elev Change: 855 m   **Season:** June to Nov.

Access: See previous hike.

The trail to Mount Fromme starts off the same as the previous hike but follows Mosquito Creek's western bank upstream instead. Within a couple minutes a sign declares that the trail is not maintained by the District of North Vancouver, warning of numerous hazards along the way. The trail is indeed rough especially at the upper end just before it meets up with the Baden-Powell Trail. Sections may even be flooded during spring runoff. The creekside route however is attractive with Mosquito Creek pouring steeply down over a course strewn with larger boulders. Photo enthusiasts may want to pack in a tripod and practice those tumbling-brook shots. To reach the creek crossing upstream at the Baden-Powell Trail should take just 40 minutes.

For an easier but longer alternative walk west along Montroyal Boulevard past Mosquito Creek, turning right at Skyline Drive. Follow the road uphill to the parking area under a BC Hydro powerline. Follow the right-of-way east (right,) staying with the road when it veers north. Continue uphill until the road intersects with the Baden-Powell Trail. Head east along the trail for a few minutes to return to Mosquito Creek.

Whichever route you take, cross the skookum iron and plank bridge over Mosquito Creek and note a side trail leading along the eastern bank of the stream. Though not the route to Mount Fromme, a brief, 10-minute stroll upstream leads to the mouth of an attractive gorge that was originally dammed as a source of water for early North Vancouver residents. The wooden dam is deteriorating now as are the wood and wire pipes.

You may also notice a faint path on the opposite bank at the foot of the dam. During times of low water, boulder hop across the creek and scramble up the steep bank to marvel at a cluster of Douglas fir giants, leftovers from when the North Shore was originally logged. Some of the behemoths have reached 2 metres in diameter and 60 metres tall.

The Mount Fromme trail proper begins a few steps east along the Baden-Powell Trail just behind two giant water tanks at the top of Prospect Drive. The trail marker states "To old Grouse Mountain Highway. 50 minutes. Trail not

Bracket Fungi

In conches, West Coast natives found the perfect punk. And we're not talking gel-topped mohicans here. By using a smouldering bit of bracket fungi clasped in a clam shell fire could be kept or transported long distance. Slow-burning bracket fungi punks were employed as mosquito coils as well.

In the photo above note the woodpecker bore holes. Parasitical fungi, insects and their feathered predators all have a role to play in reverse-engineering dead or dying trees. Eventually the entire tree will be consumed, transformed into into a nutrient-rich soil that fosters new plant life.

Nikon F; 135 mm Nikkor lens; Kodachrome 64 ISO film.

maintained." In spite of the admonishment, foot traffic is frequent enough to keep the trail open. A maze of old trails, old logging roads and the Grouse Mountain service road can sometimes make getting to Mount Fromme a confusing proposition. The first 50 minutes are steep but straightforward, leading, as the sign says, to the back door route that is still used by the Grouse Mountain Resort. Turn left upon reaching the dirt road and within a few steps expect to be confronted with a choice. The left fork is a disused logging road that eventually reconnects with the so-called Grouse Mountain Highway. The right fork is a continuation of the "Highway" which loops around to the right in a large switchback. Not always obvious, the middle route is the best option: a 20 minute short-cut named Per Gynt Trail that cuts across the aforementioned loop.

Upon regaining the old Grouse Mountain Highway turn left again. After following the service road for another 30 minutes look for numerous ribbons hanging in the trees to the right of the road. This is the steep, final fragment of the Per Gynt Trail. Forest will soon enough give way to subalpine as the trail climbs up towards Mount Fromme's North and South Peaks. Plan to take sustenance at the top while gorging on views of Lynn Valley below and Lynn Peak and The Needles beyond. Mt. Fromme was named for the CEO of the company that originally logged much of the North Shore.

Though most will want to return via the Per Gynt Trail an alternative loop exists that leads back down to Mountain Highway. Since the trail, signed to "Senate Peak (North.)", is badly marked and overgrown only the experienced should consider this shortcut.

Nestled at the foot of the draw between Mount Fromme's twin peaks lies a mountain tarn known as Meech Lake. Make for the pond after filling up on bagels and *buena vistas*. Marked with old splashes of red paint, peeling orange squares and the odd pink ribbon, the route plunges steeply down to the Grouse Mountain Highway. At the bottom the trail continues across the road as Pipeline Trail, swinging back to the first Per Gynt shortcut mentioned above.

For an easier out stick with the Grouse Mountain service road as it leads southwest to the main chalet. Numerous sideroads can be confusing but the main one is clearly marked with a sign stating that the top of the mountain is up and to the right. The road will switchback across Blueberry Ski Run several times before reaching the resort proper. The tourist trap boasts giftshops, resturants and a pub overlooking Vancover where nachos and suds are features of the house. Hiking out on the Grouse Grind is free but a quick exit via the tram will cost an $5. At the base of Grouse Mountain the **#236 Lonsdale Quay** bus leads to the North Vancouver SeaBus terminal. For a faster, all-bus route, transfer to the **#246 Vancouver** or **#246 Park Royal** bus at the intersection of Capilano Road and Ridgewood Drive. The former operates during daytime peak hours Monday to Saturday while the latter will take you as far as the corner of Marine Drive and Garden Avenue at any other time before proceeding on the West Vancouver. Transfer to the connecting **#240 Vancouver** bus to reach downtown.

Alternately, take the **#232 Phibbs Exchange** bus to Edgemont Village and transfer to the **#246** as described above. 🐾

Baden-Powell Centennial Trail

A project initiated by the Boy Scouts and Girl Guides, the Baden-Powell Centennial Trail was constructed in 1971 to commemorate British Columbia's first 100 years as a province. This 41.7-km trail stretches from Horseshoe Bay in the west, across the south-facing slopes of the North Shore Mountains to Deep Cove in the east.

Most of the trails on Canada's rugged west coast have a lot of vertical mixed in with their horizontal. This trail is no exception. Over the course of the Baden-Powell Centennial Trail you can expect to encounter nearly 5 km of elevation change. You'll climb 2438 metres and lose slightly more, 2530 metres, on the downside. Nearly half of your elevation gain will be in the first section alone.

The trail is readily accessible at many points along its length using public transportation and is best undertaken over a number of days. The Baden-Powell Trail is especially popular in the springtime for pre-season conditioning while most hiking routes in the province of are still under snow. The route cuts across a large number of administrative areas. For that reason you will find great variety in the quality of maintenance and signage along the way. Though closed to mountain bikes expect to encounter cyclists at any point on the trail. Keep in mind that if you choose to complete any sections of the trail in the opposite direction from those described below your time could vary considerably depending on the slope. 🐾

Silhouetted Sentinels
At the metropolitan fringe, the Baden-Powell Trail offers ancient trees and stupendous views overlooking Georgia Strait.

Nikon F
135 mm Nikkor lens
Kodachrome 64 ISO film.

Horseshoe Bay to Cypress Provincial Park

Level: Difficult   **Distance:** 8½ km   **Time:** 6 h

Elevation Change: 1040 m   **Season:** May to Nov   **Map:** 92 G/6

Access: For details on getting to Horseshoe Bay see Appendix on page 320

Get off the **#250 Horseshoe Bay** bus near the end of the line immediately after passing first Gleneagles Golf Course and then an elementary school on the left in quick succession. The bus will stop just before a stop sign on a short but steep uphill grade. Follow the green highway sign to the right across an overpass to Highway 99. The trailhead is just a short distance east, back in the direction of Vancouver, after you cross the busy highway. Exercise caution at this intersection as motorists are usually accelerating and jockeying for position on the treacherous road to Squamish and Whistler.

From the trailhead the route climbs very steeply, leading first to Eagle Bluff [1094 m] then on up to Black Mountain [1217 m]. Both prominences offer spectacular views of Howe Sound, Vancouver Island and the City of Vancouver. On a clear day the American San Juan Islands can be seen due south while Mt. Baker may be visible in eastern Washington State.

Black Mountain is home to a record-sized Mountain Hemlock. Though, at 44.8 metres, it is not the tallest on record, its 5.46 m girth is a species first.

The going gets easier after Black Mountain as the trail winds down into Cypress Bowl at the heart of the Provincial Park.

If enamoured with big trees, a side trip to the south side of Yew Lake will reveal the world's chubbiest balsam or amabilis fir, a whopper at 7.14 metres around at the base and 43.9 metres tall.

Nothing is uglier than a ski hill bereft of snow and Cypress Bowl is no exception. In the off-season the park is not serviced by any kind of public transportation other than an expensive taxi ride. If you do not plan to continue hiking beyond the park you should ideally arrange for someone to pick you up at the ski lodge parking lot. Hitchhiking is also a possibility but just keep in mind that the most dangerous creatures in the wilderness are not the animals. Never hitchhike alone and, for obvious reasons, women should never hitchhike.

The hardiest souls will want to continue walking through the park and beyond to the British Properties. That route is detailed below. 🐾

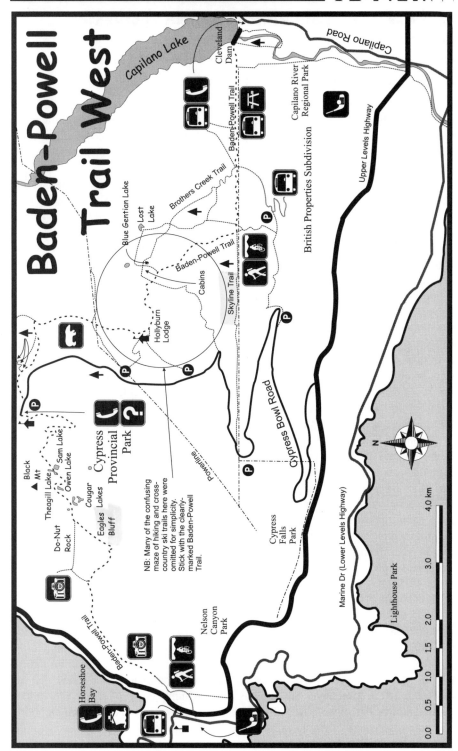

Baden-Powell Trail West

Capilano Lake

Cleveland Dam

Capilano Road

Baden-Powell Trail

Capilano River Regional Park

British Properties Subdivision

Upper Levels Highway

Blue Gentian Lake

Lost Lake

Brothers Creek Trail

Baden-Powell Trail

Skyline Trail

Cabins

Hollyburn Lodge

Cypress Bowl Road

Cypress Falls Park

Black Mt

Theagill Lake

Sam Lake

Owen Lake

Cougar Lakes

Do-Nut Rock

Eagles Bluff

Cypress Provincial Park

NB: Many of the confusing maze of hiking and cross-country ski trails here were omitted for simplicity. Stick with the clearly-marked Baden-Powell Trail.

Powerline

Nelson Canyon Park

Horseshoe Bay

Baden-Powell Trail

Marine Dr (Lower Levels Highway)

Lighthouse Park

N

0.0   0.5   1.0   1.5   2.0   3.0   4.0 km

Cypress Provincial Park to British Properties

Level: Difficult   **Distance:** 8 km   **Time:** 4 h

Elevation Change: 560 m   **Season:** May to Nov   **Map:** 92 G/6

Access: Beg a ride, Hitchhike, Take a Taxi or Walk as above.

However you reach Cypress Park in order to start the second leg of the Baden Powell Trail be sure to pause a moment to appreciate the 1200 year old yellow cedar which stands across from the turn off to the cross-country skiing area. Not only is it the world's oldest, at 6.2 metres in circumference and 40 metres tall it is one of the largest of its kind in existence.

Near the main ski lodge you'll find a large map and information board. Behind that and to the right the Baden-Powell Centennial Trail continues through one of the world's best remaining stands of yellow cedar. Also known as cypress trees, the park is named after these aromatic conifers. At 0.6 km a side trail leading to Mt Strachan reveals a number of ancient trees of note including Canada's largest mountain hemlock and the Hollyburn Giant, a massive yellow cedar measuring 3.2 m across. The Old Strachen Trail loops back to the Baden-Powell. At the junction of Hollyburn Mountain Trail, turn right and follow the popular Pacific Run cross-country ski trail down under the power line to First Lake and Hollyburn Lodge. Pay close attention to trail markers throughout the park and beyond as a bewildering labyrinth of poorly marked routes can easily lead to confusion for newcomers to the area. Compared to the first section detailed above this one is gently sloping for the most part. After the lodge Baden-Powell Centennial Trail is also called Grand National Trail. You'll pass through a large community of recreational cabins nestled in the forest then parallel Lawson Creek for two and a half km. The attractive forest is dark and cool on a hot summer day, ideal for those backlit morning mist shots that seem to define the temperate rain forest for so many.

Upon reaching Skyline Trail big tree enthusiasts will want to take a short side trip. Turn right and head west, past Lawson Creek to a point along the power line where a sign indicates a short side trail leading off to the right towards the renowned Hollyburn Fir. At a time when England's Alfred the Great was kicking Danish butt and Vikings from Norway were discovering North America the Hollyburn Fir was laying down roots on the opposite end of the continent. The 1100 year old Douglas fir boasts a girth of three metres and height of 150 m. Like many of the North Shore's surviving big trees the top of Hollyburn Fir has long since been snapped off by a west coast gale. Turn-of-the-century loggers were under the misconception that such broken-topped trees were rotten to the core and hence a waste of time to handsaw through. As a result, many such broken behemoths survived.

Just past the junction with Skyline Trail you'll encounter a branch leading to Millstream Road in West Vancouver. To leave the trail turn left and follow Millstream Road a couple paces down to Eyremount Drive then turn left and continue descending for 10 minutes to the busstop on the corner of Eyremount and Crestwell Drive. From here take the **#254 British Properties** bus to Park Royal shopping center where you can change to a **#250 Vancouver** bus or a bus with the numbers #251 #252 or #253 bound for downtown Vancouver. The **#254 British Properties** bus, operating on an hourly schedule, also goes to Vancouver during peak hours weekdays only. 🐾

British Properties to Grouse Mountain

Level: Moderate   **Distance:** 5 km   **Time:** 1½ h

Elevation Change: 240 m   **Season:** May to Nov   **Map:** 92 G/6

Access: #250, #251, #252 or #253 bus from West Georgia Street to Park Royal. Change to the #254 **British Properties** bus and get off at the corner of Crestwell Drive and Eyremount Drive and follow the latter uphill to Millstream Road. The trailhead should be self-evident from the corner.

This section is the least interesting and, except for the big trees near the start of the trail, could otherwise be easily skipped without missing a thing. From the end of the previous section the Baden-Powell Centennial Trail flattens out, continuing for 1½ km through the forest past Brothers Creek before cutting downhill through the suburbs again.

To reach the big trees follow the Brothers Creek Trail uphill, passing through a large stand of western red cedar before crossing a bridge to the opposite bank of Brothers Creek. Follow the fire access road here through an exquisite grove of ancient cedars, some boasting a diameter of 7½ metres. Before snapping off all your film continue down along the fire access road to reach the ghostly Candelabra Fir. Though dead, this 61-metre leviathan is not down. Just beyond the dead one a 43 metre Douglas fir can be found still thriving. Return to the fire access road and continue downhill to return to the Baden Powell trail.

You'll spend much of the next two kilometres travelling along a narrow power line right-of-way of behind the houses of local residences. Mercifully the final third of the trail plunges steeply down through Capilano River Regional Park ending up at Cleveland Dam. Walk across the top of the Dam and on to Capilano Road. The #236 **Lonsdale Quay** bus will take you to the North Vancouver SeaBus terminal from which downtown Vancouver is just a 20-minute boat ride away. To end up on West Georgia Street instead transfer to the #246 **Vancouver** or #246 **Park Royal** bus on Capilano Road just after the Capilano Suspension Bridge tourist trap. The latter bus is bound for West Vancouver necessitating yet another bus transfer at the corner of Marine Drive and Garden Avenue after the evening rush hour Monday to Saturday and all-day Sunday. With luck you'll meet the connecting #240 **Vancouver** bus for the Lion's Gate Bridge crossing. Alternately the #232 **Phibbs Exchange** bus will take you to Edgemont Village where you can link up with one of the #246 buses mentioned above.

If you wish to continue hiking the Baden-Powell Trail from Cleveland Dam you'll have to walk about 1½ km up Nancy Greene Way to Grouse Mountain to find the trailhead once again. 🐾

Grouse Mountain to Lynn Valley Road

Level: Difficult   **Distance:** 8.3 km   **Time:** 3 h

Elevation Change: 120 m   **Season:** April to Nov   **Map:** 92 G/6

Access: **#240 15ᵗʰ Street** bus (or **#246 Lonsdale Quay via Highland** bus when available during peak hours Monday to Saturday) from West Georgia Street to the corner of Marine Drive and Capilano Road in North Vancouver. Change to (or stay on) the **#246 Lonsdale Quay via Highland** bus to the corner of Capilano Road and Woods Drive. Change to the **#236 Grouse Mountain** to the end of the line.

When you arrive at Grouse Mountain walk back east towards Nancy Greene Way and you'll see an information sign and probably a lot of stretching athletes up the hill and to the right [east] of the main offices. The trendy Grouse Grind and the Baden-Powell Centennial Trail share the same trailhead. The former route, which nearly everybody will take, goes straight up the face of Grouse Mountain. You are marching eastward to the sound of a different drummer. At first you'll gain 135 m of elevation on a moderate slope. After 40 minutes or so the trail will flatten out then begin sloping downwards, a tendency it will follow for most of the day. For the most part this section of trail is quite rough and poorly maintained though the signage, like all those sections in North Vancouver, is excellent. This hike passes through typical second growth rain forest with very few viewpoints. If you wish to cut the hike short there are several escape routes along the way. The first one is 2½ km into the hike. Just before reaching Mosquito Creek you can follow the road down to Skyline Drive. At the corner of Montroyal Boulevard catch the **#246** bus. Mountain Highway, 5½ km further on, is another obvious egress point. Follow the road down to McNair Drive where you can catch the **#210 Vancouver** bus bound for Burrard SkyTrain station. The dirt road is gated above the Baden-Powell trail and leads via a roundabout way to the back door of Grouse Mountain. This area is particularly popular with mountain bikers.

Continuing eastward from this point Baden-Powell trail soon becomes notably steep descending through a series of switchbacks. At the bottom of the steepest part the trail intersects paved Lynn Valley Road. Turn right here. You'll find the nearest bus stop just beyond the gate on Dempsey Road. The **#228 Lonsdale Quay** bus runs at half-hour intervals, more frequently during rush hours, and will connect you up with the **SeaBus** bound for downtown Vancouver. Alternately, if you walk a block west to the corner of Underwood Avenue and Dempsey Road you can catch the more direct **#210 Vancouver** bus every 30 minutes. 🐾

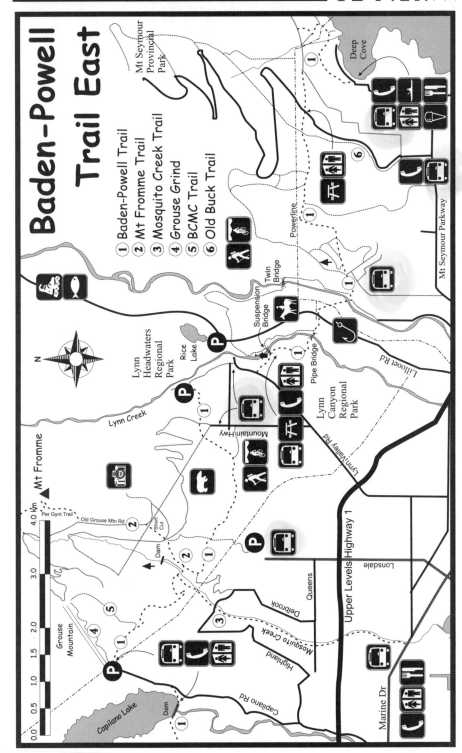

Baden-Powell
Trail East

1. Baden-Powell Trail
2. Mt Fromme Trail
3. Mosquito Creek Trail
4. Grouse Grind
5. BCMC Trail
6. Old Buck Trail

Mt Seymour Provincial Park

Deep Cove

Powerline

Mt Seymour Parkway

Twin Bridge

Suspension Bridge

Lynn Headwaters Regional Park

Rice Lake

Lillooet Rd

Pipe Bridge

Lynn Canyon Regional Park

Lynn Creek

N

Mountain Hwy

Mt Fromme

Lynn Valley Rd

Per Gynt Trail

Old Grouse Mtn Rd

Short Cut

Dam

Delbrook

Upper Levels Highway 1

Lonsdale

Queens

Grouse Mountain

Mosquito Creek

Highland

Capilano Rd

Capilano Lake

Dam

Marine Dr

4.0 Km
3.0
2.0
1.5
1.0
0.5
0.0

Lynn Canyon to Hyannis Drive

Level: Moderate   **Distance:** 3.9 km

Time: 2 h   **Elev. Change:** 60 m

Season: April to Nov   **Map:** 92 G/6 & 92 G/7

Access: Bus #229 services the trailhead and can be reached in one of two ways. Cross to North Vancouver's Lonsdale Quay on the **SeaBus** and change to the **#229 Phibbs Exchange via Westlynn** bus. Alternately take the **#210 Upper Lynn Valley** from Dunsmuir Street next to Burrard SkyTrain station. At Phibbs Exchange change to the **#229 Lonsdale Quay via Westlynn** bus. Whichever direction you come from get off the #229 at Peters Road and walk east to Lynn Canyon Park.

Skunk Cabbage

Though not in themselves palatable, skunk cabbage leaves had a zillion uses around the aboriginal kitchen. The unusually large leaves were ideal for lining and covering containers, lining steam pits, making fruit leather and sun drying seafood.

Bears are known to bung themselves up by ingesting copious quantities of mud just prior to settling in for that long winter nap.

Come springtime they seek out the laxative properties of skunk cabbage to -- *stand back* -- flush the system.

Illustration by Manami Kimura

This section of trail resumes some 2 km from where the last one left off. From the Ecology Centre at the heart of Lynn Canyon Park cross the suspension bridge, pausing the mandatory moment to ogle the frothy tumult below. From the bridge turn immediately downstream looking for the distinctive Baden-Powell trail markers. Heavy foot traffic in the canyons has created numerous intertwined routes that can be confusing. No need to cross the bridge at Twin Falls unless you require a second gawk at the gorge. After some 25 minutes or so of easy hiking through the floodplain forest you'll come to a boardwalk over a skunk cabbage patch from which you'll begin climbing steeply out of the canyon via a series of switchbacks. You have now reached the 2.7 km mark. Once on top you'll need to cross dusty Lillooet Road and find the trail again some 50 metres to your left [north.] The end of this section is just 1.2 km further on. Soon you'll come up on a huge powerline right-of-way beneath the gaze of Mount Seymour. In early summer you'll likely find plenty of plump huckleberries here but keep your ears and eyes alert at all times since black bears cherish this tart fruit too. Next the trail plunges down a steep staircase to cross a pipe-bridge over the Seymour River and climbs back up the other side to Riverside Drive. This area is not serviced by public transportation so you'll have to continue on through a muddy, uphill section before finally emerging on Hyannis Drive. If you have had enough for one-day turn right and continue on past Berkley Avenue to the first bus stop. Bus **#214** will take you down the hill to Phibbs Exchange where you may change to the **#210** bus to downtown Vancouver. Otherwise, if Deep Cove is your destination, plunge back into the forest and continue the next section as detailed below. 🐾

Hyannis Drive to Deep Cove

Level: Moderate   **Distance:** 7.2 km

Time: 4 h   **Elevation Change:** 275 m

Season: Year Round   **Map:** 92 G/6 & 92 G/7

Access: Take the **#210 Upper Lynn Valley** from Dunsmuir Street next to Burrard SkyTrain station to Phibbs Exchange. Change to the **#214 Blueridge** bus to Hyannis Drive. Walk west past Berkley Avenue to the trailhead on your right.

After climbing at a moderate pace for 2.3 km, you'll reach Mount Seymour Provincial Park where the terrain begins its descent towards Deep Cove 4.9 km to the east. On the way you'll pass a branch leading up to the historic Mushroom Parking Lot. Just fifteen minutes out of the way, you'll be rewarded by great views of the lower mainland from the picnic area. Consider returning to the Baden-Powell trail in a loop via the Old Buck Access Trail and a short segment of the Old Buck Trail itself. The detour avoids backtracking while adding only 10 minutes to your hike. For those wishing to bail out at Mount Seymour Road hourly bus service is 2 km down the hill near the park headquarters on Indian River Road. The **#215** bus will take you to Phibbs Exchange where you have to transfer to the **#210 Vancouver** bus. Continuing eastward through the park you'll soon come to Indian River Road which you'll have to follow a short distance to a power line right-of-way. From here the trail will soon lead south to a rocky bluff with magnificent views of Indian Arm and Deep Cove. The final leg of the Baden-Powell trail cuts back west again through a short but extremely pretty section of lush west coast rain forest. Turn right at the end of the trail and then left on the next street. The charming community of Deep Cove offers enough of the usual tourist treats to satisfy even the hungriest hikers. At the foot of Gallant Street pick up either the **#211** or **#212** bus to Phibbs Exchange. A quick change to the **#210 Vancouver** bus will take you downtown. 🐾

Ancient Trail Marker
A little hard to read perhaps but the plaque states "Baden Powell Trail To Skyline Drive
90 Minutes." Or so it used to. As the tree heals its wound is gradually covering the trail marker up. Eventually it should disappear inside the tree altogether.

Canon AE-1
50 mm lens
Kodacolor 200 ISO film

Deeks Bluffs Trail

Level: Easy   **Distance:** 7 km o/w

Time: 4 h o/w   **Elevation Change:** 385 m

Map: Squamish 92G/11   **Season:** Year Round

Access: See **Getting to Whistler** on pg 335

Wild Rose

This budding celebrity is popular enough to have been immortalized on license plates in four American states and one Canadian province, Alberta. Even before the Euro-invasion wild roses and their fruit, called "hips," were a mainstay in the medicine chests of nearly every nation on the continent. Whether a cure-all or just sound nutrition, rose hips are indeed generously endowed with vitamin C as well as beta-carotene, vitamins E, B and K. While rose hips are widely available as commercial herbal teas and jams, the tough outer rind can be chewed as is at trailside. Just peel and separate from the seeds, prior to chomping. Add wild rose petals to outback salad for both colour and delicate flavour.

Illustration by Manami Kimura

The bus driver should have no trouble stopping on the wide shoulder in front of the trailhead to Deeks Lake. Knowing in advance that the stop is immediately past a small sign for Bosco Creek, on the long straightaway leading up to the hill above Porteau Cove Provincial Park should be helpful however.

From the road the trail shoots straight up the shoulder of the mountain over a short section of creekside switchbacks. Once you reach the top of the bluffs however the main trail turns right onto an abandoned logging road and continues gaining altitude at a more modest pace. Turn left instead to explore the nearby quarry, now abandoned, that once belonged to the Deeks Sand and Gravel Company.

Back on the main trail, begin looking for a branch to the right after 45 minutes or so. Having located the Bluffs Trail, leave behind the trail to Deeks Lake and head down towards the highway for a few minutes. Another right hand branch leads up to a viewpoint overlooking the islands of Howe Sound, an ideal spot for lunch.

Descend to the Bluffs Trail and continue first west then south. The whole area is a nest of disused logging roads but the main route should be obvious. Expect to encounter numerous viewpoints as you make your way along the bluffs high above Highway 99. Eventually the trail begins to descend again, gradually at first then just before the end of the trail, very steeply. Back at the busy Sea to Sky Highway cross the road and look for a pull-out from which to flag down the next Vancouver-bound bus. 🐾

Deeks Lake Trail

Level: Difficult   **Distance:** 13 km r/t   **Time:** 7 h r/t

Elevation Change: 980 m   **Map:** Squamish 92G/11   **Season:** July - Oct

This thigh-burner starts out the same as the previous walk. Instead of turning off at the Bluffs Trail keep following the logging road for another 20 minutes as the trail gradually turns inland meeting up with the Old Deeks Lake Trail. Both trails join now, following a route parallel to Deeks Creek that is decidedly up. The logging road dwindles down to foot track just before it detours up and around a landslide area. The bypass is well-delineated with orange markers. Phi Alpha Falls will be first heard then seen as you approach the last steep set of switchbacks before climbing over the lip above your destination. Deeks Lake is a beautiful mountain jewel surrounded by scree slopes, old-growth forest and areas of open scrub. Mount Windsor is directly east while to the north Deeks Peak lords over the lake that shares its name. Both were named for John Deeks who, in 1910, created the lake to provide a dependable water source for his quarrying operations far below. Tarry awhile over lunch, a refreshing dip or lakeside snooze before undertaking the knee-gnashing descent. Return to where you started or, for a change of pace, follow the Old Deeks Lake Trail out to the highway. Be sure to return before the last bus passes by. 🐾

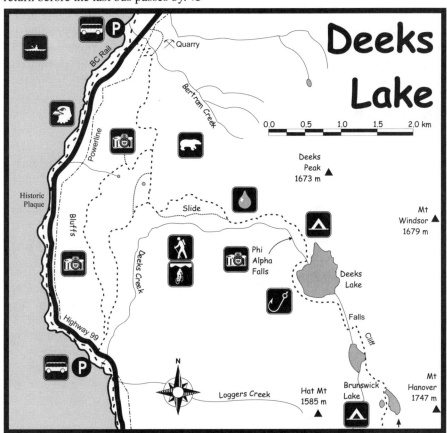

Phyllis Creek

Level: Moderate **Distance:** 16 km r/t **Time:** 7 h r/t

Elevation Change: 460 m **Map:** Squamish 92G/11 **Season:** Year Round

Access: See **Getting to Whistler** on page 335

Easy hikes are few and far between in the rugged mountains of the Sea to Sky corridor. The hike up Phyllis Creek is a happy exception. Get off the bus or train at Porteau Cove Provincial Park and look for the trailhead along the highway, 300 metres due south of the park entrance. The trail, marked with orange tape, services this and the following hike. From the outset the route is decidedly up, cutting under BC Hydro transmission lines within a few minutes before rounding massive granitic outcrops towards the south. Continue southwards and away from your destination until the trail begins paralleling a raging brook. Climb a short distance along the waterfalls to the top of the bluffs before turning northwards (left) onto an overgrown service road. The trail continues more or less along contour lines through ancient forest for more than an hour before circling eastwards around behind the Furry Creek Golf and Country Club. The creek in all her springtime fury should be plainly audible from the viewpoints. From the last of these the route drops steeply down an overgrown logging spur before reaching the active service road and powerline at the bottom. A left turn leads down to Furry Creek, the golf course and Highway 99 while a right parallels Phyllis Creek to her source. Continuing southwards, when you reach a fork in the road veer right as the left branch leads to Mount Capilano. Continue a short distance before crossing to the opposite bank of Phyllis Creek. Follow the power lines up through second growth forest to reach first Marion Lake then Phyllis Lake at 518 m elevation.

Mount Capilano

Level: Difficult **Distance:** 26 km r/t **Time:** 11 h r/t

Elevation Change: 1680 m **Map:** Squamish 92G/11 **Season:** July to Oct

Access: See **Getting to Whistler** on page 335

The approach to Mount Capilano begins the same as for the above hike. Instead of following Phyllis Creek to her headwaters veer left and cross the waterway. The route continues over an old, badly-eroded logging road above the banks of Furry Creek to just beyond Beth Creek. Watch for the trail to Mount Capilano leading off to the right of the road bed, rising through a series of switchbacks. The steep track quickly leaves logging's legacy behind, giving way to old-growth forest before reaching the shores of Beth Lake. The deep mountain lake is an ideal place to break for lunch before pushing on to the 1686-metre crown of Mount Capilano.

From the lake work down and around, first westwards then south up towards a ridge that leads ultimately to the barren, rocky summit of Mount Capilano. Perseverance is rewarded by a stupendous panorama extending from the North Shore Mountains and the Lions to the south, the islands of Howe Sound and the craggy Tantalus Range splayed out across the western horizon. Garibaldi Park's trademark peaks rise in the distance to the north.

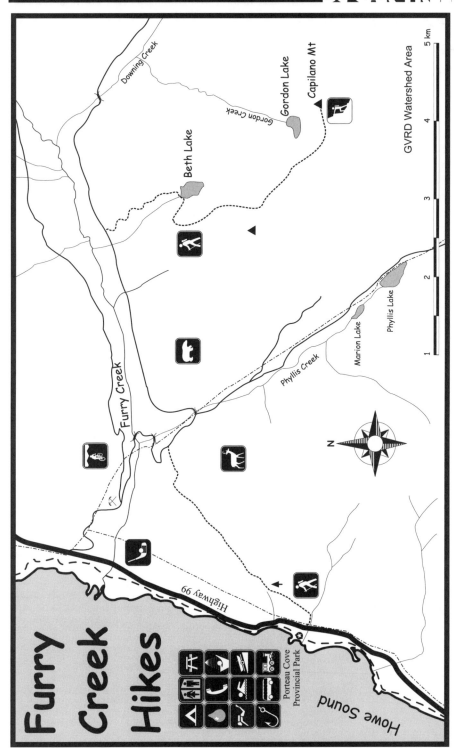

Furry Creek Hikes

Downing Creek

Beth Lake

Gordon Creek

Gordon Lake

Capilano Mt

Furry Creek

Phyllis Creek

Phyllis Lake

Marion Lake

Highway 99

Porteau Cove Provincial Park

Howe Sound

GVRD Watershed Area

N

1 2 3 4 5 km

Petgill Lake

Level: Challenging   **Distance:** 9½ km r/t   **Time:** 6 h r/t

Elev. Change: 640 m   **Map:** Squamish 92G/11   **Season:** April to Nov

Access: See **Getting to Whistler** on page 335

Take the bus as far as Murrin Provincial Park, a popular picnic and swimming area at the edge of Highway 99. Trout fishing in well-stocked Browning Lake is also possible but since a highway runs by it pack your fly rod into Petgill Lake for a more tranquil experience. You'll easily find the trailhead just beyond the park in the direction of Squamish and Whistler. From the highway the well-defined trail begins climbing straight up to a series of viewpoints overlooking Howe Sound. As you move away from the noisy transportation corridor the trail widens into a disused logging road which continues first eastward over fairly level ground then turns southward before abruptly swerving eastward on to a narrow footpath once again. Continue climbing over the shoulder that leads up to Goat Ridge before dropping down to Petgill Lake at 610 m elevation. The route on to Goat Ridge itself is much more demanding and may be better left for another day. To complete the circuit of Petgill Lake should take 30 - 40 minutes before retracing your steps back to Murrin Park. While waiting for the return bus be sure to check out the rock climbers who like to practice their bouldering skills on the rocky bluffs adjacent to Browning Lake. 🐾

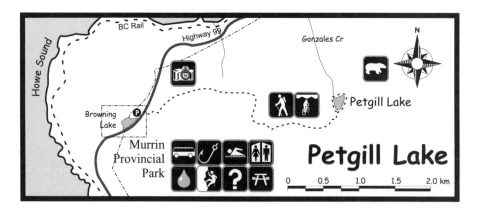

The Chief & Squaw

Route:	Distance:	Time:	Level:	Elev Change:	Season:
1st Peak	6 km	2 h r/t	Easy	620 m	March to Nov
2nd Peak	9 km	3 h r/t	Moderate	600 m	March to Nov
3rd Peak	11 km	4 h r/t	Moderate	600 m	March to Nov
Squaw	15 km	5½ h r/t	Challenging	550 m	March to Nov

Access: See **Getting to Whistler** on page 335   **Map:** Squamish 92G/11

When you get off the bus at the Stawamus Chief viewpoint, look up. Chances are there will be any number of groups hanging off the imposing granite monolith above you. This is "The Grand Wall," one of North America's most famous free climbs. The good news is you won't be scaling the Chief in that fashion.

Stawamus Chief Provincial Park now includes 40 wilderness and 15 vehicle camp-sites that were created following a prolonged bout of civil disobedience. Following many years of "guerrilla camping" by a growing corps of dedicated cliff hangers the provincial government finally decided to get with the program and build a proper camp-site with toilets at the site. The park has since become a veritable mecca for climbers from all over North America attracted by some of the longest, most accessible free

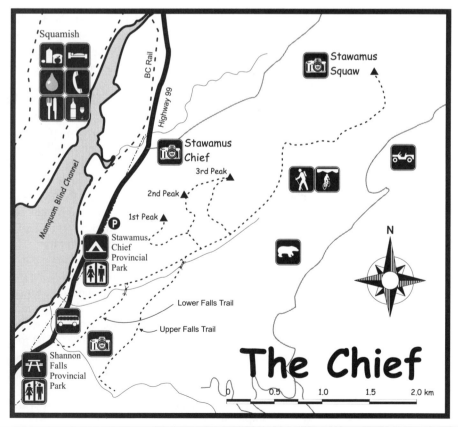

climbing routes on the planet. There are more than 280 different ascents up The Chief. Perhaps they don't know what you do, there's a much easier back door.

Walk southwards, working around behind the base of the Chief in counter-clockwise direction. Once you locate the trailhead in behind the solid rock wall scramble over the boulder that blocks the entrance and begin climbing the steps

Monster Monolith
The Chief dominates the view overlooking Howe Sound on a misty day. Taken from the trail to Diamond Head.

Nikon F
135 mm Nikkor lens
Kodachrome 64 ISO film.

in earnest. The well-used trail paralleling Olesen Creek eventually branches into four separate routes. One will take you as far as the site of a forest fire lookout perched atop Stawamus Squaw 7 km away. The others lead to the Stawamus Chief's triple peaks.

The first two branches to the right lead to Shannon Falls and are detailed below. Almost immediately a left branch leads up to the first and second peak. The first peak is a mere 3 km away; straight up mind you but mercifully short. The second peak is 4½ km away while the third one is 5½ km from the start of the trail. The third peak can be accessed either from the top of the second peak or from the main trail following Olesen Creek. This latter route eventually branches with the left fork extending up to the third peak. The Chief's distant mate will be found at the end of the right fork. The views from all four are spectacular, encompassing a panorama that includes the striking peaks of Garabaldi Park to the east, the Squamish Valley to the north and Howe Sound laid out at your feet to the west and south. The scene is marred only by the urban and industrial landscape of the city of Squamish and the Woodfibre pulp mill beyond. From atop the Chief consider you are standing on the world's second largest freestanding granite outcropping, topped only by the Rock of Gibraltar.

Choose a route suited to your schedule or camp out and undertake all four. 🐾

Shannon Falls

Route:	Distance:	Time:	Level:	Elev Change:	Season:
Falls Bottom	2 km	45 min r/t	Easy	75 m	Year Round
Falls Top	4 km	1½ h r/t	Moderate	385 m	March to Nov

Access: See **Getting to Whistler** on page 335   **Map:** Squamish 92G/11

From the trailhead described above two additional routes lead to 335 metre-high Shannon Falls where tour bus after tour bus drops off its cargo of flash happy visitors. The first trail is just a single kilometre long and, after crossing Olesen Creek, leads to the bottom of the falls where most of the shutter bugs congregate. The second footpath also crosses the creek, just before the fork leading to the Stawamus Chief's first and second peaks. Continue climbing steeply to the top of the cascade 1½ km away. Very few of the bus-bound ever make it this far. 🐾

Lowe-Tek

You're all fleeced up in Patagonia. You've donned Gore-Tex gaiters and those low top Hi-Tec's. Hoist up that high tech Lowe pack and, damn, you look good. You look the part. But do you look your very best?

What about personal grooming for the rugged outdoors man or woman? Uncommonly tough males may want to limber up each morning with a vigorous rub down using a cedar bark sponge soaked in octopus broth. That should get the old blood moving. Or so thought coastal native groups who used this very treatment on young sons to ensure they grew up dauntless. Those who practice no trace camping may even be tempted to drink the bath water.

And what about for the ladies? Stand aside Oil of Olay: native herbalism offers more support than a cosmetics counter. Want soft, supple skin while out in the elements? Simple. Concoct a skin cream out of deer belly fat and cottonwood resin. Melt the two ingredients together and pour into a hollow bull kelp bulb. Once it sets peel away the kelp and smear it on: Voila! Eternal youth.

A similar mixture of deer fat and hemlock resin makes for a quick and dandy sun screen. Who needs pink zinc anyhow?

Since those prehistoric-looking horse tails contain silica they make for a perfectly eco-friendly manicure. Native women on Vancouver Island are said to have added a little salmon slime for lubrication to buff fingernails to a gleaming lustre.

To keep dandruff, mites and other pests at bay, boil a little cow parsnip with chokecherry, red willow branches (and eye of newt if you have it.) This traditional scalp rinsing solution is even said to prevent grey hair.

When that little visitor arrives on the trail finely pounded red cedar bark, tree lichen and spagnum moss can all be used for feminine protection.

And for fresh backcountry breath try chewing on the rhizomes or roots of the common licorice fern. Or, in its place, the resin of hemlock trees is reputed to make a fine chewing gum. Like Trident, it has no added sugar. 🐾

Cal-Cheak Trail

Level: Easy   **Distance:** 4 km o/w

Time: 1½ hr o/w   **Elevation Change:** 10 m

Map: Brandywine 92J/3 **Season:** May to October

Brandywine Falls
Brandywine Creek meets an untimely end, dropping off a cliff into a gorge of its own making.

Nikon F
135 mm Nikkor lens
Kodak Plus X Pan 135 ISO film

Access: See **Getting to Whistler** on page 335

The best way to access this trail would be BC Rail. The railroad right-of-way parallels historic Pemberton Trail for the most part, crossing it at a couple points. There is even a whistle stop called McGuire near the north end of the trail but, alas, the train won't stop there no matter how hard you whistle. The next best alternative is the dependable Whistler-bound bus. Since the turn off to Cal-Cheak Forest Recreation Area may be difficult to find for some drivers, jump out, figuratively-speaking of course, at Brandywine Provincial Park instead. From the parking lot walk over to Brandywine Falls before beginning the hike in earnest. The Falls is best viewed in the morning when fingers of sunlight stream in to light up the mist and canyon walls below the 66-metre falls.

The Pemberton Trail was originally the only transportation route from Squamish through to Pemberton providing a vital link between the aboriginal peoples of the coast and those of the interior. Later, pioneers and prospectors trod the forest footpath in search of a better life. Little remains of the trail today though this little 4-kilometre section should be sufficient to take you back in time while leading over to Cal-Cheak Forest Recreation Area.

This section of the Pemberton Trail is known as the Brandywine/Cal-Cheak Trail and can be accessed by crossing back over the railroad tracks from the waterfall and making an immediate right. Near the beginning, the trail cuts across a ridge above tiny Swim Lake. There are some undulating sections and staircases to be negotiated but the trail is generally easy and should take just an hour and 20 minutes to complete. On the way look for outcroppings of columnar basalt and other signs of volcanic activity, leftovers from the cataclysm that created nearby Black Tusk and The Barrier. The trail flattens out for the last kilometre or so. Near the end the trail passes by the disused whistle stop of McGuire before reaching Callahan Creek.

The Ministry of Forests Recreation Site is just across the suspension bridge. This route could also be undertaken as a very easy backpacking overnighter. Rustic campgrounds and a picnic area are situated here at the confluence of the Cheakamus River and Callahan Creek. Due to high recreational use in the area drinking water should be boiled or treated with iodine. Both waterways are heavily laden with glacial till. Camping is possible too at Brandywine Provincial Park. While the water is better the price is also higher and the highway noise thunderous.

No need to walk all the way back to Brandywine Provincial Park to catch the return bus to Vancouver. Instead follow the dirt forest access road north for a kilometre to Highway 99. Cross the highway and stand in a visible location. Be sure to leave during daylight so the driver has plenty of time to safely pull over. Wave a jacket or $50 bill as the bus approaches. 🐾

Stinging Needles

Roll in a patch of *stinging nettle* and you'll think it's a spelling mistake. Nettle's stinging needles, as whispy as whiskers, are hollow and filled with formic acid which can cause burning, even blistering. Though aboriginal medicinal uses were various the principle technological use was as a source of hemp-like fiber for making thread and string. Stalks were picked late in the year when prickles had largely dropped off. Fibers were separated by rubbing or beating and then spun into thin threads. Those in turn could be braided to form thicker, stronger twine for weaving fine cloth, making fish nets and fishing line and, rarely, string bikinis.
Illustration by Manami Kimura

Brew Lake

Level: Difficult   **Distance:** 12 km r/t   **Time:** 7 h r/t

Elevation Change: 1036 m   **Map:** Brandywine 92J/3   **Season:** July to Oct

Access: See **Getting to Whistler** on page 335

Though Brew Lake must be accessed via the BC Railway right-of-way it is not possible to do so via the BC Railway passenger service. Instead, take the bus as far as Brandywine Falls Provincial Park. Before beginning your hike in earnest be sure to take a moment to check out Brandywine Falls. Brandywine Creek tumbles 66 metres down into a gorge of its own creation, filling the air with a fine cloud of mist. Return to the railway tracks and follow them west towards the Sea to Sky Highway. The rail bed turns abruptly south on the other side of Highway 99, continuing in a straight line for 1.8 km before making another sharp westward turn. Continue along the tracks until just 200 metres before this latter turn where you will find the well-marked trail to Brew Lake and beyond. At all times when following the railway right-of-way remain alert to the approach of freight and passenger trains as well as the fire-suppression crews which follow them.

The elevation gain is unrelenting, rising first over treed slopes then steeper, switching back and forth over rocky terrain. Pause from time to time to not only catch your breath but take in the views across the valley towards Garibaldi Provincial Park. By the time you have dropped down through alpine meadows to the shores of Brew Lake you will have climbed 1036 metres over six kilometres. Small rainbow trout are abundant in Brew Lake. The ambitious could set up a base camp at the lakeside from which to explore the open alpine ridges thereabouts. The route to Brew Mountain continues for 1.6 additional kilometres with a further elevation gain of 280 metres. 🐾

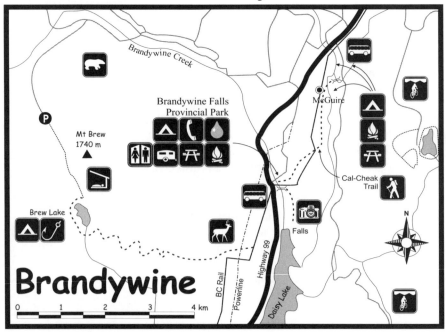

Wedgemount Lake

Level: Difficult   **Distance:** 18 km r/t   **Time:** $8\frac{1}{2}$ h r/t

Elevation Change: 1189 m   **Map:** Whistler 92J/2   **Season:** July to Sept

Access: See **Getting to Whistler** on page 335

Get off the bus where a blue BC Parks sign indicates Wedgemount Lake. If the bus driver doesn't know where that is tell him to look for a turnout just 11 km north of Whistler Village. From Highway 99 cross the BC Rail tracks and the Green River before turning left onto the abandoned logging road that will serve as a trail for the first 3 km. After the first two kilometres the trail becomes very steep, an attribute it will retain for the rest of the hike.

Soon after crossing the log bridge over Wedgemount Creek you'll be engulfed by a forest of old-growth conifers marking the boundary of Garibaldi Provincial Park. This is what the surrounding countryside used to look like. The forest gradually begins to thin out as altitude is gained eventually giving way to scrub and talus. This last pitch, known as the "Stairmaster," is the steepest of all but those who persevere will be richly rewarded.

Turquoise Wedgemount Lake lies at the foot of a nest of stupendous glacier-clad peaks. Garibaldi Park's highest, 2686 metre Wedge Mountain, dominates the picture. A single arm of Wedgemount Glacier reaches down to gently touch the lakeshore at its far end. Perched above the near end is the beehive-shaped shelter erected by the B.C. Mountaineering Club. For those willing to grunt up the trail with a full backpack there is also a wilderness campsite. Whether on an overnighter or an extended day trip be sure to leave enough time to explore the glacier close up. Never, of course, cross an

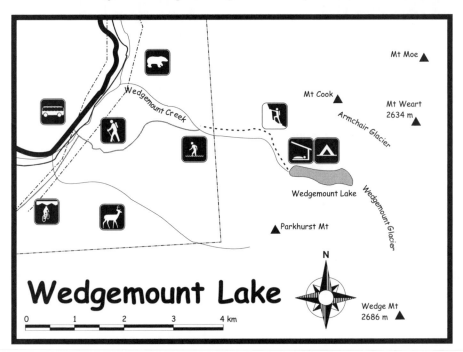

Wedgemount Creek · Mt Moe · Mt Cook · Mt Weart 2634 m · Armchair Glacier · Wedgemount Lake · Wedgemount Glacier · Parkhurst Mt · N · Wedgemount Lake · Wedge Mt 2686 m

0   1   2   3   4 km

icefield without the proper training and equipment. Extra caution should also be taken when making the return descent, especially when laden with gear.

Leave It To Beaver

Heading off for another night of logging, Canada's symbol leaves a wake sparkling in the deep shadows of dusk. By a weird quirk of evolution, beavers are unable to digest the twigs, bark, and bits of wood they typically feast on. Instead, when the mass of cellulose reaches a beaver's lower intestine it is digested by a bacteria colony. Nutrients are released but since the rodent's lower intestine is incapable of absorbing them they are expelled in the usual way. The feces are then re-consumed to allow the upper intestine to absorb the nutrients.

Nikon F
135 mm Nikkor lens
Kodachrome 64 ISO film.

Glacial-fed streams and lakes contain an inordinate amount of clay suspended in the water, hence the lovely bluish-green colour. Look for water trickling down from the melting snow pack for drinking instead. Due to the elevation you should even be able to find patches of the white stuff well into September. 🐾

Backpacking

Checklist

❑ **Backpack** lined with orange, jumbo-sized plastic garbage bags.

❑ **Sleeping Bag**; Avoid down unless planning to do a lot of winter camping. Feathers get soggy under typical "wet coast" conditions.

❑ **Ensolite Foam Pad**; Lighter and more useful than the popular Therm-A-Rest, foam pads can be used for comfort around the camp without worrying about burns and punctures. In emergencies, foam can be cut up and used for splint pads or backpack repair. Yellow foam pads also can be used to signal with.

❑ **Tent** or bivy sack

❑ **Stove**; Avoid the ones which require disposible butane cannisters.

❑ **Cooking Gear**; Eat directly from the pot and avoid carrying bowl and plate.

❑ **Water Bottle**; Keep it handy and rehydrate often.

❑ **Flashlight** or headlamp and batteries.

❑ **Duct tape**; 1001 uses from repairing packs, kayaks, boots, etc.

❑ **Nylon Cord**; 20 metres or more. Ideal for hanging food, tarps, wet clothes, etc.

❑ **First Aid Kit** and the knowledge to use it.

❑ **Knife**; Swiss Army: good, Rambo: bad.

❑ **Whistle**

❑ **Topographical Map & Compass**

❑ **Personal clothing**; Lightweight, quick-dry, clothing suited to layering. Avoid cotton as it dangerously conducts heat away from the body when wet.

❑ **Anorak** or other weather-resistant shell. Breathable fabrics are ideal.

❑ **Sun hat**; Wide-brimmed or with neck flap.

❑ **Sunglasses** with UV filtration

❑ **Sunscreen** & lip salve

❑ **Moleskin**; lots if prone to blisters

❑ **Mosquito Repellant**

❑ **Matches** & firestarter

❑ **Hiking Boots**; Well-broken in *before* the trip.

❑ **Socks**; Ultra-thin polypropolene undersocks used in combination with thicker wool socks will help keep feet dry and prevent blisters. No cotton.

❑ **Camp Shoes**; Back up footwear with the emphasis on comfort; should be durable enough for hiking in if necessary. Sandles are inadequate for the job.

❑ **Camera** and plenty of film

❑ **Personal effects**; Keep it light. First timers always bring too much.

❑ **Toilet paper**

Garibaldi Lake

Level: Difficult   **Distance:** 11.8 km o/w

Time: 5 h   **Elevation Change:** 1210 m

Season: June to October

Map: 92 G/14 Cheakamus River & 92 G/15 Mamquam Mountain. A full-colour plastic map of the entire Garibaldi Region is available from Lower Mainland bookstores. Published by International Travel Maps at a scale of 1:100,000. They forgot to include a scale but that's 1 cm = 1 km. The only other drawback is contour intervals are based on older government charts expressed in feet rather than metres. Conversion yields intervals of 61 m, not exactly a dream number to navigate with.

Grousing About The Alpine
With feathered feet and camelion-like plumage, the ptarmagin is well-equipped to endure the hardships of winter. This one is outfitted in summer camouflage.

Nikon F
135 mm Nikkor lens
Kodachrome 64 ISO film.

Access: The bus to Whistler [See Appendix **Getting to Whistler** Page 335] will drop you off at a side road 37 km north of Squamish on Highway 99. Make sure the driver completely understands where you want to get off. There should be ample room for the bus to pull over at the turn off. Look for signs along the Highway indicating Garibaldi Provincial Park, Black Tusk.

Though steep, the route into this part of Garibaldi Provincial Park can be undertaken as a day trip for those who are reasonably fit. Rushing through the Black Tusk area, however, seems somehow sacrilegious given the sights you will necessarily miss.

After getting off the bus follow the paved side road 2½ km east to the Rubble Creek parking lot. Be thankful you don't have a car to park here as, on a typical weekend, at least some of them will be broken into. The trail proper begins from here and you will be gaining elevation for most of the day, climbing steeply through a seemingly endless succession of switchbacks. The trail, sometimes derisively referred to as "Garibaldi Highway," is wide and well-maintained, capable of accommodating heavy summer foot traffic. At the 6 km mark the trail forks with the left branch leading to Taylor Meadows campsite just 1½ km further on. Continue climbing for three kilometres in the opposite direction in order to reach Garibaldi Lake campsite. Huts have been erected at both campsites but, unless you relish the idea of field mice crawling across your face while you sleep, bring a tent. Snowshoers and nordic skiers will find the well-equipped huts a godsend during the winter. Because of ease of access from Vancouver both campsites are usually over-full on weekends during the summer. For that reason a weekday visit to the Black Tusk area is strongly advised. 195,080

hectare Garibaldi Provincial Park is the busiest in British Columbia. Camping at Taylor Meadows costs $5 while sitting up a tent at the more popular lakeshore campsite costs twice as much.

Continuing along the right fork you'll soon encounter a viewpoint overlooking The Barrier, the giant volcanic dam that created Garibaldi Lake when a river of lava, ash and cinder spewed out of Mt. Price some 11,000 years ago. For the most part, area lakes drain through, not over, the porous volcanic stone with just puny Rubble Creek visible on the surface. The area below the unstable Barrier has been declared a Civil Defence Zone and, while it isn't expected to come crashing down into the valley any day soon, an earthquake could trigger just such a cataclysm. The Barrier has spawned massive landslides as recently as1855.

Following the viewpoint, the trail soon begins to level out before descending to the park headquarters and camping area in front of the aptly named Battleship Islands. Either Taylor Meadows or Garibaldi Lake are ideally situated base camps for exploring the Black Tusk Meadows and Panorama Ridge high above. Pit toilets are available at both campsites but you will be expected to pack out any refuse you create. Fires are prohibited throughout this area. 🐾

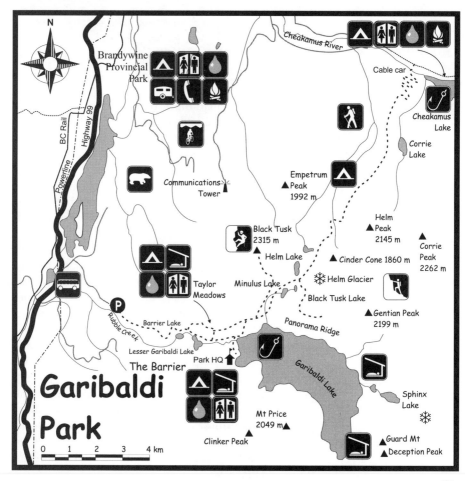

Black Tusk

Level: Moderate **Distance:** 14 km r/t

Time: 5½ h **Elevation Change:** 850 m

Season: June to Oct **Access:** See previous hike.

A pilgrimage to the Tusk is *de rigueur* though climbing to the 2316 m summit is not recommended without special

West-Facing North Face
Black Tusk dominates the view from a cliffside condo perched high atop Panorama Ridge.

Nikon F
28 mm Nikkor lens
Kodachrome 64 ISO film.

equipment. The trail to Black Tusk climbs away from Garibaldi Lake for three kilometres before rejoining the trail from Taylor Meadows campsite at Black Tusk Meadows. Expect the meadows to be alive with colour in the springtime, a verdant canvas splashed with purple heather and lupins, fiery red Indian paintbrush and golden butter cups all visited time and again by the busiest of bumblebees. Please remain on trails at all times to avoid disturbing this fragile landscape.

Continue through the meadows for a short distance before veering left on the fork that leads 2½ km up through loose talus to the base of the Tusk itself. This striking monolith is thought to be a volcanic plug; a column of solidified lava left behind as the cone is eroded away. The trail ends at the base of the only safely climbable chimney to the top.

Novices should not attempt to scale the 100 metre route without benefit of ropes, helmet and the guidance of more experienced climbers. Always ascend or descend one at a time as the crumbly volcanic material presents considerable hazard to those below. The view from the top is without peer, extending from the Tantalus Range in the southwest and turquoise Garibaldi Lake at the foot of Panorama Ridge across to the Fitzsimmons Range in the northeast behind Whistler Village. 🐾

Panorama Ridge

Level: Moderate   **Distance:** 15 km r/t

Time: 5½ h   **Elevation Change:** 630 m

Season: June to Oct   **Access:** See previous hikes.

If the scenery from the top of Black Tusk was not enough then gaining the summit of Panorama Ridge will more than satisfy. Follow the same route from camp to where you zigged left to the Tusk. Zag to the right instead, this time, continuing along the main trail. The trail forks again at the divide between two watersheds with the right fork leading up to Panorama Ridge itself. Either before or after mounting the ridge be sure to leave enough time to explore the geological wonders along the left fork as well. This route leads over the divide, across the cinder flats, then steeply down to the cable car across the raging Cheakamus River. Follow it past Helm Lake to Cinder Cone, a tiny, 200 metre tall, extinct volcano at the foot of Helm Glacier. On a hot day the cool air and eerie blue light inside the ice caves below the glacier will provide respite from the sun. Backtrack now to the junction leading to Panorama Ridge where you'll begin climbing almost immediately. The route follows a shoulder southward up to the east-west running ridge. From the summit gaze south across azure Garibaldi Lake to the appropriately named Table silhouetted against the glaciers clinging to stately Garibaldi Mountain in the distance. 2049 metre Mount Price and Clinker Peak off to the right are extinct volcanos, as are 2675 metre Castle Towers and Phyllis Engine directly east. Look north to take in a panorama -- thus the name --- that encompasses Black Tusk, Cinder Cone and Helm Glacier. From the top of the ridge retrace your steps back to camp. Experienced and well-equipped mountaineers may want to continue following Panorama Ridge in a circuit that sweeps across the eastern arm of the ice field along Gentian Ridge to 2145 metre Helm Peak before descending steeply to the foot of Helm Glacier. This route is not for the inexperienced however as some climbing is involved. Be sure to rope your party together before venturing on to the ice field, Tom. 🐾

Krumholtz

Trees clustered together in the sub alpine stand a much better chance of surviving the harsh conditions. Called *krumholtz*, these tree islands are miniature ecosystems unto themselves, providing mutual protection against the elements while acting as a catch basin for moisture. A krumholtz provides habitat for lesser plant species as well as insects, birds and mammals big and small. Usually trees in the krumholtz, German for "crooked wood," are old if not ancient, stunted by a short growing season, harsh weather and a paucity of nutrient-rich soil. Branches tend to flourish on the downwind side only.

Illustration by Manami Kimura

Singing Pass Loop

Level: Moderate   **Season:** July to October

Distance:	Musical Bumps Route 9 km o/w	**Time:** 7 h
	Fitzsimmons Creek Route 11 km o/w	**Time:** 8 h
Elevation Change:	Roundhouse to Flute Summit	+152 m
	Flute Summit to Russet Lake	-945 m
	Russet Lake to Singing Pass	+305 m
	Singing Pass to Whistler Village	-610 m

Map: 92 J/2 Whistler. A full-colour plastic map of the entire Garibaldi Region is available from Lower Mainland bookstores. Published by International Travel Maps at a scale of 1:100,000. They forgot to include a scale but that's 1 cm = 1 km. The only other drawback is contour intervals are based on older government charts expressed in feet rather than metres. Conversion yields intervals of 61 m, not exactly a dream number to navigate with.

Access: [See **Getting to Whistler** Page 335.] The Whistler Express gondola will be found on the edge of the main village.

The trailhead to Singing Pass starts from British Columbia's premier four-season resort community. Visitors and newcomers to the West Coast may want to combine this moderate backpacking trip with a day or two spent exploring and relaxing in Whistler Village afterwards. Mountain biking, river rafting, golf are just a few of the summer pursuits popular here.

Until recently most hikers reached Singing Pass via the Fitzsimmons Creek access road, driving to within 7 km of the alpine pass. Washouts along the old logging road now preclude vehicle access. And while hikers and mountain bikers still use the road most visitors to this part of Garibaldi Provincial Park follow the "Musical Bumps" route instead.

While purists and the very frugal may insist on reaching the trailhead on foot, trudging up through the open gashes slashed out of the forest for skiers makes for pretty dull hiking. The majority grudgingly dish out the astounding $21 required to ride the Whistler Express gondola up to the Roundhouse restaurant at the top of the mountain. The lift operates daily during high season from the last week of June through to the last week of September.

With most, but not all of the elevation already gained, check the map and information board after unloading to find the start of the Harmony Lake Trail. While trails snake around either side of Whistler glacier the left fork via Harmony Lake is shorter. After reuniting, the route scoots up and over one of Whistler Mountain's sprawling shoulders before dropping down again to Burnt Stew Lake. M-m-m... What's for lunch?

The trail rises again up and around the "Musical Bumps," past krumholtz, threading a path through seemingly endless rocky meadows. The faint path first skirts around to the east of Piccolo Summit then cuts over the top of 1981 m Flute Summit just a kilometre away before finally weaving 1½ km back around to the north and east of Oboe Summit.

Typically, during July and August the meadows are alive with a brilliant pastiche of wildflowers: splashes of yellow, purple and blue, white and red against the backdrop of glacial Cheakamus Lake far below and distant crags draped in ice. Stay on the trail to avoid unnecessary damage to the fragile alpine landscape.

After rounding Oboe Summit the route drops down again to Singing Pass less than a kilometre away. Just prior to reaching a *You Are Here* sign complements of BC Parks note the return trail via Fitzsimmons Creek branching off to the left.

Continue on, the best views can be had from a ridge just a mere 500 metres beyond Singing Pass. When drinking in the panorama of snow and glacier-covered peaks note Russet Lake nestled at the base of Fissile Peak. Make for the acorn-shaped cabin at the north end of the lake to set up tents. The cabin was built by the Alpine Club of Canada whose members frequently ascend the peaks and ice fields hereabouts. Unless planning to join them on the precipices, Russet Lake is the end of the road for backpackers.

Retrace the two kilometres back to Singing Pass where hikers are confronted with a choice. The shortest route back is the way you came, 8 km up and over the Musical Bumps to the gondola which, incidentally, ceases operations at 8:00 PM every evening. The loop route paralleling Fitzsimmons Creek is longer [10 kilometres] and while it

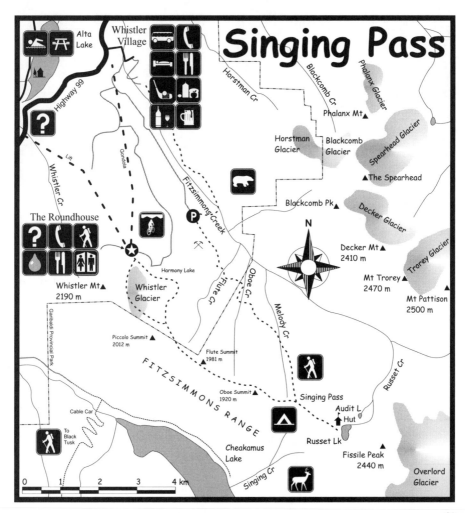

passes through a delightful old-growth forest, half of the route passes through some of the forest industry's finest clearcuts. On the upside it's downhill all the way.

From Singing Pass the trail drops down through alpine meadows parallel to the course of Melody Creek. Gradually the stunted *bonsai* trees of sub alpine merge into a forest

Mine Shaft
Ore cart rails lead into the gaping cavern of an abandoned mine along the lower half of the Sining Pass Route.

Nikon F
28 mm Nikkor lens
Kodachrome 64 ISO film

with trees getting larger as you drop into the valley. As you turn away from Melody Creek the forest becomes a mature stand of timber.

The boundary of Garibaldi Provincial Park is easy to recognize as the forest beyond it has been obliterated. The view does not improve for the rest of the journey though just past the boundary check out an abandoned gold mine at trail side. The gaping cavern, shored up with heavy wooden beams, and rusty ore cart rails are reminiscent of some cheesy western movie and seem somehow out of place here in the British Columbia outback.

Soon after the mine you'll reach the parking lot from which hikers traditionally accessed Singing Pass. An alternative route drops from the parking lot directly down across Fitzsimmons Creek picking up a service road along the fringes of Blackcomb Mountain. Though more scenic, this less direct route entails crossing Fitzsimmons Creek which may be a torrent early in the season.

Except for a few washed out sections the 5 km from the parking lot to Whistler Village are uneventful. Stay alert for black bears which tend to proliferate in clearcut areas. The end of the dirt road joins Blackcomb Way just behind the main bus loop in the Village. Splurge a little if you can afford it and soak all the trail dust off in a private hot tub. Budget accommodations are also available. 🐾

Whistler Village

Location	Notes
Whistler Mountain 1-888-284-9999 932-4211 [604] 687-7507 in Vancouver www.whistler-blackcomb.com	Accommodations Gondola to Musical Bumps Route: Summer 10 am - 8 pm
Fireside Lodge 2117 Nordic Drive, Whistler BC 604-932-4545 (604)932-3994 FAX	A hostel with dorm and private rooms, common bathrooms, kitchen, lounge, and games room Bring your own bedding and towels. On bus routes but a little far from the centre of things
Central Reservations 1-800-944-7853 604-664-5625	Hotel or Condo Accommodations
Hostelling International - Whistler; 5678 Alta Lake Rd, Whistler, BC (604) 932-5492; (604) 932-4687; whistler@hihostels.bc.ca;	
Whistler Backpackers Guest House, 2124 Lake Placid Rd., (604) 932-1177, Whistler, BC	
Seppo's Log Cabin, 7114 Nesters Rd., (604) 932-8808; Whistler, BC	
UBC Whistler Lodge; 2124 Nordic, Rd. Whistler (604) 822-5851; (604) 932-6604 (604)822-9019 FAX whisbkgs@ams.ubc.ca http://www.ams.ubc.ca/whistler/	
Whistler Travel Infocenter (604) 932-5528 (604) 932-3755FAX www.whistlerweb.net/library/cocinfo.htm	

Henrietta Lake

Level: Difficult   **Distance:** 10 km o/w   **Time:** 5 h

Elevation Change: 1475 m   **Season:** June to Oct   **Map:** 92 G/11

Access: Getting there is as simple as hopping a bus destined for Whistler [See **Getting to Whistler** Page 335.] You'll want to ensure that your bus connects reasonably well with the ferry schedule opposite. For example, catching the 8 AM bus on Georgia Street will get you to Darrell Bay just in time for the 9:30 AM ferry. You may have to run, particularly if the driver drops you off at Shannon Falls, slightly beyond your destination. Be sure to inform the driver of your special needs when you board.

Unlike various trails in Garibaldi Park, Henrietta Lake and beyond are rarely visited by more than a couple groups at a time. Perhaps the infrequent ferry service, the proximity of a pulp mill or the long tramp along an inactive logging road is a turn off for many purists. Whatever the case if you do decide to check out this area you'll more than likely find it deserted.

The crossing of Howe Sound takes about 25 minutes and costs nothing since the ferry is provided as an employee shuttle by Western Pulp. Veer left after disembarking and sign in at the first aid post. As a safety precaution and a condition of using company property all hikers must sign in and sign out again on their return. Staff will direct you along the railway away from the mill proper to a flight of stairs leading to dormitories and a cookhouse. A service road beyond cuts up behind the smoking, steaming mill

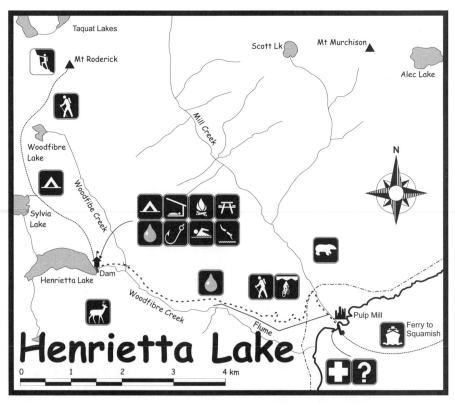

itself. Yes, the mill stinks, really stinks, but keep in mind that the route you are about to enjoy would not exist without the presence of the mill. The service road will take you steeply up through a series of switchbacks, under a large powerline and up into the Woodfibre Creek Valley quickly leaving the sights, sounds and, hopefully, smells of heavy industry behind. At each branch of the road take the right fork to remain on the mainline.

At kilometre four you may enjoy a brief side trip to check out the flume which supplies the mill with water. A 15 minute stroll along the boardwalk-topped flume itself takes you to the intake pond. On a hot summer day this enticingly deep pool offers an icy jolt that will take your breath away. A metal grill separates the intake from the pool so there is little danger of being sucked down the flume. During times of high water, however, excess spills over the front of the pool creating a waterfall and considerable peril. Use your own judgement and keep in mind that whatever you do on company property is at your own risk. At the very least, top up water bottles here.

At kilometre six the logging road abruptly ends at a sturdy aluminum footbridge. Steep suddenly becomes steeper as you follow a series of switchbacks up the last pitch before Henrietta Lake. As the narrow trail winds upward through an attractive old growth forest it crosses and re-crosses remnants of a rail lift that was once used for hauling construction materials up to the lake when it was dammed in 1947.

Near the end of the trail you'll come across a strange looking structure. Keep out! It provides access for engineers from the pulp mill to the underground shaft that drains the lake.

At Henrietta Lake you'll find the aforementioned dam, a rather rundown but watertight cabin, a rustic picnic table and a floating platform perfect for hot day dips of the skinny variety. The water of Henrietta Lake is surprisingly warm, bearable at any rate and supports a healthy, if over-fed, trout population. Try fly fishing later in the season—say September or October—once the bugs have bugged off for good.

Since water flows were once manually controlled the cabin originally served as a hermitage for on-site staff. Now, with the advent of automation, the cabin is still maintained as emergency shelter. Visitors are welcome to use it but are requested to clean up after themselves. Being mouse-infested, it is suggested that this resort be used only as a last resort, particularly since mice droppings as close as eastern Washington state have been linked to the deadly hanta vi-

Woodfibre Ferry Schedule

Leave Darrell Bay	Leave Woodfibre
7:15 AM*	8:15 AM
8:30 AM	9:00 AM
9:30 AM	10:00 AM
11:30 AM	12:05 PM
1:30 PM	2:00 PM
3:30 PM	4:15 PM*
4:45 PM	5:15 PM
5:45 PM	6:15 PM
7:25 PM	8:10 PM
8:35 PM	9:00 PM
9:30 PM	10:00 PM
11:30 PM	12:10 PM

*Crowded due to Shift Change

rus. Outside there are comfortable campsites for up to two tents.

Behind the cabin the trail leads past a sturdy helipad and begins climbing steeply towards Mt Roderick. Look for a rusted diesel "donkey" in the bush to the right. Being less travelled the trail is somewhat overgrown with blue huckle-

Lakeside Refuge
The water-tight cabin overlooking the dam at Henrietta Lake.

Nikon F
28 mm Nikkor lens
Ektachrome 100 ISO film.

berry bushes in places but is otherwise in good condition. Remember, bears also find the fruit delicious.

Once on top you'll continue climbing the ridgeline past Sylvia Lake. The best camping is to be had beyond the rock slide. Or take the high road and continue past tiny Woodfibre Lake and on up to the summit of Mount Roderick at 1475 metres. A stupendous view on all sides is the reward for making the ascent. 🐾

Sunshine Coast Trail

Map: Powell River Visitors Bureau has produced a brilliant map of the entire region detailing, not only the Sunshine Coast Trail, but the Powell Forest Canoe Route and Desolation Sound. The full-colour map includes topographic informa-tion, logging roads, and other routes of interest to mountain bikers, horseback riders and hikers. Key scuba diving, kayaking, climbing and camping locations are also highlighted. Details on how to obtain a free copy of this excellent resource are included in the information grid following this article. Geological Survey of Canada 1:50,000 series sheets for the trail are 92 F/15 & 92 F/16.

The community of Powell River has it all, a remote, multi-day canoe route, a kayak-er's paradise and now a 175 km bush trek. The first two, the Powell Forest Canoe Route and Desolation Sound are detailed on pages 314 and 306 respectively. The latter Sun-shine Coast Trail is the most recent development and, though complete, upgrading is expected to continue for some years yet. The entire trail is marked with bright orange squares though more detailed signage will be gradually added. Some campsites are rustic in the extreme but then again that's why we go there. The trail is so new in fact that this author has yet to hike its entire length. I did however live in Powell River for five years and have tramped and camped throughout the region including many of the areas embraced by the new trail. Since that was well-before the trail was ever con-ceived the description below will be necessarily scant.

Though on the British Columbia mainland, Powell River is an isolated community sandwiched between Desolation Sound to the north and Jervis Inlet to the south. The Sunshine Coast Trail runs from land's end at Sarah Point southward to the end of the road at the Saltery Bay ferry terminal. Ferries connect the mill town with Comox on Vancouver Island and, via the Sechelt Peninsula, to the Lower Mainland. Twice-daily bus service provides a car-free link from Vancouver. Refer to **Getting to the Sunshine Coast** on page 333 for full details.

Stage 1: Sarah Point to Malaspina Road

Level: Moderate   **Distance:** 21.3 km   **Time:** 2-3 days

Elevation Change: 340 m   **Season:** Year-round

Catch the first bus of the day to reach the trailhead by late afternoon. From the bus depot in Westview hop in a cab to complete the road portion of the journey. Taxi fare to Lund should be around $30. From here a water taxi, costing $50 for up to six people, will be required to reach Sarah Point. Advanced reservations are a must.

There are a number of rustic campsites at the beginning of the trail. The sun-baked bluffs of Sarah Point itself are an ideal perch from which to witness the renowned sunsets of the Sunshine Coast. Load up on water, however, before boarding the water taxi as the point is dry. If blustery weather rather than a gentle sunset greets you then push on to Myrmidon Cove 4 km away on the more protected side of Malaspina Penin-sula. Myrmidon Cove is endowed with water but no other amenities. On the way expect pleasant views overlooking Desolation Sound and one small beach at Feather Cove, 2.8 km from the beginning of the trail.

Ocean views and saltwater access will continue off and on through much of the next day. Early-rising bird watchers will want to approach Hinder Lake quietly to avoid scaring the waterfowl away. Use extra care in the vicinity of Hinder Lake as it is a source of water for nearby residents and hikers alike. The Knob [km 7.6] in particular provides vistas of Okeover Inlet. At km 9.6 a side trail leads down to a campsite on Cochrane Bay endowed with both water and oysters. Be sure to check with the Red Tide Hotline before

The Incredible Hulks
Nothing bespeaks "Powell River" better than the hulks, a ring of cement cargo ships adjacent to the city's pulp mill. The WWII leftovers were purchased, stripped then put into service as a deep water breakwater surrounding the mill's log pond. While the ships leak and list they have served as an inadvertent landmark for decades.

Nikon F
28 mm Nikkor lens
Kodachrome 64 ISO film

harvesting the latter.

Alternately join the resident beaver for a snack any day of the week at [km 12.1] Wednesday Lake. The feature of the beaver lodge is double-digested bark. If you thought to pack along a lightweight fly rod then perhaps you can tease a trout or two out of the pond and into the frying pan instead. The campsite at Wednesday Lake has drinking water, a pit toilet and the plaintive cries of loons to lull you into slumber. Rather than scooping water directly from the lake, dip into the outfall just beyond the camp to reduce the amount of suspended particulate matter. Lest the beaver sports a fever treat all water to be on the safe side. Giardia is no way to start a vacation.

Gwendoline Hills Trail

The final 9 kilometres on this first stage of the Sunshine Coast Trail are the most taxing. Though you might find a trickle here and a drip there, a reliable source of drinking water is nonexistent. Likewise, there are no established campsites along the way. The trail primarily winds through forest including the occasional pocket of old-growth with viewpoints few and far between. Take them in whenever they crop up. Just past Wednesday Lake a short side trail leads to a viewpoint overlooking Okeover Inlet. At the 16 km mark views in the opposite direction overlooking the Strait of Georgia can be had from Manzanita Bluffs.

A rustic campsite with water and picnic table has been established just 100 metres beyond the end of this section at Fern Creek but far superior alternatives abound just a short distance down Malaspina Road. Okeover Inlet Provincial Campground offers the least developed facilities but running water and pit toilets will be appreciated. If undertaking the Sunshine Coast Trail in small, easily-digestable segments or otherwise wanting to bailout at this point call for a taxi from the government wharf here. Nearby Y-Knot Campsite [(604) 483-3243] offers basic camping plus hot showers. Just prior to the end of the trail a well-marked side trail leads to Cedar Lodge B & B [(604) 483-4414] for those in dire need of both a hot water soak and a pillow. Reservations are required.

Stage 2: Malaspina Road to Powell Lake

Level: Moderate   **Distance:** 29.9 km   **Time:** 2-3 days
Elevation Change: 140 m   **Season:** Year-round

From the start at Malaspina Road the Thunder Ridge Trail passes through second-growth forest with a sprinkling of old-growth. These lone ancients are likely seed trees that were left behind when the forest was originally downed. One big and gnarly Douglas fir of note measures 2.3 metres through the middle. Big Gnarly, as the locals coincidentally call it, will be found 3.5 kilometres from the start of this section at km 24.8. One further ancient giant overlooks the 28.5 km mark.

The 3.6 km stretch of trail from Plummer Creek Rd. [25.2 km] to Southview Road is flat and easy so expect to make good time. The middle part of Toquenetch Trail, as this section is called, follows a small creek where spawning salmon may be spotted from late summer onwards. Upon reaching Southview Road [28.8 km] turn left and cross the bridge, taking the first right which should be marked Homestead Campsite. Just beyond this intersection look for the trail plunging back into the forest on the left. Homestead Campsite, with creek water, an outhouse, fire pit and picnic tables, will be found a short distance from the little-used side road.

The next 8.9 km section, knitting together the Marathon and Appleton Canyon Trails, is also fairly easy going with varied scenery. Each step now takes you further from the coastal environment as the trail winds inland. A number of bluffs in the vicinity of km 31.6 afford welcomed views. Linger to enjoy them as the trail continues through a horror-show clear-cut immediately upon leaving the bluffs. Follow plastic survey tape and metal markers for approximately 200 metres to pick your way through the mayhem. Reiveleys Pond [km 33.5] too may dispense a few moments of quiet reflection though on a hot day a cool dip might be a more satisfying reward for your efforts.

The campsite at Appleton Creek offers the usual primitive amenities. Sixty metres past the main site the trail forks with the left leading to Wilde Road and an outhouse and the right continuing through Appleton Canyon. Follow the latter route to reach a succession of tumbling waterfalls and numerous suitable campsites at creekside. The two-kilometre Appleton Canyon is undeveloped at this time so the usual cautions re-

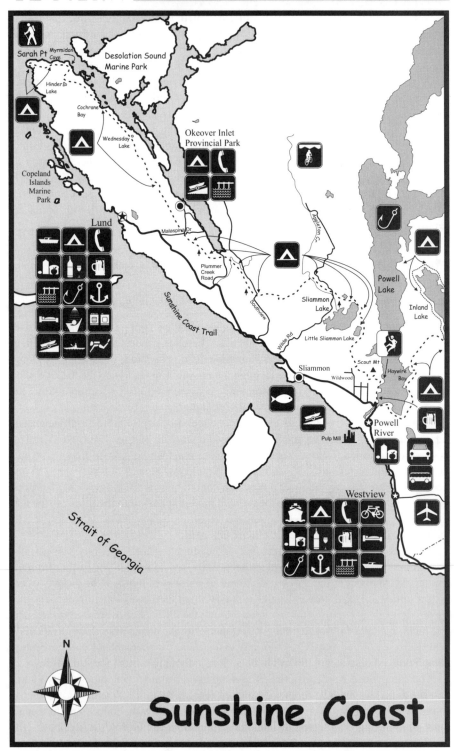

Sunshine Coast

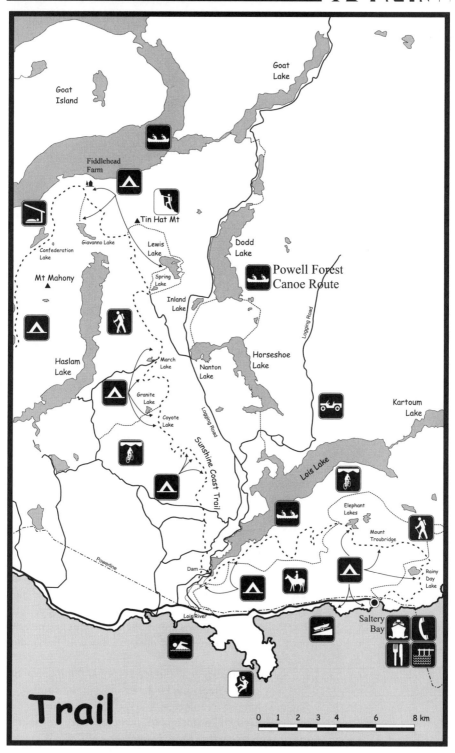

Goat
Lake

Goat
Island

Fiddlehead
Farm

▲ Tin Hat Mt

Giavanno Lake

Lewis
Lake

Dodd
Lake

Confederation
Lake

Spring
Lake

Powell Forest
Canoe Route

Mt Mahony
▲

Inland
Lake

Logging Road

Haslam
Lake

March
Lake

Nanton
Lake

Horseshoe
Lake

Kartoum
Lake

Granite
Lake

Logging Road

Coyote
Lake

Sunshine Coast Trail

Lois Lake

Elephant
Lakes

Mount
Troubridge

Powerline

Dam

Rainy
Day
Lake

Lois River

Saltery
Bay

Trail

0   1   2   3   4   6   8 km

garding wilderness sanitation apply. Upon reaching Wilde Road [km 37.7] turn right and look for the Sliammon Lakes Trail 40 metres downhill on the opposite side of the road.

Wilde Road to Wildwood

While Wilde Road leads down to Sliammon Indian re-

Full Moon
Sometimes the sun shines where the sun don't shine on the Sunshine Coast. Nothing beats a skinny dip on a sweltering day. When washing up be sure to suds and rinse well-back from the water's edge to avoid polluting nature's cistern.

Nikon F
135 mm Nikkor lens
Tri-X Pan 400 ISO film

serve and fish hatchery, the Sunshine Coast Trail continues east, skirting the edge of Powell River's wildest, wooded suburb 8 kilometres away. Initially the route marches through forest of mixed second and old-growth reaching Theyetl Lake [km 38.8], Sliammon Lake [km 39.2], Dogleg Pond [km 41.5] then Little Sliammon Lake [km 42.5] in quick succession. Numerous campsites have been established along the way with only those on Sliammon Lake boasting outhouses. All of the lakes are stocked with trout and offer birding opportunities. At km 44.9 the trail abruptly veers left onto an old logging road. Follow the road for 700 metres to a wide turnaround with left and right branches. The right branch leads to Sutherland Street in Wildwood while the left is called Scout Trail and is the continuation of the Sunshine Coast Trail. The road branches to the right again after 100 metres, finally petering out after 800 metres or more to become a proper footpath. If in doubt stay with the orange markers.

As you gradually gain altitude numerous bluffs open up. The best view hereabouts however is from the summit of Scout Mountain 20 minutes or so off the main trail at km 47.4. Nearly two kilometres following this detour the trail empties onto a gravel road. Though Powell Lake is clearly visible to the left don't be beguiled as your route continues to the right, 40 metres uphill. Less than a kilometre later the trail spills out into Kinsmen Park at lakeside. At the 50 click mark this is the end of the second stage and fittingly the Shinglemill Pub & Restaurant next door is open for business. Unless continuing deeper into the hinterland call for a cab from the pub after toasting your success. Kinsmen Park is, incidentally, the end of the Powell Forest Canoe Route.

Stage 3: Powell Lake to Fiddlehead Farm

Level: Easy   **Distance:** 31 km   **Time:** 2-3 days

Elevation Change: 570 m   **Season:** June - Oct

If continuing the Sunshine Coast Trail from the previous stage then cross the Powell Lake bridge and, if in need of provisions, follow the road into the old townsite area. A number of small shops and restaurants will be found adjacent to the pulp mill. To regain the trailhead look for a dirt road veering to the left immediately after crossing the bridge at km 50.5. The trail follows a disused side track at the end of the road, 80 metres away. 700 metres further on the route double backs to the right and uphill. If you reach an active log dump then you have missed the turn off. Climb a hundred metres or so up to an active logging road then turn right, looking for orange trail markers some 70 metres down the road on the opposite side from which you came. From the outset the trail climbs steeply over rocky slopes but in little over a kilometre it will bring you back down to Mowat Bay [km 52.8]. Though camping here is not possible swimming certainly is. The small park has a boat launch, washrooms and a snack bar. Look for the trail to resume behind the volleyball courts at the waters edge. A short distance along the trail a sign will confirm that you are plodding along Tony's Trail as the next 5.5 km section to Haywire Bay Regional Park is called.

The route from Mowat Bay to Haywire Bay [km 58.3] is uneventful save for Wednesday Point at km 55.4 which is an ideal spot to skinny dip or even set up a waterfront home for the night. After crossing the bridge at km 57 turn left and follow the logging road downhill to the boat launch. The lakeside trail is on the left near the bottom of the road and leads, half a click away, to the Haywire Bay camping area. Though just 7.8 km beyond the bridge at Powell Lake, the facility here is a sheer delight to footsore travelers, offering a chance to tidy up with hot showers. If such organized camping is not your thing however, pick up the trail, this time to Lost Lake, about 150 metres past the entrance to the camping area.

Lost Lake and Inland Lake

Thus far the hiking on Stage 3 of the Sunshine Coast Trail has been relatively easy with much of the first 8.5 kilometres being both well-traveled and well-maintained. At km 59 however bushwhacking may be necessary, depending on the season, as pioneer species rush to fill the gap in the forest created by a recent clearcut. Watch carefully for trail markers and black bears. A kilometre later the trail moves up to old-growth topped bluffs. Tiny Lost Lake is not so much missing as it is misplaced. You'll find it at km 62. Look for carnivorous, jewel-dappled sundew at the swampy foreshore. Half a kilometre past the pond the trails zigzags 30 metres to the right down a disused logging road before resuming its march towards Inland Lake. Though the trail forks a few minutes

further on, both forks lead to Inland Lake. During wetter times the left fork is reportedly dryer.

The hard-packed, gravel surface of the Inland Lake Trail is level and even wheelchair accessible. Turn right upon reaching it and circle the lake in a counter clockwise direction. There are many sites suited to picnicing, camping swim-

Shiver Me Timbers
A common problem when logging old growth is that the wood shatters on impact. The weight of the ancient tree far outstrips its internal strength so it simply explodes as it slams into the steep mountainside. The chainsaw rendered this magnificent cedar into just so much slash.

Nikon F
28 mm Nikkor lens
Ektachrome 200 ISO film

ming or fishing along the circle route with outhouses established at regular intervals. The Sunshine Coast Trail veers off to the right [km 66.8] onto a footpath called Confederation Lake Trail after four kilometres of very easy lakeside walking. Stay with Inland Lake trail for 500 metres past the turn off to reach Antony Island, reportedly the best camping in the area. Spend the night here and you will understand why the locals call this Loon Lake.

Onward and Upward

Next morning backtrack to the sign for Confederation Lake fully prepared to overcome the most demanding section of trail yet. The path climbs to an altitude of 630 metres as it cuts through significant stands of ancient forest. Expect to encounter blowdowns, some of them quite huge, particularly in the spring and early summer. At the far end of Confederation Lake at km 74.1 look forward to finding all the comforts of home. There is a cozy cabin capable of housing six for a night and a picnic area complete with spiffy biffy. Prior to being swallowed up by forestry mega-giant Weyerhaeuser, McMillan Blodel set aside Confederation Lake and environs for posterity.

As you'll be losing the elevation you gained the previous day the final 7.3 km section of trail from Confederation Lake to Fiddlehead Farm [km 81.4] should prove easier going. At the height of summer however finding water along the way may be difficult. Err on the side of caution and pack enough to meet your needs from the outset. On the way the monotony of forest trudging is regularly broken up by bluffs overlooking Powell Lake and Goat Island to the north.

For a bit of wilderness luxury look for the turn off to Fiddlehead Farm at km 80.5. The 33 hectare international wilderness hostel boasts a wood-fired sauna, budget-priced rooms, campground and farm-fresh viands. Those hoping to return to civilization the easy way can board a speed boat back to the Shinglemill Pub & Restaurant at the bottom of Powell Lake for $20. Runs back to town are generally scheduled for Mondays and Fridays and, like the hostel, are available by prior arrangement only. Those intent on keeping to the wilderness as much as possible should detour to Giavanno Lake for a more primitive camping experience.

Stage 4: Fiddlehead Farm to Lois R

Level: Demanding   **Distance:** 46.6 km
Time: 3-5 days
Elevation Change: 1067 m
Season: June - Oct

Having come this far, the summit of Tin Hat Mountain is an option which should not be missed. Those on a time budget can scale the peak as an out and back overnighter from Fiddlehead Farm. Only those well-equipped and absolutely sure of their abilities should consider undertaking the climb to 1067 metres as a day trip. If pushing on down the Sunshine Coast Trail then consider the panorama from the top of Tin Hat as just a side trip on the long trek southwards. The turn off to the mountain is just over six clicks from the hostel. Leave backpacks securely behind at the crossroads to make the 1.3 km climb unencumbered. Many backpacks have detachable day packs or fanny packs for carrying food, first-aid kit and all-weather clothing in just this kind of situation. From the top the panorama stretches for a full 360 degrees to embrace over 30 Lakes, the Rainbow Range to the north and, to the north-east the South Powell Divide. Be sure to complete the ascent in a timely fashion as Spring Lake, a suitable, if undeveloped site to put up for the night, lies an additional six clicks from the detour. Much of the route cuts through virgin groves of forest that the loggers bypassed. A number of abandoned lumber camps will be encountered on the way to Goat Lake Road. Having flourished a century or more ago most have been reduced to moldering ruins largely reclaimed by the forest they set out to topple.

From Spring Lake a little-used logging spur leads two

Labrador Tea
Forgot the tea bags and dying for a cuppa? Look around the camp. Chances are your drippy socks are draped over a *Labrador tea* bush. Steep the leaves, but not the socks, in boiled water for a tea that was enjoyed by more North American Indians than any other kind. Don't actually boil the leaves however as boiling releases a chemical called ledol which has a number of unpleasant side effects. Pregnant women should avoid Labrador tea altogether. As a mild narcotic, Labrador tea was also an essential ingredient in kinnikinnik, a tobacco-less smoking mixture used by native groups throughout much of North America. *Illustration by Manami Kimura*

kilometres to Lewis Lake where you'll find a real campsite complete with outhouse.

Home on the Range

The next morning embark on a track along the crest of the Smith Range which divides the lakes arrayed along the

Weather or Not
One of nature's wonders, the weather, wears many faces. Expect to see most of them during the course of any undertaking of the Sunshine Coast Trail. We may sometimes curse these raindrops when out and about in the middle of it. Water from above, more than any other factor however, has shaped the west coast world we have come to love.

Nikon F
28 mm Nikkor lens
Kodachrome 64 ISO film

first half of the Powell Forest Canoe Route from Haslam Lake which supplies Powell River with its drinking water. A number of suitable tent sites will be found in the vicinity of March Lake 7 km beyond Spring Lake but push on another six clicks to reach Coyote Lake before dark to slice the remainder of this stage in half. The terrain as far as March Lake is relatively flat though expect to be slowed by deadfalls as these sections are infrequently traveled and maintained. Save time for refreshment with an icy dip in Elk Lake before proceeding to the bluffs in the vicinity of Granite Lake. Patches of old-growth around Coyote Lake will provide welcomed relief from the late afternoon sun.

Anticipate steeper terrain along the final 13 kilometres to Goat Lake Main Road though thankfully more elevation will be lost than gained. Walt Hill and Blue Ridge both provide vistas of the surrounding countryside. If running short of time plan on putting up at the picnic area, mile 4 on the Goat Lake Mainline. During times of higher than average fire danger expect to hear a procession of logging trucks and crummy crews heading into the bush well before first light the next morning. Three kilometres further down the Sunshine Coast Trail a bona fide campsite has been established on the banks of the Lois River. Deep pools in the canyon downstream from the dam are popular with locals and visitors alike but be forewarned if a siren blows clear the banks of the river as the sluice gates upstream are about to be opened. Many locals refer to the popular swimming hole as Eagle River.

If completing this stage of the Sunshine Coast Trail as a self-contained unit scamper 2 km downstream to Highway 101. Then wait for the bus on the opposite side the road according to the schedule in the appendix of this book.

Stage 5: Lois Dam to Saltery Bay

Level: Difficult   **Distance:** 42 km

Time: 3-4 days   **Season:** June - Oct

Elevation Change: 1280 m

This is the final section of the Sunshine Coast Trail in more ways than one. Much of the route was little more than a sketch on a map until the summer of 1998 when it was roughed out in its entirety. And rough it is though volunteers from the Powell River Parks & Wilderness Society continue to upgrade every part of the trail whenever weather and time permits. The group deserves our applause and admiration first and foremost for having the vision to even conceive of such an undertaking. One thing which sets this project apart is the willingness of PRPAWS to eschew bureaucracy and get on with the project even when confronted with jurisdictional arcania that could easily have stalled similar projects for decades. The thousands of hours of hard labor donated to the Sunshine Coast Trail have literally put Powell River on the map.

From the campground on Lois River the trail leads upstream for a kilometre to the dam [km 133] then continues along the eastern shore of Lois Lake for 6.8 kilometres to a primitive lakeside campsite. On the way at km 136 you'll pass the start of the Powell Forest Canoe Route at a campsite operated by the British Columbia Forest Service. Picnic tables and outhouses comprise the amenities here. Once the trail leaves the lakeside expect to gain altitude, slowly a first then more steeply as the route switches back and forth up 10 kilometres to the tiny Elephant Lakes. There are no amenities to speak of but camping is permitted at the lakes which are situated more or less at the halfway point on this last stage of the trail.

The next campsite is 8.5 kilometres away atop Mt. Troubridge [km 157.2], a demanding uphill slog that reaches an altitude of 1280 metres. On the way up the footpath passes

Magic Mushrooms
They grow 'em big hereabouts. The mushrooms we see popping up all over the place after an autumn rain are in reality just the "fruit" of much larger organisms called mycelium, a rootlike structure comprised of gazillions of fine threads growing beneath the ground. Think this one is big? A mycelia found in Washington state is thought to be the world's largest organism, spreading itself across several counties. When conditions are right the mycelia sends up its 'shrooms to reproduce by spreading its spores on the wind.

Nikon F
135 mm Nikkor lens
Kodak Plus-X Pan 125 ISO film

through magnificent stands of ancient Douglas fir and yellow cedar. What goes up must come down however and the knee-burning descent to the end of the trail at Saltery Bay, 17.8 kilometres away, should take similar time and effort. On the way you'll pass a campsite at Rainy Day Lake [km 166.4.] Breaking the descent into two may be well-advised depending on your transportation arrangements. Those returning to Vancouver will want to catch the bus on board the ferry from Saltery Bay to Earls Cove. 🐾

Sunshine Coast Trail

Location	Notes
Pacific Coastal Airlines (604) 273-8666 1-800-663-2872 webmaster@pacific-coastal.com www.pacific-coastal.com	M-Fr 6 flights daily Sat 3 flights daily Su 5 flights daily $182 return taxes included
Powell River Taxi Company (604) 483-3666	
Fiddlehead Farm Box 421 Powell River, B.C. (604) 483-3018 Radio Tel. (604) 485-3832 FAX retreat@fiddleheadfarm.org	Wilderness Retreat located on the Powell Forest Canoe Route Be patient when calling the radio telephone. Let it ring many times.
Red Tide Alert Hotline (604) 666-3169 (604) 666-0583	Desolation Sound Area 15
Powell River Chamber of Commerce 6807 Wharf Street (604) 485-4051 (604) 485-2822 FAX chamber@prcn.org www.discoverpowellriver.com	Travel Information

Stein River Valley

The *Hidden Place* it was called and hidden it remained for some 7000 years. To the Nlaka'pamux Indians who lived at its mouth it was a mystical valley, at once the abode of spirits and the provider of sustenance.

Early European explorers corrupted its Nlaka'pamux name to a more pronounceable *Styne.* The *Hidden Place* had been found. Yet as time and new traditions Anglicized its name to *Stein,* the valley remained largely untouched by the wanton greed that had begun to lay waste to other nearby wildernesses piece by piece.

Geography and a marginal endowment of industrial resources have served the spirits of the Stein well. While every neighbouring watershed has endured the brutality of chainsaw and bulldozer the Stein remains today much the same as the *Hidden Place* that has long provided medicine and meals for the Nlaka'pamux.

Island in a Sea of Stumps

Often called an *island in a sea of stumps,* the Stein is characterized by rugged, steep-sided slopes, U-shaped from wave upon wave of glaciation The valley bottom is surprisingly flat with a nearly level pitch, making it ideal for hiking and backpacking.

Fully six of the 12 biogeoclimatic zones found in B.C. are represented in the Stein watershed. Such diversity supports mountain goats, black bears, mule deer, moose, wolverine, coyote, marten, mink and beaver and provides the grizzly bear with its last refuge in the southwest corner of the province.

Such diversity moreover has traditionally provided the Nlaka'pamux with an abundance of fresh green shoots, berries, roots, tubers, meat and fish.

More than a larder, the *Hidden Place* is the last refuge of a pantheon of spirits who once guided all aspects of Nlaka'pamux civilization. The imprint of the gods is felt at every step along the river. Numerous "power spots" – high ledges, caves, natural grottos – dot the landscape, bearing yet the visions of dreamers and shamans in the form of wondrous rock paintings centuries old.

Of some 36 know heritage sites in the Stein, with as many more at its mouth, 14 have been daubed with the blood-red representations of mystical events. Often pictured on the rocky tableaux are images of guardian spirits who revealed themselves to native youths during solitary coming-of-age rituals.

The modern day hiker encountering these images can sometimes sense the true power and force of mystic imagination.

Hands Off

It should go without saying that these pictographs are treasures of the Nlaka'pamux and should be accorded all due respect. To mar, deface, or otherwise despoil these treasures is not only rude and ignorant, it is highly illegal. Since the skin contains oils and acids even lightly touching them can cause irreparable damage.

Other vestiges of the Nlaka'pamux linger in the Stein. At its confluence with the Fraser where the Indians wintered in gigantic pithouses can still be found the shallow depressions of their winter storehouses. In the same area a boulder carved with petroglyphs can also be beheld.

Upstream at Stryen, Teaspoon and Earl Creeks hikers will encounter numerous cedar trees with large, rectangular strips of bark missing. Somewhat unromantically labelled *culturally modified trees (CMT's)* by the archaeological community, these small groves of cedars were an important source of fibre for clothing, cord, roofing, insulation, basketry and even diapers. So rare and important in fact was cedar bark that the Nlaka'pamux were willing to walk some 22 km round trip to collect it.

Rough hack marks at the top and bottom of each bare patch, the work of sharp-edged stones, would date the harvest to before the appearance of Europeans with their high tech implements of steel. Only small patches of bark were removed to allow for the survival of the relatively rare cedar trees. That they continue to live today, attests to the truly conservationist nature of the Nlaka'pamux.

The Stein watershed was formally declared Stein Valley Nlaka'pamux Heritage Park on November 23, 1995 following a hard-fought 20-year battle to protect the wilderness, historical and anthropological features of the region from industrial development. The park is jointly managed by the provincial government and the Lytton Indian Band.

Stein Traverse

The route as described through the lower canyon is part of a longer trail known variously as the Stein Traverse or the Stein River Heritage Trail. The 75 km traverse starts at the end of a remote four-wheel-drive road in the alpine and is not readily accessible via public transportation. The lower canyon of the Stein where the traverse ends is accessible however, leading to a wilderness area of striking diversity and beauty. The route detailed below takes a minimum of four days, including travel time, though the Stein Valley can be enjoyed as a simple overnighter. Alternately, many more days could easily be spent exploring this fascinating watershed.

With accessibility problems and requiring experience and route finding skills well beyond the scope of this book, the demanding Stein Traverse has not been included. The 51 km Mini-Traverse on the other hand follows a well-marked trail from Blowdown Pass to the headwaters of Cottonwood Creek then on down to the Stein River itself, following the lower canyon route described below in reverse. 🐾

Stein Lower Canyon to Mid-Valley

Level: Moderate   **Distance:** 29.3 km   **Time:** 2 - 4 days

Elevation Change: 537 m   **Map:** 92 I/5   **Season:** Mar to Oct

Access: Greyhound services Lytton, the nearest community to the Stein Valley trailhead, twice daily. [See **Getting to Hope & Lytton** on page 337.] As no taxi or other public transportation services exist it will be necessary to arrange for a lift 6.8 km to the trailhead through the Lytton & District Chamber of Commerce. See below for details. If arriving in Lytton without making prior arrangements negotiating with local residents on the main street is also effective and should cost between $10-25 each way. Be sure to arrange for a pick up at the end of your trip as well. Traffic is very limited along the access road so hitchhiking is not a particularly viable alternative. The ferry across the Fraser River, a unique, water-powered craft, does not operate during the heaviest days of spring runoff. If planning to go to the Stein at any time from May through early July check with travel information in Lytton or contact the department of highways to ensure that the ferry is indeed operating.

Assuming you arrived in Lytton on the morning bus you'll likely reach the trailhead in the early afternoon, too early to set up camp. Those arriving later will find excellent camping at the trailhead on Van Winkle Flats. Water is 300 metres down the main trail at Stryen Creek but an outhouse, large fire pit and grassy, open terrain characteristic of the interior dry belt combine to make for an ideal place from which to get an early morning start. As the Stein River itself can be heavily laden with glacial till, topping up with water from clear-running side creeks whenever possible is advisable.

Trailhead to Devil's Staircase: 5.3 km

Just beyond Stryen Creek you'll encounter the first "power spot," a granite outcropping where puberty rituals were once commonplace. Imagine nearly naked young Nlaka'pamux children left here in the dark, in the cold, often alone, filled with fear and awe and hunger until in a waking dream they encountered their personal spirits. The bizarre creatures daubed in scarlet onto the cliff face are the representations of those visions, the spirits which would guide them and fortify them for the rest of their lives. Their transition to adulthood complete, these young native people were free to return to their tribe accompanied by a newfound strength and purpose.

The trail continues over fairly even terrain for the next 5 km before reaching the ominously named Devil's Staircase. The forest cover of the lower canyon is refreshingly different for those used to the lush vegetation of coastal British Columbia. Here ponderous ponderosa pine with striking jigsaw-puzzle bark and lodgepole pine predominate in the arid, rocky terrain. There is little understory vegetation and lichens cling to every surface. The luminous yellow wolf lichen is particularly conspicuous, a warning to hungry ungulates to stay clear. Morels, gigantic shaggy manes and pine mushrooms pop up following the autumn rains. All are easily recognizable and delicious and the latter *matsutake* in particular are harvested by local natives for shipment to Japan where they may fetch $30 - $100 or more per mushroom in the supermarkets. In late summer and fall look for spawning salmon whenever the trail veers near the river bank. Pink, coho and chinook salmon all fight for spawning sites in the gravel of the Stein River with odd-numbered years seeing the heaviest returns of spawning pinks. By November most will have been reduced to spent carcasses, scant pickings for scavenging ravens, marten and bear. At the foot of the Devil's Staircase a side trail leads to a pleasantly situated campsite. Mount the "stairs" instead and zigzag up to the 400 metre mark where the trail crosses a wide scree slope then descends to the valley bottom again before repeating the manoeuvre up and over rocky talus one more time. While care-

Abandoned Home
Earl's Cabin has remained empty since World War I claimed the trapper. Perhaps Earl's lost treasure will always remain a mystery.

*Nikon F
28 mm Nikkor lens
Ektachrome 100 ISO film*

fully picking your way over these rocky slides note the relatively large, well-formed crystals of mica and quartz. This one kilometre section of trail is by far the most difficult though very few should find it taxing in the extreme. At the foot of the second talus slope a series of pictographs can be found on the cliff faces some 100 metres downstream.

The main route continues upstream through a small cedar grove, winding along the river until the 8.3 km mark where you'll encounter a teepee on the benchland above the river. Innumerable tent sites, a pit toilet and bear-proof food locker juxtaposed against steep cliffs towering overhead on the other side of the river completes the picture. The teepee stands as a monument to the protest rallies throughout the Stein Valley in the late 1980s during the campaign to save the Stein Valley from certain annihilation at the hands of the logging interests. No need to be beguiled by this attractive site however as excellent camping can be found in many places from here to Cable Crossing.

Pause a moment at Teaspoon Creek 1.2 km further on to contemplate the so-called "culturally modified trees" that abound in the large cedar grove here. During the dog days of summer the cool darkness here will be most welcome.

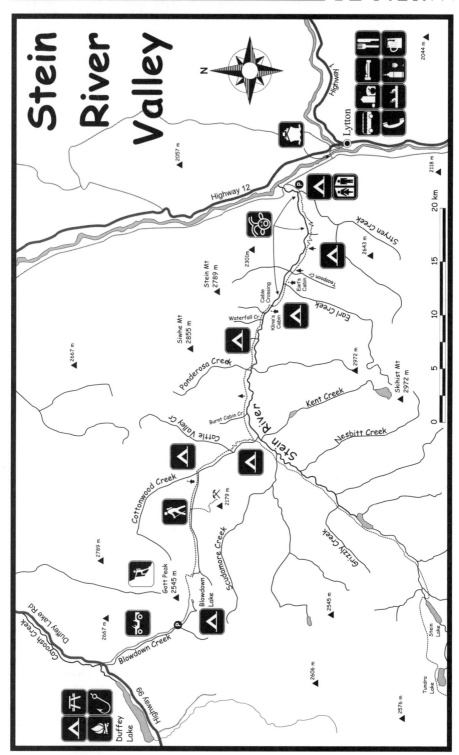

Stein River Valley

N

Highway 1

Lytton

Highway 12

▲ 2044 m

▲ 2057 m

▲ 2118 m

P

Stryen Creek

▲ 2643 m

Stein Mt
▲ 2789 m

2301m ▲

Cable Crossing

Teaspoon Cr

Earl's Cabin

Siwhe Mt
▲ 2855 m

Waterfall Cr.

Kline's Cabin

Earl Creek

▲ 2667 m

Ponderosa Creek

▲ 2972 m

Skihist Mt
▲ 2972 m

Kent Creek

Burnt Cabin Cr.

Stein River

Nesbitt Creek

Cattle Valley Cr.

Cottonwood Creek

▲ 2179 m

Scudamore Creek

Grizzly Creek

▲ 2789 m

Gott Peak
▲ 2545 m

Blowdown Lake

▲ 2667 m

P

▲ 2545 m

Duffey Lake Rd

Cayoosh Creek

Blowdown Creek

Highway 99

▲ 2606 m

Tundra Lake

Stein Lake

▲ 2576 m

Duffey Lake

20 km

15

10

5

0

Devil's Staircase to Buried Treasure: 5.5 km

Keep an eye open for the glint of buried treasure as you cover the next 1.2 km to Earl's Cabin. Once the home of trapper Fred Earl, the original cabin was abandoned when Earl went off to fight for God and country during World War I. Regrettably, Earl never returned leaving behind rumours of a $12,000 cache of gold which he had reportedly panned from the creek that bears his name. The cabin which occupies the site at present is a reconstruction. The forest hereabouts was opened up considerably during the forest fire of 1994 as Earl's cabin became ground zero in the battle against the blaze. A rough helicopter landing pad and base camp were then hewn from the forest. The understory vegetation has recovered though the scorched bark of larger trees hereabouts should provide a sober reminder to keep fires small when you must keep them at all.

Earl's Cabin to Cable Crossing: 2.4 km

The main trail follows Earl Creek upstream to a small bridge before returning to the banks of the Stein River. The next 1.3 km are easy going, leading to a point where the trail is squeezed between rocky bluffs and the cascading river itself. Though in recent history some sections of the cliff have collapsed, the rest of the face is alive with surreal creatures daubed in haematite-based pigments.

Continuing on for another 15 minutes or so you will come to a large forest campsite complete with the usual amenities. The cable car, 13.2 km from the trailhead, is nearby. Another trapper's cabin will be found about 300 metres beyond the campsite on the same side of the river. This cabin was built in 1953 by Adam Klein who began trapping in the area some 28 years earlier after running away from home at the age of 18.

If you prefer a more open setting to camp in, cross the river one at a time on the rickety cable car that dates from 1986 when the Western Canada Wilderness Committee sought to encourage recreation in the area as a way of building support against planned logging. Be sure to unhook the cable car from the landing when finished so other hikers can also cross here. Continue upstream another few minutes along the foot of a field of huge boulders. After spring runoff a large island in the centre of the river makes an ideal site for camping under the stars. To reach the island it may be necessary to get your feet wet crossing a flood channel. Camping here is not recommended during the spring or during periods of high rainfall.

Common Plantain

What drives the home gardener mad is good news for the outback-bound as *common plantain* is common indeed. Young leaves can be eaten as is like lettuce while the more mature ones benefit from steaming or boiling like kale or spinach. Chop and season before eating. Common plantain is a good trailside source of vitamins C, A and K. Much like aloe, a poultice of crushed plantain leaves is said to be a beneficial treatment for burns and insect stings.
Illustration by Manami Kimura

Cable Crossing to Ponderosa Shelter: 7.8 km

From Cable Crossing the dry, arid benchlands give way to the interior Douglas fir zone. Huge cottonwoods, aspen and poplar are common along the river's edge while the underbrush has suddenly become thick, sometimes impenetrable. Due to reduced traffic and abundant vegetation the trail narrows considerably and can be quite overgrown and

Cable Crossing
Whe-e-e-e this is fun! One at a time please. The Stein River is fast and deep and the cable car remains the only way across.

Nikon F
28 mm Nikkor lens
Ektachrome 100 ISO film

marshy in the spring. The 7.8 km to Ponderosa Shelter can be undertaken as an out and back day trip with limited gear or, for those with time on their hands, a camping destination in itself. On the way to Ponderosa Shelter you'll cross a number of creeks in quick succession. The first suitable campsite is at Waterfall Creek. Just 400 metres beyond note the beaver pond from which you'll soon climb above the valley bottom. The trail skirts the edge of a succession of "granite gardens" before returning to the flood plains below. Just 20 minutes further on take the left fork of the trail to reach Ponderosa Shelter, an attractive wilderness campsite complete with dilapidated wooden structure.

Most weekend warriors never tread beyond Ponderosa Shelter though the description continues to Cottonwood Creek 8.3 km away through similar, mid-valley, terrain. Returning to the trailhead 21 km away is best done over two days with the bulk of the distance being accomplished on the first day. The remainder can be undertaken prior to making a rendezvous with your prearranged shuttle.

Ponderosa Shelter to Cottonwood Cr: 8.3 km

Those continuing deeper into the valley will encounter the remains of a log lean-to 400 metres beyond Ponderosa Shelter. The next kilometre brings welcomed if brief respite from the marsh and mosquitoes as the forest opens up somewhat before reverting to wetlands once again. Note in passing that many of the red cedars here too bear the marks of fibre harvesting dating to pre-European times. At about the halfway point between Ponderosa Shelter and Cottonwood Creek climb the bluffs for a panorama of the mid-valley. From here swamp gives way to open forest once again all the way to Burnt Cabin Creek where you'll find a rustic campsite. Continuing on to Cottonwood Creek, the trail follows the river through the flood plains once more, passing through stands of ancient cottonwood then over a boulder garden just one kilometre from the campsite. Attractive Cottonwood Falls is just a few minutes upstream from the camp.

The other campsite near Cottonwood Creek has been set aside as a Youth Rediscovery camp, part of a program aimed at putting native youths in touch with their heritage.

One of the back doors on the Stein Valley, Blowdown Pass, can be reached from Cottonwood Creek campsite. Follow the Blowdown Pass Trail for about half an hour to reach a viewpoint well above the valley bottom. Hiking the 33 km through to Duffy Lake Road is certainly possible though such an uphill undertaking is complicated by a complete lack of public transportation alternatives between Pemberton and Lillooet. Hitchhiking remains viable along this paved wilderness highway for the truly determined. Rather than climbing out of the Stein Valley, follow the route in reverse instead, starting high near Duffy Lake and working down from Blowdown Pass to Cottonwood Creek following the Stein to the trailhead at Van Dyke Flats. The alpine scenery is certainly worth the extra hassle involved. This mini-traverse is detailed below. 🐾

Nodding Onion

Packing fresh veggies along on the trail may be impractical due to weight or time considerations. Widely-available *nodding onion* imparts a welcomed taste of green to almost any dish except granola perhaps. Both white bulb and green stalk can be used like green onions or chives. Rubbing the crushed bulbs on exposed skin is said to keep mosquitoes, black flies and maybe even your traveling companions away. Nodding onion is commonly available throughout the province though toxic *death camas* looks deceptively similar to *nodding onion* to the uninitiated. To verify, crush a bit of the plant. Only the edible species gives off an unmistakable onion smell.

Illustration by Manami Kimura

Stein Valley Mini-Traverse

Level: Difficult

Time: 5+ days

Season: June to Sept

Distance: 51 km

Elevation Change: 1870 m

Map: 92 I/5 & 92 J/8

Access: From Vancouver take the bus to Pemberton [See **Getting to Whistler** Page 335] and, as prear-ranged, meet the driver from Pemberton Taxi who will take you some 60 km further along the Duffy Lake Road to the Blowdown Pass area where this route begins. 3½ km beyond the Duffy Lake East Recreation Site the driver should turn right onto a disused logging road marked with a "No Through Road" sign. With luck the mainline will be passable for the next 9 km. If luck is not on your side and you find the road washed out you'll have to hoof it uphill the rest of the way in. Stay on the mainline all the way until you reach a large flat parking area at about the 9 km mark. Take the first branch line to the left after this and con-tinue for another 1½ km to the beginning of a private mining road. Contact the B.C. Forest Service in Lil-looet to check road conditions ahead of time. Follow the mining road in towards Blowdown Pass.

Culturally Modified Trees
Western red cedar, the most important source of fiber to natives on the west coast, was not plentiful for those who lived in the Stein River Valley. Many cedar trees still bear evidence of cedar bark harvesting. While the outer bark is brittle and incredibly itchy, the inner bark is soft and pliable and can be woven into durable clothing and baskets.

Nikon F
28 mm Nikkor lens
Ektachrome 100 ISO film

Depending on how far you've already had to hike you may want to make pretty Blowdown Lake your destination for the first night on the trail. From the start of the Silver Queen Mine road the lake is just 3 km away while windy Blowdown Pass is a further kilometre. Many different routes emanate from the alpine pass. True fanatics may want to set up a base camp from which to explore the wide open alpine hereabouts before continuing on the Mini-Traverse proper. Gott Peak to the north and Gotcha Peak to the south are popular half day ascents, both requiring route-finding skills.

From Blowdown Pass at 2150 m our route continues east along the mine road for 8½ km, dropping gradually at first then more steeply before taking up a course parallel to the South Fork of Cottonwood Creek. Abruptly the road crosses a bridge over Cottonwood Creek, heading off in a southerly direction. Continue hiking east along the north side of the creek for 15 minutes or so. Where the road plunges down towards the creek bed you'll find a well-defined trail to the east, continuing to parallel the creek. Follow this trail for 5 km down through the meadow, passing a disused trap-per's cabin just before the confluence of Cottonwood Creek's north and south fork. The best camping in the area is on the opposite side of the waterway. From Blowdown Pass to Cot-tonwood Junction expect a descent of 1170 m over 13½ km.

The trail next drops steeply south into the Stein River

Valley continuing to follow the course of Cottonwood Creek. The trail is well-defined with little underbrush but your progress may be impeded again by deadfalls. No longer a hindrance, fallen logs will get you across Cattle Valley Creek 4½ km further on. The campsite here is well-established but Cottonwood Creek camp is just 3½ km away at the bottom of the valley. To reach it you'll have to negotiate a succession of switch-backs over loose talus, following rock cairns where the footpath is not obvious. Pause in your route finding from time to time to enjoy the view of the valley laid out below. From Cottonwood Junction to the banks of the Stein is 8½ km with an elevation loss of just 390 m but the going can be taxing at times paticularly if the trail has not been recently cleared of deadfalls.

At the bottom you'll find the campsite just beyond the Stein Valley Heritage Trail. Follow the previous hike description in reverse to reach the community of Lytton at the confluence of the Fraser and Thompson Rivers. 🐾

Stein Valley Information

Location	Services	Notes
Greyhound Bus Lines Pacific Central Station (604) 482-8747 1-800-661-8747 www.greyhound.ca	$34.99 One way	**Vancouver to Lytton** 7:30 AM - 11:55 AM 5:45 PM - 10:20 PM **Lytton to Vancouver** 6:30 AM - 11:00 AM 4:30 PM - 9:15 PM
B.C. Department of Highways (604) 660-9770	Lower Stein highways information	Call to check whether the reaction ferry is operating on the Fraser River at Lytton during spring high water.
Lytton & District Chamber of Commerce P.O. Box 460 Lytton, B.C. V0K 1Z0 (250) 455-2523 (250) 455-6669 Fax lyttoncc@goldtrail.com	Local travel information	Will arrange for a shuttle in advance from Lytton to trailhead in the Lower Stein with locals. One week's notice is required.
Pemberton Taxi (604) 894-1111	Upper Stein Trailhead Shuttle	Pemberton to Blowdown Pass or Lizzie Lake Areas approximately $100 per group. Actual drop off will depend on road accessibility.
B.C. Forest Service Lillooet (250) 256-7531	Administers access roads to Stein Headwaters.	For information on logging road conditions leading to varios backdoor routes into the Stein Watershed.

Nicomen Lake

Level: Moderate

Time: 4 Days

Season: July -Sept

Distance: 42 km o/w

Elev Change: 1280 m

Map: Manning Park 92H/2

Fancy Stance
Hoping for a career in modelling, this chubby buddy poses for the camera outside Manning Park Lodge. A huge colony of ground squirrels greets visitors throughout the summer, retiring to their snug, subterranean city for the ski season.

Nikon F
135 mm Nikkor lens
Kodachrome 64 ISO film.

Access: See **Getting to Manning Prov Park,** pg 338.

Backpacking in British Columbia has its ups and downs. Usually, however, there seems to be a little too much of the former.

Nicomen Lake offers newcomers to the sport a welcomed respite. Though long enough at 42 km to present a challenge, the choicest route is predominantly downhill.

The trailhead starts from the parking lot below Blackwall Peak where chubby marmots will doubtless be begging for handouts. From Manning Park Lodge it will be necessary to cross busy Highway 3, heading left on the parallel access road. Find a safe place to hitchhike the 8 km up to the top of the dusty access road.

Heather Trail starts from an elevation of 1920 metres at the Blackwall Peak parking lot. Hikers will immediately begin dropping into sub-alpine meadows. Soon the path, actually an old fire access road, will level out. By the time you reach Buckhorn camp, just five clicks from the start, you will be gaining altitude again.

Buckhorn is the perfect place to stop for lunch if you got an early start or to set up camp if rushing out after work.

Expect company at meal time, since whisky-jacks here have long since grown accustomed to begging handouts from hikers. Otherwise known as grey jays, these bold creatures will make short work of any rations left unattended.

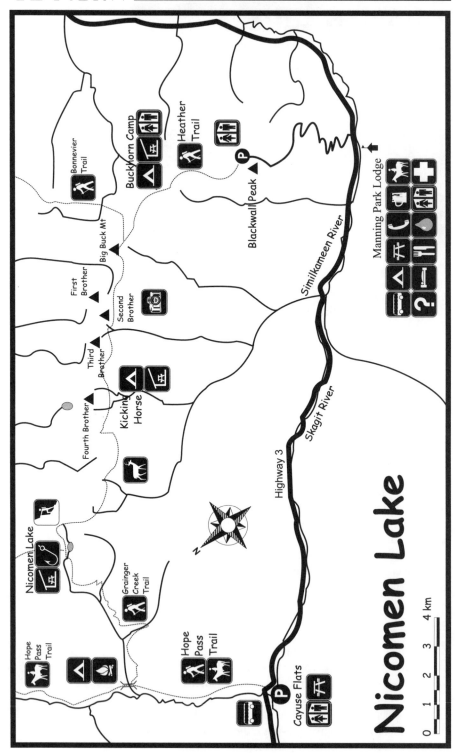

Nicomen Lake

Bonnevier Trail

Bucknorn Camp

Heather Trail

Blackwall Peak

Big Buck Mt

First Brother

Second Brother

Third Brother

Fourth Brother

Kicking Horse

Manning Park Lodge

Similkameen River

Skagit River

Highway 3

Nicomen Lake

Grainger Creek Trail

Hope Pass Trail

Hope Pass Trail

Cayuse Flats

0 1 2 3 4 km

Since many day trippers usually turn back at Buckhorn one can expect more solitude from this point on. Expect to do some puffing too since the slope from here is decidedly up for the next five km. This section of trail passes through the site of an old forest fire. Gladly, the forest is slowly reclaiming its own.

Buckhorn Birds Beg Bagles
A frisky Whisky-Jack spirits lunch away from one unhappy camper. AKA Canada Jay, Grey Jay and "Camp Robber," the Whisky-Jack amazingly has never developed a fear of humans and will greet hikers, demanding a hand-out, whenever we trespass in their high elevation domain.

Nikon F
135 mm Nikkor lens
Kodachrome 64 ISO film

A Family of Peaks

At click seven the Bonnivier Trail breaks off to the right, continuing another 22 km towards the park's East Gate. Continue upwards and onwards however, towards the foot of First Brother Mountain.

The main trail levels out at this point, skirting the shoulders of Second and Third Brother Mountains, but the truly gung ho may want to shed their backpacks and race to the summit. While a relatively easy climb, leave plenty of time to reach Kicking Horse Camp 3½ km further along.

With ample water, a toilet and even a rustic shelter, Kicking Horse is an ideal spot to camp on the first day out. Building campfires in the fragile sub-alpine is not only considered bad form, it is prohibited.

Since most hikers, constrained by the demands of real life, will turn back at Kicking Horse the trail narrows somewhat from this point on. While the scenery has been nothing short of magnificent thus far, the best is yet to come.

The next 7½ km is comprised of gently rolling meadows splashed with every imaginable shade of purple, red, white, yellow, blue and green. Since human traffic is limited hikers can expect to encounter mule deer grazing against a backdrop of distant rugged peaks on all sides.

You will be gradually losing altitude all day until reaching the razor-edged summit of Nicomen Ridge. From here the trail plunges steeply down a series of switchbacks for

Nicomen Ridge
A steep set of switchbacks leads quickly down to Nicomen Lake. Pikas and Marmots have established lively communities on the talus slopes adjacent to the lake. On one occaision we noticed a wolverine chasing down lunch too. Luckily the groundhog it coveted escaped into a rocky refuge.

Nikon F
28 mm Nikkor lens
Kodachrome 64 ISO film

two kilometres to the edge of the blue jewel of Nicomen Lake.

Even with restraint your descent will be fast. Loose rock presents considerable hazard here so caution should be exercised at all times. Avoid taking short-cuts between the switchbacks as this will needlessly erode already unstable slopes.

Nicomen Lake is perfectly suited for a second night's stopover. Rustic camping areas can be found at several points along the lake.

Rock slides at the foot of Nicomen Ridge are an excellent place to observe the communal activities of large colonies of hoary marmots and pikas, small relatives of the Energizer Bunny that look like rats with big ears, bulbous eyes and furry tails. On one occasion we even spotted a wolverine at relatively close range. Infamous for their ferocity, sighting one of these creatures is sure to send shivers.

If you haven't been toting a collapsable fly rod you will now wish you had. Nicomen Lake is home to thousands of small but voracious mountain cutthroat trout. Most are of the catch and release variety but consult Fish and Wildlife Branch regulations for exact details on size and catch limits.

Down, Down, Down ...

From Nicomen Lake you will begin losing altitude at a much faster pace. During the next 11 km sub-alpine will quickly give way to interior dry belt forest of pine, fir, spruce and hemlock. On the forest floor expect to find an inordinate variety of unusual moulds and fungi. Be sure to pack ample water since supplies are limited along this section of trail.

Smarmy Marmot
Catching a few rays on a hot spring day, hoary marmots never venture far from the protection of their dens. Marmots prefer building their dens under rocky skree, making it hard for predators like badgers or wolverines to dig them out.

Nikon F
135 mm Nikkor lens
Kodachrome 64 ISO film

Camping on the third and final night is best at the Grainger Creek - Hope Pass Trail junction. Though rustic, this site is equipped with a fire grate and outhouse.

Those with time on their hands may want to explore, unencumbered, along the Hope Pass Trail, a circuitous route horse riders often use to reach Nicomen Lake.

The final leg of this four day route is a mere 8 km, largely downhill that ends at Cayuse Flats on highway 3 near the West Gate of Manning Park. To flag down the bus, look for a section of road with wide shoulders and ample visibility near this day use area. Drivers will only stop if safe to do so. The Greyhound should pass by between 12:30 PM and 1:00 PM each day. 🐾

Juan De Fuca Marine Trail

Level: Moderate   **Distance:** 47 km   **Time:** 4+ Days

Terrain: Undulating   **Map:** 92 C/9 & 92 C/8   **Season:** Mar - Oct

Access: The Juan de Fuca Marine Trail is directly accessible from Vancouver but an early start is a must. The Pacific Coach Lines bus bound for Victoria leaves Pacific Central Station at 5:45 AM each morning, reaching its destination at 9:15 AM. Catch the West Coast Trail Express from in front of the bus terminal at 700 Douglas Street at 9:30 AM. Expect to reach the trailhead at around noon. This shuttle service connects to the southern terminus of the West Coast Trail as well as any of four access points along the Juan de Fuca Trail. Reservations are required. See below for further details. See Getting to Tsawwassen on page 321 for alternative schedule information between downtown Vancouver and the provincial capital.

The 707 hectare Juan de Fuca Marine Trail connects Botanical Beach Provincial Park in the north to China Beach Provincial Park 47 km to the south. The popularity and global renown of the nearby West Coast Trail made convincing argument for the preservation of other examples of the unique environment along Vancouver Island's west coast. The Juan de Fuca Trail was officially commemorated in 1994 as a tribute to the Commonwealth Games held in Victoria that year. Creation of the trail would not have been possible without generous donations or exchanges of land from Western Forest Products and TimberWest and support from the Pacheenaht First Nation. As many as 100 local, primarily native, youths were engaged in the creation of the trail through a provincial government work experience program. Construction of the trail pumped $8½ million into the local economy.

Time your visit to the Juan de Fuca Marine Trail to take advantage of the lowest possible tides. Not only will your progress along the beaches be enhanced, but innumerable natural phenomena become accessible when the tide drops below one metre.

Botanical Beach

The northern trailhead starts at the end of Cerantes Road, 2.5 km from the hotel and government wharf in Port Renfrew. Since we are following the trail in reverse, working through the easiest sections while our packs are heaviest and conditioning possibly not at its best, this hike starts at kilometre 47, counting down as we proceed. Be sure to check the notice board at the trailhead for up-to-the-minute trail condition reports as well as tide tables posted for the benefit of those who may have forgotten this essential information when preparing for the trip. Be sure to correct tide tables for daylight savings time where appropriate.

Botanical Beach was the site of a marine biology research station sponsored by the University of Minnesota from 1900 to 1906. The Juan de Fuca Marine Trail proper skips much of the rich intertidal zone at Botanical Beach. If arriving at the trailhead at low tide plan on spending some time exploring the tide pool-pocked reef and unique geology of the foreshore between Botany Bay and the start of the trail itself before setting out.

The coast parallels a fault line along the colliding North American and Juan de Fuca Plates. As a consequence, much of the foreshore is an odd mixture of volcanic and metamorphosed sedimentary rocks.

At the far eastern end of the Botanical Beach low tide reveals three sea caves. Keen eyes may discern even keener eyes gazing back from a giant eagle nest nestled atop an ancient spruce. Though camping is actually frowned upon here, this secluded corner would be an ideal spot to pitch a tent if arriving later than anticipated. The site boasts both

Gawking Gullivers
Three other-worldly creatures steal the sun, striking terror into the hearts of the Lilliputian community of a tide pool at Botanical Beach. Tiny fish dart for cover, hermit crabs duck into their borrowed hermitages while their less-armoured brethren scramble under rocks and plants until the towering menace retreats trailwards.

Nikonos V
35 mm Nikkor lens
Kodachrome 200 ISO film

water and driftwood though building a fire too early is sure to catch the keenest eyes of all: those of the park ranger.

Botanical Beach to Parkinson Creek 10 km

The first 10 kilometres of the Juan de Fuca Marine Trail follow a route through climax forest of mixed cedar and hemlock just beyond a barrier of thick salal that rims the rocky shore. Though sometimes cursed by coastal hikers, this salal and other shoreline vegetation provides the important function of "pruning" the gusting wind blowing in from the ocean, thereby protecting the forest which rises behind it. Numerous breaches in this cover provide ample access to the unusual geology of the coast all the way to Providence Cove. The trail is generally easy with many boardwalk sections during the first 4 km. Past Tom Baird Creek watch for sea lions basking on the rocks. Anticipate many muddy sections as you climb up towards Soule Creek [km 43.]

Tiny, well-protected Providence Cove was once an important seasonal village for the ancestors of the Pacheenaht nation. Camping and fires are prohibited at the steep, pebble beach now but forest campsites, bear caches and pit toilets will be found ½ km further on at Payzant Creek [km 40.] Situated high above the stream, the site is accentuated by a delightful waterfall. Tent pads are poorly engineered, however, and fill up with rain water during even moderate sprinkles. There is no direct beach access here.

Except at high tide, less than a kilometre from the bridge at Payzant Creek, you'll have an opportunity to leave the forest and explore along the expansive intertidal shelf for

Risin' and Shinin' at the Crack of Noon
The patter of rain and the melody of Payzant's tumbling waterfall were enough to keep this young hiker snug in his sleeping bag until well-after the early birds had captured all of the worms.

Nikonos V
35 mm Nikkor lens
Kodachrome 200 ISO film

nearly one and half clicks. Backtracking will be necessary to regain the trail as there is no access at the eastern end.

At Parkinson Creek [km 37.2] there are no camping facilities but you will find a parking lot, pit toilets and an information board. Minute Creek Forest Service Road provides access through the logging clearcuts from Highway 14, 3.8 km away.

You'll also find very extraordinary seal caves just west of the mouth of Parkinson Creek. The caves are only accessible from the beach during the lowest of tides. Watch for a side trail near the Parkinson Creek trailhead that leads down to a viewpoint. From the bluff peer back west to glimpse the well-concealed seal nursery.

Parkinson Creek to Sombrio Beach 9 km

Push for Kuitshie Creek 4 km further on before camping for the night. In addition to forest campsites and pit toilets the secluded beach is an ideal place from which to enjoy the long, slow evenings of early summer. Along the way hikers are periodically treated to *buena vista*'s from the bluffs overlooking Juan de Fuca Strait. Such views must be paid for however and the trail exacts its toll in the form of deep ravines, exposed roots, mud holes, deadfalls and numerous

Juan de Fuca
Marine Trail

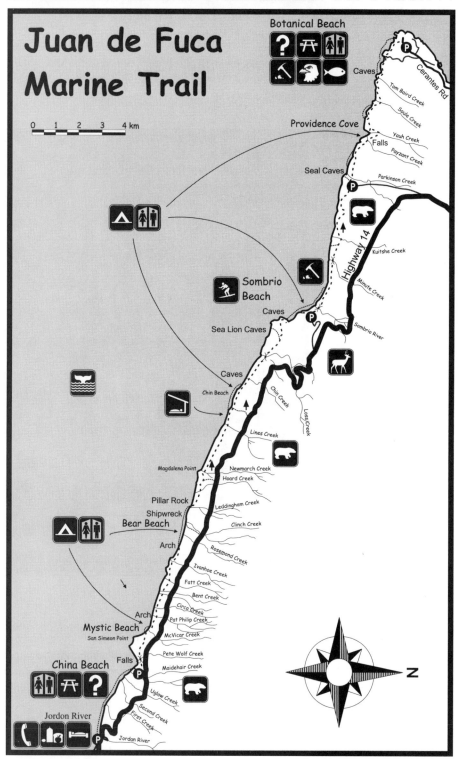

Botanical Beach

Caves

Cerantes Rd

Tom Baird Creek

Soule Creek

Providence Cove

Yauh Creek

Falls

Payzant Creek

Seal Caves

Parkinson Creek

Highway 14

Kuitshe Creek

Minute Creek

Sombrio
Beach

Caves

Sombrio River

Sea Lion Caves

Caves

Chin Beach

Chin Creek

Loss Creek

Lines Creek

Magdalena Point

Newmarch Creek

Hoard Creek

Pillar Rock

Leddingham Creek

Shipwreck

Bear Beach

Clinch Creek

Arch

Rosemond Creek

Ivanhoe Creek

Fatt Creek

Bent Creek

Circa Creek

Arch

Pat Philip Creek

Mystic Beach

McVicar Creek

San Simeon Point

Pete Wolf Creek

Falls

Maidehair Creek

China Beach

Jordon River

Uglow Creek

Second Creek

First Creek

Jordan River

N

0 1 2 3 4 km

117

stairs to be overcome. As contracted staff spend an inordinate amount of time chasing down delinquent hikers, trail maintenence suffers. Hikers on the other hand are often loathe to pay for such poorly maintained trails. Much of the Juan de Fuca Marine Trail is reminicient of the West Coast Trail of yesteryear: knee-deep mud and ankle-busting roots

Taking A Breather
This tired hiker finds a spot of sunlight in the forest gloom to stay warm while taking a rest. Sweating from physical exertion can quickly cause a chill whenever you take a break. Slip on a jacket or find a sunny spot when the lunch bell rings.

Nikon F
135 mm Nikkor lens
Kodachrome 200 ISO film

that slow progress down to a crawl.

Just a kilometre before Kuitshie Creek the trail winds past a small grove of ancient cedars that the loggers missed.

The next 5 kilometres to Sombrio Beach through a swath of regenerated second growth are uneventful except for a camping spot at Little Kuitshie Creek [km 33] cut from an impenetrable wall of salal. Expect the usual amenities. Tent sites are gravel-topped and drain well.

Slightly more than a kilometre beyond Little Kuitshie Creek you'll encounter a suspension bridge across the ravine at Minute Creek. From here the closest approach to Sombrio Beach is just 2 clicks away. The proximity of logging clearcuts can be unsightly at times. Of more concern to hikers, these open gashes in the forest promote the proliferation of berries which can support an inordinate numbers of bears. Of the three coastal hiking routes detailed in this book the Juan de Fuca Marine Trail boasts the largest concentrations of these foraging omnivores. Failure to practice no-trace camping or hang food beyond the reach of bears is an open invitation to trouble.

The expansive foreshore of Sombrio Beach is accessible more than two kilometres before reaching the Sombrio River when tides are running low. Otherwise stay with trail, a more circuitous route, until reaching the suspension bridge. Cliffs preclude foreshore navigation when the flood reaches its peak. Those taking the boulder-strewn beach route however will be rewarded with two cliff-hanging waterfalls and, at Som-

Rogue Waves

Backpackers following the intertidal shelf should be aware of phenomenon known as *rogue waves*. Unless seismic in origin, waves are usually created by the transferance of energy from wind to water. Three factors, wind speed, duration and fetch or the distance which a wind can blow, unimpeded, contribute to wave size. The energy moves wave-like through the water, displacing that water but not in fact transporting it. In other words the energy moves but the water doesn't. Long *wave-trains*, waves marching in succession, can travel over great distances across the water. At any given time the waves from several wave-trains from disparate origins may come crashing on any particular beach. Rogue waves occur when the crests of individual waves from different wave-trains momentarily coincide. In short rogue waves occur when two or more waves displace the same water at the same time. When two wave crests come together they create a bigger than average wave. When a crest and trough coincide the result is a smaller than average wave. Statistically the coincidence of two waves doubling up is thought to occur as frequently as one in 23 normal-sized waves. Certainly often enough to warrant caution whenever mucking about at the very edge of rocky shelves. When walking along the edge of metre high surf the margin of safety will rapidly disappear whenever a two metre wave hits the beach. Backpacker and knapsack may very well disappear as well if three crests overlap. Fortunately triple-sized waves are predicted to occur only once out of 1, 175 while four crests meeting simultaneously is as rare as one in three hundred thousand. A further dynamic, not fully understood yet, occurs when coinciding waves are further pumped up by ocean currents. Though not a frequent occurrence off the B.C. coast, waves on steroids have been measured as high as a 10-story building from crest to trough. Coinciding troughs are known to create momentary liquid black holes from which an unlucky freighter or tanker would be unlikely to reappear. Every year a handful of cargo ships vanish from the oceans of the earth. At least a few of these are thought to have fallen prey to rogue waves.

brio's western end, fossil beds richly-endowed with all manner of shellfish: snails, clams, dentalia and mussels.

A sturdy walking stick can save a lot of grief whenever traipsing across the rocky foreshore with heavy backpacks. Seaweed slick rocks have broken many a wrist or forearm. Even away from the beach the extra stability of a "third leg" will prove its usefulness time and again. Though any stick will do, a collapsible monopod-style walking stick or ski pole can be handy when climbing ladders or steep trails. Ski poles, however, can be slippery on rocks.

Sombrio Beach 2 km

Expect company at Sombrio Beach [km 29.] The access road, though unsurfaced, is short and well-marked with the gorgeous beaches attracting surfers, picnicking families and the overnight car-camping crowd. There are, however, numerous squeeky, wooden tent pads in the vicinity of the river mouth. Towards the eastern half more secluded spots for beach camping can be found.

Little actual sand will be found along Sombrio's white cresent. Starting at the headland in the west, the beach is comprised of basketball-sized boulders that become progressively smaller as one proceeds eastward. Around the river the rocks have been reduced to the size and shape of sun-bleached baseballs. Small pebbles and sand comprise the foreshore at the headland on the opposite end. At low tide, note the sea caves too at the base of the eastern cliffs.

Whenever following a route along the beach scan the sea from time to time looking for resident orcas and Gray whales. Each spring 18,000 migrating Gray whales pass by on their way to the Bering Sea from Baja, Mexico. As you rest on a driftwood log gaze across Juan de Fuca Strait to Neah Bay on Washington's Olympic Peninsula and contemplate the revival of coastal whaling that occurred there in 1999. Were the Native American whalers simply reasserting a traditional right? Was the slaughter necessary for the band to earn back the self-esteem that had been robbed from them as their culture collapsed? Or was it just an ill-thought out act of brutality by a mob of celebrity mongerers?

Sombrio Beach to Chin Beach 6 km

The headland at the far end of the Sombrio Beach is impassible. To regain the main trail look for bright orange fish floats hanging in the trees. Most beach egress points along the Juan de Fuca Marine Trail have been marked this way. As you climb up the main trail from Sombrio Beach to

Dwarf Dogwood
Since the Dogwood is the provincial flower in British Columbia, "bunch berry," is a protected species. Following pollination and fruiting, dwarf dogwood produces a bunch of bright red berries, hence the name. Bunch berry berries are edible either raw or cooked though they are not particulary tasty. They have further been used both internally and externally to counteract natural toxins from mushrooms, poison ivy and even bee stings. Dwarf dogwood is a perennial and a perennial favourite with hikers as this low ground cover will be found along most forested footpaths on the coast. The white petal-like mane surrounding the central flower are actually specialized leaves called bracts.
Illustration by Manami Kimura

the cliff top you may realize that you're leaving the easiest hiking behind. The next 18 km are particularly demanding as the steep terrain is deeply fissured from innumerable creeks that tumble across the Juan de Fuca Marine Trail from the hills above. On the other hand you'll be passing through exquisite examples of coastal temperate rain forest. After

Cedar Bark

Next to salmon, western red-cedar was the most important resource available to coastal Indian groups. Together the two enabled natives of the Pacific Northwest to rise well above mere subsistance to a level of sophistication unmatched elsewhere in Canada.

Transportation and shelter in the form of dugout canoes and longhouses were fashioned from the strong, lightweight, rot-resistant wood as were implements too numerous to mention. The inner bark of cedar was the most important source of fiber available. Cedar bark was woven into waterproof hats and clothing, as pictured left, and all manner of basketry. Shredded bark found utility in diapers, bandages and menstral pads.

Cedar branches were processed into rope and basket making material.

Edward Sheriff Curtis Photo. Title: *A Nakaktok Chief's Daughter*. Courtesy the National Archives of Canada PA-039457.

passing Sombrio viewpoint drop your packs and explore the side trail overlooking a shelf where sea lions enjoy basking in the sun.

The main trail next climbs inland eventually following a logging road before plunging down a series of switchbacks to the suspension bridge across Loss Creek Canyon. Once across, the steep terrain with many switchbacks continues for four more kilometres, finally dumping hikers out on to the beach where a new challenge awaits.

The headland just a kilometre further on is impassible at high and even moderately low tides. If the moon is on your side you may wish to undertake a side trip before rounding the headland. During times of extremely low tide, those below one metre, an arch and several sea caves reveal themselves near the western end of Chin Beach. Explore but dally not if you want to continue on to Chin Creek for beach camping at its best. Luckily, an alternative forest route exists for bypassing this barrier. From here to Bear Beach 12 km away there are very few other camping opportunities.

Love on the Rocks
The pounding surf and plaintive cries of gulls will be the melody running through any trip to the Juan de Fuca trail.

Nikon F
300 mm Nikkor lens
Kodachrome 200 ISO film

A small grove of giant cedars is accessible via a side trail that leaves Chin Beach just east of the outhouses. It should take 35 minutes unencumbered with packs to reach the ancient big trees. A further 15 minutes will take you to Highway 14.

Chin Beach to Bear Beach 12 km

At the east end of Chin Beach too progress may be impeded by excessively high tides and no alternative exists other than staying in touch with the moon's influences and planning accordingly. The trail to Bear Beach is a demanding slog over very uneven terrain. Thankfully backpacks should be considerably lighter than when you first started out. The trail climbs steeply up to an emergency shelter perched at the top of the bluff. This cliff top condo is a great place to dry out during times of inclement weather. If you choose to tuck in here for the night the mice who got there first should quickly convince you that tenting out is infinitely preferable. The route follows the bluff high above the beach, cutting down then up again across many ravines and canyons through mature stands of second growth timber. From Magdalena Point, just past Newmarch Creek at the 14 km post, enjoy sweeping views of the Strait of Juan de Fuca before heading back into the forest, now a surviving stand of old-growth. Imagine what human events were transpiring when these giant cedars were just seedlings. The trail rises steeply for a kilometre now before plunging an equal distance back down towards the seashore. A side trail at Hoard Creek reveals a tiny secluded beach. One and a half kilometres further on, where you and Ledingham Creek both tumble out of the forest on to Bear Beach, notice Mush-

Bushwhacker Blues
Exposed roots, pools of mud, deadfalls and impenetrable salal challenge every step along the Juan de Fuca Marine Trail. Since maintenance contracts are in part tied to user fees, contract holders spend an inordinate amount of time tracking down delinquent campers, much to the detriment of trail maintenance. As one weary hiker put it: "I don't really feel very good about paying with the trail in such bad condition." Interestingly, while day-use areas tend to be very well-maintained, day users pay nothing for the facilities.

Nikonos V
35 mm Nikkor lens
Kodachrome 200 ISO film

room Rock, a geological anomaly more reminiscent of Wile E. Coyote country than coastal British Columbia. A kilometre further along the beach, just before reaching Clinch Creek, scraps of a shipwreck litter the foreshore. Depending on the tide, Bear Beach may be divided by an impassible headland just west of a Rosemond Creek. Beach campsites with pit toilets have been set up on either side of the barrier for those who are required to wait overnight for more favourable conditions. Wading around the sheer cliff walls is possible during all but the highest tides, those above three metres. If tempted to risk the crossing, attempt it only during relatively calm seas. Use a walking stick for stability and don't even dream of wading barefoot. Keep in mind too, that massive *rogue waves*, created far out in the Pacific, can crash on the beaches along Vancouver Island's west coast unexpectedly at any time, sweeping the inattentive far out to sea.

Bear Beach to China Beach 9 km

Beneath the cliffs of the east end of Bear Beach notice the wave-sculpted arch. Back track to the last orange marker and climb a unique set of stairs up the headland east of Bear Beach before encountering the rugged terrain once again. Magnificent views from the cliff tops above the beach are more than enough compensation for the steep gorges which must be overcome. Just 6 km on you'll reach sandy Mystic Beach, an inviting place to camp if waiting for transportation pick up the next day. The end of the trail at China Beach is just 2 km away! Choose your real estate early if you want to pre-empt one of the choicer spots. Mystic Beach can get crowded on blue sky weekends. While hanging out there is plenty to explore. Stretching from a sea worn arch of sandstone at the far west end this delightful beach continues eastward for less than a kilometre past a small waterfall to the cliffs of San Simon Point. As one might expect, these features are accessible at low tide only. The trail rises steeply from Mystic Beach following a route across San Simon Point and one final suspension bridge before reaching the parking lot at popular China Beach.

Trail's End: China Beach

As with Botanical Beach at the north end of the trail, the southern trailhead too is restricted to day use only. At the far western end of China Beach during tides of 2½ metres and lower, an attractive waterfall and pool are revealed where Pete Wolf Creek pours on to the beach. If time allows continue exploring the rocky shore from China Beach 2.2 km to Jordan River before your ride arrives. The shuttle is scheduled to leave Port Renfrew at 3:30 PM but is notoriously late. Wait for your pick up from the upper parking lot. 🐾

Juan de Fuca Marine Trail
Season: April - October

Contact	Notes
West Coast Trail Express 1-888-999-2288; (250) 477-8700 bus@trailbus.com; www.trailbus.com	9:30AM Leave Victoria to Port Renfrew $30 3:30PM Leave Port Renfrew to Victoria $30 Victoria P/U in front of Island Coach Lines (700 Douglas St.)
Pacheedaht First Nation Bus (250) 647-5521 or (250) 647-5556	Shuttle service; Call in advance to arrange for pick up from any of the four trailheads.
BC Parks South Vancouver Island District 2930 Trans Canada Highway Victoria BC V9E 1K3 (250) 391-2300; (250) 478-9211 FAX	Juan de Fuca Marine Trail Administration Beach camping $5 per person per night
Juan de Fuca Express Brian Gisborne 1-888-755-6578 1-877-332-5333 radio telephone juanfuca@island.net	Water Taxi Services the southwest coast of Vancouver Island
Hostelling International Victoria 516 Yates Street, Victoria BC (250) 385-4511; (250) 385-3232 FAX 1-888-883-0099 victoria@hihostels.bc.ca	
Paralytic Shellfish Poisoning Hotline (604) 666-2828	Recorded red tide information from Fisheries & Oceans Canada Check Fisheries Management Area 20

The West Coast Trail

Level: Difficult   **Distance:** 75 km   **Time:** 4 - 7 Days

Map: Provided to registrants   **Terrain:** Undulating   **Season:** May - Sept

Extending 75 km along the southwestern shore of Vancouver Island, the West Coast Trail attracts 8,600 hikers each year. Visitors, encumbered with heavy backpacks, are challenged by deep ravines with seemingly endless ladders, slippery beach trails, taxing river fords, drenching rains and, at times, knee-deep mud. Sound horrible? The rewards are less easy to enumerate but include some of the finest scenery in the world, magnificent wildlife including bears and cougars, Gray whales and orcas. For better or worse, hiking the West Coast Trail is an experience never to be forgotten. For many it may be an endurance test, but compared with the perils of a bygone era, undertaking the West Coast Trail today is, if you'll excuse the pun, a walk in the park.

Currents of Doom

Prevailing currents that sweep northward along the California, Oregon and Washington coasts run headlong into the flank of Vancouver Island as it juts out into the Pacific. Running at speeds of as much as 5 km/h, The California Current intercepts the warmer Japanese Current just offshore, creating thick banks of fog while at the same time pinning all manner of flotsam and jetsam against the rugged coastline.

Flotsam and Jetsam

Above these colliding currents, offshore winds – often raging typhoons – tend to slam everything in towards the shoreline.

Dead Reckoning

Before the advent of steam, sailing ships needed plenty of room to manoeuvre under even the best of conditions. Unfortunately for many a doomed sailor the myriad rocks, islets, reefs and shoals left little room for anything once an error had been committed.

In the early days of B.C. shipping, finding the entrance to Juan de Fuca Strait on a fine, clear day could prove demanding. Locating the strait on a dark and stormy night was a daunting, often deadly task.

Inaccurate navigational charts, a lack of navigational aids such as lighthouses, foghorns and beacons meant often near blind groping for the entrance at night in the worst possible weather. Little wonder that so many captains overshot Juan de Fuca Strait only to have their ships ravaged by the savage Graveyard of the Pacific.

Since 1854 some 70 or more ships big and small have been dashed to bits on the gnarly southwest coast of Vancouver Island. Over the decades hundreds have been killed. Some have been lucky, meeting death quickly and mercifully in the pounding, grinding surf. Those less fortunate met death slowly and excruciatingly. Spared a watery grave they huddled on wild beaches wet and cold, continually lashed by the elements, unable to kindle fire, too weak to find food until life slipped away with a shiver.

Countless others have been saved by the largely unacknowledged heroism of local natives. Time and time again the original inhabitants pulled survivors from the mayhem, provided shelter and food in the wilderness or ferried them as far away as Sooke and Victoria, at considerable personal risk, in their seaworthy dugout canoes.

In 1906, following the loss of 126 lives from the steamer Valencia, Pachena Point Lighthouse and the West Coast Lifesaving Trail were built. In addition to the rough-hewn trail, a network of rustic cabins and a telegraph line were constructed to support future shipwrecked survivors.

Lighthouse keepers and their ever-vigilant families played an increasingly important role as navigational aids were installed along the coast. Often running or rowing through many kilometres of darkness and storm, they were able to bring help to foundering vessels whenever the primitive telegraph lines failed.

Present day hikers on the West Coast Trail can scarcely conceive of the perils shipwrecked mariners faced. Often marooned in the harshest winter months, survivors had no broad avenues to follow, no suspension bridges, ferries or cable cars on which to cross rivers. There were no ladders up the sides of steep, greasy-slick ravines. Often survivors had no food, little clothing and even less hope. Yet against the odds many survived.

Anchor's Away
A poignant reminder of the countless lives lost to shipwrecks in the Graveyard of the Pacific, an anchor lies rusting on the beach.

Nikon F
28 mm Nikkor lens
Ektachrome 100 ISO film

The Litter of History

Hikers today will encounter the old telegraph wire still hanging in trees. Rescue huts decay in the forests as boilers and anchors and broken chunks of iron and steel rust on the beaches. And in the sun, in the summer, it's hard to image the hell that was the Graveyard of the Pacific.

Access

There are two ways of undertaking the West Coast Trail. From the south, starting at Port Renfrew, you can expect to get the worst over first, with your hike getting progressively easier as the days wear on. This northward route culminates in a pleasant, well-earned cruise along the Alberni Inlet from Bamfield to Port Alberni. The other possibility is start hiking from Bamfield (pop 400) undertaking the easiest sections while your backpack is heaviest. The theory is, your physical conditioning will gradually improve to meet the demands of an increasingly difficult route. The reality for those who try to undertake the West Coast Trail too quickly, however, is they may reach the difficult bottom end fatigued and stiff, heightening the potential for injury. The key, of course, is to allow plenty of time to drink in the sights and sounds. Backpacking should never seem to be a forced

march. I have met those who try to undertake the trail as an overnighter, presumably just for the bragging rights. By any definition, doing so is sheer folly.

This book will detail access and egress to both trailheads north and south but will focus on a southward route description aimed at less experienced hikers.

Getting There

The West Coast Trail Express offers one-stop shopping for transportation to either end of the trail. A fleet of maxed-out minibuses delivers hikers daily from Victoria while those originating in Vancouver can intercept a Bamfield-bound bus in Nanaimo.

Northward Ho!

If you decide to follow the trail from Port Renfrew northwards to Bamfield the West Coast Trail Express costs $30 and leaves from in front of the Island Coach Lines bus terminal in Victoria at 700 Douglas Street arriving in Port Renfrew 2½ hours later. When you finish your hike the same transportation company will pick you up at Pachena Bay near Bamfield and return you to Victoria or Nanaimo for $50. If you would prefer to avoid the dusty logging roads on the return, Alberni Marine Transportation operates a ferry service between Bamfield and Port Alberni every day in the summer except Monday and Wednesday. The ferries MV Lady Rose or MV Frances Barkley make any number of whistle-stops at cabins and fish farms along the Alberni Inlet arriving invariably behind schedule. Fortunately, bus service from Port Alberni is frequent enough to be relied upon no matter how late the ferry returns. From the Public Quay where you will get your land legs back again, the bus terminal is a mere 10 minute walk. If you've had your fill of walking, grab a cab instead. From Port Alberni, Vancouver Island Coach Lines will deliver you to the connecting Maverick Coach Lines bus in Nanaimo for the final leg of the journey back to Vancouver.

Southward Ho!

If undertaking the trail in the recommended north-south direction, arriving in Bamfield by boat is logistically difficult though not impossible. The ferries leave Port Alberni at 8 am every Tuesday, Thursday, Friday, Saturday and Sunday, too early to be accessed directly by public transportation from Vancouver which arrives at 10 AM at the earliest. The only alternative would be to arrive in Port Alberni the day before then board the ferry at the Public Quay after a good night's sleep at a nearby motel. Needless to say the logistics and cost of bus, accommodation and boat make this alternative hard to justify.

The West Coast Trail Express is both faster and cheaper, bumping and grinding its way over dirt roads from either Victoria or Nanaimo on a daily basis. Pick up in Nanaimo is at the Departure Bay Ferry Terminal at 8:45 every morning and costs $50. You'll have to be on the first ferry [6:30 AM] from Horseshoe Bay in order to connect. **[For details on getting to Horseshoe Bay see Appendix on page 320.]**

Reservation System

The recreation potential of the West Coast Trail area was recognized as long ago as

1926 when it was formally set aside as a park reserve by the provincial government. Ulterior designs on the land and its forests by the logging lobby were enough to convince the government to rescind the reserve designation in 1947. The West Coast Lifesaving Trail was simply too remote for recreational use they argued. In spite of the poor condition of the trail word gradually spread of this natural wonder until, in the 1960s, the federal government persuaded its provincial counterpart to set the land aside for broader usage. Pacific Rim National Park was born in 1970 and from that point forward recreational use exploded. By the 1990s recreational overuse, not the logging interests, was threatening the very wilderness values along the West Coast Trail so revered by users. In 1992, for the first time, a quota was imposed limiting the number of hikers that could enjoy the trail. Though trail beds, bridges and camping facilities including outhouses have steadily improved, hiker impact on the ecosystem has continued to grow causing regular reductions in the annual quota. At present only 26 users may access the trail daily from each trailhead. Twenty of those must have reservations while just six hikers are allowed on the trail from the often extensive waiting lists at Gordon River near Port Renfrew or Pachena Bay near Bamfield. Permits are issued to those on the waiting lists daily at 1 PM. Reservations can be made up to 90 days in advance but because of the demand reservations are usually gobbled up within minutes of becoming available. Those who show up at the trailhead can expect to wait for several days before getting on the trail. Those with reservations must pay a $25 reservation fee while all users must pay a $70 user fee at the trailhead and must carry a park use permit at all times while on the trail. The permit must be returned when leaving the trail. In addition to trail upkeep, the user fee pays for regular rescue patrols, pre-trail orientation, and each user receives a waterproof map and tide chart.

Parks Canada does not allow camping in the vicinity of either trailhead. Those on the waiting list can find commercial camping on adjacent Indian land. The Huu-Ay-Aht Band at Pachena Bay charges $18 per night for a campsite while the Pacheenaht Band

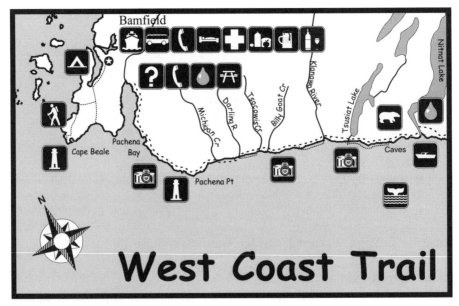

West Coast Trail

at Gordon River levies a fee of $3 per night for each tent. Some hikers resent paying to wait just to get on the trail. Keep in mind, however, that the trail cuts through Indian land at many points and without the blessing of all three local bands, hiking the trail would not be possible at all.

Wherever you may be recreating it is always a good idea to try to support the local economy in some small way either through the purchase of provisions, local transportation services, tacky tourist T-shirts, or even just a cheese burger in paradise. Those making a living from the recreational trade will prove to be invaluable allies if push ever comes to shove in the myriad land-use battles that define outdoor recreation in British Columbia.

Since inexperience is by far the greatest danger in wilderness situations Parks Canada staff have sought to improve the kind of information each trail user receives. Consequently all West Coast Trail users must now undertake an orientation session prior to starting the trail. Orientations are offered daily at each trailhead at 9:30 AM, noon, 1:30 PM and 3:30 PM. Given the importance Parks Canada places on accurate information it seems somehow ironic that whenever I've called as either a hiker, guide or as an author I have received inaccurate information or could not find answers to my questions at all.

Parks staff will try to dissuade hikers from harvesting seafood of any kind in Pacific Rim National Park of which the West Coast Trail is part. The fact remains however that doing so is entirely legal, subject to the laws of the province of British Columbia. A fishing license is of course necessary and catch limits must be adhered to. For two good reasons it is better to sample *fruits de mer* than feast on them. The obvious reason is to limit the impact visitors to the area have on marine life. The second reason is to limit the impact, including death, that marine life may have on visitors to the area. Paralytic shellfish poisoning or red tide is a seasonal toxin associated with all bivalve molluscs that can cause paralysis and death. Pigging out on mussels, clams, oysters and other species of shellfish could have dire consequences even when an area is officially open

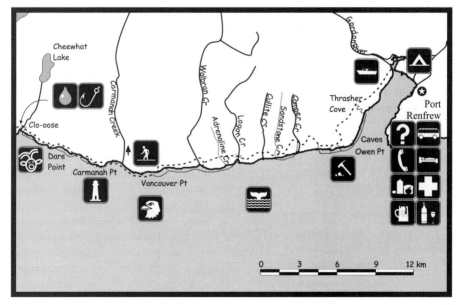

to harvesting. If intending to harvest seafood contact the red tide hotline [see info grid, page 140] before setting off on the West Coast Trail.

Every morning and every evening Parks Canada staff patrol offshore in red or gray inflatable zodiacs. Those with injuries or requiring assistance can flag the boats down at any of the following preferred evacuation sites:

Pachena Lighthouse	Carmanah Lighthouse	Camper Bay
Tsocowis Creek	Cullite Cove	Thrasher Cove
Nitinat Narrows	Logan Creek	

Being, as the Boy Scouts say, prepared is the single most important thing you can do to make your trip to the West Coast Trail a safe and enjoyable one. The trail is first and foremost a wilderness one. Bring enough food for an extra day should accident or incident demand it. Wear clothing that allows you to stay cool yet protects your skin on hot summer days. When it rains it pours on the West Coast of Vancouver Island and rain it does even in the summer months. Average annual rainfall is 120 mm. Clothing that keeps you dry and warm is just as essential. Cheap backpacks, sleeping bags, tents and footgear can cost you dearly. More than anything pack your common sense along with your toothbrush and you'll meet the elements evenly matched.

Day One — Pachena Bay to Michigan Creek 12 kilometres

After signing in at Pachena Bay at the northern end near the community of Bamfield you'll find the going very easy at first. A number of impassible headlands make beach walking out of the question until Michigan Creek. The first 10 km of the trail follow what was once a supply road for the Pachena Point Lighthouse. As a consequence the trail is generally flat and so wide that walking two abreast is possible. Just a kilometre before the lighthouse on this pretty but otherwise uneventful section of trail a viewpoint affords a view of Flat Rocks where sea lions often enjoy basking in the sun on a warm spring or autumn day. At the lighthouse you'll be greeted in your native language no matter where in the world you come from. Hikers are welcome to look around the Lighthouse grounds during posted visiting hours but keep in mind that this is home to the lighthouse keepers. Disturb nothing including the keepers as they go about their daily chores. Only recently the original tower was decommissioned, replaced with an automated light-on-a-stick. The original beacon at Pachena Point, now a Recognized Heritage Building, is the last remaining wooden lighthouse in British Columbia. The massive Fresnel lens and oil wick lamp have operated faultlessly since 1907.

Two kilometres on consider calling it a day at the popular Michigan Creek campsite[km 12.] After setting up camp check out the boiler and other rusty bits of iron from the steamship Michigan that ran aground here in January 1893 costing a number of lives.

Much of the next day will be spent hiking along the beach. Loose rocks, slippery seaweed-covered surfaces, soft sinking sand and surge channels all require special attention especially when encumbered with a heavy backpack. The majority of ankle, wrist and arm injuries occur on the intertidal shelf. A sturdy driftwood walking stick or ski pole can go a long way towards providing the additional stability needed along the shore route. Once you reach the ladders at the bottom end of the trail you'll doubtless agree that a collapsible walking stick is well worth the investment.

Day Two — Michigan Cr to Tsusiat 12½ km

From Michigan Creek the first two kilometres to Dar-

Well? Come!
An international welcome greets hikers at the Pachena Bay Light Station. Whether it is your first day or your last day on the trail the greeting is most -- um, -- welcomed.

Nikon F
28 mm Nikkor lens
Ektachrome 100 ISO film

ling River are beach accessible during all but the highest tides [below 3.7 metres.] The cable car across the Darling River [km 14] is the first of many you will encounter on the West Coast Trail. They are fun to ride on and will keep your feet dry but often the cable cars are out of order. When creeks are running low marching across them instead will save considerable time and energy. Whenever fording streams undo your waist belt and loosen your pack straps in the event that you stumble and have to quickly jettison your pack.

If the tides are in your favour, continue along the beach for a further 3 km until Tsocowis Creek. Though a forest route is available, most prefer the open coastal scenery and the ease of walking the beach route affords. Keep an eye seaward as the foreshore is popular with foraging Gray whales.

The next three kilometres to Trestle Creek follow a relatively easy forest footpath packed with historical relics. To find the trail from the beach, look for fishing floats hanging in the trees. Access points are marked this way all along the

West Coast Trail. Be sure to top up your water at Billy Goat Creek as the elixir of life can be hard to find the rest of the way to the Klanawa River. About a kilometre beyond Billy Goat Creek pause for a moment at the Valencia viewpoint to consider the victims of the shipwreck in January 1906 which ultimately led to the construction of the Pachena Point Light Station and the West Coast Lifesaving Trail. In time the sea has claimed every last remnant of wreckage leaving only the dimmest memory of the 126 people who died on the rocks off distant Shelter Bight. Those not mercifully claimed by drowning were trapped with cliffs at their backs and impassible headlands on either side. Many faced the raging sea bravely only to be exhausted and broken by hypothermia. Amazingly, 38 survivors managed to scramble to safety.

Just beyond the viewpoint you'll come across first a grader then a steam "donkey" [km 19] left behind after completion of the Lifesaving trail in 1909. The road-wide portion of the trail extended from Bamfield to the site of the *Valencia* wreck at Shelter Bight, continuing on to Carmanah Point as a well-defined trail. Beyond Carmanah the Lifesaving trail was a rough footpath hacked through the forest to Port Renfrew. Though all sections have been vastly improved, today this relativity persists.

The winch on the rocks at Shelter Bight and the anchor at Trestle Creek are thought to come from the 1923 wreck of the steamer *Robert E. Lewers*. At low tide wreckage from the Janet Cowan which sank in 1895 can also be seen at Shelter Bight [km 20.]

Either trail or beach will take you the 2½ km from Trestle Creek to the cable car crossing at Klanawa River. Since you will have already covered 11 km since Michigan Creek some will want to stop here for the night and Klanawa River [km 23] is certainly a suitable spot to pitch a tent. Many, however, will want to push on for another 1½ km through the forest to the most popular place on the West Coast Trail, Tsusiat Falls. The sandy beach, picturesque waterfall, dipping pool and sea caves are attractive enough for some hikers to camp over for several days at a time. The crowds can be insufferable however so many others would rather opt for a more wilderness setting to set up camp. The choice is yours. Assuming you fall into the latter category and decide to stop for the night at Klanawa keep in mind that the river is tidal so you may have to go upstream some distance in order to get untainted water when the tide is in. Always taste the water first before filling up to avoid contaminating your container.

Day Three — Tsusiat Falls to Dare Point 13½ km

Even if you didn't camp at Tsusiat Falls [km 25.5] you will want to stop to enjoy the scenery and snap a few pictures. From the falls the beach again affords the best hiking. Tsusiat Point a kilometre away is impassible at tides above 2.7 metres. The Hole-in-the-Wall at the point is another popular photo op. Another kilometre reveals an anchor mired in the beach near a forest access trail. The beach route continues another kilometre before Tsuquadra Point [km 29] forces hikers back into the forest for the last three kilometres before Nitinat Narrows. Tsuquadra Indian Reserve is now out of bounds since hikers in the past have desecrated important cultural sites hereabouts. The beaches along this section of trail however are very attractive with numerous sea caves revealed at low tide. Trails just before and after the reserve provide access to public portions of the beach.

Ring the dinner bell, a giant iron triangle, when you reach Nitinat Narrows [km 32] to call for the ferry across this treacherous waterway. The ferry, operated by members of the Ditidaht Indian Band from early May to early October, costs $12.50 and is the only way to cross this deep tidal river. Keep your Trail Use Permit handy to show the operator when you board. Both ferries along the West Coast Trail must be paid for in advance upon registration. On a hot day it may be possible to purchase an ice cold brew or two from

Flotsom Mobile
Beachcombing yields a colourful array of fishing floats at Tsusiat Falls.

Nikon F
28 mm Nikkor lens
Ektachrome 100 ISO film

the skipper. Remember, however, if you intend to enjoy your beer at the next campsite you are expected to carry your empties, as with all your garbage, to be properly disposed of at the end of the trail. Water is going to be a problem for the next 10 km so be sure to top up with water once you reach the opposite shore. There is excellent water to the left of the main trail just a few steps from the dock. Due to the ignorance and immaturity of hikers in the past, the Indian villages of Whyac and Clo-oose [km 35] are now off limits. Hikers must remain on the forest the trail for the next 4 km until reaching the Cheewhat River. A number of unique petroglyphs in the vicinity of Clo-oose record the passage of the paddlewheel steamer *Beaver* and other sailing ships in 1836. These treasures too are now off-limits to hikers. From one of the cliff-top viewpoints between the two villages note the anchor below, all that remains of the *Skagit* which was shipwrecked in 1906.

Meaning "river of urine," water from the Cheewhat is undrinkable. A small spring to the left of the trail just before the Cheewhat River Bridge is, in spite of the sulphuric tinge, the best water in the area. What may be caustic to humans seems oddly attractive to crabs, however. Sizable dungeness crabs often litter the bottom of the shallow Cheewhat River as it meanders out to sea below the bridge. If equipped with a fishing license you may discover the real reason for carrying that hiking stick day after day. Using the oldest trick in the book, scare the crabs with the stick towards a companion waiting in the shallows. Always grip the crabs from behind, grasping the main shell firmly between thumb and forefingers. Use any other technique and you will no doubt find out how eager indeed the crabs are to end up in a pot of boiling water.

The point of land overlooking the mouth of the Cheewhat River is also Indian Reserve and therefore out of bounds but the sandy beach beyond that and extending for nearly 1½ km to Dare Point would be ideal for camping except for the lack of water. Only one site about 1 km away has an adequate supply. Since you will have already covered 13½ km since Klanawa River setting up camp here might be well-advised.

Carmanah Giant
The world's largest sitka spruce tree, called the Carmanah Giant, leans over the creek for which it was named. The Giant's neighbors are themselves no dwarf pines. More resistant to salt than other west coast species, sitka spruce has found a niche along Vacouver Island's Pacific Rim.

Nikon F
28 mm Nikkor lens
Ektachrome 100 ISO film

Day Four — Dare Pt to Walbran Cr 16 km

You'll start the day on the forest footpath again but only for a kilometre or so. Once past Dare Point [km 37] the beach is again accessible except when tides are running below 2.1 metres. Wreckage including the anchor from the steamer Santa Rita which ran aground in 1923 can be found in a surge channel about halfway between Dare Point and Dare Beach. The headland before Dare Beach is passable at low tide but the forest route, being both faster and safer, is recommended. From Dare Beach the trail moves inland and includes some sections of boardwalk leading to Carmanah Point Lighthouse. Before leaving the beach note the unique natural breakwater off shore called the Cribs [km 40.]

The Carmanah Point Light Station [km 44] was first manned in 1891 as a complement to the Cape Beale Light Station which was established in 1874 as a reference point to assist mariners searching for the entrance to Juan de Fuca Strait.

Beyond the lighthouse you'll regain the beach once again. The trail follows a beach-only route for the next 7 km to Vancouver Point. If time is on your side, take a break at Carmanah Creek [km 46] and wade upstream 1.3 km unencumbered with packs for a look at the Carmanah Giant, the world's largest sitka spruce tree. The Carmanah Giant is 95 metres tall and 3 metres thick at the base. Carmanah Creek is also an excellent place to camp though I have seen the river and the beaches in the vicinity absolutely polluted from tens of thousands of krill-feasting herring gulls. The overwhelming stench made camping impossible.

Continuing on from Carmanah Creek looks easy. Do not be misled. The powdery sand places unique demands on your calf muscles, knees and lower back. While you will move forward at a rapid pace you'll find it exhausting work. Even at the water's edge, where the wet, packed sand is firmer, walking is never easy. Mercifully, the rocky sandstone shelves provide some relief when the tide is low. If the tide is below 3.7 metres it is possible to walk around Vancouver Point [km 51] and on to the mouth of the Walbran River [km 53.] Wading the river will be necessary, however, so this route is not recommended during spring runoff or following heavy rains. After 16 km of steady trudging you'll be more than eager to pitch the tent at this picturesque site.

Aping It Up
You'll seem more monkey than mountaineer as you climb up and up and up again on countless ladders along the southern section of trail. No bananas up top however, just another ladder to scamper back down.

Nikon F
28 mm Nikkor lens
Ektachrome 100 ISO film

Day Five — Walbran Cr to Camper Cr 9 km

Awaken well-rested after the long haul on the previous day to realize you have to undertake a mere 9 km amble today. Look a little closer at your map and notice that the terrain, relatively flat thus far, is about to undergo a dramatic transformation. The beach has suddenly become problematic forcing hikers away from the coast and into the forest. A succession of creeks big and small has cut deep ravines across your route. As you will soon discover, this day will stand out as a seemingly endless sequence of ladders, some of them broken, all of them slippery. From this day forward, when you think of the phrase "temperate rain forest" you will recall the magnificent gloom you are about to enter. Depending on the weather, you may also think of mud.

The 3 km from Walbran Creek to Logan Creek could be accomplished on the beach, at least when tides are below 2.1 metres, were it not for the dangerous surge channel at Adrenaline Creek [km 55.] Adrenaline Surge is a wide fissure that cuts through the intertidal shelf to the cliff face where a waterfall tumbles into the channel. During periods of low precipitation, and when tides are below 1.7 metres, an exposed rock in the middle of the surge channel provides a perilous stepping stone to the other side. Be forewarned: hikers have died here.

By comparison, the forest route is largely uneventful. From Walbran Creek you'll climb 150 metres or so to a boggy area, excellent mosquito habitat early in the season, before climbing ladders down into the ravine carved by Adrenaline Creek. After climbing out the other side, it will be another kilometre before you begin descending into Logan Creek canyon [km 56.] Ladders will drop you on to a suspension bridge which should not be crossed by more than six people at once. If you wish to access the beach

Bear Attack

You are far more likely to be maimed or killed in an auto accident while driving to the trailhead than from the charge of a marauding bear while recreating. The fear of bear attack far outstrips the reality. Such attacks are rare and the causes of most attacks, when they happen, are often preventable. In a typical year we can expect between 3 - 5 attacks. In the 15 years since 1985 there were just 10 deaths attributed to bears in British Columbia. Annually in excess of 200 people die on BC roads. That's more than 3000 fatalities for the same time period. Incidentally, statistics show those using public transportation have a greatly reduced risk of traffic accident.

Since bears are more than happy to avoid contact with humans, accidental confrontations should be a primary concern. On the trail staying alert, scrutinizing the trail that lays ahead of you and traveling in a group of four or more will usually be enough to avoid stumbling upon a bear. With the wind at your back most bears should be forewarned of your approach, giving them ample time to vanish into the forest. A head wind on the other hand will eliminate a bear's most important sense. A particularly blustery wind could also hamper a bear's ability to hear your approach. That leaves sight, touch and taste and bears are the original Mr. Magoo. Under these conditions or when fresh bear sign is evident assist the bear by making noise. Metallic noise, not found in nature, is thought by some to be the best. Gabbing and gaffawing among your companions runs a close second. Liven up the chatter with a few bear mauling anecdotes. That ought to add a shrill, excited edge to the conversation. Keep the group together by placing the slowest person in the lead. Even just stumbling through the bush, a group of four or five makes appreciably more noise than groups of one or two strung out all along the trail. Be extra alert also when hiking early in the morning or late in the afternoon when most creatures are more active. Huckleberry or salal berry patches too are a great place to break out the noise makers.

Everyone knows that a sow with cubs could spell trouble particularly if the she-bear perceives a threat to her offspring. A bear guarding a kill or a scavaged bag of bones can also be a particularly lethal situation. If you ever see the carcass of an animal do not stop to investigate. Clear out immediately or you too could be dead meat.

No Trace Camping is not just an aesthetic, it is a safety measure. Food should be hung where no bear can reach it. Your camp cooking area and utensils must be kept spotless and refrain from slipping a few granola bars under your pillow for and camping area follow the trail to the right once you have reached the opposite side of the span. Otherwise mount the ladders again to climb out of the ravine. There is no beach route between Logan Creek and Cullite Creek [km 58.]

The high ground is marshy once again but thankfully the trail is topped with a cedar boardwalk. Pay close attention to your footing as some boards may be cracked or broken. Always try to step across two boards at once in case one happens to give way.

---

a midnight snack or the snack might be on you.

Upon meeting a bear never turn and run. The eyes of bears, like those of most predators, are cued in to movement. Run and so will the bear, right after you. Talk to the bear in calm, reassuring tones while backing away from the situation. A bear may rear up on its hind legs, not as a prelude to attack but, to sniff the air and get a better sense of what kind of oddballs confront it. Even if the bear decides to charge stay cool. Chances are the bear is bluffing, such behavior is common in bear society. Keep backing away and keep up to chatter. If it is a grizzly confronting you, back towards a stout, climbable tree as these bears are not good climbers. By remaining calm you may avoid making one of two very unsavory choices: fighting or playing dead.

In the event of a full-blown attack which option you choose will depend on the kind of bear is involved. If a black bear attacks that obviously has cubs or a meat cache then the bear may be satisfied if it can eliminate the threat. In such a situation playing dead is preferable to fighting back as the latter will only serve to antagonize the bear. If the black bear is obviously old or injured or otherwise motivated by hunger then fight for your life as this bear views you as a food source.

Grizzly bears are simply too big and powerful to fight off and they know it. If climbing a tree is out of the question, play dead. Keep your backpack on and lay face down on the ground, spread-eagled, hands clasped behind your neck for additional protection. Brace your legs to avoid being flipped over but if flipped, roll with the momentum and try to land face down again to protect vulnerable parts such as abdomen and throat. If the bear manages to move you onto your side assume the fetal position, hands still clasped behind the neck with elbows and knees protecting chest and belly. Otherwise do not move until well after the bear has decamped, then clear out in the opposite direction.

Wearing bear bells in the backcountry may be a good idea but in those areas frequented by hikers, bears may come to associate the sound with food. Particularly in areas frequented by those overlooking the commandments of no-trace camping, a standard-issue ding-a-ling may come to be regarded as a dinner bell. Try a bell with a tone different from those purchased from outdoor stores. An increasingly common practice among bearanoid rookies is to squirt a defensive circle of pepper spray around their tent. Field research, however, has shown that far from being deterred, such a practice can actually draw bears to the site. In some cases bears have been seen rolling on the pepper-scented ground. 🐾

Repeat the up-down performance at Cullite Creek, crossing the river via cable car. Even if not camping at Cullite Cove this exquisite site is certainly worth a side trip. From the beach here I have seen a pod of killer whales swim by and on a different occasion, enjoyed watching a family of otters beachcombing in the early morning.

Gaping Grotto
Low tide reveals enormous sea caves near Owen Point. Explore, yes, but tarry not, lest the flood catch you napping.

Nikon F
28 mm Nikkor lens
Ektachrome 100 ISO film

Just ½ km further on you'll encounter the bridge across Sandstone Creek. Descend the ladders to the beach to find another exceedingly attractive campsite complete with tumbling waterfall. Those who have had enough of yo-yo hiking will be pleased to know that the beach now becomes a viable alternative again. The catch is that getting onto the intertidal shelf at Sandstone Creek may require a bit of wading and is not accessible at all when the tide is above 1.2 metres. Having gained the shelf, the beach is passable to Camper Creek when tides are below 1.7 metres. When unsure, err on the side of caution and stay with the boggy forest route. The 3½ km to Camper Creek require no tricky manoeuvring, just steady plodding. As the best, last campsite before the end of the trail, Camper Creek [km 62] can get crowded.

Day Six — Camper Cr to Gordon R 13 km

After crossing the creek on the cable car and climbing out of the ravine, the end of the trail is a steady slog through the forest mud. Alternatives that involve the beach add welcomed variation as well as significant distance to your day. At two and three kilometres from Camper Creek the beach becomes accessible once again. Take the second access route to avoid a difficult surge channel. The rocky shelf here is passable when tides are below 2.4 metres for 1 km. Most hikers then return to the forest for the duration of the trip. The geology along the next two kilometres of shelf to Owen Point, however, should not be missed. Known locally as Moonscape, the sandstone surfaces along the way have been uniquely sculpted by aeons of weather and water.

Owen Point itself is passable when the tide is below 1.8 metres. The beach route beyond that to Thrasher Cove is narrow with many loose rocks and can be clogged with driftwood making this an often demanding route. Cleft Falls and a series of delightful sea caves might just make following this route worthwhile however. As the going will be slow be sure to allow enough time to cover the 2½ km from the point to Thrasher Cove while the tide is out. Thrasher Cove is an attractive place to camp but those determined to reach the end of the trail before nightfall will have to climb 1 km steeply up to the main trail [km 70.] On the final 5 km leg of the journey you'll reach the highest point on the West Coast Trail, a viewpoint overlooking Port San Juan. Shortly thereafter [km 72] you'll encounter another abandoned steam "donkey." This one was used to log the area in days gone by. This is the only section of the West Coast Trail which suffered the bite of the cross cut saw. Compare the thick understory vegetation that has resulted with the relatively open spaces beneath the canopy of virgin forest you passed through the day before. When you finally reach the trailhead at Gordon River [km 75] wait for the herring skiff that will ferry you across to the other side. Like the ferry that took you across Nitinat Narrows, boat transportation here costs $12.50 and should have been paid when you registered. The ferry operates just four times daily at 9:15 and 11:15 every morning and at 3:15 and 6:15 in the afternoon. Your Trail Use Permit is your ticket to ride. Return your permit to the Parks Canada office at the mouth of Gordon River. For those who have to weather one more night in the area while waiting for transportation there is commercial camping nearby at the Pacheenaht Indian reserve for $8 per tent per night.

Canyon Crossing
Stout cables suspend the bridge over Logan Creek. Look down into the ravine if you dare. Pausing for snapshots is mandatory, however.

Nikon F
28 mm Nikkor lens
Ektachrome 100 ISO film

West Coast Trail
Season: May 1 - September 30

Contact	Notes
WCT Reservation Service 663-6000 (Vancouver) 1-800-663-6000 (Canada & USA) (250) 387-1642 (International)	Reservation Fee $25 Reservations may be made seven days a week between 6:00 am and 6:00 PM. Trail opens May - September with reservations available up to 90 days in advance.
Hostelling International Victoria 516 Yates Street, Victoria BC (250) 385-4511; (250) 385-3232 FAX 1-888-883-0099 victoria@hihostels.bc.ca	
Parks Canada Information (250) 647-5434	Registration Centre Trailhead Port Renfrew Trail Use Permit $75; Day Use Permit Free Orientation daily at 9:30 AM, Noon, 1:30 PM & 3:30 PM
Parks Canada Information (250) 728-3234	Registration Centre; Trailhead Bamfield Trail Use Permit $75; Day Use Permit Free Orientation daily at 9:30 AM, Noon, 1:30 PM & 3:30 PM
West Coast Trail Express 1-888-999-2288; (250) 477-8700 bus@trailbus.com; www.trailbus.com	7:00AM Leave Victoria to Pachena Bay $53 8:45AM Leave Nanaimo to Pachena Bay $53 9:30AM Leave Victoria to Gordon River $32 1:00PM Leave Pachena Bay to Nanaimo & Victoria $53 4:15 PM Leave Gordon River to Victoria $32 Nanaimo P/U at Departure Bay Ferry Terminal Victoria P/U in front of Island Coach Lines (700 Douglas St.)
MV Lady Rose Passenger Ferry Alberni Marine Transportation 1-800-663-7192; (250) 723-8313 www.ladyrosemarine.com	One Way Fare: $40 Tu, Th, Sat Year Round; Fri, Sun July & August only 8:00 AM Port Alberni - 12: 30 PM Bamfield 1:30 PM Bamfield - 5:30 Port Alberni (Always Late)
Pacheedaht First Nation Bus (250) 647-5521 or (250) 647-5556	Connects the two trailheads via logging road. $40 one way Port Renfrew 9:00 a.m. to Bamfield 12:30 p.m. Bamfield 1:00 p.m. to Port Renfrew 4:00 p.m.
Juan de Fuca Express Brian Gisborne 1-888-755-6578 1-877-332-5333 radio telephone juanfuca@island.net	Connects the two trailheads via water taxi Port Renfrew to Bamfield 4 hours one way

Vancouver Island Coach Lines (250) 388-5248 1-800-318-0818 (Gray Line) 4541 Margaret Street Port Alberni, BC	Port Alberni to Vancouver 8:15 AM - 12:45 PM 10:15 AM - 2:45 PM 12:45 PM - 5:15 PM 2:45 PM - 7:15 PM 6:50 PM - 11:15 PM	$32.50 one way 10 minute walk from Public Quay Transfer to Maverick Coach Lines in Nanaimo
Maverick Coach Lines Pacific Central Terminal Vancouver, BC (604) 482-8747	Vancouver to Port Alberni 5:45 AM - 10:00 AM 7:30 AM - noon 9:30 AM - 2:00 PM 2:00 PM - 6:30 PM 6:00 PM - 10:45 PM	$32.50 one way P/U at Main Bus Depot or any major stop on the north side of West Georgia St. Transfer to Vancouver Island Coach Lines in Nanaimo

Hanna Air Charters 1-800-665-2359	Air Charter service to Vancouver Island's West Coast
Seabeam Fishing Resort Bamfield BC (250) 728-3288	Independent Hostel
Paralytic Shellfish Poisoning Hotline (604) 666-2828	Recorded red tide information from Fisheries & Oceans Canada Be sure to check the appropriate Fisheries Management Area : Area 123 Bamfield to Pachena Point Area 21 Pachena Point to Bonilla Point Area 20 Bonilla Point to Port Renfrew Area 51 Roswell New Mexico [Alien Harevesting Only]

The Mid-Coast Trail

Level: Challenging **Distance:** 43 km

Time: 5 Days **Map:** 92 E/8 & 92 E/10

Terrain: Undulating **Season:** May - Sept

The Vanishing Wilds
Hiking along the intertidal fringe of the Mid-Coast Trail reveals virgin wilderness like beautiful Barchester Beach. Bears and wolves live here and just a few of that most dangerous game ever passes through. These eco-tourists travelled all the way from the industrial wasteland of Japan just to experience what most local British Columbians take for granted.

Nikon F
135 mm Nikkor lens
Kodachrome 64 ISO film.

Comparisons between the Mid-Coast Trail and the West Coast Trail are inevitable. And while both largely follow the beach along the western fringes of Vancouver Island, the comparison stops there.

The West Coast Trail has earned an international reputation over the years attracting as many as 9,359 hikers in a single season. Environmental degradation was inevitable. Litter and sewage and broad hiking avenues supplanted a once pristine wilderness. Foot traffic comparable to the Stanley Park Seawall forced indigenous wildlife away from the coast, forcing also Parks Canada to impose quotas for the first time in 1992.

The 43 km Mid-Coast Trail, by contrast, is a well-kept secret. Recently protected by the provincial government's Clayoquot Land Use decision, the Mid-Coast Trail remains a true coastal wilderness attracting only a handful of savvy purists every year. For the time being its relative remoteness is its best protection.

Getting There is Half the Fun

Most hikers reach the trailhead from Tofino. A few lo-

Crusty Uplift
Hiking the Mid-Coast Trail is frequently called an uplifting experience: about every 200 million years.

*Nikon F
28 mm Nikkor lens
Kodachrome 64 ISO film.*

cal bush pilots will land on Escalante beach. Though fast, this approach is not recommended for the faint of heart.

Alternately, hikers can contract the services of local guide and entrepreneur Peter Buckland who will arrange air or water transport from Tofino to his property at Boat Basin.

A third, more leisurely, route to the trailhead, relies on the expertise of local guide and fisherman Dave Ignace. The first leg of the adventure takes us over choppy waters to Hesquiat, site of a once thriving aboriginal village and Catholic mission. The name for the community is onomatopoeia, derived from the sound eel grass laden with herring roe makes as it slides through one's teeth. As the name-meister Captain John Walbran put it:

> *"At Hesquiaht village a saltwater grass called 'segmo' drifts on shore in large quantities, especially at the time of the herring spawning, which the Natives are in the habit of tearing asunder with their teeth to disengage from the grass or wee the spawn, which is esteemed by them a great delicacy."*

A tsunami in 1964 and modern maladies like small pox and urbanization have reduced Hesquiat to just the Ignace family. This is the last outpost of hospitality on the central coast. Dave and his wife Diane have established a rustic camping area and, as an added bonus will host a lavish split-salmon and crab barbecue on the beach. Anticipation of the seafood, fresh garden salad, wild blackberry flan and bonfire potatoes will fortify hikers through days of backpackers' rations.

From Hesquiat Dave's boat handling skills will be required to ferry hikers past the breakers of Estavan Point,

Peter Buckland's homey cabin at Homais Cove was originally built to accommodate hikers who passed through his property at Boat Basin following the Escalante River down to the beach. It looks like they had a whale of a rib feast. Bronto burger anyone?

Nikon F
28 mm Nikkor lens
Kodachrome 64 ISO film.

over the rollers of the open Pacific, through myriad kelp beds, reefs and other hidden hazards. At Escalante Point near the mouth of Nootka Sound it's time to bid your worthy seaman farewell, wade ashore and set up a base camp before setting out to explore the beaches to the north.

Nature Mirrors Art

From Escalante set an easy pace following the coastline southwards. Sand soon gives way to a field of gigantic, voluptuous sandstone and conglomerate formations reminiscent of Henry Moore's wildest abstract imaginings. And if Moore sensuality is not your thing you'll find a hint of Salvadore Dali's jagged dreamscapes in the massive tectonic uplifts that follow.

At Split Cape you'll encounter the only real impediment to navigation though the surge channel here is easily overcome with a quick scramble through the bushes at all but the highest of tides.

That Old Sinking Feeling

Barchester Bay affords exquisite beach camping but step quickly when fording the river here as patches of quicksand are sure to surprise. This is not the Tarzan movie variety of quicksand, however, so mucky boots are the worst you'll suffer.

Since the river at Barchester is brackish, wading upstream will be necessary to ensure fresh supplies. In fact, finding fresh water all along the Mid-Coast Trail can be a problem in the summer months with many creeks are either dry or reduced to a trickle. Keep a sharp eye open for any wet spots at the forest edge. Usable sources will often disappear under the sand upon reaching the beach. Remember to top up whenever possible, tasting first for salt contamination.

Expect to encounter black bears scavenging on the beach. On one occasion we were able to watch and photograph, from a safe distance, a sow with two cubs for about ten minutes before being discovered.

Wolves too are in abundance on this part of the coast though spotting these shy animals is no easy task. Imagine though, crawling out of your tent in the morning to discover fresh wolf tracks *on top of your own!*

In 1774 the Spanish made contact with the original inhabitants of Hesquit at Estavan Point. Now you'll find the tallest lighthouse, 39 m, on Vancouver Island. Built in 1907, Estavan Point Light Station is one of the few remaining manned lighthouses on the west coast. This will be your closest link to the outside world. Estavan Point light-

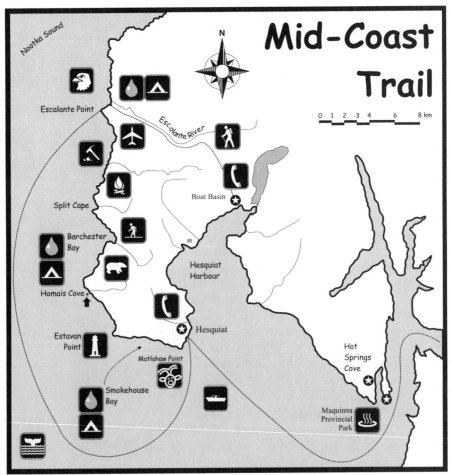

house was the only place in Canada to see action during WW II. A marauding Japanese submarine crew fired more than 25 shells at the beacon but missed every time. Maybe it is true, as the Japanese say *"Tôdai moto kurashi* - It's darkest at the foot of the lighthouse."* Following the assault, lighthouses up and down the coast were very dark indeed: blacked out in fact, until the end of the war. For its part, the submarine was sunk a few months later off the coast of New Zealand.

The beach prior to Estavan Point or the tiny one at Smokehouse Bay are perhaps the best spots for camping on the third night. If actually planning to sleep, the further from the Estavan Point fog horn the better.

A petroglyph can be found on one of the beach boulders just prior to Matlahaw Point. For those who intend to continue past Hesquiat to Boat Basin, you'll find ideal camping in the vicinity of Teahmit Indian Reserve. Perhaps it goes without saying but respect for the land should be paramount at all times. Hikers should be especially observant when crossing native lands.

At Hesquiat you will be greeted by Dave Ignace and family once again. From here he will ferry you on to Hot Springs Cove for a well-earned soak in the finest natural hot spring on the west coast.

Mid-Coast Trail

Location	Details
Dave & Diane Ignace Boat Basin Ignace 980-75 PO Box 418 Tofino, B.C. V0R 2Z0	Tofino - Escalante $500 Hesquiat - Tofino $300 Hesquiat - Hot Springs Cove $100 Hot Springs Cove - Tofino $200 Minimum 3 Maximum 6 Camping at Hesquiat $10 per tent Salmon barbecue at Hesquiat $15 per person For transportation to and from the trailhead contact Dave & Diane Ignace at Hesquiat by marine radio telephone. In British Columbia Dial 0 and ask for Operator 0711 or, if that doesn't work, ask for Campbell River marine radio operator and, when connected, ask for Boat Basin Ignace 980-75.
Tofino Backpackers Hostel, 2431 Campbell Street, Tofino, BC V0R 2Z0 (250) 726-2288	
Hostelling International - Tofino: Whalers on the Point Guesthouse 81 West Street, P.O. Box 296, Tofino, BC V0R 2Z0 (250) 725-3443; (250) 725-3463 FAX info@tofinohostel.com ; www.tofinohostel.com	
North Vancouver Air Vancouver, B.C. 1-800-228-6608 (250) 278-1608	$345 Return $130 Stand-By O/W Daily flight to Tofino/Uclulet
Maverick Coach Lines Vancouver Bus Terminal (604) 662-8051 (604) 255-1171	Leave Vancouver: 8:00 AM Daily Arrive Tofino 3:30 PM Leave Tofino: 10:00 AM Arrive Vancouver 5:20 PM Daily Leave Tofino: 4:00 PM Arrive Vancouver 11:20 PM Daily $88.45 Round Trip

Cycle Touring

Cycle Touring is the one activity that needs little advance preparation or training and can be done just about

Rural Touring
They say we never forget how to ride a bicycle. Exploring the coast by bike is certainly an unforgettable experience. And highly addictive. You'll run out of islands before you run out of steam.

*Nikon F
28 mm Nikkor lens
Plus X Pan 135 ISO film*

anywhere in the province where there are roads. If you can ride a bicycle you can hit the road. And while British Columbia is a mountainous province Vancouver Island and the Gulf Islands all offer excellent touring opportunities that are not too physically challenging.

Equipment

Given the popularity of mountain bikes in BC it's hardly a wonder that most touring is done on these slow but sturdy, low-geared conveyances. The truth of the matter is, however, that the mountain bike is really the wrong equipment for road-based touring. A touring bike will get you farther faster and in more comfort.

If you decide to rent, keep in mind that rental shops almost exclusively stock mountain bikes. There are numerous rental shops on Denman Street between Robson and

Georgia. Consider renting at your destination instead where possible and avoid some of the headaches of transporting the bike past barriers engineered primarily for cars. Rentals, where available, are detailed following the description of each outing.

Because of their tarnished image — once popular but supplanted but the far cooler-looking mountain bike — touring-style bikes can be picked up quite cheaply second hand. If you are planning to buy a used bike be sure to check out the used and consignment racks of many bike shops.

Helmets are mandatory for all cyclists in BC.

A bike rack and a set of good rear panniers is essential. Carrying your belongings in a pack on your back is not an option. Not only will your bike be top heavy and off balance, but back strain and heat exhaustion can result. Cycling, which involves the continuous movement of the body's largest muscle groups, generates a lot of heat. Your exposed back acts like the radiator of a car, channelling heat away from the body. During hot summer weather interfering with this function could have disastrous results. A few shops rent panniers but most do not. Since a good set of panniers can be had for as little as $100 it's best to make the purchase yourself. Check out the **Mountain Equipment Co-op** for the best prices in town.

Don't be beguiled by fat bike seats with lots of cushioning. These will only cause chaffing and a great deal of pain over the long haul. A slimline touring seat with very little padding will cause far fewer problems once your rear end has become acclimatized. Obviously, jumping on a new bike and heading off into the sunset is not a great way to break your butt in. Prior to attempting any multi-day excursions it is wise to spend some time day tripping around Vancouver and beyond to beef up the bottom as well as other muscles that will come in handy when slogging up hills with a fully loaded bike.

Those who plan to camp out will of course need the usual camping equipment: tent, sleeping bag, ensolite pad, cooking utensils. Equipment weight is a much more important consideration with cycling than with backpacking. One way to sidestep this whole issue would be to plan on staying at inexpensive lodges, hostels and bed and breakfasts during your trip. It goes without saying that advance reservations are a must. 🐾

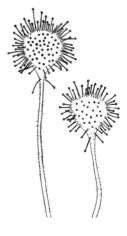

Sundew

Giant man-eating extraterrestrials? No, but you got the carnivorous part right. Tiny, insect chomping Sundew inhabit swamps and bogs, attracting bugs and keeping them interested with sticky secretions.

Not only well-adapted to dissolving gnats, indigenous peoples of the coast put sundew to work dissolving corns and warts much like a product from Dr. Scholls.

While Europeans considered the sundew to be a potent potion when fishing for romance, the Haida summoned its powers to reel in the really, big ones.

Illustration by Manami Kimura

Gabriola Island

With a permanent population of 4000, Gabriola Island is the third most populous island on the coast of British Columbia. And while Gabriola Island has been on the beaten track of intrepid Spanish explorers since the late-18th Century, it does not get as much tourist traffic as many of the other islands in Georgia Strait. Gabriola is no less fascinating and a quick burn around the island by bicycle can even be undertaken as a day trip from Vancouver. While Gabriola Island may be a bit large for some people, at 29 km, a circle tour of the island on foot is not out of the question over a long weekend. The less ambitious can tap into local knowledge through Gabriola Island Tours & Cabs, getting a lift and the lowdown at the same time. This rural island is perfect cycling territory however, and as such, the description below has been optimized for cyclists.

From downtown Vancouver pedal west along Georgia Street, across the treacherous Lion's Gate Bridge and follow the picturesque Lower Levels route along Marine Drive to Horseshoe Bay. [Non-peddlers should refer to Appendix: **Getting to Horseshoe Bay**.] Hop the ferry to Nanaimo and, after disembarking at Departure Bay, follow the noxious fumes out of the ferry terminal to Stewart Avenue. You should notice **Sealand Public Market** immediately on your left. From the foreshore here follow the seawall to the Gabriola Island ferry dock just beyond the Bastion, a historic Hudson's Bay Company fort and prominent landmark in downtown Nanaimo. Foot passengers can follow the same pleasant urban walkway or grab a cab at the ferry terminal and cover the same distance in 10 to 15 minutes for $10 or so. The **Nanaimo Seaporter** is a shuttle service that connects Nanaimo's four ferry terminals: Departure Bay, Newcastle Island, Gabriola Island and Duke Point. Though a good idea deserving our patronage, the service is a bit undependable at present.

The Gabriola Island ferry crossing takes just 20 minutes and runs once every hour from 6 AM to 11 PM. As with many of the smaller ferries on the west coast, the fare you pay includes the return voyage.

Once on *terra firma* again climb the hill, taking the first left you come to. If planning to camp you'll find waterfront tent sites less than a kilometre along Taylor Bay Road. Operated by Nanaimo and District Credit Union, **Gabriola Island Camping** is well-maintained and conveniently-located. The foreshore here alone can provide many hours of explo-

Gabriola Island Ferry Schedule

Leaves Gabriola	Leaves Nanaimo
5:45 AM	6:15 AM [3]
6:45 AM [2][3]	7:15 AM
7:50 AM	8:25 AM
9:00 AM	9:35 AM
10:05 AM	10:40 AM [2]
11:15 AM	11:45 AM
12:25 PM	12:55 PM
1:20 PM	1:50 PM
3:10 PM	3:45 PM
4:15 PM [2]	4:50 PM
5:20 PM	5:55 PM
6:25 PM	6:55 PM
7:25 PM	7:55 PM
8:25 PM	8:55 PM
9:25 PM [1]	9:55 PM
10:25 PM	10:55 PM

[1] Except Wednesdays
[2] Except Saturdays
[3] Except Sundays

ration at low tide. Photo enthusiasts especially will appreciate the endless opportunities provided by Gabriola's unique sandstone formations.

Visitors can also pitch a tent at **Page's Resort Marina** on the opposite end of the island. These latter campsites have been established for the benefit of mariners and are

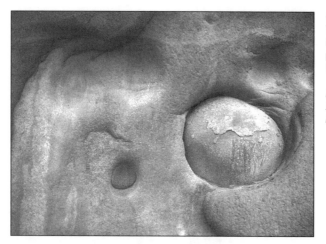

Gabriola Sandstone
Voluptuous sandstone formations of every imaginable abstraction provide tantalizing photo ops all along the shore of Gabriola Island.

Nikon F
28 mm Nikkor lens
Kodachrome 64 ISO film

not so conveniently-situated for landlubbers.

Since you probably arrived at midday or later confine your explorations to the northern tip of the island on the first day. After losing your load at the campsite continue along Taylor Bay Road a further kilometre or so until you come to Malaspina Drive at the foot of which you'll find the renowned Malaspina Galleries. These wind and wave-sculpted sandstone formations even caught the eye of Spanish explorers Galiano and Valdes in 1792. Commander Galiano's sketch of these geological features was found in an old trunk in the Museum of Madrid 100 years after he drew it. No need to decry the latter-day pictographs, graffiti that has been slopped all over these natural wonders. Instead consider it an inadvertent statement: nature's best juxtaposed with humanity's worst: yin & wanker; beauty & the Butthead; Bambi meets Godzilla perhaps. Since erosion is proceeding rapidly by geological standards, most of the paint has been sandblasted away leaving an embossed effect. The Galleries are a favourite hang out of local youths who while away the summer months baking in the reflected sunlight inside the Galleries and diving off the top into the deep waters below. Their carefree lifestyle should be the envy of every city slicker who visits the island.

From Malaspina Galleries the beach will take amblers on to **Gabriola Sands Provincial Park** during all but the highest tides while cyclists should stick with the road. A short distance past Malaspina Drive, Taylor Bay Road ends in a dirt track. The main road abruptly changes name and direction leading another half kilometre to a small shop-

Forever Young
Youth may indeed be wasted on the young but these young Gabriolans wasted no time doing what comes naturally in the spring of life: jumping off the famed Malaspina Galleries without so much as a glance towards the swimmers below.

Nikon F
28 mm Nikkor lens
Kodachrome 64 ISO film

ping mall where the essentials, wine and cheese, can be obtained. In addition to grocery and liquor stores the **Twin Beaches Shopping Centre** is home to a deli, second hand store, hair salon and auto dealership.

Across the road you'll find the entrance to Gabriola Sands Provincial Park. Locally known as Twin Beaches, this popular picnic area occupies a narrow spit with sandy beaches on either side. Leave bikes behind to explore the foreshore beyond the park where more of Gabriola's famous sandstone formations will be found. By road follow DeCourcy Road to Tinson Point and look for dedicated beach access routes between the cottages.

From Twin Beaches Shopping Centre the main drag continues on to Berry Point over a road of the same name. The expansive beach at Orlebar Point, as Berry Point is officially gazetted, is the perfect place for picking, of all things, blackberries. Picnicking and exploring tidal pools are popular pursuits as well. Later in the day snuggle into a sandstone chair to catch the sunset. Wine and cheese, anyone?

On the way back to your campsite you may be tempted to stop in at the nearby **Surf Lodge** pub. Closer to camp,

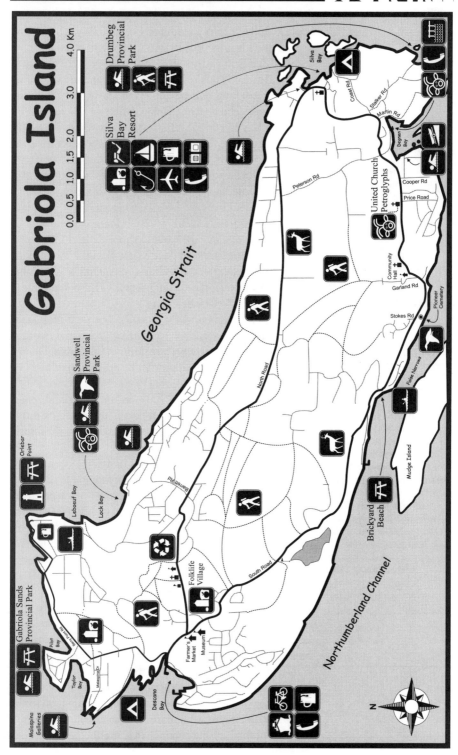

Gabriola Island

Georgia Strait

Northumberland Channel

Sandwell Provincial Park

Gabriola Sands Provincial Park

Malaspina Galleries

Drumbeg Provincial Park

Silva Bay Resort

United Church Petroglyphs

Brickyard Beach

Folklife Village

Farmer's Market

Museum

Mudge Island

Silva Bay

Coast Rd

Stalker Rd

Martin Rd

Degnen Bay

Cooper Rd

Price Road

Peterson Rd

North Road

Gabriola

South Road

Community Hall

Garland Rd

Stokes Rd

Pioneer Cemetery

False Narrows

Orlebar Point

Leboeuf Bay

Lock Bay

Pilot Bay

Taylor Bay

Malaspina Dr

Descanso Bay

Berry Point Road

0.0 0.5 1.0 1.5 2.0 3.0 4.0 Km

N

151

burgers and brew can also be had at the **White Hart Pub** overlooking the ferry landing at Descano Bay. Those staying at Page's Marine Resort will want to quench their thirst at the **Bitter End Pub** at **Silva Bay Resort**. Arrive early to get a patio seat. Those who have been camping on the island a bit too long will be edified to know that Silva Bay Resort has pay showers in addition to fine ale. Though Page's and Silva Bay Resort are adjacent to each other as the crow flies getting there follows quite a roundabout route as the road goes.

Though many have been beguiled by the notion that "Gabriola" is derived from the Spanish *gaviota* for "seagull," the actual etymology may be somewhat less fitting. According to Captain John T. Walbran, BC's foremost authority on coastal place names, Gabriola is simply a corruption of a Spanish surname. In 1791 Jose Maria Narvaez labelled the eastern end of the island *Punta de Gaviola* or Gaviola Point. Through usage over the ensuing centuries the name came to include the whole island.

Gabriola is sometimes also called "Petroglyph Island" for the simple reason that it is one of just four important concentrations of petroglyphs in British Columbia. Quadra Island, Prince Rupert Harbour and a collection of sites on the mid-Fraser River share that distinction. To date nearly 80 petroglyphs have been uncovered on the island, many quite recently. As the island develops the past is steadily being uncovered. No doubt many more of these rock carvings lay hidden under a patina of moss.

While some of the petroglyphs may have been carved during post-European times, others are thought to date back some 2000 years or more. Though petroglyphs tend to depict a pantheon of mythical beings, a cross between the temporal and imaginative realms, little is known of their purpose, use and significance. While some have suggested that they are simply prehistoric graffiti most archeologists agree this ancient art form expresses something far deeper than "Joe loves Sue," or "Grad 99."

To take in Gabriola's petroglyphs stop first at the local museum. While there are no actual petroglyphs here there are plenty of reproductions which, unlike the real thing, can be explored in tactile fashion. To make a quick and easy wall-hanging place a square of artist's canvas over the casting and rub it with conté, graphite or even chalk. When finished spray the rubbing with fixative and mount it on something stiff like plywood or particle-board. Though many of the petroglyphs are quite large some are the perfect size to

The Dancing Man, Gabriola's most famous petroglyph, had become a defacto logo for the island and its Summer Music Festival. The charming figure was a popular motif for jewelry, t-shirts and other island crafts as well. At the turn of the new millenium the savvy Nanaimo Indian Band registered the image, along with the rest of the Gabriola petroglyphs, as a trade mark, restricting use of the symbol to license holders. The band is seeking to eliminate the petroglyph copies on dislay outside the Gabriola Museum as well. Gabriola Islanders are understandably incensed. The issue is less about heritage than about profit. The irony being anyone could have registered the marks but the Nanaimo Indian Band thought of it first.

fit on a T-shirt. Using a product like Pentel's FabricFun™ Pastel Dye Sticks first make a rubbing with the waxy crayons, pressing hard to push the dye deep into the fabric. The dye must be set with a hot iron before washing or wearing your creation.

To get to the museum follow South Road away from the

Sacred Sandstone
The rocks at Gabriola's United Church site come alive in the afternoon sun. Many of the petroglyphs are nearly invisible at other times of day. Step lightly and stay on the grass.

Nikon F
28 mm Nikkor lens
Kodachrome 64 ISO film.

ferry dock past the **Agricultural Hall** where, incidentally, a colourful Farmers' Market is held every Saturday [10 AM to 2 PM] from May through September. The museum will be found just a few pedal pumps further on.

South Road continues eastward through a quiet forest landscape, passing a golf course before it begins descending a steep, 18% grade to sea level once again. Be sure to keep your speed under control on the downhill section as a sharp S-bend at the bottom could spell disaster for a runaway bike. As the road levels out you'll find Brickyard Beach off to the right. Red brick fragments attest to the brick-making operation that thrived here from 1895 until the end of World War II.

The flat lowlands provide access to a number of other beaches as well. At Stokes Road, cut past the Pioneer Cemetery to reach the tidal flats along False Narrows. Each spring seals, sea lions and eagles congregate here in the narrow passage between Gabriola Island and adjacent Mudge Island. A healthy population of resident great blue herons can usually be seen foraging at the waters edge year-round. The Community Hall just beyond Stokes Road is site of the salmon barbecue held every August.

A further 2 km down South Road behind the **United Church** at Price Road you'll find a large collection of petroglyphs. The short trail to the site is well-marked though the ancient rock carvings themselves are not easily discernible. Avoid walking on any of the sandstone outcroppings here as nearly every surface has been incised with shamanistic doodles. Thus far 56 petroglyphs have been identified at the United Church site which was once likely an important religious place for a radically different denomination.

Gossip Corner
Stop to stab some backs, sling some mud and assassinate at least a few characters under the old oak tree at Gossip Corner. In spite of the euphemisms the locals seem friendly enough.

Nikon F
135 mm Nikkor lens
Kodachrome 64 ISO film.

Probably other carvings lurk just below the thin covering of grass and moss but no doubt you will agree that they are best left as they are once you witness the tourists stomping across these sacred images. Or as an archeologist acquaintance once said perhaps they should all be covered with a layer of plastic and several tons of concrete until the human race can grow up enough to fully appreciate their significance. Like many other such sites in British Columbia you'll even find fresh graffiti scratched into the rocks here. Is there a genetic impulse to be a dork? The best time to visit the United Church site is in the early evening when the tourists are busy chomping mushroom burgers and the sun is low. As the shadows lengthen the hitherto invisible carvings spring to life filling the forest with echoes of a distant time.

Price Road itself leads to another secluded beach. From Price turn right onto Island View Drive then take a left on Grilse Road, veering right again when you reach Spring Beach Drive and continuing until you reach the beach parking area.

Yet another beach will be found less than a kilometre beyond the chapel. Turn right at Cooper Road and take an immediate left on Gray Road at the foot of which you'll find a pleasant beach on the shores of Degnen Bay. This is one of the best spots to launch kayaks and small boats.

South Road begins to climb once again but the side excursions have not quite finished. Pause a moment as well to sample the blackberries that grow in abundance along both sides of the road. Look for baby lambs frolicking at Gray's Farm in the spring.

Degnen Bay Road leads to a government wharf and pay phone. The petroglyph of a dolphin-like creature carved into a sandstone shelf at the head of Degnen Bay is a must-see but is best accessed via Martin Road across from Gossip Corner. The skeletal representation encased by the creature's outline is thought by some to signify death or passage beyond this world to another. The solitary image can only be viewed when the tide is very low. One of the early residents of Gabriola Island, Frank Degnen, reportedly deepened the outline in a misguided attempt to enhance the glyph.

Twenty hectare **Drumbeg Provincial Park** is also well worth a visit. Follow Coast Road then Stalker Road for nearly two kilometres before reaching Drumbeg Bay at the southeast corner of the island. The foreshore is comprised of a couple small gravel beaches dominated by low sandstone bluffs topped with garry oak. The park overlooks a sweeping bay studded with low rocks where sea lions sometimes congregate. As the extensive midden here suggests Drumbeg Bay was once an important seasonal encampment of the Coast Salish.

On one occasion here we had the good fortune to witness close at hand a river otter grooming itself by rubbing face and body over a patch of freshly exposed seaweed.

At low tide it is possible to follow the beach as far north as the mouth of Silva Bay though cliffs prevent access to the marinas beyond.

Once back on South Road, continue climbing past a pastoral sheep farm until you reach a quaint log church. Both Catholic and Anglican parishes have sought solace for the soul at the chapel since 1912. Across the road at Silva Bay Marina they are serving up sin in the form of frosty mugs of draft and better than average pub food. The truly devilish may want to bypass the holy Eucharist and head straight for the yam chips.

At Silva Bay the road switches gears with up becoming down. South Road becomes North Road, a generally straight route that leads down through "the tunnel," lengthy sections of forest that arch over the road. Watch for deer along the

Puffballs
Apart from being edible—and delicious at that—dried spores were used as diaper rash "talcum powder" by the First Nations of BC. Spores were also found to staunch bloodflow when placed on a wound.

At one time the brownish spores were used as a photographic flash powder. A large puffball can contain as many as 7500 billion spores. If each of these spores were to grow to maturity the next generation would form a fungus colony some 800 times the size of the earth.
Illustration by Manami Kimura

road, particularly in the early morning or early evening or after a shower. Barrett Road is the turn off to 12 hectare **Sandwell Provincial Park**. The road drops steeply at an 18% grade through many twists and turns. Be prepared to make a left at Bluewater Road then an immediate left onto Bond Street at the bottom of which you'll take another left

Swinging Season
Swing on over to Degnen Bay where the halcyon days of summer may be found lingering along the seaside at any season.

Nikon F
28 mm Nikkor lens
Kodachrome 200 ISO film.

onto The Strand which leads directly to the park itself.

From the parking lot a short, 650 metre forest footpath leads to the beach. Just before reaching the flat shoreline note the giant boulder garden. Evidence of an ancient midden left behind by the island's original inhabitants can also be seen. Facilities are minimal at Sandwell Beach, just outhouses and a couple picnic tables. Birding enthusiasts may spot something of interest in the marsh just behind the beach.

The beach itself is a delightful dark sand arc which is often deserted or nearly so. Sandwell Park, which was created in 1988, looks out across Lock Bay towards the Entrance Island Lighthouse and beyond to the mainland. The beach is home to three more petroglyphs. Two will be found above the high tide mark on a large boulder with a concave top. The carvings of simplistic faces may be obscured by driftwood logs piled up during winter storms. The third petroglyph will be found nearby and may have post-European origins. The excessive depth of the carvings suggests that a metal tool may have been used while the content, a hunter chasing down a deer, is unusual in coastal British Columbia suggesting an era of greater communication or even a European hand at work. 🐾

Gabriola Island

Location	Activity	Notes
Nanaimo Seaporter (250) 753-2118 (250) 753-2324 Fax	Shuttle service that meets most but not all ferries from the mainland. Pick up from the Gabriola Ferry dock should be booked in advance. Same price for 1 or 2 passengers. From/To Departure Bay $7 From/To Duke Point $14	
AC Taxi Nanaimo, BC (250) 753-1231 1-800-753-1231	From/To Departure Bay $9-12	
Gabriola Cabs (250) 247-0049	$20 Ferry - Silva Bay $15 Ferry - Petroglyph Park	Fares negotiable Operates 20 hours/day
Gabriola Campground 595 Taylor Bay Rd (250) 247-2079	$14/night Firewood $4.50/bundle	
Page's Resort & Marina 3350 Coast Rd (250) 247-8931 tpreeve@island.net www.island.net/~tpreeve/	Campground $12/night Cottages $70-80/day Laundry & Showers	
Silva Bay Resort Marina 3383 South Rd. (250) 247-8443	Pub & Store Pay Showers Pay Phone	
Gabriola Cycle and Kayak (250) 247-8277 (250) 247-9788 pmarcus@island.net	Kayak & cycling tours Kayak rentals	Rents kayaks to experienced kayakers only.
Casa Blanca by the Sea 1707 El Verano Drive (250) 247-9824 casablan@island.net www.island.net/~casablan/	Kayak rentals Single Fiberglass $35/day Double Fiberglass $50/day 2 Hour Full Moon Paddle $25	Operates a B & B; Kayak rentals a sideline.
Gabriola Reefs Dive Shop 3383 South Rd. nsmall@mail.island.net	Full service dive shop. Charters, rentals, airfills. Located at Silva Bay Resort Marina.	
High Test Dive Charters 3350 Coast Rd [250] 247-8931	Dive Charters located at Page's Resort & Marina	
Cycle Rentals (250) 247-9114	Located next to the ferry dock.	
Cycle Rentals (250) 247-7848		
Gabriola Tourist Information 575 North Rd (250) 247-9332 info@gabriolaisland.org www.gabriolaisland.org	Located at Folklife Village. Open May through September.	
Silver Blue Fishing Charters 210 Decourcy Rd (250) 247-8807 (250) 247-9700 Fax	22-foot SeaRay	
Pacific Spirit Airlines 3383 South Rd (250) 247-9992 1-800-665-2369	Vancouver Airport to Silva Bay $65 3 scheduled flights daily	

Galiano Island

Terrain: Hilly　　　　**Traffic:** Light　　　　**Season:** Year Round

Distance:　Ferry to Montague Harbour: 10.5 km o/w

　　　　　　　Montague Harbour to northern end: 27 km o/w

Access: See **Getting to The Gulf Islands** on pg 324.

Galiano Island is the first stop on the inter-island ferry from Tsawwassen. There are two campgrounds on Galiano Island but only the one at Montague Harbour is accessible due to a right-of-way dispute. For the foreseeable future badly-needed Dionisio Point Provincial Marine Park will remain off-limits to land-based visitors. Lodges, cabins, B & Bs and resorts abound. Too numerous to include, contact the reservation hotlines listed below to discuss your needs. The route described below assumes you are planning to camp at Montague Harbour Provincial Marine Park. If you made alternative arrangements vary the route according to your needs.

Named for the Spanish ship captain who explored the coast in 1792, Galiano Island is part of a long, undersea ridge comprised of Mayne and Saturna Islands to the south and Valdes, Gabriola, Protection and Newcastle Islands to the north. At 26 km long and just 2 km wide, Galiano is the second largest of the Gulf Islands.

From the dock climb Sturdies Bay Road for 1.9 km to the Hummingbird Pub. Just beyond this favourite watering hole Porlier Pass Road veers off to the right. You want to continue on the left branch, now Georgeson Bay Road, for a couple minutes where you'll find two general stores. The Corner Store, somewhat far from any corners, also serves as a liquor store and has a notice board where local secrets can be uncovered. The Daystar Market opposite specializes in locally grown organic produce. After stocking up on provisions you'll want to continue for 0.7 km along Georgeson Bay Road until the main route winds right onto Montague Road. Immediately the road becomes steep, getting steeper by the second. On the way up just remember what goes up must come down. And indeed you will. The ride down the other side of the hill is a scream. Don't overdo it however as manoeuvring down and around the numerous curves with a fully loaded bike could have dire consequences.

Two kilometres on, near the bottom of the hill, Montague Park Road suddenly veers off to the right. Take it if you want to set up camp right away or go straight to Montague Harbour Marina where you can purchase limited grocery items, order a bite to eat or rent kayaks. Gulf Islands Kayaking was the first and most successful company to set up a paddling business on the island. In addition to their standard offerings, the Full Moon Paddle is a sheer delight.

The very best campsites have been set aside for the campground reservations system. A signboard at the entrance to the park indicates who gets what. Any sites which are not specifically earmarked are up for grabs. If you arrive without reservations make a note of those sites which are not taken so you may make an informed selection. The walk-in sites are far superior than those designed for people with vehicles. Though it is a good idea to make reservations well in advance during the summer there is always room for an extra tent in the group camping area.

Keep a close eye on your food at all times as the racoons and crows in the park have made a profession out of pilfering whatever they can't beg. Their cuteness wears a little

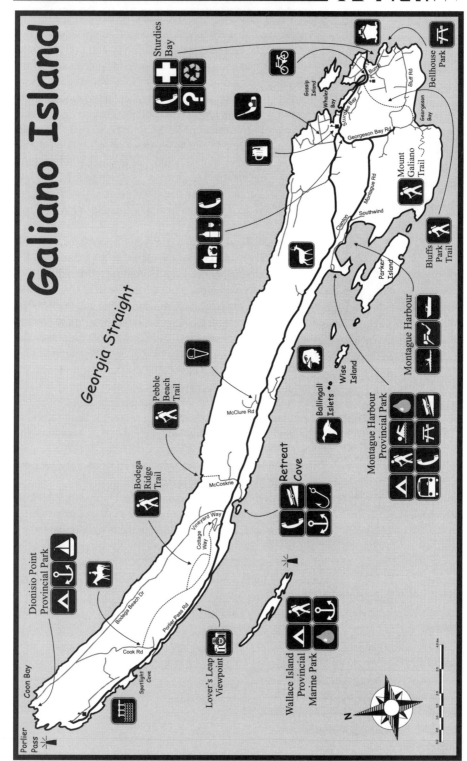

Galiano Island

Georgia Straight

Sturdies Bay

Gossip Island

Whaler Bay

Sturdies Bay

Georgeson Bay Rd

Bluff Rd

Burrill

Bellhouse Park

Montague Rd

Mount Galiano Trail

Southwind

Clanton

Parker Island

Bluffis Park Trail

Montague Harbour

Montague Harbour Provincial Park

Pebble Beach Trail

McClure Rd

Wise Island

Ballingall Islets

Bodega Ridge Trail

McCoskrie

Retreat Cove

Vineyard Way

Cottage Way

Dionisio Point Provincial Park

Bodega Beach Dr

Porlier Pass Rd

Cook Rd

Spotlight Cove

Lover's Leap Viewpoint

Wallace Island Provincial Marine Park

Coon Bay

N

thin when these bandits have gulped down the last of your hot dogs. When that happens you are not completely stranded however. Though most shops close very early on the island a bus will magically appear at the park gate at 6 PM and every hour thereafter until 11 PM. No doubt in cahoots with the racoons, the bus will take you to and return you from the Hummingbird Pub for just two dollars. This service is available nightly from the end of May to the Labour Day long weekend. There are numerous other restaurants on the island but most are in the vicinity of the Sturdies Bay ferry landing. One notable exception is La Berengerie [(250) 539-5392] on Montague Road near Clanton Road. Reservations are required to sample this fusion of French and West Coast cuisine.

Clanton Road will also take you on an exploratory ride up island, rejoining Porlier Pass Road at the top of a 0.7 km grunt. 7.8 km further on, over undulating terrain, there is an ice cream cone with your name on it. The Blue Goose Country Kitchen at the corner of McClure Road and Porlier Pass Road serves designer coffee in addition to its renowned home-made ice cream. You'll easily burn off the extra calories by the time you reach Lovers' Leap Viewpoint 7.3 km later. Jumping off is not recommended for those who are already infatuated with the island. From atop the cliff you'll be rewarded with views of Trincomali Channel, Wallace Island and Saltspring Island in the distance. Exploration of this area by kayak is detailed on page 301. If your butt isn't sore yet horseback riding opportunities exist at the Bodega Resort another 4 km down the road. The end of the road is a final four clicks away at Spanish Hill.

Chartering a boat on Galiano Island is as easy is picking up the phone. Check the list below for contact information. Fishing gear is usually included in the price. Active Pass is always popular though familiarity with currents and traffic patterns in the busy channel are recommended. Your skipper will most certainly have insight into local salmon habits.🐾

Pedal Power

Expect to discover miles of smiles on each and every Gulf Island. Though the pace of life is decidedly slower helmets are required over here too, except when grinning for the camera.

Nikon F
135 mm Nikkor lens
Kodacolor 200 ISO film.

Galiano Island Hiking Trails

Bodega Ridge

Level: Easy   **Distance:** 7 km   **Time:** 1½ h

Elevation Change: 282 m   **Season:** Year Round   **Map:** 92 B/14

Access: Just before the Lovers' Leap Viewpoint turn right on to Cottage Way. The trailhead starts from the end of the road.

The trail along Bodega Ridge is an excellent example of the concept *Think Globally, Act Locally*. When threatened with clearcut logging in 1991 locals became motivated to raise enough funds to purchase the property for posterity. Through their efforts the deal was sealed four years later. The open ridge provides magnificent views of Trincomali Channel and beyond. After feasting your eyes you may wish to turn back or continue on to Cook Road. Turn left and follow Porlier Pass Road to loop back to where you started. 🐾

Bluffs Park

Level: Easy   **Distance:** 8 km   **Time:** 2 h

Elevation Change: 180 m   **Season:** Year Round   **Map:** 92 B/14

Access: At the head of Whaler Bay about one km from the Sturdies Bay ferry terminal you'll find the trailhead on the left side of the road.

An old overgrown logging road leads to 130 hectare Bluffs Park. Follow the forested trail 2 km to reach Bluff Road. A few minutes up the road you'll find the parking area from which a trail leads to the summit. The view overlooks Active Pass and Navy Channel with North Pender Island in the distance on the right. Mayne Island is across the channel on the left. Bluffs Park was created in 1948, made possible by a generous land donation from the Belgian farming family who settled the land. To loop back to the ferry terminal return via Bluff Road to Burrill Road (2 km) then on to Sturdies Bay Road (2 km). The ferry terminal is just a kilometre down the hill. 🐾

Mount Galiano

Level: Moderate   **Distance:** 6 km   **Time:** 2 h

Elevation Change: 311 m   **Season:** Year Round   **Map:** 92 B/14

Access: Mount Galiano may be a bit far to access on foot from the ferry dock. A 4-km bicycle or taxi ride to the trailhead will solve the dilemma however. Follow a route via Sturdies Bay Road, Georgeson Bay Road, Highland Road, and Active Pass Drive to the trailhead at the end of Phillimore Point Road.

Anticipate some steep sections on the trail to the top of Mount Galiano. The last 20 minutes of the climb follows an old logging road. As you might expect the summit provides a panorama extending from Mayne Island across the twin Pender Islands to Saltspring Island on the right. You might be surprised to find a grove of Garry Oak on top, indicating how arid these islands really are. Retracing your steps off Galiano Island's highest point should take but a fraction of the time. 🐾

Galiano Island

Contact	Notes
Discover Camping (604) 689-9025 1-800-689-9025 www.discovercamping.ca	Campground Reservation Service $15 per night at Montague Harbour plus $6.42 per night [to a maximum of $19.26] reservation fee. Changes or cancellations will cost another $6.42. Recommended during high season. Make reservations up to three months in advance. Specify the more scenic walk-in campsites if available.
Go Galiano Island Shuttle (250) 539-0202	Bus/taxi transportation
Gulf Islands Kayaking (250) 539-2442 kayak@gulfislands.com www.islandnet.com/tour/	Kayak rentals , lessons & tours Single Kayak Rentals: $45/$68/$89 for 1/2/3 days Located at the dock in Montague Harbour. In operation since 1985.
Galiano Island Sea Kayaking 1-888-539-2930 (250) 539-2930	Kayak & Canoe rentals; Kayak & Catamaran tours Single Kayak Rentals: $40/$70/$100 for 1/2/3 days B & B; Located at the foot of Southwind Road. Free pickup from the ferry.
Cliffhouse Oceansports (250) 539-5239	Kayak rentals , lessons & tours Sailing charters
Galiano Diving School (250) 539-5186	PADI Certification, Equipment rentals ,Tank refills & Dive charters
Red Tide Hotline (604) 666-2828	Paralytic Shellfish Poisoning Information Information on the Gulf Islands will be found under Red Tide Area 17-2.
Galiano Bicycle 36 Burrill Road (250) 539-9906	Mountain Bike rentals, repairs and retail. Located just up the hill from the ferry.
Bodega Resort (250) 539-2677	Horseback Riding Log cabins
Canadian Gulf Islands Reservations 1-888-539-2930 (250) 539-2930 reservations@gulfislands.com	Free booking service for B&Bs, resorts, lodges, and cabins throughout the Gulf Islands.
Galiano Boat Rentals (250) 539-9828	16 and 17-foot motor boats equipped for fishing.
Retreat Cove Charters (250) 539-9981	Salmon Fishing & Sightseeing Tours
Sea Devil Charters (250) 539-2974 (250) 539-3287	Salmon Fishing & Sightseeing Tours
BC Fisherman's Unique Tours (250) 539-2278 (604) 522-4331 1-800-304-1389 Pager	Salmon Fishing & Sightseeing Tours Service to Ganges on Salt Spring Island for "Market in the Park" every Saturday 11 a.m. to 3 p.m. Reservations required.
Galiano Golf and Country Club 24 St. Andrews Street (250) 539-5533	Par 64 golf course Licensed restaurant

Mayne Island

Terrain: Rolling   **Traffic:** Light

Season: Year Round   **Distance:** 25 km

Access: See **Getting to The Gulf Islands** on pg 324.

The quiet country roads of Mayne Island are ideal for cycling though power walkers could easily tackle the pleasant byways on foot. Pedestrians have the advantage when it comes to exploring the island's hiking trails.

Manami Kimura Photo
Nikon F
135 mm Nikkor lens
Plus X 135 ISO film.

At 21 square kilometres Mayne Island is the smallest of the Gulf Islands. While summer homes abound just 900 people call Mayne Island home. By ferry from Tswwaasen you'll island-hop first to Galiano Island then on to Village Bay at Mayne Island. As the ferry from Galiano Island rounds Helen Point look for bald eagles roosting in trees above both sides of the channel. At times a dozen or more white heads can be picked out against the dark backdrop of forest. The constricted waters of Active Pass concentrate the tidal flows into and out of Georgia Strait, concentrating too the salmon which coastal eagles thrive on.

The first thing to strike one upon arrival at Mayne Island's Village Bay is a sense of desolation. Apart from an old converted bus at the ferry terminal which sometimes dispenses hamburgers there is no commercial activity. Rows of houses ring the bay at a distance and a real estate office just beyond the ferry terminal is boarded up, mission accomplished perhaps. A tourism information display fades in the sun and the ferry traffic hustle and bustle soon fades too leaving visitors wondering. Wonder not! In spite of its small size Mayne Island has all of the charms of its bigger neighbors. Follow Village Bay Road to Miners Bay to find both hurley and burly in equal quantities.

Village Bay has no village, likewise no miners will be found in Miners Bay. The miners passed through long ago. Stricken with gold fever in the 1858 Fraser River gold rush thousands of frantic fortune seekers arrived from California and beyond via Victoria. Being halfway from Vancouver Island to the mouth of the Fraser River, Miners Bay became a marshaling area for the crossing of Georgia Strait.

Unlike the previous island, Mayne is small enough to tackle completely on foot. With two private campgrounds, three grocery stores, two with liquor counters, nearly as many B & B's as there are houses and countless lodges, several pubs and restaurants and a bakery there are plenty of amenities on the island.

Both campgrounds on the Island are some distance from the ferry so, whether on foot or bicycle, it might be prudent to swing by one of the shops in Miners Bay to stock up on provisions before setting up camp. While it may cost a little more it is always a good idea to buy provisions locally thereby giving something back to the economy. Both campgrounds are equidistant from MOM's, the Mayne Open Market, and, once you settle in, it should take a mere 10 minutes by bike, 30 minutes on foot. Miner's Bay is the hub of the community so finding suitable accommodation there is a logical step. The two bedroom cabins operated by the Springwater Lodge have awesome views of Active Pass but are incompetently operated and serviced. You can expect to find broken toilets, broken heaters, broken curtain rods, missing furniture and many other signs of neglect. Nonetheless the location and the view might make these distractions endurable at least to visitors on foot. Those equipped with bicycles will find little inconvenience no matter what corner of the island they choose to snuggle into for the night.

Regardless of where you park your bike the description of Mayne Island begins in Miners Bay. Springwater Lodge is noteworthy if not for the beer and burgers, then because it has been in operation continuously since it was first built in the 1890s. From the dock next door follow Georgina Point Road northwards. Within a kilometre you'll pass quaint St. Mary Magdalene Anglican Church which was constructed

Horsetails

Some would say the first plant: ever! A gigantic earlier relative of the common horsetail thrived in the Carboniferous era and eventually became our present day coal deposits.

Containing silica, horsetails make a natural "sandpaper." On the west coast horsetails and salmon slime were used to polish masks, canoes, bone tools and soapstone pipes.

In spite of the rough texture of the stalk, the young plant heads can be eaten as asparagus.

Illustration by Manami Kimura

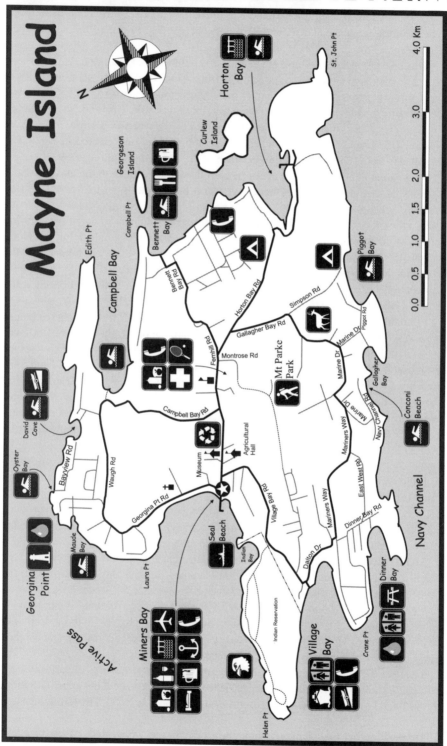

Mayne Island

N

4.0 Km
3.0
2.0
1.5
1.0
0.5
0.0

St. John Pt
Horton Bay
Curlew Island
Georgeson Island
Campbell Pt
Bennett Bay
Edith Pt
Campbell Bay
Bennett Bay Rd
Piggot Bay
Horton Bay Rd
Simpson Rd
Gallagher Bay Rd
Piggot Rd
Montrose Rd
Fernhill Rd
Mt Parke Park
Marine Dr
Gallagher Bay
David Cove
Oyster Bay
Bayview Rd
Campbell Bay Rd
Mariners Way
Marine Dr
Navy Channel Rd
Conconi Beach
Waugh Rd
Museum
Agricultural Hall
East West Rd
Navy Channel
Maude Bay
Georgina Pt Rd
Laura Pt
Seal Beach
Indian Bay
Village Bay Rd
Mariners Way
Dinner Bay Rd
Georgina Point
Active Pass
Miners Bay
Indian Reservation
Dalton Dr
Village Bay
Crane Pt
Dinner Bay
Helen Pt

in 1897 soon after the aforementioned pub opened its doors. Saturday night suds and Sunday morning solace. The churchyard ghosts can boast of one of the island's best views.

Continue along the road for 2 km to reach the lighthouse at Georgina Point Heritage Park. The park keeps odd hours, open daily from 1 to 3 PM, but is a pleasant place to stop for lunch. Capt. George Vancouver must have thought so too as he and his crew, according to local legend, visited the point overlooking Active Pass and Georgia Strait. Some careless crew member left behind a coin dated 1794 and a knife which were excavated nearly a century later when the lighthouse was first erected in 1885. The present-day light station dates from 1940 while the tower was built in 1969.

There are a number of beach access points along the north shore of Mayne Island. Just outside the park gate a tiny beach on Maud Bay at the foot of Cherry Tree Bay Road is a great place to strip and dip on a hot summer day. Similarly, Bayview Drive leads to the rocky foreshore of Oyster Bay where swimming may be out of the question but sandstone formations eroded by wind and wave are sure to tantalize. Further along Waugh Road as the main drag is called, Porter then Petrus Road will take you to the boat launch on David Cove. When Waugh Road turns abruptly south, becoming Campbell Bay Road, look for a trail leading off to the left. A delightful beach at the head of Campbell Bay will be found at the end of this short trail.

From the beach huff and puff your way for 2 km up to Fernhill Road where choices await. A left turn leads to much of the rest of the island while a right along Fernhill will take you past the Plumper Pass Lockup back to Miners Bay. The jail, which now serves as a museum, was built in 1896. The museum is open every Friday, Saturday and Sunday from 11 AM to 3 PM throughout July and August. Call (250) 539-5286 to verify. Those with an interest in gardening may want to drop in to the island's recycling center next door. The facility features a composting demonstration area as well as a deer and drought resistant demo garden. With a large, nearly domesticated deer population and just half the rainfall of Vancouver gardening can be a challenge to local residents. To contact the recycling depot call (250) 539-3380.

Follow Fernhill Road in the opposite direction to reach the island's second central business district. Otherwise known as MOM's, Mayne Open Market is less than a kilometre away from Campbell Bay Road. In addition to a market with fresh island produce and a liquor outlet, MOM's features gourmet cooking and a lineup for ice cream that really is worth lining up for. A health clinic can also be found nearby.

MOM's is at the crossroads of three separate routes. Continue along the left fork which starts out as Fernhill Road but soon becomes Bennett Bay Road to reach the waterfront 2 km away. The expansive, sandy beach at the head of Bennett Bay is popular for swimming and sun tanning while the rocky foreshore flanking it can provide hours of beachcombing at low tide. Before you drop from hunger and thirst drop in to the Mayne Inn overlooking Bennett Bay to quell the hunger pangs and sooth that parched throat. Return to MOM's for another ice cream for dessert.

The road to Horton Bay passes through more than three kilometres of pastoral scenery. Many of the orchards date to the late 19th-century when the King apple was king. Mayne Island's oldest homestead is found along Horton Bay Road. The farmhouse was built in 1871.

Tomatoes rather than apples became the crop of choice between the wars. Japanese

immigrants settled in large numbers, capitalizing on the island's rich soil and balmy climate, to develop a thriving greenhouse industry. With the outbreak of World War II more than 30 percent of Mayne Island's residents were suddenly whisked off to work camps in BC's interior, farms and livelihood confiscated.

Inactive Pass
Even threatening skies are not enough to dissuade determined fishermen from dropping a line in Active Pass. Mayne Island's Helen Point is on the left with Galiano Island on the right.

Nikon F
135 mm Nikkor lens
Kodachrome 64 ISO film.

One of the island's campsites, Fern Hollow Campground, can be found on the left side of the road. Tent sites are rustic and secluded and and cost $12 per night. Amenities are minimal and include showers, pit toilets and a covered, communal cooking area. At the end of Horton Bay Road itself there is a red and black government pier.

Gallagher Bay Road leads to the island's other campground. Calling Journey's End Farm a campground may be stretching the truth somewhat but it is possible to pitch a tent for $12. The facilities include a couple rickety tables, a toilet that is little more than a hole in the ground and a distant water supply that must be shared with the livestock. For that reason, however, you may find the campsite completely deserted. That privacy, coupled with the five star location atop rocky bluffs overlooking Navy Channel may be inducement enough to check it out. Follow Simpson Road to its end to pitch a tent.

Continue along Gallagher Bay Road to explore the southern shore of Mayne Island. The road signage is confusing hereabouts but for the most part the main route is obvious. Abruptly Gallagher Bay Road ends becoming Marine Drive right and left. The right fork is the main road while the left fork leads to Piggot Bay, a pleasant, sandy crescent facing

Saturna Island. Being exposed to driving northwesterlies, expect the beach to be choked with driftwood. Head to Piggot Bay for winter storm watching.

Marine Drive as main drag soon gives way to Mariners Way. Marine Drive as side road however leads to another sandy southside beach, this time at Conconi Reef Park near the eastern end of Navy Channel Road.

To reach Dinner Bay Park take East West Road from Mariners Way. While the beach is small the park includes a boat launch, picnic tables, public washrooms and a playground. Take Dinner Bay Road then Dalton Drive to return to the ferry terminal at Village Bay.

Mayne Island Hiking Trails

Mount Parke Park Hiking Trail

Those on foot can take a longish shortcut, returning to Village Bay from the opposite side of the island over the top of Mount Parke rather than by road around its shoulder. Mountain bikers should respect the landscape and stick to the roads. The trail to Mount Parke Park starts from the end of Montrose Road behind MOM's. Outhouses provided by the regional district are located near the trailhead. The first section is decidedly up, cutting across private property initially then, after numerous switchbacks, reaching the ridgeline 45 minutes later. At the top of the ridge the trail branches both east and west with stunning views from the cliffside to the south overlooking Saturna Island and beyond to the San Juan Islands. Follow the west [right] branch for a further 20 minutes ever upwards towards the 271 m peak which, incidentally is off-limits, being the site of a federal maritime traffic radar installation. From the gate take the service road back downhill to where it continues losing elevation as Wood Dale Drive. Within half an hour you can expect to pass under a giant arch of logs at the intersection of Village Bay Road. Take a left to reach the ferry dock in a matter of minutes or take a right to reach the next trail.

Helen Point Hiking Trail

Nearly a kilometre and a half from the ferry, where power lines cross Village Bay Road, you'll find the start of a nine kilometre hike along the foreshore bluffs of Active Pass. Since the route cuts through native Indian land it is necessary to obtain permission from the Tsartlip Band Office [(250) 652-3988] before setting out. Since access is allowed only through the good graces of the band council the tenants of no-trace hiking should be strictly adhered to. Failure to do so could result in a perpetual loss of access for the public at large.

The trail follows the powerline down towards Indian Bay before turning left to parallel the shoreline all the way to Helen Point. Hikers will pass through mature stands of mixed coniferous forest with arbutus clinging to the rocky shoreline bluffs. En route hikers may notice CMT's, cedar trees which bear the scars of fiber harvesting. These culturally modified trees are of course historic artifacts and must be treated as such. The removal or defacement of any artifact is prohibited by law.

Forest gives way to open bluffs at Helen Point, adjacent to Active Pass's narrowest

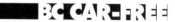
section. Tides propelled by following winds can push currents to in excess of 15 km/h here. 🐾

Mayne Island

Location	Notes
Fern Hollow Campground (250) 539-5253 640 Horton Bay Rd	$12/night; Showers and pit toilets No RV hook-ups
Journey's End Farm (250) 539-2411 Simpson Rd	$12/tent; Very primitive facilities
Canadian Gulf Islands Reservations 1-888-539-2930 (250) 539-2930 reservations@gulfislands.com	Free booking service for B&Bs, resorts, lodges, and cabins throughout the Gulf Islands.
Gulf Islands Water Taxi (250) 537-2510 (250) 537-9202 FAX watertaxi@saltspring.com	See Appendix for full schedule $15 per person, Bikes free, Kayaks $5 extra
Viable Marine Services (250) 539-3200 Tel/FAX	Water taxi, Wildlife tours, Dive charters and instruction
Mayne Island Kayak & Canoe 359 Maple Rd; Mayne Island (250) 539-2667 Tel/FAX Seal Beach, Miners Bay kayak@mayneisle.com www.mayneisle.com/kayak/	Kayak Rentals $42/day; $92/3 days Canoe Rentals $40/day; $75/3 days Complimentary ferry pick up & drop off with rental; Beachfront camping with hot tub & showers at Seal Beach
MV Albatross Scuba Diving C-30 Bayview Drive (250) 539-2437 (250) 539-3438 FAX	Full service dive charters
Harbour Air 1-800-665-0212 1-800-665-4267 (604) 688-1277 Vancouver	Daily scheduled and charter seaplane service to the Gulf Islands from downtown Vancouver $58 per person one way
Seair 1-800-447-3247	Scheduled and charter seaplane service
Cooper Air 1-800-656-0766 (604) 656-3968	Charter seplane service
Mayne Mast Charters (250) 539-3056	Fishing charters for 2-6 people aboard a 42 ft Sport Fisher; Washroom and lounge;
Island Charters (250) 539-5040 Tel/FAX	Sailboat charters aboard a 33 ft sailing yacht $160/day for 2 people; $190/day for 4 people Lunch included
Mayne Island Chamber of Commerce mayne_chamber@gulfislands.com Box 2, Mayne Island, B.C. VON 2J0 CANADA	Tourist Information

Pender Island

Terrain: Moderate - Hilly

Season: Year Round

Traffic: Light

Distance: 43 km

Access: See **Getting to The Gulf Islands** on pg 324.

Two ferries a day service the Pender Islands from Tsawwaasen and while departure times vary day to day there is always a morning sailing and an evening sailing. More importantly, all morning sailings can be reached via bus from downtown Vancouver. For precise details see **Getting to the Gulf Islands** on page 324.

Those not too keen on dragging a bike load of the gear around the island are in for some good news as well. Otter Bay Marina, around the corner from the ferry landing has tent sites, pay showers, coin laundry and groceries. Those arriving without bikes can even be accommodated with a limited number of rentals. While tent sites are far from ideal, they are indeed handy.

The Penders, North and South, were once part of the same wasp-waisted land mass. Rather than row around either end of the island, locals were in the habit of portaging over the narrow isthmus separating Browning and Bedwell Harbours. An accommodating federal government dredged a canal between the waterways in 1903 when traffic out and about the islands was decidedly of the maritime variety. As the local population grew, seeking more reliable land-based modes of transport they demanded a bridge. The provincial government responded, rejoining the islands again in 1955. Now both modes of transportation are accommodated with masted ships as tall as 8.5 m able to scoot under the overpass at high water.

More than 2500 people call the Penders home. The north island is by far the most settled of the two as pioneers began pre-empting land hereabouts in the 1800s, largely ignoring the more rugged southern end. The communities of Port Washington and Hope Bay retain a funked-up 19th-century air that is oddly reminiscent of the nearby American San Juan Islands. Groceries, crafts, fine arts and photo ops galore will present themselves as you explore this historic end of the island.

Huff and puff up the hill from the ferry terminal and turn left at Otter Bay Road to reach Port Washington 2.5 km away. On the way, golfers may be tempted by nine holes on the right side of the road. With extra tee offs for each hole and a clubhouse the truly determined can squeeze in a full 19.

At the outskirts of sleepy Port Washington note Old Orchard Farm, a Victorian homestead named for the historic fruit trees which annually yield more than 50 varieties of pear, apple and plum. Some species, delicious but not transportable, have all but disappeared in the modern world of agribusiness. Down by the government wharf false-fronted Port Washington store looks like a set from a western movie. At the end of the road turn right onto Bridges Road and loop around to a small pocket beach just minutes away. Or skip the loop to climb to the summit of George Hill instead.

To reach Hope Bay, 3 km away, two alternatives exist. The main drag, Port Washington Road, slides past Southridge Farms County Store while Clam Bay Road winds towards the coast through forested back road. The beach at Bricky Bay, where a brick works once stood, can be accessed via Coast Shale Road. Broken bits of red brick still litter the beach.

Farm houses dating from the 1890s and Hope Bay Store built in 1912 dominate the community of Hope Bay. Look for hidden treasures in the motley collection of clapboard shops near the dock. Locally fashioned clothing, jewelry, pottery and glassware are all offered up for discriminating buyers.

From Hope Bay follow Bedwell Harbour Road for 3 km down island past the oldest church on the island, a homestead dating from 1895 and the pioneer cemetary where the makers of early local history pre-empted their last bit of turf.

Just before reaching the local airstip the road drops down through a steep s-turn, ending on a long straightaway. As traffic tends to bottleneck here, slowdown to avoid mishap. Near the end of the straightaway further traffic congestion may be found in the vicinity of Driftwood Centre where residents do much of their shopping. A supermarket, bakery, liquor store and laundromat provide the essentials of island existence. Visitors can browse the gift shops or have their questions answered at the tourist information center. Be sure to check the bulletin board for the lowdown on upcoming shindigs. Homegrown music, theater and dance productions are regularly mounted by the more expressive hereabouts. Everything *but* homegrown will be on sale every Saturday morning when islanders show up to show off their green thumbs and creativity at the Farmers' Market. Seasonal veggies, herbs and fruit fresh from the farm are offered for sale alongside textiles, hand-painted stationery, dried flowers, pottery and much more. The herb superb? Ask around.

Even during the dog days of summer the worst of Pacific Coast weather should be anticipated. Take a cue from the Boy Scouts and *Be Prepared.*

Tom Simons Photo

Just across from Driftwood Centre, Hamilton Road leads down to a beach of the same name and Bedwell Harbour Island Resort next door. All three marinas on the two Penders have facilities directed at the tenting public including tent sites, pay showers and coin laundry machines. The latter may come in handy if exploring several islands over many days. Camping in the open, grassy field edging the beach here can be a noisy affair with more of a carnival, than wilderness air but the sun deck, suds and pub food come highly recommended.

The more solitude-inclined will want to push 2 km further on, climbing the hill beyond Driftwood Centre to Prior Centennial Provincial Park where campers can seek refuge in the cool forest darkness. Unless arriving with reservations you are likely to find the campground full during the height of summer as its popularity far outstrips the meager

17 campsites which are available. Though ideally situated for exploring the island, services are rustic when compared to the marinas. Pit toilets and a hand pump for water are the extent of the plumbing provided here. Please help conserve water whenever visiting the Gulf Islands as the elixir of life can be scarce on these arid rocks.

For a change of pace dismount and follow the Heart Trail from the campsite to a low prominence overlooking Browning Harbour. The trail eventually connects up with a Minotaur's labrynth of roads, crescents and cul-de-sacs known collectively, sometimes derisively, as Magic Lake Estates. The 1960s real estate development sparked a fierce debate that eventually led to the creation of a political body called the Islands Trust in 1974. Much like a mayor and city council, the Trust tempers unbridled development through the creation of zoning bylaws throughout the Gulf Islands.

Though the residential neighborhood could easily be skipped several notable beaches lie beyond. Head to either Thieves Bay or Shingle Bay on Swanson Channel for a dip of the salty variety or detour to the estate's namesake to dunk your toes in freshwater instead. While at Magic Lake be sure to take in the Golf Island Disk Park too. BYOF. There are no green fees at the 18-pole frisbee fairway. A couple of other secluded beaches will be found in the vicinity of Peter Cove 5 km away at the far eastern end of North Pender.

One of the best beaches in the Penders is nearby at the head of Bedwell Harbour. Little-known Medicine Beach was obviously home to a sizable native Indian settlement as evidenced by the millions of broken clam shells strewn along the foreshore. Such "kitchen middens" are commonplace on the coast of British Columbia, mute evidence of the breadth of pre-European civilization. The saltwater marsh behind the midden, habitat for rare plants and a wide variety of waterfowl, is uncommon in the Gulf Islands. To reach Medicine Beach and the neighboring convenience store from Prior Centennial Provincial Park leave Canal Road where it abruptly zigs to the left, continuing straight on Aldridge Rd. for a short distance to the junction of Schooner Way and Wallace Rd. Medicine Beach is on the left while the grocery store is on the right.

Zigging down Canal Road and zagging past the school and health center are necessary to continue exploring southwards. Hosteling *aficionados* should keep an eye out for the turn off to Cooper's Landing which provides budget accommodations under the aegis of Hosteling International. Kay-

Kitchen Midden

A typical west coast kitchen midden, exposed by wave and rain erosion. The seasonal nomads who occupied pre-European British Columbia left behind evidence of their passing: huge mounds of fire ashes, discarded clam shells, fish and other bones. The size and depth of these shell heaps is a good indication of the size and age of the settlement that once flourished here. These historic, cuturally rich garbage dumps are protected by law and cannot be disturbed except by wind and wave.

Nikon F
28 mm Nikkor lens
Kodachrome 64 ISO film.

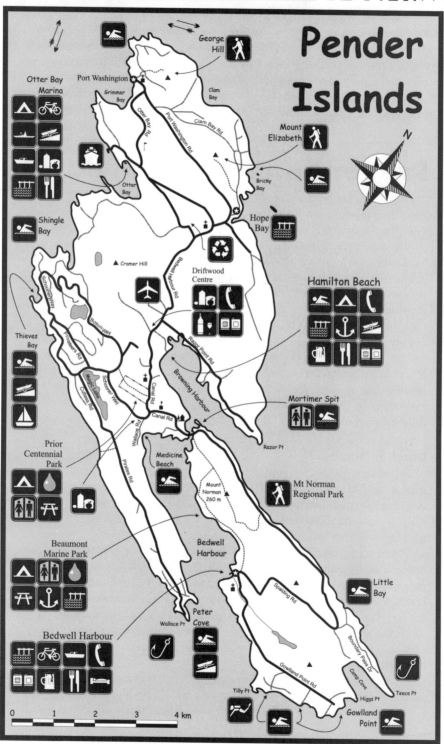

Pender Islands

George Hill

Otter Bay Marina

Port Washington

Grimmer Bay

Clam Bay

Otter Bay Rd

Port Washington Rd

Clam Bay Rd

Mount Elizabeth

Bricky Bay

Shingle Bay

Hope Bay

Cramer Hill

Bedwell Harbour Rd

Driftwood Centre

Hamilton Beach

Thieves Bay

Schooner Way

Privateers Rd

Bosun Way

Magic Lake

Schooner Way

Cutlass Rd

Canal Rd

Browning Harbour

Razor Point Rd

Mortimer Spit

Canal Rd

Wallace Rd

Prior Centennial Park

Pirates Rd

Medicine Beach

Razor Pt

Mount Norman 260 m

Mt Norman Regional Park

Beaumont Marine Park

Bedwell Harbour

Spalding Rd

Little Bay

Bedwell Harbour

Peter Cove

Wallace Pt

Boundary Pass Dr

Camp Cove

Gowlland Point Rd

Tilly Pt

Higgs Pt

Teece Pt

Gowlland Point

0   1   2   3   4 km

aking, canoeing, whale watching and scuba diving can all be undertaken through the facility. The turn off to Cooper's Landing is just before the Canal Bridge on the left.

Prior to becoming a shortcut for early pioneers, for 5000 years in fact before the arrival of a few hearty Spanish and British explorers, the isthmus was a safe haven for an extended family tribe of original inhabitants who flourished on the resource-rich west coast. Though much evidence of their habitation was destroyed when the canal was dredged, the midden, known as the Helisen Archeological Site, was thoroughly

Preventing Hypothermia

If you've ever been so cold that your teeth started chattering and your body began to shiver uncontrollably then you've experienced mild hypothermia. Most of us have been there, particularly when we were kids for indeed children are particularly prone to this potentially deadly condition.

Simply put, hypothermia occurs when heat loss from the body outstrips heat production. Even during mild weather hypothermia can occur for outside temperature is just one of a number of factors which contribute to the onset of the condition. A tired cyclists cruising through the countryside on a fine spring day could be a potential hypothermia victim. If tired, the cyclist's energy reserves are already waning. Being, in all likelihood, sweat-soaked, the cyclist's garments will be sucking heat away from the body at a rate 240 times faster than at the start of the day when presumably the cyclist was dry. Even on a windless day the speed of the cyclist creates its own wind multiplying the rate of heat loss exponentially. Exertion is also contributing to the cyclist's quandary by causing dehydration through sweating and breathing.

Dumb is Dumber

All of these factors working in concert, dehydration and fatigue; outside temperature and dampness could spell disaster. The cyclist's inexperience more than anything else could prove deadly. Ignorance is the number one cause of this number one recreational killer. Armed with knowledge the cyclist can take simple precautions and avoid hypothermia in even its mildest form.

A savvy cyclist will dress in layers, shedding them as body temperature rises, donning them again as it drops. The inside layer will be a thin synthetic such as polypropylene that whisks moisture away from the body. Intermediate, insulative layers will be loose-fitting and made of fleece or wool. A breathable shell made of Gore-Tex will complete the package, acting as a barrier to rain, fog or condensation but at the same time allowing sweat in the form of water vapor to escape. Gloves, possibly in layers, and an insulating helmet liner complete the ensemble of a well-prepared cyclist.

Knowledge will further tell the cyclist that both water and energy will require regular replenishing and by habit the cyclist will frequently consume high-energy foods such as granola bars, trail mix and the like. Such foods contain sugars excavated in the 1980s.

On the opposite side of the bridge an immediate right on Ainslie Point Road provides access to hiking trails to the summit of Mount Norman or along the foreshore to Beaumont Provincial Marine Park. From the 260 metre summit of the former a panorama of the Gulf and San Juan archipelago is revealed. The latter hike leads to a secluded arc of sand and gravel along the shores of Bedwell Harbour. Tenting is possible but access is either on foot or by boat only. As campsites abound on the Penders save

which provide immediate energy, carbohydrates which release their energy over a moderate period of time and oils and proteins which take the longest to be processed into usable energy by the body. That energy propels the bicycle forward, keeping the cyclist warm at the same time.

The informed cyclist will also recognize that chills and shivering are the earliest signs of hypothermia's onset. The cyclist will know that decision-making will soon become confused and coordination impaired if the condition is allowed to progress. Immediately the cyclist will switch from recreational mode to a survival-bent one, seeking ways to stabilize net heat loss from the body core.

Stumbles, Fumbles, Mumbles and Grumbles

If hypothermia progresses our cyclist must rely on companions to correctly assess the situation. The inexperienced may fail to notice the violent shivering, slurred speech, clumsiness, even irrationality that indicate their buddy is already suffering from moderate hypothermia. If they fail to intervene and the body core temperature of the victim continues to drop then unconsciousness, coma and finally death, all consequences of late-stage hypothermia, can be expected.

Treatment protocols of moderate to advanced hypothermia are complex and ever-changing. In the normal course of things, when adequate preparation and prevention measures are strictly adhered to, no one should ever get beyond the initial symptoms. Accidents do happen, however and a kayak spill in the west coast surf or a slip into an icy creek while hiking could be just the kind of event to precipitate the rapid onslaught of life-threatening hypothermia. The Wet Coast of British Columbia is aptly nicknamed because the conditions which prevail on Canada's west coast are ideal for hypothermia. Anyone, even casual recreationalists, who venture into the wilderness should consider taking a wilderness first-aid course which includes training in hypothermia prevention and treatment. Slipstream Wilderness First Aid offers regular, certified training at many levels of proficiency geared specifically for outdoor recreational settings. Contact them as follows:

Slipstream Wilderness First Aid; 50B Cambridge Street, Victoria, BC, Canada V8V 4A8; 1-800-760-3188; (250) 388-0633
www.slipstreamadventures.com; firstaid@slipstreamadventures.com

this delight for some future paddle trip.

Much more accessible, Mortimer Spit will be found to the left of Canal Road just seconds beyond the bridge. The peaceful crescent of gravel and shell has seen tragic times as well. The conquest of native populations throughout the New World was an often bloody affair. And while the taming of coastal British Columbia cannot be compared to the massacres which occured throughout Latin America and the American Southwest it was not without its frictions either. In 1863 two white settlers camping on Mortimer Spit were set upon by three native men and a woman while they slept. In the ensuing fracas one of the settlers was killed while the other was wounded. White justice of course carried the bigger stick and the male natives eventually swung from a rope.

Continuing down island, the next eight kilometres pass through a sparsely populated rural landscape. Just 10 percent of Pender residents live on the south island. A side trip down Boundary Pass Drive leads to Little Bay another pocket beach favored by those seeking seclusion. From here to Bedwell Harbour the main route follows Spalding Road through mature coniferous forest before culminating in a series of steep turns leading down to the five star Bedwell Harbour Island Resort. Tenting is possible here too but is clearly a sideline as the resort complex boasts an onshore hotel, restaurant, pub, grocery store and houses Canada Customs depot for mariners arriving from across the border.

The final 3.5 km dash down island follows Gowlland Point Road through more forest landscape, past a couple of side roads to the beach. Craddock Road too leads to the the foreshore near Tilly Point, a spot popular with scuba divers drawn to a network of underwater caves. A gravel beach at Drummond Bay can be accessed by turning off on Higgs Road.

Gowlland Point is a favorite spot for winter storm watching or at any time when the sun is shining. Poking around tide pools and wave-carved caves, exploring the grassy headland above the beach or simply lazing in the sun are all just rewards for the long, 20 click pedal down island. The U.S. border is just two kilometres offshore. Small wonder that Pender Island was once the staging area for smugglers running whiskey and rum into the parched, prohibition-era San Juan Islands visible in the distance. 🐾

Seasonal Seascapes
A maritime still-life awaits in every quiet cove throughout the Gulf Islands.

Nikon F
300 mm Nikkor lens
Kodachrome 200 ISO film.

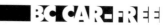

Pender Islands

Location	Notes
Canadian Gulf Islands Reservations 1-888-539-2930; (250) 539-2930 reservations@gulfislands.com	Free booking service for B&Bs, resorts, lodges, and cabins throughout the Gulf Islands.
Otter Bay Marina 2311 McKinnen Road, Pender Island, BC, V0N 2M0 (250) 629-3579; (250) 629-3579	Camping Bike Rentals
Kayak Pender Island (250) 629-6939 kpi@gulfislands.com www.kayakpenderisland.com	Kayak Rentals; Tours & Lessons Located at Otter Bay
Port Browning Marina Resort (250) 629-3493; (250) 629-6585 FAX www.portbrowning.com	Camping $10/night
Bedwell Harbour Island Resort 9801 Spalding Rd South Pender Island, B.C. V0N 2M0 1-800-663-2899 (250) 629-3212 ; (250) 629-6777 FAX	
Hostelling International-Pender Island Cooper's Landing; 5734 Canal Road, Pender Island, B.C. V0N 2M1 1-800-921-3111; (250) 629-6133; (250) 629-3649 FAX info@cooperslanding.com cooperslanding.com	Dorm and Lodge from $20/night Bike Rentals $30/day Kayak Rentals $25/2 hours Dive Charters
Pender Island Taxi (250) 629-9900	
Gulf Islands Water Taxi (250) 537-2510; (250) 537-9202 FAX watertaxi@saltspring.com	See Appendix for full schedule $15 per person, Bikes free, Kayaks $5 extra
Viable Marine Services (250) 539-3200 Tel/FAX	Water taxi, Wildlife tours, Dive charters and instruction
Harbour Air 1-800-665-0212; 1-800-665-4267 (604) 688-1277; (604) 278-3478	Daily scheduled and charter seaplane service to the Gulf Islands from downtown Vancouver $58 per person one way
Seair 1-800-447-3247; (604) 273-8900	Scheduled and charter seaplane service
PenderIsland Visitor Info Centre (250) 629-6541; (250) 629-6541	Tourist Information

Saltspring Island

Terrain: Very Hilly   **Traffic:** Heavy

Season: Year Round   **Distance:** 73 km

Access: See **Getting to The Gulf Islands** on pg 324.

Beaver Point

The grassy headlands along the south-western corner of Saltspring Island make Ruckle Provincial Park an ideal spot to sit and watch the world go by. Geologically it's a topsy-turvy world, however. While much of the Gulf Island chain is comprised of rather youngish sandstone, conglomerate and shale, the lower third of Saltspring is made up of far more ancient igneous rocks, primarily granite, pushed up through the sedimentary layers by a volcano wannabe. Generally the dividing line between the two land masses runs down the Fulford Valley from Beaver Point to Mount Maxwell Park. At either location it is possible to straddle 400 million year old Devonian period stone and Cretaceous layers just an eighth as ancient. Volcanic action pushed the elder stone upwards some 180million years ago, and while it was eventually covered with the same silt as the rest of the island, Pleistocene glaciation scoured it clean. Adjacent sedimentary layers are typically 4 km thick.

Nikon F
28 mm Nikkor lens
Kodachrome 64 ISO film

With more than 10,000 permanent residents spread over 180 square kilometres, Saltspring Island is the largest, most-populated of the Gulf Islands. As a consequence the island is well-serviced by BC Ferries. Direct service from the lower mainland is still abominable though, with only two sailings a day connecting Tsawwassen with Long Harbour on Salt-spring. Both disembark late enough to reach by Translink, too late in fact for the early birds among us to catch any worms. The first sailing of the day usually leaves during late morning, sometimes even in the early afternoon. This would be a travesty if a workaround didn't exist. Fortunately sailings bound for Swartz Bay near Victoria depart much more frequently: hourly during summer high season and every odd hour before June or after September.

Upon arrival in Swartz Bay turn around and immediately board another ferry, this time headed for Fulford Harbour on the southern end of Saltspring Island. These ferries operate at approximately 90 minute intervals taking just 35 minutes to shuttle across Satellite Channel. When purchasing your ticket in Tsawwassen ask for a "Throughfare Ticket" which gives you both ferries for the price of the ill-conceived direct route. Arriving in Fulford Harbour has the additional advantage of being handy to Ruckle Park, without

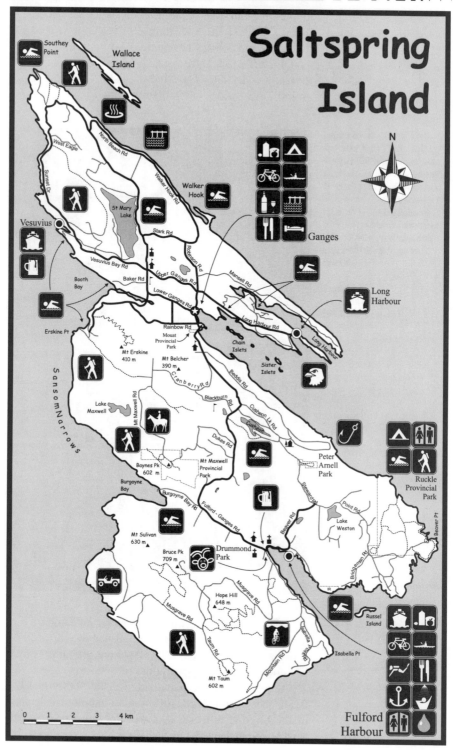

Saltspring Island

Southey Point

Wallace Island

West Eagle

North Beach Rd

Walter Hook Rd

St Mary Lake

Walker Hook

Stark Rd

Vesuvius

Vesuvius Bay Rd

Robinson Rd

Ganges

Baker Rd

Booth Bay

Upper Ganges Rd

Lower Ganges Rd

Mansell Rd

Long Harbour

Erskine Pt

Rainbow Rd

Mouat Provincial Park

Long Harbour Rd

Long Harbour

Sansom Narrows

Mt Erskine 410 m

Mt Belcher 390 m

Cranberry Rd

Chain Islets

Sister Islets

Lake Maxwell

Mt Maxwell Rd

Blackburn Rd

Beddis Rd

Cusheon Lk Rd

Cusheon

Peter Arnell Park

Baynes Pk 602 m

Mt Maxwell Provincial Park

Dukes Rd

Ruckle Provincial Park

Burgoyne Bay

Burgoyne Bay Rd

Fulford - Ganges Rd

Stewart Rd

Point Rd

Lake Weston

Beaver Rd

Bridgeman Rd

Beaver Pt

Mt Sulivan 630 m

Bruce Pk 709 m

Drummond Park

Russel Island

Musgrave Rd

Hope Hill 648 m

Isabella Pt

Musgrave Rd

Taum Rd

Mountain Rd

Isabella Point Rd

Mt Taum 602 m

Fulford Harbour

0 1 2 3 4 km

N

a doubt the finest campsite in all of the Gulf Islands. For that reason the route as described in this book will start at the southernmost ferry terminal and work northwards.

One further advantage of arriving in Fulford Harbour is the ready availability of both bicycle and kayak rentals. Upon arrival most traffic will follow the main road to the left

Stone Chapel

Picturesque St Paul's chapel, Saltspring's oldest, was erected in 1880. Originally constructed out of wood, the stone facing seen here was added during the 1950s. A number of itinerant Kanaka's, native Hawaiians and some of the earliest homesteaders, found their final resting place in the cemetary out back after carving a home out of the island wilderness.

Nikon F
28 mm Nikkor lens
Kodachrome 64 ISO film

around the head of the inlet. If planning on camping then head right on Beaver Point Road instead to reach Ruckle Provincial Park 10 clicks away. Peddling, paddling or even just hoofing it are all possibilities.

Acquired from the pioneering Ruckle family in 1974, the 480 hectare provincial park features interpretive displays of the original homestead, a working farm operated by Ruckle descendants, 7 km of shoreline to explore and more than 70 walk-in campsites situated on grassy bluffs with stunning views overlooking Swanson Channel. As a bonus not a single site is available for the gas-guzzling RV set. On the downside, popularity means people and the campground can be packed on a summer long weekend; a good time to stay away. Consider visiting on the shoulder season or better yet in the dead of winter to experience the site in all its desolation. Ruckle Park is an ideal spot for storm watching if properly equipped. Reservations are not possible or necessary.

To begin exploring the island in earnest backtrack to Fulford Harbour or consider taking a shortcut along Steward Road. The latter leads through Peter Arnell Park to the Saltspring Island Hostel. Hosteling is a great alternative to camping especially for those traveling solo, enabling cyclists to lighten their load considerably while having the opportunity to meet other like-minded people. Cusheon Lake Road reconnects with the main thoroughfare, Fulford-Ganges Road, just beyond the lake for which it was named. A short, 1.8 km section of Steward Road is unpaved.

The long cut has its appeal too so back-peddle to Fulford Harbour. Just a kilometre from the ferry terminal charming Saint Paul's Church, built in 1880, sits on a rise overlooking the harbour. Pause for pictures, picnic, or petinence but not for long. Why is it whenever we find a charming church in the Gulf Islands there is usually a pub lurking nearby? Contemplate that question over a frosty, frothy mug or two at Fulford Inn just down the road. The south island watering hole is actually equidistance from St. Paul's and another church, Saint Mary's, that was erected 6 years later. If planning to peddle in from Ruckle Park for a pint o' bitter in the evening keep in mind that the park gate closes at sunset. Slamming into it in a suds-induced fog is no way to leave your mark on the island.

Just across the street from the pub, Isabella Point Road leads to a number of secluded beaches and a little-used hiking route to the top of Mount Taum. Closer at hand take Musgrave Road to Drummond Park for a look at Saltspring's most famous petroglyph. Thought by many to be the image of a seal, the rock carving was moved to its present location from the foreshore of Fulford Harbour.

Musgrave Road, an unsurfaced service road, provides mountain-bike equipped riders with bone-crunching access to a number of hiking trails including Mount Taum, Hope Hill, and Bruce Peak. All boast panoramas overlooking the Gulf and San Juan Islands while only Hope Hill is without a collection of transmission towers on top. Hiking stats for each destination are listed below. Cars and trucks also ply the dusty access roads.

Destination	Trailhead via	Hiking Distance	Elevation	Ability
Hope Hill	Musgrave 3.5 km	5 km r/t	648 m	Moderate
Bruce Peak	Musgrave 10 km	6 km	709 m	Challenging
Mount Taum	Taum Rd 13 km	Negligible	602 m	Easy

From Isabella Point Road Fulford-Ganges Road cuts 3 km across island, marching through open pasture land, verdant in spring, turning golden later on. Burgoyne Bay Road continues straight connecting up with the opposite shore 1.5 km away while the main drag climbs northwards up a long hill. On the straightaway up top look for Dukes Road to begin scrambling to the top of Baynes Peak. The other, more popular route to

Mount Maxwell Provincial Park can be found a further click and a half towards Ganges. Turn left on Blackburn Road which leads past Blackburn Meadows, one of the island's two 9-hole golf courses. Upon reaching Cranberry Road turn left and follow the signs ever upwards. All too soon pavement gives way to rough, secondary road. Since the route to the top is well-marked it is well-traveled as well. A handkerchief over the mouth may help ameliorate dust kicked up by approaching vehicles. Rather than biting dust, park your bikes at Saltspring Guided Rides instead and hoof it uphill on the back of beast. The riding stable will accommodate groups as small as two people.

Baynes Peak is only a short distance from the end of the access road. Steep cliffs along the southern edges of the park present considerable danger while affording magnificent views of Fulford Valley, Burgoyne Bay and Vancouver Island beyond it. Step gingerly if fog grips the summit.

What goes up must come down but by all means maintain a controlled descent to avoid becoming a hood ornament. Stay with Cranberry Road to coast most of the way into Ganges. On the outskirts of town note Mouat Provincial Park on the left. Other than being central to all parts of the island and convenient to all manner of services, the campground has little to recommend itself. But then again, what was that they said about location, location, location?

Ganges is indeed the commercial heart of, not only Saltspring but, the whole chain of southern Gulf Islands. Visitors with the urge to consume will find more than enough quaint little gift shops and galleries and funky fashion boutiques to satiate even the most jaded consumer appetites. Cap off that buying spree by taking in the Saturday morning market at the oceanfront on Ganges Harbour. Candles, raku pottery, stained-glass, hand-woven goods, health and beauty concoctions and a cornucopia of organic produce from the island larder will be on display throughout the summer. During fall, in the run-up to xmas, a series of craft shows are mounted at different community halls around the island. Many of the goods are sold nowhere else in the world at no other time ensuring that your purchases are indeed unique. Visiting the island at that time of year is a great way to escape the city and wrap up that xmas shopping in one fell swoop. Many artists and artisans open their studios to the public every autumn as well. A complete listing of participating studios is published each year. Contact tourist information for details of both venues.

A quick walk-through Ganges village will encourage other appetites is well. Choosing from the breadth of cuisine offered by island eateries can be difficult. Notably, Moby's Pub showcases island musical talent every weekend.

From Ruckle Park, Ganges is 23.5 km. From Fulford Harbour it is 14.5 km. Ganges and Long Harbour are six clicks apart while the loop around the north end of the island is 29.5 km. To embark on this latter circle tour leave the urban center behind via Lower Ganges Road. En route up island you'll pass by the second golf course before reaching an intersection with Upper Ganges Road. Turn left here to reach Vesuvius Bay where Saltspring's third ferry terminal will be found. The frequent shuttle scoots across Stuart Channel to Crofton on Vancouver Island. Those with time on their hands may want to consider looping back to Vancouver via Crofton, Chemainus and Ladysmith to Nanaimo where the ferries to Tsawwassen, Gabriola Island [p 148,] Newcastle Island [p 209] and Horseshoe Bay will be found.

The Vesuvius Inn, famed for its sunsets, serves up drinks, dinner and darts daily. As the name suggests Sunset Drive reveals the orange orb as well while passing through a sparsely populated rural landscape. Just before reaching West Eagle Road you'll pass the trailhead in to Channel Ridge, an easy 9 km return toddle into the local watershed.

Outdoor Market
The reknowned Ganges Market in the Park gets underway at 8 AM every Saturday from April to October in Centennial Park. Cottage industry treasures beckon from tables, blankets, even in the backs of pick-ups. More than 100 vendors in all offering their wares until 4 PM. Cyclists travelling light can still stop by to sample the output of magical island kitchens.

Nikon F
28 mm Nikkor lens
Kodachrome 64 ISO film

The foreshore at northern Southey Point is minuscule but Jack Foster Trail leads 2 km in to a secluded beach opposite Wallace Island. Look for the trailhead on the right after turning onto Southey Point Road. Loop around to North End Road to avoid retracing your steps.

North End Road offers two possible routes for returning back down the island. The most direct route cuts down the middle of the island passing close to St. Mary Lake. Access to the lakefront is extremely limited however belonging to private residences or countless lodges and B & Bs. Turn off onto North Beach Road instead for an oceanfront route that provides plenty of beach access.

Salty Springs Resort, at the roadside here, is the only place on the island where the public has access to the artesian wells for which the island was named. Guests at the resort can enjoy a mineral bath supplied by one of the springs. Altogether 14 minerals springs have been identified at the northern end of the island, all on private land. The largest feeds a 25 m pond ringed with salt crystals. Incidentally, though the earliest settlers soon dubbed the island "Salt Spring," it was officially known as Chuan Island in 1854, being renamed Admiral Island after Admiral Baynes in 1859. The name meisters in Ottawa finally got with the program in 1905, creating the compound "Saltspring" out of the original. Baynes may have lost his title but was able to retain the mid-island peak as his own.

The lagoon created by a protruberance called Walker Hook can be accessed at the bottom of Fort Street. A good spot for launching kayaks, Walker Hook is the last point of access before the road veers inland again, making a beeline back to Ganges. Those planning to take the direct ferry back to Tsawwassen should turn off at Long Harbour Road. 🐾

Saltspring Island

Location	Notes
Salt Spring Island Hostel 640 Cusheon Lake Rd (250) 537-4149	Three dormitories with shared kitchens Teepee camping
Canadian Gulf Islands Reservations 1-888-539-2930; (250) 539-2930 reservations@gulfislands.com	Free booking service for B&Bs, resorts, lodges, and cabins throughout the Gulf Islands.
Gulf Islands Water Taxi (250) 537-2510; (250) 537-9202 FAX watertaxi@saltspring.com	See Appendix for full schedule Interisland: $15 per person, Bikes free, Kayaks $5 extra
Viable Marine Services (250) 539-3200 Tel/FAX	Water taxi Wildlife tours, Dive charters and instruction
Prince of Whales Ocean Tours (250) 656-8788	Whalewatching and wildlife tours Water Taxi
Salt Spring Taxi (250) 537-9712	Taxi and guided tours
Saltspring Kayaking & Cycle 2923 Fulford-Ganges Road (250) 653-4222; sskayak@saltspring.com www.saltspring.com/sskayak	Bike rentals & repairs; Rent: $25/day $10 delivery of bike to any corner of the island Kayak rentals & tours; Rent: $45/day Kayak renters must have wet exit proficiency. Two locations in Fulford Harbour and Ganges
Sea Otter Kayaking 149 Lower Ganges Road 1-877-537-5678; (250) 653-4875 FAX kayaking@saltspring.com	Kayak rentals & tours
Salt Spring Marina 1-800-334-6629; (250) 537-9100 jsmall@saltspring.com www.saltspring.com/rentals	Kayak, Boat Rentals & Fishing Charters
Island Escapades 118 Natalie Lane 1-888 529-2567; (250) 537-2537 escapades@saltspring.com	Kayak Tours
Harbour Air 1-800-665-0212; 1-800-665-4267 (604) 688-1277; (604) 278-3478 (250) 537-5525	Daily scheduled and charter seaplane service to the Gulf Islands from downtown Vancouver
Salt Spring Island Tourist Information 121 Lower Ganges Road; Saltspring Island (250) 537-5252; (250) 537-4223; (250) 537-4276 FAX chamber@saltspring.com	Tourist Information

Saturna Island

Terrain: Fairly Flat

Season: Year Round

Traffic: Light

Distance: 34 km

Access: See **Getting to The Gulf Islands** on pg 324.

Saturna Island is hard to get to and the locals are usually content to keep it that way. With just 350 permanent residents to service, ferry sailings to the island are extremely limited. From Vancouver it is impossible to reach the morning sailing out of Tswwaasen by bus on any day except Saturday. Typically the second and last sailing occurs in the early evening which means visitors will arrive on Saturna at dusk or after dark with just enough time check-in. Since the ordeal is further complicated by stops at other islands and usually one transfer along the way, a trip to Saturna Island usually takes about three hours.

On a Friday for instance visitors could board the 6:30 PM ferry, arriving at around nine o'clock. They could then spend a full two days cycling and hiking then leave on the four o'clock boat on Sunday, arriving back in Tswwaasen by 7 PM. Due to the oddball schedule a simple day trip is out of the question.

The best way to reach Saturna Island is from one of the other Gulf Islands in the context of a longer, multi-day exploration of the archipelago. Visit Saturna last, then, after a day or two of exploration, return to the city on an early-morning run midweek or the late-afternoon one on the weekend. At times it may be practical to hop from one of the other Gulf Islands to Swartz Bay near Victoria then scoot over to Saturna.

Finding a place to put up for the night is likewise complicated by Saturna Island's overprotective populace. In spite of the fact that the provincial government ministry responsible for parks has long sought to open up its holdings at Winter Cove to camping, fierce local opposition has thus far prevented any such action. And while residents have valid concerns regarding forest fires or way-of-life the less patient among the recreating public sometimes chalk their motives up to mere selfishness. Certainly the self-interest of lodge and B & B owners is well-served by disallowing camping island-wide. A smaller, monied class of tourist is attracted while the budget traveler is discouraged from visiting Saturna by a lack of services. Parks, ferry deficits and infrastructure are all covered by general revenue however, so the island does not belong just to the Islanders. Currently there is no camping whatsoever on the island.

In spite of these controversies and hardships Saturna Island is well worth a visit, not least because the seasonal invasion of visitors that plagues other islands is noticeably absent in this out-of-the-way corner of the gulf.

The price of solitude may come higher but includes a shower. Reservations are a must as Saturna Island boasts just two lodges and a handful of B & Bs and becoming stranded during high season is a real possibility. Most of the B & Bs are located near the ferry terminal in the vicinity of Lyall Harbor, an obvious choice if arriving in the evening.

Progress, in the form of Saturna Lodge, blasted its way onto the accommodation scene late last century. Not only does the luxury resort offer all of the usual facilities, it includes development of strata title condominiums and comes attached to coastal British Columbia's first vineyard and winery. 1999 saw production of the first local vintage. Needless to say local wine figures prominently in the lounge and dining room.

The lodge, with just seven rooms, overlooks Boot Cove off Payne Road.

At the very opposite end of both the island and the political spectrum, East Point Resort features six rustic housekeeping cottages and could not be more in keeping with the island ethos. Located on secluded beachfront with views

Canadian Gothic

Like a scene in some windswept gothic novel, East Point bears the brunt of foul weather arriving from the south and east. The exposed headland is ideal for winter storm watching, summer whale watching, anytime bird watching but never clock watching. Like the birds, time flies by down here.

Nikon F
28 mm Nikkor lens
Ektachrome 200 ISO film

overlooking Tumbo Island, East Point Resort also offers boat rentals for those interested in exploring the offshore islands. Fishing and crabbing off East Point is reportedly the best in the Gulf Islands.

All politics aside, to begin exploring Saturna Island follow East Point Road from the ferry landing at Saturna Point past the government wharf and community hall. The latter structure, built in 1933, serves as locus of a farmers market every Saturday all summer long. The commercial heart of the island lies three kilometres from the ferry at the crossroads of East Point Road, Narvaez Bay Road and Harris Road. Funky Saturna General Store is the place to stock up on groceries, wine and other necessities before proceeding into the hinterland.

From the crossroads here East Point Road drops down to Sunset Boulevard which in turn leads a short distance to a small gravel beach at the head of Lyall Harbour. Not ready for a dip? Proceed uphill again for another four clicks to where East Point road suddenly veers right. Veer left instead to reach the waterfront at Winter Cove Provincial Marine Park just a kilometre away.

Top up with water here and set aside at least an hour to loop past marshes and shoreline north to the open waters of

Pastoral Scenery
Feral goats and tame island deer have all but vanished but the neighbour's sheep move wraith-like in and out of the early morning mist atop Mt Warburton Pike. The reknowned view will have to wait for the fog to burn off.

Nikon F
135 mm Nikkor lens
Ektachrome 200 ISO film

Georgia Strait. Tidal currents through Boat Passage, as the narrow gap between Saturna and Samuel Island is called, can reach in excess of 7 knots or 13 k/mh. From shore the turgid waters of Boat Passage are a sight to behold. From the cockpit of a kayak they are best avoided altogether though experienced paddlers may enjoy the thrill of shooting the chute. In a pinch the rocky point overlooking the passage can be portaged over.

As mentioned, 91 hectare Winter Cove Provincial Marine Park was at one time destined to be the site of a wilderness walk-in campground though local opposition put that idea on hold. Now it is the site of the annual Canada Day Lamb Barbecue. Imagine the carcasses of freshly slaughtered baby lambs roasting on giant skewers around a huge bonfire and perhaps you can picture this traditional event. Some may question why such a hedonistic bacchanal can occur on public lands while something as innocuous camping cannot. Direct your questions to BC Parks.

Back on the saddle, East Point Road will now take you for a 10.5 kilometre sprint along the northern coast of Saturna Island. You can expect to pass numerous points of beach access. The waters adjacent to Russell Reef in particular are ideal for swimming. At times the forest canopy arches over the road while at others tremendous vistas of Georgia Strait and beyond are revealed.

While there may be little or no traffic always pedal in

single file as you never know what may come barrelling around the next corner. Six clicks into this coastal byway the road passes through native reserve lands. Shortly thereafter the final four kilometres of road becomes Tumbo Channel Road.

A federal light station dominates East Point. The beacon was established in 1888 following a shipwreck two years previously on Boiling Reef. Surrounded by a Regional Park since 1996, the grounds are now open to the public though the lighthouse remains off-limits.

The bluffs hereabouts offer unobstructed views of the American San Juan Islands and beyond to distant Mt. Baker. Closer to shore the reefs and kelp beds just off East Point are a pelagic bird watchers' paradise. Tidal currents which rip eastward through Tumbo Channel on both the ebb and the flood churn up feed for a myriad of species.

East Point is also considered the Gulf Islands' best site for land-based orca watching. The whales, usually members of the K pod, are said to pass by nearly every day from May through November in their never-ending quest for salmon.

At the foreshore expect to find pebble and shell beaches edged by wind and wave-whipped formations of sandstone and conglomerate. Photo opportunites abound of course as do chances to explore the watery microcosms left behind as the tide recedes. Sun supplicants no doubt can find a secluded pocket beach on which to worship.

Cliffside Road offers an alternative route for the return journey. As the 2.5 km road begins looping back to re-join the main road look for a trailhead on the left side of the road. Just three kilometres round-trip, this amble follows the rocky bluffs above Fiddlers Cove. The arid heights are typical Gulf Islands: sun-burnt meadows dotted with gnarled arbutus. As the trail passes through Indian reserve lands contact the joint owners for permission to enter prior to visiting. The Tsawout band office can be reached at (250) 652-9101 while the Tseycum Indian Band phone number is (250) 656-0858. Please respect the land and the spirit of any posted signs.

To explore other corners of the island return to Saturna General Store. Narvaez Bay Road leads 8 km through the heart of Saturna Island to the waterway named for Captain Jose Maria Narvaez of the Spanish schooner *Saturnina* in 1791. The island of course took its name from the sailing vessel which Narvaez commanded. The foreshore is inaccessible though the 16 click ride passes through pastoral scenery bereft of vehicle traffic. Look for deer grazing at the side of the road particularly at dawn and dusk.

Harris Road follows the valley bottom between Mt. Fighter and Mt. Warburton Pike. Those in the mood for a thigh burner should ascend Saturna's highest mountain (490 m) via Staples Road. Be prepared to dodge both deer and feral goats while navigating the narrow dirt track. The latter are descendants of livestock brought to the island by the earliest homesteaders. To reach the summit of Mt. Warburton Pike on foot, park bikes at the end of Harris Road. A couple of trails emanate from here.

The course to the left leads to the aforementioned peak with its crown of TV towers and beyond to Brown Ridge Nature Trail. Eight kilometres round-trip, the cliffside route reveals a panorama extending from the nearby Pender Islands and southward to include the San Juan Islands and distant peaks in Washington's Olympic National Park. As this hike passes over private property respect the privilege or lose it.

Three-kilometre Quarry Trail also begins at the end of Harris Road. Setting out on a powerline right-of-way the route soon veers off to the right, dropping down to an unsurfaced road. Follow the road right to reach pretty Saturna Beach at Thompson

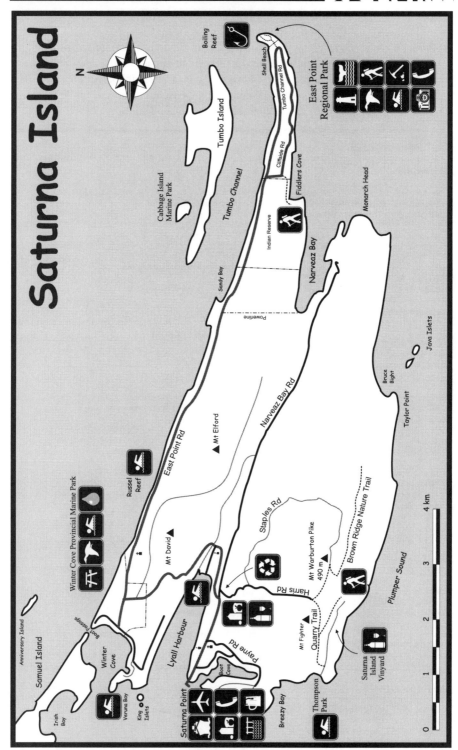

Saturna Island

N

Boiling Reef

Tumbo Island

Tumbo Channel

Cabbage Island Marine Park

Shell Beach

Tumbo Channel Rd

Cliffside Rd

Fiddlers Cove

East Point Regional Park

Sandy Bay

Indian Reserve

Narveaz Bay

Monarch Head

Powerline

Java Islets

Narveaz Bay Rd

East Point Rd

Mt Elford

Bruce Bight

Taylor Point

Russel Reef

Mt David

Staples Rd

Mt Warburton Pike 490 m

Brown Ridge Nature Trail

Winter Cove Provincial Marine Park

Harris Rd

Mt Fighter

Quarry Trail

Plumper Sound

Anniversary Island

Samuel Island

Irish Bay

Winter Cove

Boat Passage

Veruna Bay

King Islets

Lyall Harbour

Payne Rd

Boot Cove

Saturna Point

Breezy Bay

Thompson Park

Saturna Island Vinyard

0   1   2   3   4 km

Park. A left turn here leads to Saturna Island Vineyards where tours are offered daily from 11:30 AM to 4 PM June through October.

Arrive early at the ferry dock in preparation for the return voyage. While doing so will ostensibly ensure your passage on the infrequent vessel, more importantly it is a handy excuse to pay homage at the pub next door. The Lighthouse Pub is an ideal vantage point from which to survey the coast for approaching mariners while sampling the indigenous service, suds and supper. 🐾

Saturna Island

Location	Notes
Canadian Gulf Islands Reservations 1-888-539-2930; (250) 539-2930 reservations@gulfislands.com	Free booking service for B&Bs, resorts, lodges, and cabins throughout the Gulf Islands.
East Point Resort; (250) 539-2975; Saturna Island, British Columbia, V0N 2Y0	Cabins with kitchenettes Boat rentals
Saturna Lodge & Resturant 130 Payne Rd; Saturna Island, B.C. 1-888-539-8800; (250) 539-2254 (250) 539-3091 FAX rpage@pronet; www.saturna-island.bc.ca	Styled after a French country inn
Saturna Island Vineyards P.O. Box 54, 8 Quarry Road Saturna Island, B.C. V0N 2Y0 wine@saturnavineyards.com (250) 539-5139; (250) 539-5157 FAX	Wine & vineyard tours Wine shop Wine tasting
Gulf Islands Water Taxi (250) 537-2510; (250) 537-9202 FAX watertaxi@saltspring.com	See Appendix for full schedule $15 per person, Bikes free, Kayaks $5 extra
Viable Marine Services (250) 539-3200 Tel/FAX	Water taxi, Wildlife tours, Dive charters and instruction
Bike and Boat Rentals (250) 539 3041	
Saturna Island Kayaking 121 Boot Cove Road (250) 539-5553 rbruce@gulfislands.com	5 minute walk from ferry landing Single: $70/day; $80/2 days; $25/additional day Double: $90/day; $105/2 days; $35/additional day $10 kayak delivery or pick up charge
Boot Cove Kayak (250) 539 3421	
Harbour Air 1-800-665-0212; 1-800-665-4267 (604) 688-1277; (604) 278-3478	Daily scheduled and charter seaplane service to the Gulf Islands from downtown Vancouver $58 per person one way
Seair 1-800-447-3247; (604) 273-8900	Scheduled and charter seaplane service
Cooper Air 1-800-656-0766 (604) 656-3968	Charter seaplane service
Kenmore Air 1-800-543-9595	Charter seaplane service
Saturna Island Tourism Association www.saturnatourism.bc.ca	Tourist Information

San Juan Islands

Access: To get to the American San Juan Islands from Vancouver take the Tsawwassen Ferry to Swartz Bay. [See **Getting to Tsawwassen** on page 321.] From the ferry follow traffic along Highway 17 towards Victoria, watching for directional signs to Sidney, BC. Follow the signs left on to McTavish, proceed one block, then turn left on to Lochside. Peddle north along the sea shore to Ocean Avenue, across from the Information Center. Turn right on Ocean Avenue continuing to the terminal entrance at 2499 Ocean Avenue. The route is well-marked from the Highway 17 turn-off to the terminal entrance.

There is only one ferry daily from Sidney to the San Juans. Leaving at just before noon, it makes one stop at San Juan Island before proceeding to Anacortes, Washington. Upon arrival at 3 PM it is necessary to clear customs before turning around and lining up to reboard the ferry an hour later. This time the destination is Lopez Island. From here cyclists can island hop at leisure. Frequent sailings on the inter-island ferry provide links to Shaw, Orcas then San Juan Island in turn with the cycling becoming more demanding as each island is conquered. At the end of it all, pick up the international run at Friday Harbour on San Juan Island for the crossing back to Sidney.

Washington State Ferries

Sidney, BC: (250) 381-1551 or (250) 656-1531

USA: 1-888-808-7977 (Washington only) or (206) 464-6400

Internet: www.wsdot.wa.gov/ferries

San Juan Island Ferry Eastbound Daily

Leave Sidney	Leave Friday Harbor	Leave Orcas	Leave Shaw	Leave Lopez	Leave Anacortes
-	6:00	-	-	6:45	7:30
-	6:15	7:15	7:00	-	-
-	-	7:05	7:15	7:45	8:25
-	8:10	-	-	8:55	9:35
-	8:35	9:25	9:40	10:00	-
-	-	10:30	9:50	11:00	11:40
-	11:35	-	-	-	12:40
-	-	-	-	12:55	1:35
-	12:00	12:50	1:05	1:25	-
11:50	1:50	-	-	-	3:05
-	-	2:40	2:00	-	3:30
-	2:30	3:20	3:35	3:55	-
-	4:05	-	-	4:45	5:25
-	-	5:50	5:20	-	6:40
-	5:30	6:20	6:35	6:55	-
-	6:40	-	-	-	7:55
-	7:45	-	-	8:25	9:05
-	-	8:30	8:00	8:55	9:35
-	-	10:50 SaSu	10:30 SaSu	11:15 SaSu	11:55 SaSu
-	11:40 Fri	10:50 Fri	10:30 Fri	-	12:45 Sat

San Juan Island Ferry Westbound Daily

Leave Anacortes	Leave Lopez	Leave Shaw	Leave Orcas	Arrive Friday Harbor	Arrive Sidney
5:45	6:30	7:15	6:45	-	-
6:20	7:10	-	-	7:40	-
-	-	7:05	7:25	8:15	-
7:50	-	-	9:00	9:45	11:15
8:45	9:30	9:50	10:00	-	-
10:00	-	-	-	11:05	-
-	10:10	10:35	11:00	11:40	-
11:55	12:35	-	-	-	-
-	1:30	1:05	12:50	2:10	-
1:05	-	2:00	2:10	-	-
2:00	2:50	-	-	3:20	-
-	4:00	3:35	4:30	5:10	-
4:10	5:00	5:20	5:30	-	-
5:00	-	-	-	6:15	-
5:45	-	-	6:45	7:25	-
-	7:00	6:35	-	7:50	-
7:00	7:45	8:00	8:10	-	-
8:25 Ex Fri	9:15 Ex Fri	9:35 Ex Fri	9:50 Ex Fri	10:30 Ex Fri	-
8:25 Fri	-	-	-	9:40 Fri	-
9:30 Fri	10:15 Fri	10:30 Fri	10:50 Fri	11:30 Fri	-
9:30 SaSu	10:15 SaSu	10:30 SaSu	10:40 SaSu	-	-
11:00 Fri	11:55 Fri	-	12:25 Sat	1:05 Sat	-

Lopez Island

Terrain: Fairly Flat

Season: Year Round

Traffic: Light

Distance: 53 km

Access: See section intro, **The San Juan Islands,** on pg 191.

Since pedalling Lopez Island's 53 km circuit is easy, cyclists will have plenty of time to explore the foreshore, stop for a refreshing dip in Hummel Lake or photograph the ample agricultural artifacts of the island's frontier era. Farming continues to be the principle industry here.

While there are numerous inns and B & B's to choose from venture not to Lopez without reservations. Most rooms throughout these islands are booked up as much as 6 months in advance. Campers too may find both Spencer Spit State Park and Odlin County Park full to bursting during the high season summer months.

From the ferry both of the island's campgrounds are nearby. Since campgrounds throughout the San Juan Islands fill up fast, securing a campsite should be a high-priority. Setting up camp early not only reserves a spot for the night, but allows you to leave behind most of your gear. Of course valuables such as camera and cash should never be left unattended. Neither park on Lopez Island has showers so embark on a clockwise tour around the island, ending up towards the end of the day in the Fishermen Bay - Lopez Village area where showers, laundry and provisions can all be had.

Odlin County Park, on the sunset side of the island, is just 1½ km from the ferry dock. Altogether Odlin County Park boasts 30 campsites and a sandy beach overlooking Upright Channel. With luck, one of the more secluded beachfront bicycle campsites will be available.

If full, sprint across to the sunrise side via Port Stanley Road to Spencer Spit State Park. The park can accommodate 49 groups, including 18 walk-in campsites for cyclists and kayakers above the beach.

To begin your explorations head down island towards Hunter and Mud Bays, avoiding Center Road, the island's busiest, wherever possible. At the end of Islandale Road you'll find a public wharf on the little peninsula separating both bays. Public access to the waterfront can be had further along Mud Bay Road and again near the end of Sperry Road. Unlike in Canada where 98 percent of all foreshore belongs to the Crown and is publicly accessible, in the U.S. most beaches are part of the private property above them and owners can and do enforce their ownership.

En route to the beach, at the corner of Mud Bay Road and Mackaye Harbor Road, you'll find the Islandale Bicycle Rest, a small picnic area set aside for cyclists. Picnic tables, outhouses and shade have been provided for the comfort of the many two-wheeled tourists who visit Lopez each year. Not surprisingly water, that scarcest of commodities, is not available.

There are two more noteworthy points of waterfront access on the southeast corner of Lopez Island. Hughes Bay County Park off Watmough Head Road features a gravel beach at the bottom of a steep, wooden staircase. Mackaye Harbor Road leads to Agate Beach Picnic Area where again all the amenities except water are available. Working around to the west cyclists will find a boat launch at Mackaye Harbor and a public pier at historic Richardson. The latter was once a busy fishing and steamship port from which the island's produce reached markets in Seattle.

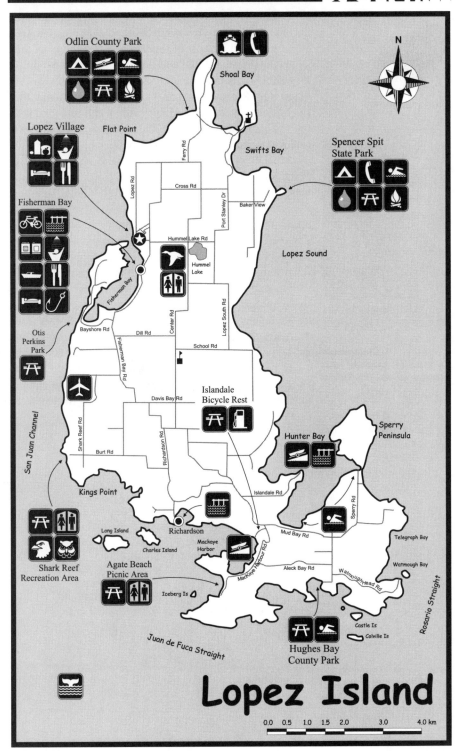

Odlin County Park

Lopez Village

Fisherman Bay

Otis Perkins Park

Shark Reef Recreation Area

Shoal Bay

Flat Point

Swifts Bay

Spencer Spit State Park

Cross Rd

Baker View

Lopez Sound

Ferry Rd

Lopez Rd

Port Stanley Dr

Hummel Lake Rd

Hummel Lake

Lopez South Rd

Bayshore Rd

Dill Rd

Center Rd

School Rd

Fisherman Bay Rd

San Juan Channel

Davis Bay Rd

Islandale Bicycle Rest

Hunter Bay

Sperry Peninsula

Shark Reef Rd

Richardson Rd

Burt Rd

Kings Point

Islandale Rd

Sperry Rd

Long Island

Richardson

Mackaye Harbor

Mud Bay Rd

Telegraph Bay

Charles Island

Agate Beach Picnic Area

Aleck Bay Rd

Watmough Bay

Iceberg Is

Watmough Head Rd

Rosario Straight

Juan de Fuca Straight

Castle Is

Colville Is

Hughes Bay County Park

Mackaye Harbour Rd

Lopez Island

0.0 0.5 1.0 1.5 2.0   3.0   4.0 km

From Richardson take Burt Road across island to reach the old-growth forest reserve at Shark Reef Recreation Area. Birders with an interest in waterfowl will want to set their sights on Hummel Lake while those captivated by predatory habits will find a variety of raptors but no sharks at Shark Reef Recreation Area. The old-growth sustains a variety of owls while the nation's symbol can be found nesting in the topmost branches. Rather than a beach expect to find rocky shelves along the foreshore.

Shark Reef Road leads back up island past the local airport. Pick up Fisherman Bay Road to reach the island's commercial heart. Along the way take a side trip down Bayshore Road to reach the narrow neck of land which separates Fisherman Bay from the more open waters of San Juan Channel. The road continues along the spit past the picnic area at Otis Perkins Park to eventually end at private property.

A number of services related to maritime recreation as well as public laundry and showers facilities, a bike rental shop, restaurants, a dive shop and a motel can be found at the settlement of Fisherman Bay. Just minutes further along the road at Lopez Village groceries, public showers, accommodations, restaurants and even a museum will be found.

Lopez Road will take campers back to Odlin County Park while those staying at Spencer Spit State Park can follow Hummel Lake Road to return to camp. Fishermen can cast in the lake for trout and bass. 🐾

Soaring Seaward
A mature bald eagle looking for sharks, no doubt, at Shark Reef Recreation Area.

Nikon F
300 mm Nikkor lens
Kodachrome 200 ISO film

Shaw Island

Terrain: Flat   **Traffic:** Light

Season: Year Round   **Distance:** 22 km

Access: See section intro, **The San Juan Islands,** on pg 191.

At 20 square kilometres, Shaw Island is the smallest, least developed of the San Juans. A general store, a historical society museum and a county campsite comprise the amenities on Shaw Island. The cycling circuit is a mere 22 km of well-paved country roads from which you'll glimpse virgin stands of timber, historic farms and an active commercial salmon fishery. You may even want to scout the beach for agates at South Beach County Park [(206) 468-2580.]

Arrive early at Shaw Landing and head directly for the only campsite on the island. If in need of provisions pause for a moment after disembarking from the ferry. The general store at Shaw Landing is the only place on the island where groceries can be procured. Be forewarned that, since the Little Portion store is operated by a group of Franciscan nuns, it remains closed on Sundays.

To reach the park follow the road around the head of Blind Bay, turning left upon reaching Squaw Bay Road. South Beach County Park, about a kilometre further on, sadly has just 12 tents sites. If you find it full you may wish to do a quick circuit of the island then catch the ferry onward to Orcas Island in the afternoon. Those who crave a certain amount of solitude far from the hurly burly of other more tourist-infested campgrounds will find South Beach County Park a sheer delight however. The south-facing beach, a crescent of fine sand and gravel nearly a kilometre long, winds around the

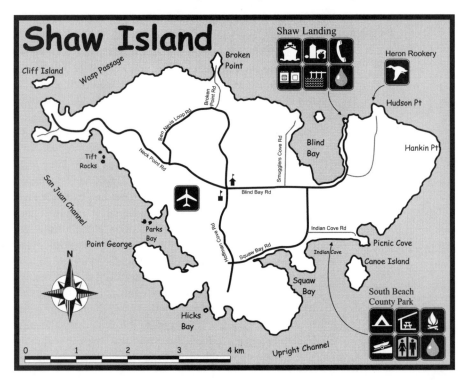

peninsula along the east side of Indian Cove and into Squaw Bay. Enjoy taking long walks, beachcombing and observing the abundant shore birds here as the rest of the foreshore of Shaw Island is off-limits due to the tyranny American real estate law. The shore at the western end of the island is a nature preserve.

Cyclists are limited to exploring the rural nature of in-

Free-Car Tourist
Though the tourists can drive them mad, locals are quick to lend a hand when disaster befalls island visitors. Being picked up by a pick-up is a sure fire pick-me-up when stranded by mechanical problems.

Nikon F
28 mm Nikkor lens
Kodachrome 64 ISO film

land Shaw Island rather than the maritime features ringing it. From South Beach County Park continue along Squaw Bay Road making a right at Hoffman Cove Road. At the island's principal intersection you'll find the Little Red Schoolhouse which still operates as a one-room school for the children of Shaw Island's 163 year-round residents. Kitty-corner to the historic school a log cabin serves as the island's museum. Visitors are welcome every Monday and Saturday.

Continue peddling north along the Ben Nevis Loop Road turning right where it rejoins Blind Bay Road. If time allows follow Neck Point Road 5 km out and back for more of Shaw Island's pleasant rural landscape. If unable to camp over on Shaw Island follow Blind Bay Road all the way back to the ferry landing. A short detour along Smugglers Cove Road reveals more of the island's foreshore. Smuggling, incidentally, has a long history throughout the San Juan Islands. A myriad of islands and heavy maritime traffic have made eluding interdiction easy. Illegal immigrants from China, wool, whisky and, to this day, British Columbia's fine hemp products, have all found their way into the States from its neighbour to the north via these waters.

Orcas Island

Terrain: Hilly   **Traffic:** Heavy

Season: Year Round   **Distance:** 77 km

Access: See section intro, **The San Juan Islands,** on pg 191.

Campgrounds, B & B's and vacation resorts abound on Orcas Island. In fact, the only thing more plentiful is the number of tourists who invade the island every summer. For that reason dropping in without reservations during high season is pure folly. If camping out it will be necessary to cycle from the ferry terminal across island for 20 to 30 km fully laden with gear. With the exception of the private campground at West Beach Resort on the northwest corner of Orcas Island, most camping will be found on the eastern half of the Island. Unlike the previous two islands, Orcas Island is a rugged, mountainous rock with many hills to be overcome. Demanding, yes, but most certainly worth it.

Being a mecca for vacationers, Orcas Island, boasts a profusion of services. Restaurants, groceries and the like are usually just around the next corner.

From the ferry follow the aptly named Horseshoe Highway around Eastsound, the deep fjord which nearly severs Orcas Island in two. A longer, alternative route follows White Beach Road and Dolphin Bay Road around the shoulder of Mt. Woolard enabling cyclists with gonzo thigh muscles to avoid a good portion of the busy Horseshoe Highway. Pause for a well-earned moment of reflection at marshy Killebrew Lake. While RV camping is allowed here tents are not as there are no facilities of any kind.

The village of East Sound at the head of the like-named waterway is the urban centre of Orcas Island. Stock up on provisions here, get bikes fixed if necessary and plan a visit to the Orcas Island Historical Museum. Housed in six log cabins dating to the island's pioneer era, the museum features displays of first nations culture as well as that of the settlers who supplanted them.

Orcas Island is rich in architectural history as well. Many of the island's resorts were originally constructed according to Victorian-era models as hideaways for Seattle's hoi polloi. The Orcas Hotel above the ferry terminal dates from the opening moments of the last century while the Post Office at Deer Harbor commenced operations in 1883. Rosario Resort got its start of in 1904 as the residence of industrialist and former Seattle mayor Robert Moran. Much of the wealthy ship builder's estate was eventually donated to the state park system. Moran State Park is the result of that gen-

Fireweed
Gashes in the forest caused by fire, blowdown or human intrusion are quickly filled in by pioneer species such as fireweed or salal. Quick growing red alder and maple soon take over, being themselves supplanted in turn by Douglas fir once soil has stabilized. Eventually shade tolerant climax species such as western red cedar and western hemlock will come to dominate. The whole process can take centuries if not millenia. Immature fireweed plants can be cooked whole like broccoli while the young leaves can be used as salad greens. Fireweed is high in both beta-carotene and vitamin C.
Illustration by Manami Kimura

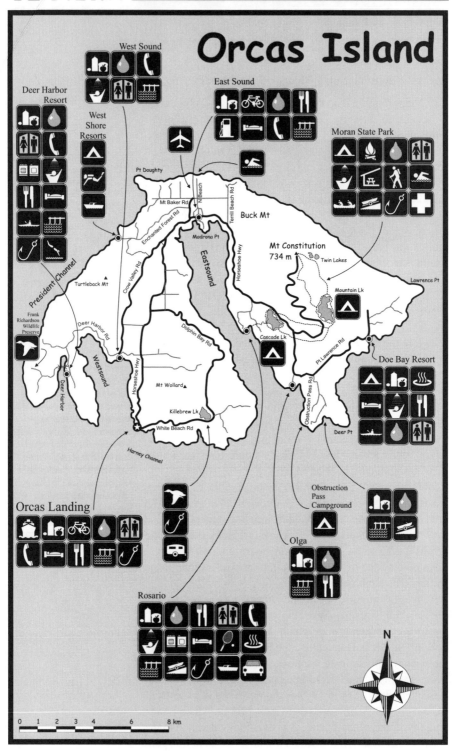

Orcas Island

West Sound

Deer Harbor Resort

West Shore Resorts

East Sound

Moran State Park

Pt Doughty

Mt Baker Rd

N Beach

Terrill Beach Rd

Buck Mt

Madrona Pt

Mt Constitution
734 m

Twin Lakes

Enchanted Forest Rd

Eastsound

Horseshoe Hwy

Crow Valley Rd

Turtleback Mt

Mountain Lk

Lawrence Pt

President Channel

Frank Richardson Wildlife Preserve

Deer Harbor Rd

Dolphin Bay Rd

Cascade Lk

Doe Bay Resort

Westsound

Horseshoe Hwy

Deer Harbor

Mt Wollard

Pt Lawrence Rd

Obstruction Pass Rd

Deer Pt

Killebrew Lk

White Beach Rd

Harney Channel

Orcas Landing

Obstruction Pass Campground

Olga

Rosario

N

0 1 2 3 4 6 8 km

erous act of philanthropy.

Madrona Point, named for the arbutus trees which flourish on the rocky bluffs there, once served as a burial ground for the local Lummi Indians. Less than half a kilometre from East Sound, Madrona Point is an ideal spot from which to enjoy lunch and south-facing views overlooking Eastsound. As with the rest of the San Juan Islands, legal access points to the foreshore can be few and far between. Just east of Madrona Point, at the foot of Lover's Lane, Fishing Bay Waterfront Park provides additional access to the beach overlooking Indian Island.

The first campgrounds along Horseshoe Highway will be found on the shores of Cascade Lake in Moran State Park. There are two additional campgrounds higher up at Mountain Lake while walk-in sites are located in between. Altogether there are 166 campsites spread through five separate campgrounds within the park including 15 sites set aside specifically for cyclists and those who arrive without motor vehicle transportation. Those who arrive without reservations can only count on misery.

For camping with an ocean view try the Obstruction Pass Campground just beyond the settlement of Olga. Just nine campsites, all without water, populate this tiny timbered point. Designed specifically for kayakers, cyclists and hikers, there are no drive in campsites. The rocky bluffs and gravel beach are ideal vantage points from which to toast the setting summer sun.

A further 10 walk-in campsites can be found on the shores of Doe Bay. Even when full, wayward cyclists can usually find a foothold somewhere on the property. More than a campground, organic cooking, whole earth crafts and rustic accommodation make Doe Bay Resort perfect for groovin' on a sunny afternoon. A relaxing, *au naturel* dip in the mineral hot tub is *de rigueur*. Be sure to wear some flowers in your hair.

The high point of Orcas Island— literally — is Mount Constitution. On an exceptionally clear day Mt. Baker, Mt. Ranier and even Vancouver, B.C. are visible from the stone observation tower at the 734 m summit. The truly gung-ho may want to try cycling up the road to the top of Mt. Constitution. Hiking is the recommended approach.

Altogether Moran State Park has 50 km of hiking trails suited to nearly every ability level. Extending from sea level at Rosario and connecting both Cascade Lake and Mountain Lakes, a network of trails continues via Twin Lakes to reach the mountaintop. Very few trails are open to terrain-crunching mountain bikes.

Leave enough time on your return to the ferry landing to finish your explorations of the western half of the island. A thin sliver of beach is accessible at the end of North Beach Road near the island's air strip. To avoid retracing your route follow a circuitous route along the Enchanted Forest Road, Crow Valley Road and Deer Harbor Road to visit West Sound village and historic Deer Harbor. Birders may spot something out of the ordinary at the Frank Richardson Wildlife Preserve. Follow Sunset Beach Road to reach the eight hectare marsh. 🐾

Orcas Island

Location	Notes
Dolphin Bay Bicycles (360) 376-4157 or (360) 376-3093 www.rockisland.com/~dolphin/	Bike Rentals, Repairs & Sales
Orcas Island Eclipse Charters 1-800-376-5655; (360) 376-4663	Whale Watching Tours
Deer Harbor Charters 1-800-544-5758; 360-376-5989 chartert@rockisland.com	Whale Watching Tours; Boat Rentals
Moran State Park (360) 376-6173; 1-800-452-5687	Camping Reservations & Information
West Beach Resort (360) 376-2240	Camping Reservations & Information Kayak Tours & Rentals
Obstruction Pass Park (360) 856-3500	Camping Reservations and Kayak Rentals
Doe Bay Village Resort (360) 376-2291	Camping Reservations & Information
Crescent Beach Kayaks (360) 376-2464	Kayak Rentals
Black Fish Paddlers (360) 376-4947	Kayak Rentals & Tours
Osprey Tours (360) 376-3677	Kayak Tours
Shearwater Kayak Tours (360) 376-4699	Kayak Tours
Orcas Outdoors (360) 376-4611 orcasoutdoors@thesanjuans.com	Kayak & Yacht Tours
Spring Bay Inn Kayak Tours (360) 376-5531	Daily 2 Hour Guided Paddle 5 - 7 PM
Walking Horse Country Farm 1-877-376-9423; (360) 376-5306 stay@walkinghorsefarm.com	Horseback Riding
Orcas Taxi (360) 376-8294	Tours & Taxi Services
Lodging Information Hotline (360) 376-8888	Orcas Island only accommodation info
Orcas Island Chamber of Commerce (360) 376 - 2273 www.orcasisland.org	
Amante Sail Tours (360) 376-4231	Sail Tours for 2-6 people
Biplane Senic Flights (360) 376-2733	Open cockpit tour of the islands
Brisa Charters (360) 376-3264	3 hour tours aboard classic 45 foot sloop
Resort at Deer Harbor (360) 376-4420	Hotel, Marina and Kayak Rentals
Rosario Resort 1-800-562-8820; (360) 376-2222	Hotel, Marina and Boat & Car Rentals

San Juan Island

Terrain: Hilly **Traffic:** Moderate

Season: Year Round **Distance:** 72 km

Access: See section intro on page 191.

San Juan Island is the last of the four big islands in the

Canadian Honkers
The Canadians tend to stand out from the crowd down here.

Nikon F
28 mm Nikkor lens
Kodachrome 64 ISO film

San Juan Group that draw thousands of cyclists every year. The terrain and length of the cycling circuit, 72 km, is similar to that of Orcas though the scenery is far more diverse.

The island is unique in that rudimentary public transit exists, reaching most points of interest as it loops around the island on a 40 minute schedule. As a consequence, those not willing or able to explore the island on two wheels can do so on foot.

Campgrounds abound on San Juan Island but still arriving without reservations during high season is not recommended. The ideal place to set up a tent is San Juan County Park. Situated midway along the west coast of the island, cyclists can set up a base camp from which to explore the 41 km southern half of the island one day and the shorter, 31 km opposite end the next. Though San Juan County Park officially has only 11 individual campsites and no water, dozens more can pre-empt a piece of turf in the group campground. Bottled water and a few other essentials can be purchased in the park store. The real reason San Juan County Park is so popular has little to do with its amenities or lack thereof. Rather, orcas plying the waters of Haro Strait can often be seen from the foreshore and the bluffs overlooking Smallpox Bay. From the ferry slip Beaverton Valley Road provides the most direct access to the campground.

San Juan Island is the island of choice for cetacean watch-

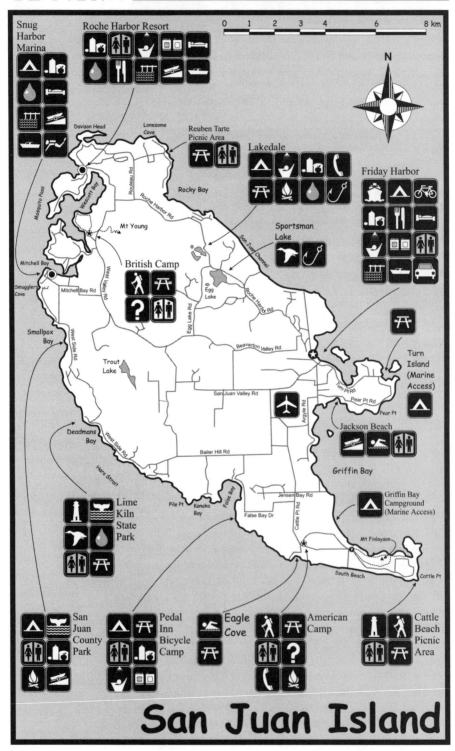

Snug
Harbor
Marina

Roche Harbor Resort

Reuben Tarte
Picnic Area

Lakedale

Friday Harbor

Davison Head

Lonesome
Cove

Rouleau Rd

Westcott Bay

Roche Harbor Rd

Rocky Bay

Mosquito Pass

Mt Young

San Juan Channel

Mitchell Bay

British Camp

Egg
Lake

Sportsman
Lake

Smugglers
Cove

Mitchell Bay Rd

West Valley Rd

Egg Lake Rd

Roche Harbor Rd

Smallpox
Bay

West Side Rd

Trout
Lake

Beaverton Valley Rd

Turn
Island
(Marine
Access)

Turn Pt Rd

Deadmans
Bay

West Side Rd

San Juan Valley Rd

Pear Pt Rd

Pear Pt

Argyle Rd

Jackson Beach

Haro Strait

Bailer Hill Rd

Griffin Bay

Lime
Kiln
State
Park

Pile Pt

Kanaka
Bay

False Bay

Jensen Bay Rd

False Bay Dr

Cattle Pt Rd

Griffin Bay
Campground
(Marine Access)

Mt Finlayson

South Beach

Cattle Pt

San
Juan
County
Park

Pedal
Inn
Bicycle
Camp

Eagle
Cove

American
Camp

Cattle
Beach
Picnic
Area

San Juan Island

ing. The Whale Museum in Friday Harbor is a must-see. Many commercial whale watching packages include a stop at the public education facility as part of the tour. As part of its ongoing research, the museum maintains a toll-free hotline (1-800-562-8832) for reporting whale sightings. Confirmed recent sightings are then noted on the museum's web-

Garry Oak
Though never common, garry oak has established a niche along the foreshore of the San Juans, the Gulf Islands and Vancouver Island. With arbutus, garry oak shares a fondness for dry, rocky habitat which cannot sustain the more usual west coast conifers. The two deciduous species taken together lend a unique air to the island environment.

Nikon F
28 mm Nikkor lens
Kodachrome 64 ISO film

site at www.whale-museum.org.

From May through September each year more than 80 individual orcas in 3 pods take up residence in the waters of the San Juan Islands. Attracted by Canadian salmon returning to the Fraser River via American waters the orcas and their smaller cousins, Dall's and Harbor porpoises, are a delight to thousands of vacationers. Though the population of the Southern Resident Community has remained stable for several decades the Canadian government declared the orcas "threatened" in 1999 due to concerns about pollution, growing maritime traffic and, particularly, over-fishing by American commercial interests.

Whale watching excursions come in many flavours from 60 foot motor cruisers, zippy, little zodiacs and kayak-based paddle tours. And while joining a tour may offer a certain amount of certainty doing so is certainly not necessary. The favourite location for land-based whale watching is just 4 km south of San Juan County Park at Lime Kiln Point State Park. The site of Lime Kiln Lighthouse since 1919, the rocky bluffs here provide the best vantage anywhere for viewing orcas, minke whales and porpoises. If statistics are anything to go by, in past mid-summers orcas passed by at least once a day 77% of the time. On a typical summer day foraging cetaceans may pass by several times. Plan on a picnic and several hours spent lounging in the sunshine to catch a glimpse. The decrepit kilns at the park attest to a once thriving lime industry on the island.

Continue exploring southward on scenic West Side Road. If you reach False Bay, 8½ km further on, at low tide plan on getting muddy while exploring the extensive tidal flats. Sandals or a pair of neoprene beach booties will save your costly cycling shoes from the ravages of salt water.

Near the southern entrance to False Bay the Pedal Inn campground caters exclusively to the cycling set. This is a full-service, private campground that features 25 walk-in sites, pay showers, laundry facilities and even a limited supply of groceries.

Unlike other destinations in the San Juan Islands, the archipelago's namesake offers generous access to the waterfront for landlubbers. The peddling public can thank a potato pilfering porker for this happy state of affairs. The slaughter of a Hudson's Bay Company pig in 1859 by an American settler sparked a controversy that became known as the "Pig War." As tensions heightened British and American forces set up encampments at opposite ends of the island. More about boundaries than bacon, the border war fortunately was never fought. Instead the dispute was eventually arbitrated by Wilhelm I of Germany. The Kaiser ruled in favour of the American claim to the pork and the British finally cleared out in 1872. Both garrisons are now national historic parks.

Nearly the whole southern end of the island is devoted to the San Juan Island National Historical Park's American Camp. Interpretive history displays with staff dressed in period costumes, extensive beaches and easy hiking trails are the legacy of one time bilateral belligerence.

A succession of low rocky headlands and crescents of sand comprise the shore south of the interpretive displays. These finally give way to 3 km long South Beach. The whole public foreshore extends nearly 6 km. Flanking the American Camp, Eagle Cove to the west and Cattle Beach picnic area to the east provide additional points of access. The former is a popular swimming hole while the latter features a lighthouse overlooking San Juan Channel.

On the opposite side of the peninsula a 5 km trail follows the shore of Griffin Bay as far as an inaptly-named cove called Fish Creek before looping back through grassy pastures and over the knoll called Mount Finlayson. En route look for feral rabbits grazing at the edge of forest cover. The bunnies, which once reached a population of over a quarter of a million, are thought to be descendants of livestock brought to the island by 19th-century settlers.

Stay with Cattle Point then Argyle Road to return directly to the commercial heart of the island. Friday Harbour is 10 km up island. For a less direct approach take a 5 km detour looping first along Pear Point Road and then back via Turn Point Road to experience more of the island's charming waterfront. On the way expect to encounter popular Jackson Beach, a small spit of sand adjacent to a cannery. Further along a small beachfront picnic site will be found opposite Turn Island Marine State Park.

Friday Harbour, the largest community in the San Juans, bustles with gift and craft shops, cappuccino bars and restaurants of every variety. Yet in spite of the trend towards commercialization in recent years Friday Harbour still retains much of its rural ambiance. In addition to the aforementioned Whale Museum, Friday Harbor boasts a historical museum as well. The San Juan Island Historical Museum is housed in a 19th-century farmhouse furnished and refurbished to the standards of the day.

To continue exploring the highways and by ways of the northern end of the island leave the Friday Harbor on the Roche Harbor Road. Within 7 km you'll reach marshy Sportsman Lake, a favourite haunting ground of birders.

Roadside Repairman
Nothing like a dozen or so broken spokes to ruin your day.

Nikon F
28 mm Nikkor lens
Kodachrome 64 ISO film

Lakedale Campground, just a click and a half further down the road, will strike terror into the very heart of every solitude-seeking cyclist. The commercial campground boasts 120 sites, 10 of which are dedicated to cyclists. Visitors can enjoy the full range of services including pay showers, a well-supplied grocery store, canoe and rowboat rentals and even, of all things, pay fishing.

Seclusion of sorts can be found way off the beaten track at the Reuben Tarte Picnic Area at the northwest corner of the island. Birders and scuba divers in particular are drawn to the quiet beachfront here.

Historic Roche Harbour Resort boasts bed and board fit for the heads of state, or fit, at least, for American Presidents Teddy Roosevelt and William Howard Taft who both stayed at the venerable waterfront lodge. The opulent resort was once home to a bustling community of lime makers. Even if ostentation is not your thing the historic buildings and the lime kilns and quarry operations should not be overlooked. Roche Harbour was once the west coast's largest lime producing operation with an output of 15,000 barrels of lime daily.

To reach the second half of the San Juan Island National Historical Park follow West Valley Road south for 6 km from Roche Harbor. Many of the original buildings still exist at English Camp. In addition to historical displays visitors can enjoy two pleasant hikes at English Camp. One excursion winds for just a click and a half around Bell Point, following the shoreline of Garrison Bay and Westcott Bay through an landscape dominated by arbutus and fir. The second trail, somewhat longer and steeper, climbs past the British Cemetery to the summit of Mount Young. For good reason the British kept a lookout posted on the 180 metre peak. As now, observers then could enjoy a panorama encompassing the whole San Juan-Gulf Islands archipelago, extending as far as the Olympic Mountains to the southwest and Mt. Baker to the east while watching for the approach of menacing ships. Round trip to the top is 3 km.

The final stop on our circle tour of San Juan Island is Snug Harbor Resort on Mitchell Bay. Though catering to the yachting set, camping, groceries and water may be of interest to cyclists as well. San Juan County Park is just 3 km further along.

From San Juan Island hop on board the ferry once more, this time headed back for Sidney, B.C. on Vancouver Island. If intending to continue exploring this archipelago by bicycle you will no doubt find the name, the country and even the atmosphere has changed. Now called the Gulf Islands, the pace of life seems to slow considerably. As actively as tourism has been pursued in the San Juans, it has been shunned by many who have come to the Gulf Islands seeking peace and an escape from the hurley burly of the complex modern world. 🐾

Oregon Grape
Looking much like tiny concord grapes on a holly bush, the intensely sour fruit of the Oregon grape is loaded with Vitamin C. Munch them directly from the bush for a surefire pucker or render them into sugar-loaded jelly for a more palatable treat. Traditionally Oregon grape berries were mashed with other, sweeter berries to enhance their flavour. The inner bark of both stems and roots was a source of brilliant yellow dye during pre-European times. The source of the colour, an alkaloid called berberine, is known to possess antibiotic properties that are still used to combat both internal and external infections. An extract concocted from the roots is used by modern-day herbalists to correct a wide range of liver, kidney and urinary tract problems.

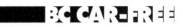

San Juan Island

Location	Notes
San Juan County Park (360) 378-2992	Camping Reservations
Pedal Inn Bicycle Park (360) 378-3049	Camping Reservations
Lakedale Resort 1-800-617-2267; (360) 378-2350	Camping Reservations
Snug Harbor Resort (360) 378-4762	Camping Reservations; Whale Watching; Kayak Rentals
Town & Country Trailer Park (360) 378-4717	Camping Reservations
Island Bicycles; Friday Harbor (206) 378-4941	Bike Rentals & Repairs
The Whale Museum 1-800-562-8832; www.whale-museum.org 62 First Street North, Friday Harbor	Whale sightings hotline to report sightings only Recent sightings listed on website.
Western Prince Cruises 1-800-757-6722; (360) 378-5315	Whale Watching
San Juan Excursions 1-800-809-4253; (360) 378-6636	Whale Watching; Kayaking Tours
San Juan Safaris 1-800-451-8910; (360) 378-2155	Whale Watching; Kayaking Tours
Adventure Kayak Tours 1-888-858-5296; (360) 378-5296	Whale Watching; Kayaking Tours
San Juan Boat Tours 1-800-232-6722; (360) 378-3499	Whale Watching
Sea Quest Expeditions (360) 378-5767	Whale Watching; Kayaking Tours
Maya's Whale Watch Charters (360) 378-7996	Whale Watching
Salish Sea Charters (360) 378-8555	Whale Watching
San Juan Kayak Expeditions (360) 378-4436	Kayak Tours & Rentals
Leisure Kayak Rentals 1-800-836-1402; (360) 378-5992	Kayak Rentals
Outdoor Odysseys 1-800-647-4621; (360) 378-3533	Kayak Tours
Crystal Seas Kayaking 1-877-732-7877; (360) 378-7899	Kayak Tours
San Juan Transit (800) 887-8387; (360) 378-8887; santran@rockisland.com	Shuttle Service to lodges and campgrounds, departing every 40 minutes. Guided tours of the island and taxi services also available.
Bob's Taxi (360) 378-6777	Guided Island Tours and Taxi Service
Roche Harbor Resort 1-800-451-8910; (360) 378-2155	Boat Rental
San Juan County Visitor Information Service (888) 468-3701; (360) 468-3663 visitorinfo@interisland.net; www.guidetosanjuans.com	
B & B Association of San Juan Island (360) 378-3030 or (360) 378-2881 FAX secretary@san-juan-island.net www.san-juan-island.net	Lodging Hotline for Bed & Breakfast Accommodation on San Juan Island
San Juan Island Chamber of Commerce (360) 378.5240 chamber@sanjuanisland.org; www.sanjuanisland.org	

Weekend Getaways

A weekend getaway differs from a day trip or a full-blown backpacking or other outback adventure in that usually participants will have to pack tents, sleeping bags, food, electric hair dryer and other necessities but they won't have to carry this camping gear very far. In the Getaways detailed below public transportation will take you almost as far as the campsite. Dragging along the gas barbecue is still out of the question.

Kayaking is not for everybody. Seniors, kids or the slightly aquaphobic may however wish to enjoy some of the natural wonders kayakers take for granted. Many of the tours outlined under Sea Kayaking could easily be reconstituted as Weekend Getaways and enjoyed from the vantage point of a power launch instead. A visit to Hot Springs Cove in Clayoquot Sound, for example, or to Princess Louisa Inlet and the twin rapids in that area can be exhilarating. Both places can be easily accessed through local eco-tour companies. Combine that with the hospitality and comfort of a B & B and you have a Weekend Getaway suited to nearly any taste. The information grid following each outing in the Kayaking section lists available tours.

The Gulf Islands are ideally suited to cycle touring and, as such, have been fully described in that section on page 146. All are compatible with the concept of a walking tour as well with some caveats. Mayne, Saturna and Gabriola Islands are certainly small enough to be explored on foot over the course of a two or three day period. Tramping about Galiano Island and the Pender Islands is also pleasant but more than a simple weekend may be required to fully appreciate these bigger rural islands. Salt-spring Island is by far the biggest and, depending on which of three possible ferry terminals you arrive by, may require a taxi pick up at the ferry. Many B & B owners are willing to include shuttle service in the price of the room.

Camping at Porteau Cove, Stawamus Chief or Brandywine Falls Provincial Parks could turn day hikes to Marion & Phyllis Lakes [Page 64,] the Chief or Squaw [Page 67,] Cal-Cheak [Page 70] or Brew Lake [Page 72] into easy overnighters. 🐾

Newcastle Island

So you'd like to get-away-from-it-all but don't know where to start. Start off slow with a visit to Newcastle Island Marine Park.

Just off shore from downtown Nanaimo, it's the perfect spot for a day trip or even an easy going overnighter. Unlike so many other wonderful places, it's easy to get to Newcastle Island using public transportation, faster and cheaper in fact than taking your own dinosaur along. Hop a Nanaimo-bound ferry in either Tsawwassen or Horseshoe Bay, then grab a cab on the other side. [See Appendix **Getting to Horseshoe Bay** on page 320 or **Getting to Tsawwassen** on page 321.] For an $8 taxi ride you'll be at the Newcastle Island ferry dock in a matter of minutes. The **Nanaimo Seaporter** will whisk you from ferry terminal to ferry terminal for slightly less when it is available. Look for the shuttle bus when exiting the terminal or call in advance in order to have it

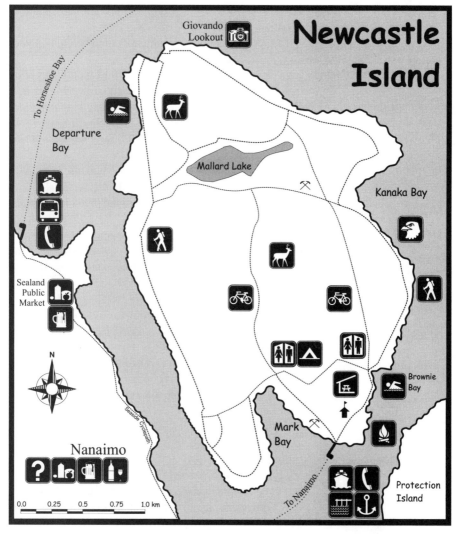

meet you on arrival.

As an alternative you can either take a bus or walk between the two ferries. The **#2 Hammond Bay** bus runs at half-hour intervals from Departure Bay ferry terminal to downtown Nanaimo. Get off at the corner of Wallace and Comox Streets and walk back towards the civic arena behind which you'll find the Newcastle Island Ferry dock.

Nanaimo's Harbourside Walkway leads directly to your destination along the waterfront. After arriving on Vancouver Island you'll find the start of this pleasant seawall route at Sealand Oceanarium & Market just east of the ferry terminal entrance. Total walking time is about 45 minutes.

The Newcastle Island foot passenger ferry runs regularly in the summer months so if you miss one stay cool, there will be another one along in a few minutes. Kind of like dating, isn't it?

And speaking of dating, romance could be high on your list in this tranquil, idyllic setting.

As you step off the ferry you'll find plenty of picnic tables and wide grassy fields perfectly suited for frisbee, football or other fun.

At the edge of the forest there is ample camping so set up that tent and set out to explore the many wonders of this small isle.

Newcastle Island is rich in history. Middens, essentially stone age garbage pits made up of clam shells, fish bones and wood fire ash, bear testimony to the prehistoric Indian villages that once flourished here.

In the mid-1800s frenetic coal mining activity threatened the island's tranquillity. Bits of coal can still be found littering the beaches and airshafts that extend deep into the gloom of yesteryear attest to Nanaimo's colourful coal mining past.

From 1910 a small fishing community was established by Japanese-Canadians on Newcastle Island until, well, you know what we did to them at the time of World War II.

And for many years the Canadian Pacific Steamship Company operated a holiday resort on Newcastle Island, the main pavilion of which still stands as a visitor centre and museum.

You'll also find an old sandstone quarry that at one time supplied grindstones for pulp mills throughout the Pacific Northwest.

Yet with all that past activity, Newcastle Island is still an excellent example of the unique west coast island environment characterized by mixed deciduous and coniferous for-

Stonecrop
This unique succulent prefers dry rocky outcrops or shelves suited to few other plants. The crisp, young leaves of stone crop can be eaten raw or steamed. Being well-adapted to retaining moisture, the leaves can be an emergency source of water as well. Mashed, stone crop is valued as a burn or wound treatment as well.
Illustration by Manami Kimura

est, with Garry Oak and Arbutus predominating near the foreshore.

Expect to find lots and lots of feral bunnies hopping about. Could it be they too have been seduced by the island's romantic charms?

Black-tailed deer have also proliferated. The best time to see these shy, gentle creatures is early in the morning. While campers sleep the dog-sized deer sneak out to graze the dew damp grass.

As you explore the forests and seashore of Newcastle Island be sure to keep a sharp eye out for bald eagles perched high in old fir snags.

You'll have to call for a cab [see below] on the return journey. There is a pay phone on Newcastle Island so you can call just before boarding the ferry and have your ride waiting for you when you reach the other side. If vandalized, you'll have to wait, then cross the Island Highway to use the pay phone at the beer and wine shop. 🐾

Newcastle Island

Contact	Phone Number	Service
Swiftsure Taxi	(250) 753-8911	
AC Taxi	(250) 753-1231	
Nanaimo Seaporter	(250) 753-2118 (250) 753-2324 Fax	Shuttle service that meets most but not all ferries from the mainland. Same price for 1 or 2 passengers. From/To Departure Bay $7 From/To Duke Point $14
Newcastle Island Ferry	(250) 753-5141	Operates on the hourly schedule during the high season. Only operates on sunny weekends during the winter.
Newcastle Island	(250) 754-7893	For camping information.
Nanaimo Regional Transit System	(250) 390-4531	#2 Hammond Bay bus every 30 minutes to downtown Nanaimo. from Departure Bay Ferry Terminal.
Tourism Nanaimo	1-800-663-7337 1-250-756-0106	
Aqua Motion Water Taxi 21 Pirates Lane Nanaimo, BC	(250) 716-6623 (250) 755-1269 Fax	Located in the Nanaimo Harbour, Water Taxi, Tours and Sightseeing, Kayak Rentals

Keats Island

Access: Take the bus to Horseshoe Bay [See Page 320] and catch the ferry to Langdale [See Page 333] on the Sunshine Coast. Crossing time is 40 minutes. As you step off the loading ramp of the Langdale ferry you'll find the tiny ferry to Keats Landing immediately on your right. Since this ferry services both Gambier Island and Keats Island make sure you get on the correct sailing. Published schedules are sometimes altered on the fly to accommodate weekend rushes. The trip to Keats usually takes just 10 minutes. Getting a good connection on the return trip is often impossible so be sure to bring a book or magazine to make time stuck in the ferry terminal bearable.

Keats Island Ferry

Crossing time 10 ~25 minutes. Some sailings stop at Gambier Island or Eastbourne before arriving at destination. Holiday Mondays follow Sunday schedule.

Leave Langdale		Leave Keats Landing	
Time	Day	Time	Day
7:30 AM	Daily	7:40 AM	Daily
8:10 AM	Daily	8:25 AM	Daily
10:10 AM	Daily	10:50 AM	Daily
1:55 PM	Su	2:10 PM	Su
3:00 PM	Daily	3:25 PM	Daily
5:00 PM	Su	5:15 PM	Su
5:15 PM	M-Sa	5:30 PM	M--Sa
6:20 PM	F	6:55 PM	F

Alternate Transportation to Keats Island

Gibson's Water Taxi (250) 886-0226
Cell: 240-4109
Located in Gibsons

Gambier Water Taxi (250) 886-8321
Cell: 740-1133
Located in Gibsons

Cormorant Marine (604) 250-2630
Located in Horseshoe Bay Regularly scheduled service to Gambier Island

Mercury Launch & Tug (604) 921-7451
Located in Horseshoe Bay Regularly scheduled service to Eastbourne

Like Newcastle Island, Keats Island is home to a Provincial Marine Park. Though well-known among mariners, the park at Plumper Cove is a well-kept secret among landlubbers. Similar also to the previous getaway, two ferries are required to get there. Unlike Newcastle, however, only a small portion of Keats has been accorded park status.

From Keats Landing it is a 2 km hike to the park itself. Walk directly up the hill from the dock, taking a short-cut across the expansive lawn dotted with summer cottages. At the top of the hill you'll come across a gravel road. To your right you'll see a large kids camp. Go left along the road instead for a few hundred metres until you see a building with a sign that says simply: "BC Hydro." A trail plunges into the bush just to the right of this building. Since there are numerous branch trails watch signs carefully to ensure you take the correct route. Follow the mainline marked with yellow squares and a few decrepit signs that indicate "Marine Park." The trail is maintained by the local resident who originally constructed it to keep trespassers off his own property. Still, expect to have to scramble over or under numerous deadfalls along the otherwise well-kept trail.

Camping

Unlike Newcastle Island and most other parks in the islands of the Gulf of Georgia, fires are permitted at all of the 20 walk-in campsites at Plumper Cove. Since prevailing winds come from the direction of the yacht anchorage choose your site wisely so your fire pit is on the lee side of your tent and picnic table. Arriving midweek or early on the weekend will ensure you have choices to make. Late comers may have no choices at all during busy, summer long-weekends. Worry not, however, as there is plenty of overflow camping space in the grassy field that serves as a picnic area. No fires allowed here however. Reservations are not possible at this time on Keats Island.

Cold drinking water is only available from a hand pump. Pit toilets will provide a rustic element to your camping experience but be forewarned to bring toilet paper as supplies, though replenished daily, sometimes run out.

One of the finest features of Plumper Cove is the grassy headland that overlooks Shoal Channel to the west. Use this romantic vantage point to witness the slow summer sunsets that have made the Sunshine Coast famous. As the sky colour deepens from orange to red to purple, stars flicker on as do the lights of Gibsons across the Channel and, further off, Nanaimo on Vancouver Island. And while consuming alcohol is forbidden—if tolerated—in all provincial Parks a robust Bordeaux in a coffee mug goes a long way towards satisfying both park regulations and the mood of the moment.

Hiking Trails

There are three trails of note on Keats Island. The first one is a simple loop trail that extends past the last campsite, climbing up to an elevation of 120 metres to a treed ridgeline before doubling back to reconnect with the park proper. Yellow ribbons and plastic squares mark the Loop Trail. From the summit it may be possible to spot deer grazing in sunny forest glades below. Trail length is a mere 1½ km.

A second trail climbs 216 metres to the top of Stony Hill. Follow the trail back

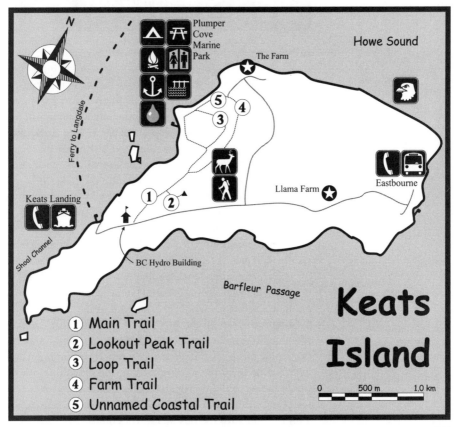

Plumper Cove Marine Park

Howe Sound

The Farm

Ferry to Langdale

Keats Landing

Eastbourne

Llama Farm

Shoal Channel

BC Hydro Building

Barfleur Passage

Keats Island

① Main Trail
② Lookout Peak Trail
③ Loop Trail
④ Farm Trail
⑤ Unnamed Coastal Trail

0   500 m   1.0 km

towards Keats Landing for about 20 minutes in order to access the Lookout Peak Trail. An old, somewhat faded wooden sign marks the trail that then branches off up the slope from the main trail. Follow green markers to the summit after another half hour of upward plodding.

The third route starts out the same as the Loop Trail but branches off to the left after just a few minutes. Watch care-

Dally Llama
The locals on Keats Island are anything but local. This llama mama hails from the Bolivian Andes, well-beyond spitting distance away.

Nikon F
135 mm Nikkor lens
Ektachrome 100 ISO film

fully for the intersection as it is not marked in any way. This unnamed route follows well-above the shoreline until connecting up with a one lane forest track that soon leads past a place called, for obvious reasons, simply "The Farm" by locals. From The Farm the road turns inland and uphill for some 40 minutes or more sometimes paralleling an electric powerline on the right. Eventually you'll reach the main gravel road that connects Keats Landing with the village of Eastbourne. Take a left here and continue up and down a number of rolling hills. After a further 25 minutes or so you'll see a llama farm of all things. Feel free to stop and take pictures of these woolly cousins to the camel but beware: the fence is electrified and llamas, being territorial by nature, spit as a defence mechanism against intruders. Better pack along some lens cleaning paper as a precaution.

From the Double K & J Corral, as the llama farm is called, another 25 minutes will take you as far as the "bus stop" in Eastbourne. Though the bus stop sign looks suspiciously like one of Vancouver's old BC Transit signs don't plan on taking the bus back this year at any rate. The bus stop is an example of local humour, providing the occasional bit of light-hearted retribution against the seasonal invasion of city slickers to this quiet rural backwater. Tourists sometimes wait for hours for the bus that never comes.

Eastbourne, site of a tiny government dock and the best beach on Keats, is just a further five minutes to the right and downhill from here.

A fourth trail, an alternative to the Eastbourne route just described, will be mentioned but is not recommended. Called the Farm Trail, this poorly marked and overgrown path cuts across the island from near the beginning of the Lookout

Fishy Business
The fish are biting on Keats Island and this young Islander proudly reels them in.

Nikon F
135 mm Nikkor lens
Ektachrome 100 ISO film

Peak trail to the Farm. Ironically the Farm Trail slices through by far the most beautiful forest scenery on the island. Following a number of dry and not-so-dry stream beds, the farm trail often disappears altogether and only a careful search for orange trail markers or ribbons will reveal its course. Fear not, though, since Keats Island is so small that after stumbling around in the forest lost for a couple hours you are bound to happen upon one of the routes that crisscross the island. Use common sense however and don't stumble alone. 🐾

Gambier Island (Halkett Bay)

Access: From Horseshoe Bay via water taxi. For details on **Getting to Horse-shoe Bay** see Appendix on page 320. The water taxi leaves from the foot of the red-railed government wharf 1½ blocks to the south [left] of BC Ferries foot passenger entrance. To arrange for drop off at Halkett Bay on Gambier Island contact Cormorant Marine. Reservations are a must. Drop off or pick up in the course of one of their regularly scheduled runs costs $14 per person while a custom shuttle over to Halkett Bay costs $65 per group one way. Scheduled runs as below during spring, summer and fall. Be sure to schedule your pick up as well as drop off to avoid becoming stranded. Call for winter schedule.

Water Taxi: Cormorant Marine (604) 250-2630

Friday: 5 PM and 7 PM and sometimes early afternoon.

Saturday: 9 AM and sometimes early afternoon.

Sunday: 5 PM and 7 PM and sometimes an extra run later in the evening.

The hike to the top of Mount Artaban can be easily done as a day trip but secluded Halkett Bay is the perfect place for an overnighter. If your private yacht is at the dry cleaners you can still reach Halkett Bay Provincial Marine Park via water taxi. Beyond the dock and to the left you'll find a number of rustic campsites, some with picnic tables. Since most visitors float in on their own boats you'll likely have the camping area to yourself. The surrounding maple forest is not so common in coastal British Columbia. The high, bright green canopy arches, cathedral-like, over the dark empty spaces below. Like many island parks, campfires are not permitted here. The shore-based facilities include pit toilets but not drinking water. Fill up a big jug on the wharf in Horseshoe Bay and carry water ashore. The tap is just to the right of the water taxi ramp. If you run out there is a clear running brook in the park but water should be boiled or treated with iodine before drinking.

Halkett Bay at one time served as a seasonal camp for members of the Squamish nation. Collecting clams was the main activity here as the midden above the beach reveals.

In springtime you'll be sharing the bay with flocks of nesting Canada geese. When exploring the rocky islets at low tide approach with caution lest you startle the geese away from their nests. They will not return a gesture, however. These highly communal creatures will most surely keep you awake much of the night calling in newcomers, shouting out warnings and chattering about goose stuff. If sleep isn't a high-priority, witnessing their interactions is certainly fascinating and far more fruitful than counting sheep. 🐾

Mount Artaban

Level: Challenging   **Distance:** 10 km

Time: 5 h   **Elevation Change:** 614 m

Map: See pg 36 or 92 G/6   **Season:** Year Round

The trail to Mount Artaban parallels the brook up the hill behind the campground. After 40 minutes or so on this old logging skid road you'll reach a T-junction with a directional sign. United Church Camp Fircom lies to the left while our destination will be found ever uphill in the opposite direction. As you proceed in a large arc you'll leave the maple forest behind, rising into more open terrain. Soon you'll reach another fork in the trail. A few steps to the left will take you to a viewpoint with a cross on top while a few steps to the right will yield another sign at the top of a large clearcut pointing out the way you want to go. The most obvious trail, a kind of over-grown logging spur, goes nowhere. From the directional sign you should re-enter the forest, mature conifers this time, almost immediately and soon begin losing elevation before the trail flattens out. You'll be following the contours for quite some time before you meet the next trail junction. Downhill and to the left connects with Gambier Estates while you want to go, you guessed it, up and to the right. The next stretch of trail is the longest and gets progressively steeper as you approach the summit of Mount Artaban. The first 45 minutes will be spent rising through a mossy gully before the trail cuts to the right steeply upward the summit. The last 5 minutes will be spent scrambling up and over steep rocky outcrops. At the top, the perfect place for lunch, you'll discover the remains of a former fire surveillance tower and magnificent views of Anvil Island and the Howe Sound Mountains. 🐾

Gander Gumption

This hearty honker defends its nesting site against all comers. From the beach at Halkett Bay we were treated to a rare showing of gander gumption. A dog escaped from one of the yachts with the intention of trashing the nesting sites just for the sheer delight of it. The clueless canine was subsequently led on a 40 minute swim all around the bay by the whole conspiring flock. Finally the mangy mutt returned, exhausted by its ordeal, to its, by now, livid owner. Not a single gosling was ever molested.

Nikon F
135 mm Nikkor lens
Kodachrome 64 ISO film

Horseback Riding

Riding in British Columbia means western riding. English-style is widely available too but requires an expensive, long-term commitment in the form of lessons and practice.

A Horse is a Horse Of Course, Of Course...
...unless of course the horse is still a colt. Sporting a punk hairdo and unbridled curiosity, this little colt demands grass from the dudes.

Nikon F
135 mm Nikkor lens
Kodachrome 64 ISO film

Western-style trail riding, on the other hand, can be enjoyed as a simple day outing. Most trail rides are conducted on either quiet country roads or tranquil forest horse trails. After a quick briefing on the basics, jump on and ride off into the sunset: Trail rides are led by expert guides the first few times. Once you prove your horse-handling skills, however, many stables will allow customers to take the horses without supervision. If you bring a sweaty horse back after your ride, or otherwise abuse your horse you will never be allowed to ride at that stable again.

Technique

A horse is not a car, it's a big, dumb animal that looks to the rider on its back for clear, precise instructions. More than anything it wants to know who is the boss and it will be constantly testing the rider to see what it can get away with. The horse will not respect you if you try to be nice and gentle with it. Your horse will appreciate firm, unambiguous signals.

By and large, riding stable horses are docile creatures content to follow the guide horse's lead. Nonetheless, for safety and other reasons, keeping your horse under control at all times is essential.

Getting On

Always mount from the horse's left side. Grip the reins and the saddle horn in your left hand. Reins should be tight enough to prevent the horse from moving forward but not so tight that it begins to move backwards. Next place your left foot in the left stirrup and grasp the back of the saddle with your right hand. Putting most of your weight on your right leg, bounce once, twice, building momentum, then push off the ground the third time. Transfer your weight to your left leg and push up while pulling yourself up with both arms. As your left leg straightens swing your right leg over the horse and seat yourself in the saddle. Slip your right foot into the right stirrup.

Staying On

Always sit upright, not slouched, with a straight back. Your knees should be bent somewhat in the stirrups enabling you to transfer your body weight to your legs. You will want to stand slightly when galloping or trotting so you don't smash your crotch against the saddle.

Hold the reins in your left fist as you would an ice cream cone or computer joystick. The reins should be grasped firmly passing first through the bottom of the fist with the end sticking out of the top of the fist.

Keep the reins in the resting position with your fist almost touching the back of the horse's neck. There should be enough slack for the horse to hold its head normally but not enough for the horse to lower its head and graze. Whenever the horse tries to eat grass or leaves during the ride pull back HARD on the reins or your problems will never end. Remember, the horse isn't starving, it's testing you. You won't make a friend if you allow it to eat, you'll make an enemy.

Moving Forward

Say "Hyaaaa!" forcefully and kick the horse hard in the flanks with your heels at the same time. The harder you kick the faster you will move and the more respect the horse will have for you. Don't worry about hurting the horse, you aren't strong enough. Horses routinely kick each other and rarely suffer permanant damage. Don't give wimpy little pokes with your heel unless you want to convince your horse that it is the one in command.

Stopping or Slowing

If you have been keeping the proper amount of slack in the resting position stopping should be as simple as pulling back firmly, but not jerking, on the reins. At the same time say "Woa!" in a loud, deep voice with falling intonation. By the time your hand reaches the saddle horn the horse should begin stopping. Once the horse has reached the desired speed or completely stopped you may relax and return the reins to the resting position. Keep in mind that, if all of the horses in your group begin running yours will want to follow the herd and run too. Instead of yanking back on the reins in terror just relax, transfer your weight to the stirrups and enjoy the ride.

Backing Up

Reversing your horse is the same as stopping except that you'll pull back a few centimetres further and hold that position until you've backed up far enough.

Turning

From the resting position pull hard left to go left or hard

Howdy Pardner!
Italo, owner of Mustang Stables takes a mean hombre out for a wrangle or two in the back forty. (Cowboy talk is *de rigueur*.)

Nikon F
50 mm Nikkor lens
Ektachrome 100 ISO film

right to go right, much the same as you would on a computer joystick in the middle of a Wing Commander dog-fight. You'll be pulling much harder in the saddle however.

Getting Off

Dismounting your steed is not just a reversal of the mounting procedure. As with Getting On the reins should be tight enough to prevent the horse from moving forward but not so tight that the horse begins to move backwards. Stand up in the stirrups and, still holding the reins, grasp the saddle horn and shift your body weight to your left leg. Twist your body clockwise as you swing your right leg up and over the back of the horse, grasping the back of the saddle with your right hand in the same motion. Now lean into the horse and shift your entire body weight to your straightened arms. Kick your left leg free of the stirrup and allow your body to slide down the horse's flank so that both feet touch the ground at the same time. Be sure your legs are free of the stirrups so that, in the event that the horse suddenly bolts, you won't be dragged by the leg.

Hold your horses until the guide can come over and tie it securely. 🐾

Riding Stables

Alpine Riding Academy has an excellent location making this an attractive place for both guided trail riding suited to beginners and more formalized riding lessons. Trail rides start at $30 for the first hour, $52 for two hours including guides and taxes. Those with a proven riding ability can rent for $20 per hour. Western-style lessons are available for $178 for 5 lessons. Reservations are a must at Alpine since this small but popular stable is often booked solid up to a week in advance, especially on weekends.

Situated just next to BC Hydro's Buntzen Lake Reservoir Recreation Area, riders have access to many kilometres of forest riding trails. For equestrian trails in the park see page 40. While most trails are ideal for novices, experienced riders will enjoy the challenge of Lake View Trail, portions of which are steep, narrow and rough.

Alpine Riding Academy is easy to get to from downtown Vancouver though time consuming. See Appendix **Getting to Buntzen Lake** on page 334 for transit details.

Other riding stables are included below but are not presently accessible in car-free fashion from downtown Vancouver. 🐾

Horseback Riding Stables

Stable	Rentals	Lessons	Notes
Alpine Riding Academy 3170 Sunnyside Port Moody, B.C. (604) 469-1111.	Western	Western	Reservations Required Staff impatient at times
Golden Ears Riding Stable 13175 - 232nd Street Maple Ridge, B.C. (604) 466-1399 (604) 463-8761	Western	Western English	Big and impersonal with top quality facilities. Staff sometimes have a surly attitude.
Mustang Riding Stables 22947 - 132nd Avenue Maple Ridge, B.C. (604) 467-1875	Western	Western English	The personal touch. Facilities pretty basic but staff very helpful. Willing to transport horses up to Golden Ears Provincial Park
North Shore Equestrian Centre 1301 Lillooet North Vancouver, B.C. (604) 988-5131		Western English	No Rentals
Back in the Saddle Again 1-888-449-3264 (604) 534-3264 (604) 530-5673 FAX www.trailridesbc.com	Western	Western English	Trail rides and rentals. Access to 14 km of trails in adjacent Cambell Valley Park 5-Star facility
Riverside Equestrian Centre 13751 Garden City Richmond, B.C. (604) 271-4186		Western	No Rentals

Whale Watching

There are two kinds of whale watching in British Columbia: Orca watching through-out the summer months and Gray whale watching in spring and fall.

Orcas

Orca whales, also called Killer Whales, are actually the largest member of the dolphin family. Of the nearly 500 known orcas off the coast of British Columbia some 60% are members of resident pods and generally survive by following large schools of salmon and other fish. The other 200 or so orcas are known as *transients* and predate primarily on seals and other sea mammals.

Orca pods are organized along family lines with the eldest female orca dominating. Average pod size is from 5 to 20 individuals though pods of up to 45 orcas are not uncommon. A typical orca is just 2½ metres at birth and grows up to 8 metres for a mature cow, 10 metres for an adult bull. Cows live as long as 75 years while bulls are lucky to reach 50.

Gray Whales

Except for a few year-round residents, Gray whales, are usually seen migrating past the British Columbia coast on their way to the Bearing Sea in the spring or back south to coastal Mexico in the fall. The biannual march of these cetaceans is the longest migration of any mammal on earth. Grays are suspected of navigating by using the globe's magnetic field as a compass..

Baja California is the midwinter scene of both mating and calving. Since cows will carry their offspring for a full year mating occurs every other year. Without a suitable source of food in Mexico they begin their 8000 km northward trek as soon as these rituals are completed, living exclusively off thick deposits of blubber in the meantime. Every March and April some 18,000 members of the Pacific herd pass Vancouver Island's western shores in small family groupings. Swimming slowly but steadily these monsters can cover a mere 60-80 km per day.

Once they reach the Arctic Ocean and coast of Siberia the Grays gorge themselves on billions of tiny sandworms, sand fleas and other crustaceans which are sucked up from the sea floor in and filtered through the whales' baleen plates. Once the whales have replenished their reserves of blubber they begin yet again their southward swim, driven by the urgency of the calves growing within the pregnant cows.

From early May onwards whale watching excursions switch focus to the resident Gray whales which feed on the beaches of Clayoquot Sound. Transient orcas, seals, sea lions and harbour porpoises and the odd minke or humpback whale are often sighted as well.

While the fall migration reaches its peak off the coast of Vancouver Island in December whale watching tours are usually popular from September through to the end of October. Heavy winter weather and short daylight hours preclude a longer season.

Orca Watching: Northern Vancouver Island

By far the best place to view orcas is in the Johnstone Strait/Blackfish Sound area of northern Vancouver Island. Robson Bight, where orcas mysteriously congregate to rub against submerged rocks, is an especially important part of the northern residents' habitat and, as such, was formally protected in 1982 as an ecological reserve. This tiny portion of Johnstone Strait is therefore off-limits to humans.

On one occasion I witnessed from close quarters, two or three pods of orcas feasting on salmon in a narrow passageway between islands. On another occasion our boat was surrounded by a giant pod of some 200 Pacific White-Sided dolphins. On all sides the frisky creatures danced and dove, surfing in the bow wake, seeming to play tourist tag with the awestruck onlookers, zigging and zagging from port to starboard and back again.

In addition to orcas and dolphins, expect to see colonies of basking Harbour seals, porpoises, Stellar sea lions and maybe even a minke whale or two. Minkes are the smallest of the baleen whales.

Telegraph Cove, where most formal whale watching tours in the Johnstone Strait area begin, is not at all easy to get to. While most whale watchers drive, there are a couple alternatives. **Maverick Coach Lines** services Port McNeill on a twice daily basis. Be forewarned though: it's a gruelling nine hour slog. For those with money to burn it is possible to fly from Vancouver to Port Hardy via **Pacific Coastal Airlines**. From the airport Port Mcneill is a 90 minute taxi or limo ride. See **Getting "Up Island"** on page 331.

Upon reaching Port McNeill walk to the Alert Bay Ferry dock at the foot of the main drag and head immediately to Cormorant Island. [See schedule] Be prepared to discover a island steeped in 'Namgis history and tradition. The charms of Alert Bay far outweigh any advantages of staying in either Port McNeill or Telegraph Cove. The tiny fishing community of Alert Bay, population 691, boasts the world's tallest totem pole, a gigantic longhouse with colourful frontispiece, fascinating U'Mista Cultural Centre, an ecological preserve oddly called Gator Gardens, native burial grounds, a very photogenic chapel dating from the 19th century as well as ample opportunity to fish for salmon or watch for orcas.

Based in Alert Bay on Cormorant Island, **Seasmoke Tours** offers 5-hour whale watching tours from the deck of a 44-foot [18.3 m] sloop. Under ideal conditions this vessel

Alert Bay Ferry Schedule

Departing Alert Bay	Departing Port McNeill
7:00 am	8:40 am
9:25 am	10:10 am*
	11:10 am*
12:00	12:45 pm
	1:45 pm
3:00 pm	3:45 pm
5:30 pm*	5:45 pm
	7:15 pm
8:15 pm	9:15 pm
10:30 pm	

Sailing time : 40 minutes
Contact: (250) 956-4533
*Dangerous cargo run every 2nd Tuesday. No passengers; Call (250) 956-4533

with its teak and Honduran mahogany cabin, polished brass fittings and low profile would be perfect for checking out the sea mammals. The north coast, however, rarely boasts ideal conditions. Inclement weather is not uncommon even during the dog days of summer. The cabin cannot comfortably accommodate a full complement of 14 passengers so some customers must necessarily brave the elements for an extended period of time. Obviously the elderly and those with children would be less than satisfied with such arrangements. The crowded, sloping decks are also not really practical for serious photography either. On the other hand, Seasmoke Tours boasts a 90% plus success rate backed up with the offer of a free, second day of whale watching in the event that the elusive orcas cannot be located.

Alternately you can take a $20 foot passenger ferry, directly to Telegraph Cove. This historic boardwalk community is certainly worth visiting though camping here is not recommended. Unfortunately, the private campground operated by **Telegraph Cove Resorts** is perhaps the world's worst, obviously ripped out of the forest in a simple grab for money. Not only is it ugly but it is noisy with campsites cramped together to maximize profits. Bathrooms and showers are filthy. The only plus is the proximity to Telegraph Cove itself.

Whale watching tours in Telegraph Cove are operated by **Stubbs Island Charters** and depart from the main wharf in the tiny tourist community. Tours are conducted from one of two 60-foot sea craft capable of transporting 40 or more passengers. An optional lunch can be booked in advance for $8 but is pretty dull stuff. Bring your own.

All whale watching vessels are certified for passenger service by the Canadian Coast Guard. Additionally, most boats are equipped with hydrophones to eavesdrop on the underwater vocalizations of whales. Passengers on all whale watching tours are advised to bring extra warm clothing even on the hottest of days as weather on the north coast can change abruptly with little warning.

Most whale watching companies offer two tours a day. The second one is usually the best bet not least because it allows you to sleep in. Often much of the first tour is spent just locating the whales. By the time they have been found it may be time to return to port. Once they've been spotted there is enough local marine and air traffic to keep track of each pod's movements while loading customers for the second tour of the day.

Salmon and ground fishing charters are easily arranged in Port McNeill, Telegraph Cove or Alert Bay. Combining a

Orcas

Distinctive dorsal fins allow scientists to identify individuals in the field. Under scrutiny, unique personalities manifest themselves alongside species-wide traits. Should orcas be captured, put into cramped pools to perform circus tricks for the consuming masses? View these gentle giants on their own terms just once and you'll most likely agree they do not belong in jail. The lives of captive orcas are often woefully short.
Illustration by Manami Kimura

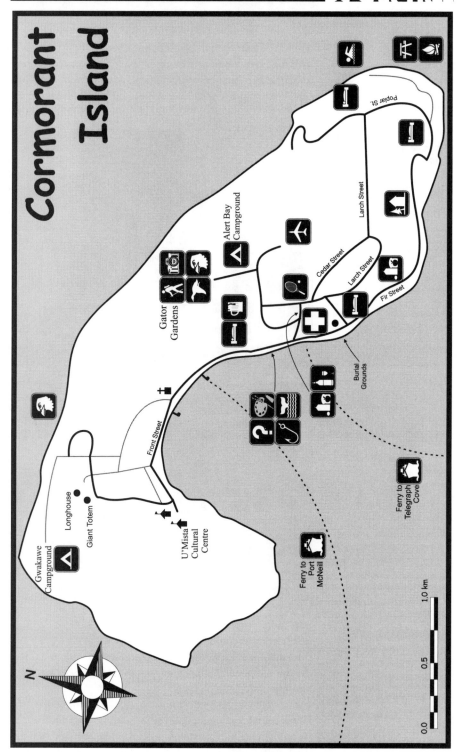

Cormorant Island

Gwakawe Campground

Longhouse

Giant Totem

U'Mista Cultural Centre

Front Street

Gator Gardens

Alert Bay Campground

Poplar St.

Larch Street

Cedar Street

Larch Street

Fir Street

Burial Grounds

Ferry to Port McNeill

Ferry to Telegraph Cove

N

0.0   0.5   1.0 km

day of fishing with whale watching is certainly a possibility and can even be a very cost-effective option if travelling in a group of four or more. Before booking a fishing charter be sure the boat is equipped with a good marine radio to zero in on the chit-chat between dedicated whale watching vessels. Your skipper should also have radar to follow the whales

Cormorant Island
Totems old and new stand sentinal over grave markers at historic Alert Bay. This one states:
*"Kla LiLiKla Ke
Died April 8 1928
Chief of the Nimpkish Tribe"*

*Nikon F
200 mm Nikkor lens
Kodachrome 64 ISO film*

into more open water even when the fog banks roll in. In addition to the contacts provided below ask at the local travel information center, your motel or campground or even at the dock to find a skipper willing to take you out on a private excursion.

For the truly adventurous a number of companies offer kayak rentals and guided kayaking adventures to Johnstone Strait. A multitude of steep-sided islands, fog, heavy maritime traffic and raging riptides makes doing it yourself ill-

advised for all but the most experienced paddlers.

Orca Watching Northern Vancouver Island
June - October

Location	Notes
Pacific Hostel Alert Bay, BC V0N 1A0 Tel: (250) 974-2026	$15 per night
Stubbs Island Whale Watching PO Box 2-2 Telegraph Cove, BC 1-800-665-3066 or (250) 928-3185 or (250) 928-3117 (250) 928-3102 Fax stubbs@island.net Website: www.stubbs-island.com	Orca Watching 4 Hr Motor Yacht Tours; $60; Max Passengers: 48 Lunch $8
Seasmoke Tours PO Box 483 Alert Bay, BC 1-800-668-6722 or (250) 974-5225 (250) 974-2266 Fax seaorca@island.net Website: www.seaorca.com	Orca Watching 5 Hr Sailing Yacht Tours; $80; Guaranteed sightings Max Passengers: 14
Starline Tours Port McNeil, BC 1-888-755-2233 or (250) 956-2233 starline@pinc.com Website: carver.pinc.com/~starline	Orca Watching 6 Hr Motor Yacht Tours $55 Max Passengers: 40
Sure Hit Charters & Tours; PO Box 587 Port McNeill, BC 1-888-817-3474 or (250) 956-3474 surehit@capescott.net Website: www.capescott.net/surehit	Personalized whale watching and fishing charters.
Headwind Charters PO Box 319, Alert Bay, BC 1-800-947-2032 or (250) 974-2032 headwind@island.net Website: www.alertbay.com/headwind	Personalized whale watching and fishing charters. $60/ per hour. 6 person maximum
Fish Hound Charters PO Box 1063 Port McNeill, BC (250) 956-2344	Personalized whale watching and fishing charters.
Magic Dragon Charter PO Box 410, Sointula, BC (250) 974-8080	Personalized whale watching and fishing charters. Hiking and caving tours available.
Viking West Charters Box 113 Port McNeill, BC (250) 956-3431 or (250) 956-3431 Fax vikingwest@capescott.net	Personalized whale watching, native heritage, diving and fishing charters. $80/ per hour. 12 person maximum. Zodiac charters $40 per hour.
Little Rock Kayaks & Adventures PO Box 479 Alert Bay, BC (250) 974-2221	Guided tours: $125/day Kayak rentals: $40/$65/$90 for 1/2/3 days
Cormorant Seakayaking PO Box 17 Sointula, BC (250) 973-6033 lulin@north.island.net Website: www.island.net/~lulin/	Kayak rentals: $40; $35 for additional days Also operates a B & B
Telegraph Cove Sea Kayaking Rentals 1-888-756-0099 or (250) 928-3030	Guided tours: $125/day Kayak rentals: $45/$80/$105 for 1/2/3 days
Foot Ferry Telegraph Cove - Alert Bay - Sointula 1-800-668-6722 or (250) 974-5225; (250) 974-2266 Fax seaorca@island.net Website: www.seaorca.com	$20 return Alert Bay to Telegraph Cove Service every two hours during high season from 8:30 am to 8:30 PM
Forty K Taxi Alert Bay, BC (250) 974-5525 or (250) 974-5464	Though Cormorant Island is small enough to walk everywhere taxi available if pressed for time or have too much stuff to carry.
Maverick Coachlines (604) 662-8051 Vancouver	Bus Service $71.65 one way $139.65 return, Departing 6 am and 10 am daily Returning 9:15 AM daily from Port McNeil
Pacific Coastal Airlines Vancouver, B.C. (604) 273-8666 or (604) 273-6864 Fax	Daily Flights to Port Hardy
Alert Bay Tourist Information Centre 118 Fir St. Alert Bay, BC (250) 974-5213 or (250) 974-5470 Fax	

Orca Watching: Victoria

Joining an orca watching tour in Victoria harbour on the southern tip of Vancouver Island is much easier than up island but the experience may be far less rewarding. With luck you may see a few orcas but chances are you'll only encounter seals and sea lions or a few small pods of porpoises or the occasional minke or Gray whale. With a company like **Seacoast Expeditions** from May 15 to September 15 it is possible to participate in a Guaranteed Killer Whale Sighting program. For an extra $5 participants who are available for more than one day are given a pager and are alerted when contact with orcas has been made. They must then scramble down to the dock to meet their tour boat and are then whisked off to sea. Chances are you'll then see a transient or two but not large feeding pods as on the north island tours.

If seeing orcas is your main objective, go north. If however you look on the tours out of Victoria as just an adventure and seeing orcas as a bonus then these tours are great value for the money [See below.] You'll be screaming over the ocean on small, open but very sea-worthy seven metre zodiacs with just 11 other passengers. In two or three hours you'll see excellent examples of west coast scenery, spot seals, sea lions and proud bald eagles. Dolphins and porpoises are likely to be encountered, minke and Gray whales are a possibility and orcas, well, they're a bonus. 🐾

Orca WatchingVictoria
April - October

Location	Service	Notes
Seacoast Expeditions Victoria Inner Harbour Oceane Pointe Resort 45 Songhees Road 1-800-386-1525 (250) 3832254 (250) 383-3834 FAX whales@seacoastexpeditions.com www.seacoastexpeditions.com	Orca Watching 3 Hr Zodiac Tours $79 adult $59 youth	Season: April - October Up to 5 tours daily during summer peak season. Access via Harbour Ferry in front of Empress Hotel Guarenteed Sighting option available
Ocean Explorations Victoria Inner Harbour 1-888-442-6722 (250) 383-6722 (250) 383-6749FAX www.oceanexplorations.com	Orca Watching 2 Hr Zodiac Tours 3 Hr Zodiac Tours	Season: April - October Up to 6 tours daily during summer peak season. Guarenteed Sighting option available
Great Pacific Adventures Victoria Inner Harbour 1-877-733-6722 (250) 386-2277 (250) 386-3370 FAX whales@greatpacificadventures.com greatpacificadventures.com	Orca Watching 2 Hr Zodiac Tours $55/35 3 Hr Zodiac Tours $75/45	Season: April - October Up to 8 tours daily during summer peak season.
Oak Bay Beach Hotel 1175 Beach Drive Victoria, B.C. 1-800-668-7758 (250) 592-3474 (250) 598- 6180 FAX sales@oakbaybeachhotel.bc.ca	Luxury Hotel with 46-passenger Motor Yacht Orca Watching Tours $79/adult $39/children	Season: March - October Seaside location Fishing & sightseeing cruises available English-style Pub.

Gray Whale Tours

Gray Whale watching usually takes place on the west coast of Vancouver Island in the Pacific Rim National Park area. Tours originate in either Tofino or Uclulet. The area is serviced by both bus and air from Vancouver. For details on **Getting to Tofino** see Appendix on page 329.

Ecotourism

A United Nations flotilla of sorts sets out from Tofino to view the migrating monsters. Ecotourists like these from Columbia, Mexico, Switzerland and Japan are an important, renewable source of pollution-free revenue for coastal communities formerly dependant on ripping a livelihood out of the forest and fisheries alone.

Nikon F
28 mm Nikkor lens
Kodacolor 100 ISO film

As with orca tours, Gray whale watching is done from either small, manoeuvrable zodiacs or larger motor yachts. As the Tofino area is exposed to the open Pacific, however, you may want to take seasickness pills prior to boarding just as a precaution. Large swells, originating off Japan, are carried across the ocean on the Japan Current to break like thunder on the BC coast. Wild northern weather can whip those swells up into frenzy.

A German tourist and the skipper of a zodiac from Jamie's Whaling Station were killed in 1998 when a freak wave broadsided the usually seaworthy craft. Some tours may be cancelled due to stormy conditions. Tour operators will usually explore more protected water when poor conditions prevail. Needless to say the chances of seeing the migrating behemoths is almost nil whenever this occurs. The protected inlets around Tofino offer a chance to spot resident Gray whales, orcas, dolphins and porpoises or scavenging wolves and bears on shore. Informed operators will also take the time to explain the various controversies surrounding the Clayoquot temporal rainforest.

No matter the weather conditions be sure to carry along some extra clothing including hat and gloves, jacket and extra sweater.

Though camping in Pacific Rim National Park is an ideal way to explore this part of the coast the weather can be uncooperative during prime whale watching season. A new shuttle service has been inaugurated to ferry people between the national park and Tofino or Uclulet. To avoid the commute, put up at a centrally located hotel like the Maquinna Lodge instead. Though not luxury accommodation, the Maquinna Lodge is comfortable and close to tours, grocer-

Lichens

Lichens are composite organisms made up of a fungus and an algae living in perfect symbiosis. The fungus provides algae habitat while the algae feeds the fungus. Hair lichens were processed into a winter staple by the indigenous peoples of western Canada. The "Old Man's Beard" was steamed in underground pits, mixed with berries then sun-dried to make yummy carbo-rich cakes that could be easily stored or carried.

Lichens are an essential winter food source for large mammals. One dimension of the old growth forest debate which we hear so much about is essentially over lichens. The organisms proliferate in ancient forests but not in young second growth. Deer and elk populations boom in logging clearcuts, thriving on pioneer species. Come winter, however, they find little food. Starvation and a weakening of the species ensues leading to an explosion of cougar populations. As the number of ungulates diminishes the predators look to nearby human habitat for sustenance: cats, dogs and children. Such marauding cougars are invariably slaughtered by wildlife officers though the unhappy situation is part of a dynamic authored by ourselves.

Nikon F
28 mm Nikkor lens
Ektachrome 100 ISO film

ies, restaurants, pubs and gift shops. Be prepared to entertain yourself in the evening hours however, as Tofino is hardly an urban centre by anybody's definition.

The five-star Canadian Princess Resort has put together an excellent, whale-watching package for the spring season only. As a bonus the cheapest accommodation is aboard the 70 metre long Canadian Princess which was built in 1932 and served as a survey vessel until 1975. Now it serves as the centrepiece of the Resort itself. While ship accommodation is somewhat more rustic than that on shore, all state-rooms have a sink and bunkbeds with shared bathrooms. Ship accommodations can be a bit noisy: creaking and groaning throughout the night. What, however, could be more in tune with the romance of high seas adventure than "roughing it" for a night on a charming old vessel? Shore-based accommodations are 2-4 person deluxe suites with private amenities.

Canadian Princess Resort customers receive a slight discount on bus transportation from Vancouver or Victoria and will be dropped off and picked up at the resort. 🐾

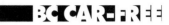

Gray Whale Watching Information

Location	Details
Remote Passages Central Tofino 1-800-666-9833 (250) 725-3330 (250) 725-3380 FAX webmaster@remotepassages.com www.remotepassages.com	3 Hr Zodiac Tours $59. 7 Hr Zodiac Tours $89 incl. stop at Hot Springs Cove. Pelagic bird watching tours also available. Maintains online Whale Report at website.
Jamie's Whaling Station 1-800-667-9913 (250) 725-3919 jamies@jamies.com www.jamies.com	2 Hr Zodiac $50; 2 Hr Motor Yacht Tours $70. Sightings guaranteed March to October or you go again free. Hot Spring tour also available $75. Bear watching tour also available May - Sept $59. Has offices in both Tofino & Ucluelet.
Chinook Charters 1-800-665-3646 (250) 725-3431	2 Hr Motor Yacht Tours $50. Fishing charters also available.
Subtidal Adventures 1950 Peninsula Rd. Ucluelet, BC 1-877-444-1134 (250) 726-7336 (250) 726-1292 chinook@cedar.alberni.net www.chinookcharters.com	3 Hr Zodiac or Motor Yacht Tours $35. Pelagic bird, humpback whale or Broken Islands nature watching tours also available.
Canadian Princess Resort Ucelet, B.C. 1-800-663-7090 (250) 598-3366	Fishing Resort with spring whale watching package. 3 Hr Whale-watching tour $39/$29 (Adult/Child.) Double/Triple /Quadruple Ship Stateroom -$49 /$59 /$69 Ship Stateroom Weekend Rate $10 off for weekdays. Fly-in fishing tours available.
Whalers on the Point Guesthouse 81 West Street, Tofino, BC (250) 725-3443 (250) 725-3463 FAX info@tofinohostel.com www.tofinohostel.com	Hostelling International Members $22/night. Guests enjoy substantial discounts with select local merchants and outfitters.
Vargas Island Inn and Hostel, Box 267, Tofino, BC VOR 2ZO (250) 725-3309	Accessible only by boat. Phone ahead for boat transport. 1910 Tudor-style Heritage House. Gorgeous Beach; Wilderness Hiking.
Maquinna Lodge 1-800-665-3199 (250) 725-3261	Inexpensive hotel accommodation. Pub; Resturant; Cold beer and wine store. Discount for whale watchers.
Pacific Rim National Park 1-800-689-9025	Camping at Green Point; 94 drive-in sites, 54 walk-in sites.
Tofino Taxi (250) 725-3333	Taxi Service, Shuttle to Park, Airport & Ferries.
Island Link 1-877-954-3556 (250) 726-7779 www.newshuttle.com	Shuttle between Tofino & Ucluelet to Long Beach and the Airport. Full schedule in Appendix.
North Vancouver Air Vancouver, B.C. 1-800-228-6608 (604) 278-1608 travelinfo@northvanair.com	$345 Return Full Fare; $250 Return Stand-By. Daily flight to Tofino/Uclulet . Full schedule in Appendix.
Maverick Coach Lines Vancouver Bus Terminal (604) 662-8051 (604) 255-1171	Leave Vancouver: 8:00 AM Daily Arrive Tofino 3:30 PM . Leave Tofino: 10:00 AM Arrive Vancouver 5:20 PM Daily. Leave Tofino: 4:00 PM Arrive Vancouver 11:20 PM Daily. $88.45 Round Trip.

Bird Watching

Of course the esoteric pursuit of bird watching can be undertaken in just about any corner of the province. There are, however, several major ornithological events that at-

Fuzzy Fella
The dying rays of the sun revealed this Saw Whet owl catching a few extra winks just prior to the night shift. Though not visible here, this little guy left a mouse hanging in a nearby branch, a post-nap snack no doubt. When looking for these elusive creatures peer up into the branches of a tree near the trunk. Most owls prefer dark, well-protected hollows from which to wait out the daylight hours. A flock of crows screaming at an unseen menace is a good clue that an owl has been spotted.

Though the acuity of owl eyesight is widly-know their hearing is even more impressive. Owls have developed three dimensional hearing. Natural selection has endowed these raptors with offset earholes: one hole is located noticably higher on the sides of their heads. So accurate indeed is their hearing that owls can snatch up a rodent in total darkness or even through a layer of snow. The curious behaviour owls sometimes exhibit of bobbing their heads around is, in reality, an attempt to focus their ears . By changing the position of their ears relative to the noise, owls can more precisely locate and identify the source of the sound.

Nikon F
300 mm Nikkor lens
Kodacolor 100 ISO film

tract a broader, more common curiosity. British Columbia is an important stop on the migratory flyways of numerous species including black brant geese on Vancouver Island, snow geese, snowy owls and sandpipers in the Fraser River Delta and Boundary Bay and bald eagles to a number of coastal British Columbia rivers. These cyclical events attract photographers and naturalists from all over the world.

For up-to-date information on birding phenomena such as the arrival of the snow geese or rare bird sightings contact:

Vancouver Bird Alert Hotline: (604) 737-3074
Website: www.birding.bc.ca
Sponsors: Vancouver Natural History Society and Wildbirds Unlimited

Snow Geese

Autumn is the season when the snow geese pass through the Fraser River Estuary. Over the course of one or two days in October wave after wave of the small white geese arrive – some 30,000 in all – in a spectacle that is sure to move even the thickest-skinned urbanite. The snow geese gener-

ally arrive in early October from Wrangel Island in the Aleutian Island chain and refuel by feasting on the buried stems of marsh plants. Many will continue on to California much like the human variety of "snow bird" though large flocks will winter over in the Lower Mainland, moving on to the Skagit River delta in Washington state in January. By February the northward migration begins again with B.C. as the final staging area before the flight back to Siberia. With daily new arrivals the numbers gradually build up until the whole gaggle takes flight, *en masse,* every April, drawn northwards yet again by the urge to procreate. In spite of their impressive presence, the snow goose has experienced a drastic decline in its numbers since the 1960s when an estimated 400,000 snow geese made the annual migration to the Arctic. Though staging a comeback through efforts of conservationists, the population today hovers at just a quarter of its former glory.

The George C. Reifel Migratory Bird Sanctuary located on Westham Island is the best place to view the snow geese.

Seizin' Quackers
At least a gaggle and a half reaches for the sky in unison when a bald eagle drops by for lunch. Taking advantage of the chaos, the eagle plucks a duck from a nearby pond instead.

Nikon F
300 mm Nikkor lens
Ektachrome 200 ISO film

Time your visit to the wildlife sanctuary, admission $3.25, to coincide with high tide, preferably in the early afternoon. As the water rises giant flocks of the snow geese will be forced away from the distant water's edge to fields more readily visible from the dikes of the refuge.

The white-phase Lesser Snow Geese of the Fraser River Estuary are small by goose standards, weighing in at just

Aerobatics

Incoming snow geese signal their approval of the landing zone with a synchronized roll. Consensus reached, the raucous lot on the ground directs their airborne cousins in.

Nikon F
300 mm Nikkor lens
Kodachrome 200 ISO film

2½ kg. Typically, their black-tipped wings stretch a mere 90 cm. Though the plumage of adult snow geese is white note the rusty red colouring of their faces and heads, permanently stained from mucking about in iron-oxide rich soil after edible roots. Like most of their kind, snow geese are a gregarious, raucous lot with those on the ground imploring, with high-pitched honks, those swirling overhead to join them. From time to time, a marauding eagle may force the entire flock into the air in a cacophony of whistling wings and startled goose chatter. Be sure to be in prime goose-viewing position as day turns to dusk since the snow geese will take flight once again as they return to the sea for protection overnight.

November is officially Snow Goose Month at the bird sanctuary but, as an added bonus, mid-November happens to coincide with the return of trumpeter swans as well. Watch for these larger birds in smaller flocks. Though also white, they can be easily distinguished on the wing by longer necks, slimmer bodies and an absence of black wing tips. The world's largest concentrations of trumpeter swans will be found here.

Numerous other species call Reifel refuge home as well. Blinds and viewing platforms have been erected to enhance the viewing experience while minimizing the impact of human presence on indigenous wildlife. On weekends, volunteers will scour the habitat for anomalous wildlife, setting up a spotting scope and providing interpretation to visitors whenever they encounter something of interest. Expect to see hunting hawks, roosting saw-whet owls in addition to the more pedestrian variety of waterfowl.

The George C. Reifel Migratory Bird Sanctuary is unfortunately not serviced directly by Translink. The **#601 South Delta** bus, operating on half-hour intervals, will deliver you to within 7 km of the wildlife refuge. The **#601 South Delta** originates adjacent to the Burrard Street SkyTrain Station in downtown Vancouver. Get off the bus at

Hey Pumpkin Head!
Any October visit to Reifel Refuge is sure to be greeted by the powerful potentate of pumpkins, pictured here at Westham Island Herb Farm [4690 Kirkland Road.] In step with the season the farm annually features whimsical pumpkin and harvest displays, u-pick pumpkins, a haunted greenhouse, herbs and jams for sale and, each evening during the final two weeks prior to Halloween, over 150 carved and lighted pumpkins.
Bicycles are an ideal way to explore rural Westham Island. Fortunately the #601 South Delta bus is equipped with bike racks. From Ladner Exchange make a left then follow Harvest Drive south, continuing west along 44th Avenue. Continue westward until reaching River Road. Swing left and follow the river until a sign for George C. Reifel Migratory Bird Sanctuary directs you across the bridge to Westham Island. Stay with the main road as it twists and turns through the pumpkin dotted landscape to reach the wildlife refuge.

Nikon F
28 mm Nikkor lens
Kodachrome 200 ISO film

Ladner Exchange some 45 minutes later and, if feeling rich, grab a cab at the taxi stand or transfer to the **#606** or **#608 Ladner Ring** bus to wheel a further 1½ km closer to your destination. The **Ladner Ring** bus operates only during peak hours Monday through Saturday. Disembark at the corner of River Road and 46A Street fully prepared to cover the final 5½ km to the George C. Reifel Migratory Bird Sanctuary on foot. Given that the route cuts across the pleasant rural landscape of Westham Island, serious consideration should be given to hiking particularly for those looking for photo opportunities. Sunshine and pumpkins is one obvious subject which should present itself every autumn. After getting off the bus walk westward along River Road until Westham Island Road. Turn right and cross the one-lane Canoe Pass Bridge, following the road to its end at the bird sanctuary.

Taxis should be waiting at Ladner Exchange and should cost around $15, cost-effective if travelling in a group of four or five. Contact Delta Sunshine Taxi by phone at (604) 594-5444 or (604) 592-0111. Pay phones are available at both Ladner Exchange and the George C. Reifel Migratory Bird Sanctuary. Hitchhiking back to Translink territory is another alternative, keeping the usual safety caveats in mind.🐾

Snowy Owls

Access: See Getting to Boundary Bay below.

Bald Eagles, red-tailed hawks, harriers, long-eared owls, short-eared owls and their prey are a common sight from the dikes of Boundary Bay in any season. In fact this is truly raptor heaven. Particularly harsh arctic winters however drive the massive Snowy Owl south and west in search of alternative food supplies. Many of these itinerant *ookpiks* end up in Boundary Bay feasting on fowl rather than their customary lemming diet. As you continue walking along the dikes 1½ km northward from the park entrance you'll notice a collection of greenhouses at the foot of 64th Street. On a good day careful scrutiny of the structures around the farm here may reveal as many as a couple dozen of the fluffy white raptors.

Female Snowy Owls are generally larger with more brown-dappled colouring to blend in with their arctic tundra nesting sites. Nesting females exclusively incubate the eggs and guard and tend the chicks while the males concentrate on providing meat for the mother and hatchlings.

Depending on the severity of northern and inland weather, the season for viewing Snowy Owls typically extends from November to February though very few *ookpiks* may reach the coast during particularly balmy winters.

The hawks, harriers and short-eared owls will usually be quite active, patrolling the marsh lands on the ocean side of the dike for ripe rodent. Along the ditches on the opposite side of the dike scan for long-eared owls roosting in the shadows of bushes and trees. If quiet, you can expect to get as close as 2 metres to these slumbering guys. Photographers will want to use a flash with telephoto attachment. 🐾

Getting to Boundary Bay

Getting to Boundary Bay is as easy as hopping the **#601 South Delta** bus at Burrard Skytrain Station. The bus runs every half hour [hourly weekends before 11 am] and, during peak hours, crosses three zones and takes about an hour. The bus stops momentarily at Ladner Exchange but you won't need to transfer. Jump off at the corner of 56th Street and 16th Avenue instead, cross the busy main street and continue walking east along 16th for 20 minutes or so until you reach Beach Grove Road. Take a left and you'll find the GVRD Park one block ahead. The trees on your left as you enter the park are a favourite perching place for Bald Eagles. The **#601 Vancouver** bus will return you to where you started in reverse *déja vu*.

Most bird watching is done from the dikes though at high tide the beach will afford better views of feeding shorebirds. At low tide exploring the extensive mud flats of Boundary Bay is not recommended. Quicksand and in-rushing tides can be perilous. Becoming stranded far from shore is a very real possibility. The best time to see active feeding, particularly from owls, is from late afternoon on to dusk. 🐾

Sandpipers

Access: See Getting to Boundary Bay below left.

The passage of the snow geese coincides with the arrival of migrating western sandpipers. During April and May each spring half a million of the Alaska-bound shorebirds

Great Blue Heron
Sporting long, wispy plumage on the crown, breast and back, this Great Blue Heron is all gussied up for the spring breeding season. The fish and frog breath and croaking monotone are an added attraction. Any takers?

Nikon F
300 mm Nikkor lens
Plus-X Pan 125 ISO film

pass through the Fraser delta and Boundary Bay pausing for just three days to refuel on intertidal zone invertebrates. Breeding and rearing in the glow of the midnight sun is a brief affair with most adults returning to the Lower Mainland from June to mid-July. Juveniles are abandoned after a relatively brief period of parental care and remain behind to fatten and strengthen until late in the summer, passing through the Pacific Northwest in August and September on their way to points as far south as coastal Peru and Chile. 🐾

Bald Eagles

Relatively large winter runs of spawning chum and, every other year, pink salmon in a number of coastal B.C. rivers attract nearly half of all of North America's bald eagles. Each winter B.C.'s resident population of some 12,000 of

Snapshot
Serious photographers will want to bring their longest lenses to shoot the Brackendale Eagles. Even with a 1100 mm mirror lens I had to use a 2X extender to reveal sufficient detail. With direct sunlight and fast 400 iso film I still had to reduce my shutter speed to one fifteenth of a second.
On warm days the eagles are more active. Try panning with a medium telephoto as they cruise by low overhead, as right. If you have one bring your polarizing filter too in case you need to cut past the surface glare of the river.

Nikon F
135 mm Nikkor lens
Kodak 5247 Movie Film 80 ISO

the once endangered raptors swells to over 30,000 with birds drawn from Alaska, the Yukon, Alberta and as far away as Wyoming and Arizona. The Squamish River, halfway between Vancouver and Whistler, is particularly bountiful and has attracted as many as 3,766 of these normally solitary birds in one season.

Eagles begin flocking in as early as November each year and lingering on until the following February. From late December to early January the transient eagle population reaches its peak, making the holiday season an ideal time to visit. A high point of this natural wonder is the **Annual Eagle Census** which takes place on January 15 each year. Volunteers are always needed for this chore so it's a good chance to get involved, meet others who share a love of and fascination with nature and be part of an important event.

Getting There

The cheapest, easiest way to simply get a glimpse of this marvel is to take the **BC Rail** passenger train or the **Maverick Coach Lines** bus connection to Squamish. Once you

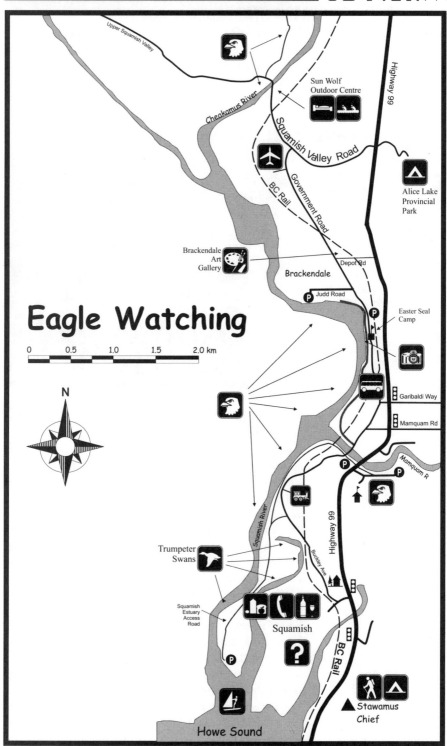

Eagle Watching

Upper Squamish Valley

Cheakamus River

Sun Wolf Outdoor Centre

Squamish Valley Road

Highway 99

Government Road

BC Rail

Alice Lake Provincial Park

Brackendale Art Gallery

Brackendale

Depot Rd

Judd Road

Easter Seal Camp

Garibaldi Way

Mamquam Rd

Mamquam R

0   0.5   1.0   1.5   2.0 km

N

Squamish River

Trumpeter Swans

Highway 99

Buckley Ave

Squamish Estuary Access Road

Squamish

Stawamus Chief

BC Rail

Howe Sound

arrive be prepared to walk [See map.]

If you arrive by rail follow Buckley Avenue south for a half kilometre or so until you reach the first right. Take it and immediately on your right you'll see the high dikes which flank the Squamish River. Clamber up on the banks and, if you haven't seen any eagles yet, you should begin

Squamish for the Squeemish
Though hardly rip-roaring whitewater, the wintertime face of the Squamish River reveals the intricate web of life. The very survival of many species including eagles and seagulls , mink, marten and coyotes depends on the timely demise of spawning salmon. A float tour reveals many parts of the Squamish River that would be otherwise inaccessible on foot.

Nikon F
300 mm Nikkor lens
Ektachrome 200 ISO film

spotting them directly across the river. These few stragglers are nothing: the best is yet to come. Continue following the river upstream, crossing the mouth of the Mamquam River via the Government Road bridge, not the railway bridge. Whenever crossing railway tracks here use extreme caution as the crossing is not controlled and speeding freight trains are frequent along the busy BC Rail tracks. From the Government Road bridge peer into the crystal clear water to spot spawning salmon early in the season or their spent carcasses later on. Decay is slow in the icy water so eagles and other scavengers will continue feeding on them well into February. From the bridge stay with the dike following the Mamquam River downstream past the local animal shelter and sewage treatment plant. Near the end of the dike trail you'll reach Eagle Run where the largest number of Eagles are concentrated.

If you arrive by bus simply take Government Road north for less than a kilometre. As soon as you see the dikes on your left you have reached Eagle Run. The main viewing area is directly across from Easter Seal Camp Squamish.

If you are arriving by car pool you'll want to turn off the Sea to Sky Highway 99 at the Squamish McDonald's. Almost immediately on your right you'll find Buckley Avenue. Turn here and continue north until the first set of railway tracks. If you take a sharp left here you may see the trumpeter swans which make Squamish Estuary their home. Since swans are not our main objective you'll probably want to continue along Buckley Road until you reach Eagle Run in front of Easter Seal Camp Squamish.

Of Eagles and Men

Photo opportunities abound here. Not only are the eagles themselves a majestic subject but the spawning salmon and their spent carcasses provide a bittersweet foil to the elegy of survival, of renewal acted out each winter on the banks of the Squamish. Keep in mind that by as early as noon in the dead of winter the eagles perched in the trees across the river will be in the shadows. An early start is recommended.

Depending on the weather and the time of winter most eagles may be inactive, conserving their energy in an effort to survive the long cold winter. You may note the pecking order of eagle society among those actively feeding. Juveniles, those without the distinctive white head of the Bald Eagle, will defer to their seniors, waiting impatiently as the elder birds feast on carrion.

Later in the season as food becomes scarcer, watch as eagles rely on sea gulls to pull salmon carcasses up from the depths of the river. The giant raptors will then swoop in, commandeering the yummy victuals for themselves. You are sure to catch a whiff reminiscent of cod liver oil as the birds tear at the decaying flesh.

A word of warning: never approach too closely to the eagles or disturb them in any way. Winter is a difficult time for these birds and flying uses up crucial energy reserves. If distressed too often eagles may not survive winter's torments.

Package Tours

A unique way to see the wintering bald eagles is to join a float tour. These river rafting packages [see table below] are reasonably priced and allow participants the opportunity to see parts of the Squamish River not normally accessible to road-bound naturalists. Tours are generally interpretative though the knowledge of guides and quality of the information varies somewhat. Usually you can arrange to be picked up at the railway or bus station prior to the tour. Don't expect a raging, whitewater experience, however. Water levels are quite low in all rivers throughout winter so you can expect rafting to be a serene, slow-paced experience emphasising harmony.

In addition to river rafting, the **Sun Wolf Outdoor Centre** has ten rustic riverside cabins, fireplace-equipped, for those who would like to combine eagle viewing with a romantic overnight getaway.

Nature Venture Tours solves the transportation problem by including van pick up and drop off in Vancouver. Their *Eagles of the Pacific* package emphasises nature interpretation, a great way to learn about eagles while seeing them in their natural habitat.

Squamish Eagle Watching

Location	Notes
Sun Wolf Outdoor Centre 70002 Squamish Valley Rd Brackendale, BC 1-877-806-8046 (604) 898-1537 sunwolf@sunwolf.net	Eagle Float Rafting Tours $79 Historic 1930's fishing lodge has ten cabins with fireplaces Call for Squamish pick up
The River League 805 W 18th Avenue 1-800-440-1322 (604) 687-3417 (604) 687-3413FAX iankean@riverleague.ca www.riverleague.ca	Rafting: Weekdays $39 Rafting: Weekend $59
Annual Eagle Festival Brackendale Art Gallery (604) 898-3333 gallery@mountain-inter.net	Numerous events, special guests, annual eagle count, refreshments, eagle displays & information Free
Maverick Coach Lines Vancouver Bus Terminal (604) 662-8051	For schedule information see getting to Whistler on page 335
BC Rail Passenger Station 1311 West 1st Street North Vancouver (604) 984-5246	For schedule information see getting to Whistler on page 335
Squamish Hostel 38490 Buckley Avenue 1-800-449-8614 (604) 892-9240 (604) 815-0041Fax hostel@mountain-inter.net	Popular with rock and ice climbers, and windsurfers from all over the world
Rare Bird Hotline (604) 737-3074 www.birding.bc.ca	Vancouver Natural History Society Recorded information about recent rare bird sighitigs.

Brant Festival

The first weekend of April is a rite of spring for the folks who live on the mid-coast of Vancouver Island. As early as February small flocks of Pacific Black Brant Geese begin returning to the Parksville and Qualicum Beach areas. [See **Getting "Up Island"** on page 331.] By mid-March the annual "sea goose" migration is in full swing, peaking a month later in the middle of April. By the time it is over in mid-May some 20,000 of the small geese will have passed through, stopping to rest up and feed on eelgrass, green algae and herring roe before continuing their northward journey.

Wintering in Baja California and adjacent mainland Mexico, the brant follow the coast northward until reaching British Columbia. As the Pacific coast north of Vancouver Island is rugged and rocky most brant wing towards the northwest from this last staging area to begin the transoceanic flight to breeding grounds in Siberia, Alaska and the Canadian Arctic. Altogether this three month journey covers more than 10,000 kilometres. Interestingly the southward migration in the fall follows a more direct route across the open Pacific. Only in the spring do the Brant grace the British Columbia coast with their presence.

To celebrate this annual return local businesses and naturalists have inaugurated the Brant Festival. Brant viewing areas have been established at Rathtrevor and Qualicum Beaches with telescopes and nature interpretation provided. Peripheral events include art shows, photo exhibitions, a wood carving contest, craft fair, Native Indian-style salmon barbecue, Native dance displays, special children's events and environmental displays.

To be completely honest, unless you are a bird watching fanatic, the Brant Festival is neither awesome nor profound. It is, however, interesting. To make a trip to Vancouver Island simply for this event may be disappointing to some. Coupled with a cycling weekend or a trip to the Pacific Rim area, the Brant Festival could provide a more than satisfying glimpse of one of nature's marvels. 🐾

Brant Festival
Parksville-Qualicum Beach: First Weekend in April

Location	Services
Mid Island Wildlife Watch Parksville, BC (250) 248-4117	Birding and other wildlife information
Brant Wildlife Festival Box 327 Parksville, B.C. CANADA V9P 2G5 (250) 752-9171; (250) 752-2766 FAX www.island.net/~bfest	Brant Fetival Informatioin Festival dates and events and prices Event registration recommended
Visitor Info Centre Parksville, BC (250) 248-3613	General travel and accommodation information
Island Link 1-877-954-3556; (250) 954-3556 www.newshuttle.com	Shuttle between Nanaimo & Qualicum Beach Full schedule in Appendix.
Visitor Info Centre Qualicum Beach, BC (250) 752-9532	General travel and accommodation information
Rathtrevor Beach Parksville, BC (250) 689-9025	Beachside Provincial Park & Campground 174 Campsites. Advance reservations recommended in April.

BC Birding Checklist

Loons
- ❑ Red-throated Loon
- ❑ Pacific Loon
- ❑ Common Loon
- ❑ Yellow-billed Loon

Grebes
- ❑ Pied-billed Grebe
- ❑ Horned Grebe
- ❑ Red-necked Grebe
- ❑ Eared Grebe
- ❑ Western Grebe
- ❑ Clark's Grebe

Alcids
- ❑ Common Murre
- ❑ Thick-billed Murre
- ❑ Pigeon Guillemot
- ❑ Marbled Murrelet
- ❑ Kittlitz's Murrelet
- ❑ Xantus's Murrelet
- ❑ Ancient Murrelet
- ❑ Cassin's Auklet
- ❑ Parakeet Auklet
- ❑ Crested Auklet
- ❑ Rhinoceros Auklet
- ❑ Tufted Puffin
- ❑ Horned Puffin

Tubenoses
- ❑ Black-footed Albatross
- ❑ Laysan Albatross
- ❑ Short-tailed Albatross
- ❑ Northern Fulmar
- ❑ Mottled Petrel
- ❑ Pink-footed Shearwater
- ❑ Manx Shearwater
- ❑ Flesh-footed Shearwater
- ❑ Buller's Shearwater
- ❑ Sooty Shearwater
- ❑ Short-tailed Shearwater
- ❑ Black-vented Shearwater
- ❑ Fork-tailed Storm-Petrel
- ❑ Leach's Storm-Petrel
- ❑ Red-tailed Tropicbird
- ❑ Magnificent Frigatebird

Pelicans & Cormorants
- ❑ American White Pelican
- ❑ Brown Pelican
- ❑ Brandt's Cormorant
- ❑ Double-crested Cormorant
- ❑ Red-faced Cormorant
- ❑ Pelagic Cormorant

Jaegers & Skuas
- ❑ South Polar Skua
- ❑ Great Skua
- ❑ Pomarine Jaeger
- ❑ Parasitic Jaeger

- ❑ Long-tailed Jaeger

Gulls & Terns
- ❑ Heermann's Gull
- ❑ Franklin's Gull
- ❑ Little Gull
- ❑ Black-headed Gull
- ❑ Bonaparte's Gull
- ❑ Mew Gull
- ❑ Ring-billed Gull
- ❑ California Gull
- ❑ Herring Gull
- ❑ Thayer's Gull
- ❑ Iceland Gull
- ❑ Lesser Black-backed Gull
- ❑ Slaty-backed Gull
- ❑ Western Gull
- ❑ Glaucous-winged Gull
- ❑ Glaucous Gull
- ❑ Great Black-backed Gull
- ❑ Sabine's Gull
- ❑ Black-legged Kittiwake
- ❑ Red-legged Kittiwake
- ❑ Ross's Gull
- ❑ Ivory Gull
- ❑ Caspian Tern
- ❑ Elegant Tern
- ❑ Common Tern
- ❑ Arctic Tern
- ❑ Forster's Tern
- ❑ Aleutian Tern
- ❑ Least Tern
- ❑ Black Tern

Herons & Allies
- ❑ American Bittern
- ❑ Least Bittern
- ❑ Great Blue Heron
- ❑ Little Blue Heron
- ❑ Green Heron
- ❑ Black-crowned Night-Heron
- ❑ Great Egret
- ❑ Snowy Egret
- ❑ Cattle Egret
- ❑ White-faced Ibis
- ❑ Wood Stork

Waterfowl
- ❑ Fulvous Whistling-Duck
- ❑ Great White-fronted Goose
- ❑ Emperor Goose
- ❑ Snow Goose
- ❑ Ross's Goose
- ❑ Canada Goose
- ❑ Black Brant
- ❑ Mute Swan
- ❑ Trumpeter Swan
- ❑ Tundra Swan
- ❑ Whooper Swan
- ❑ Wood Duck

- ❑ Gadwall
- ❑ Falcated Duck
- ❑ Eurasian Wigeon
- ❑ American Wigeon
- ❑ American Black Duck
- ❑ Mallard
- ❑ Blue-winged Teal
- ❑ Cinnamon Teal
- ❑ Northern Shoveler
- ❑ Northern Pintail
- ❑ Garganey
- ❑ Baikal Teal
- ❑ Green-winged Teal
- ❑ Canvasback
- ❑ Redhead
- ❑ Ring-necked Duck
- ❑ Tufted Duck
- ❑ Ruddy Duck
- ❑ Greater Scaup
- ❑ Lesser Scaup
- ❑ Steller's Eider
- ❑ Spectacled Eider
- ❑ King Eider
- ❑ Common Eider
- ❑ Harlequin Duck
- ❑ Surf Scoter
- ❑ White-winged Scoter
- ❑ Black Scoter
- ❑ Oldsquaw
- ❑ Bufflehead
- ❑ Barrow's Goldeneye
- ❑ Common Goldeneye
- ❑ Smew
- ❑ Hooded Merganser
- ❑ Red-breasted Merganser
- ❑ Common Merganser

Cranes & Allies
- ❑ Yellow Rail
- ❑ Virginia Rail
- ❑ Sora
- ❑ Common Moorhen
- ❑ American Coot
- ❑ Sandhill Crane
- ❑ Whooping Crane

Shorebirds
- ❑ Black-bellied Plover
- ❑ Lesser Golden-Plover
- ❑ Mongolian Plover
- ❑ Snowy Plover
- ❑ Semipalmated Plover
- ❑ Killdeer
- ❑ Black Oystercatcher
- ❑ Black-necked Stilt
- ❑ American Avocet
- ❑ Greater Yellowlegs
- ❑ Lesser Yellowlegs
- ❑ Spotted Redshank
- ❑ Wood Sandpiper

Solitary Sandpiper
Willet
Wandering Tattler
Spotted Sandpiper
Terek Sandpiper
Upland Sandpiper
Whimbrel
Bristle-thighed Curlew
Far Eastern Curlew
Long-billed Curlew
Hudsonian Godwit
Bar-tailed Godwit
Marbled Godwit
Ruddy Turnstone
Black Turnstone
Surfbird
Red Knot
Sanderling
Semipalmated Sandpiper
Western Sandpiper
Red-necked Stint
Little Stint
Temminck's Stint
Least Sandpiper
White-rumped Sandpiper
Baird's Sandpiper
Pectoral Sandpiper
Sharp-tailed Sandpiper
Rock Sandpiper
Dunlin
Curlew Sandpiper
Stilt Sandpiper
Spoonbill Sandpiper
Buff-breasted Sandpiper
Ruff
Short-billed Dowitcher
Long-billed Dowitcher
Common Snipe
Wilson's Phalarope
Red-necked Phalarope
Red Phalarope

Vulture, Hawks & Falcons
Black Vulture
Turkey Vulture
Osprey
Bald Eagle
Golden Eagle
White-tailed Kite
Crested Caracara (1)
Northern Harrier
Sharp-shinned Hawk
Cooper's Hawk
Northern Goshawk
Broad-winged Hawk
Swainson's Hawk
Red-tailed Hawk
Ferruginous Hawk
Rough-legged Hawk
Eurasian Kestrel
American Kestrel
Merlin
Gyrfalcon

Peregrine Falcon
Prairie Falcon

Owls
Barn Owl
Flammulated Owl
Western Screech-Owl
Great Horned Owl
Snowy Owl
Northern Hawk Owl
Northern Pygmy-Owl
Burrowing Owl
Spotted Owl
Barred Owl
Great Gray Owl
Long-eared Owl
Short-eared Owl
Boreal Owl
Northern Saw-whet Owl

Goatsuckers
Common Nighthawk
Common Poorwill

Gallinaceous Birds
Chukar
Gray Partridge
Ring-necked Pheasant
Blue Grouse
Willow Ptarmigan
Rock Ptarmigan
White-tailed Ptarmigan
Ruffed Grouse
Spruce Grouse
Sage Grouse
Sharp-tailed Grouse
Wild Turkey
Mountain Quail
California Quail
Northern Bobwhite

Pigeons & Doves
Rock Dove
Band-tailed Pigeon
Oriental Turtle-Dove
White-winged Dove
Mourning Dove

Cuckos
Black-billed Cuckoo
Yellow-billed Cuckoo

Kingfishers
Belted Kingfisher

Woodpeckers
Pileated Woodpecker
Common Flicker
Lewis's Woodpecker
Red-headed Woodpecker
Yellow-bellied Sapsucker
Red-naped Sapsucker
Red-breasted Sapsucker

Williamson's Sapsucker
Downy Woodpecker
Hairy Woodpecker
White-headed Woodpecker
Three-toed Woodpecker
Black-backed Woodpecker

Hummingbirds & Swifts
Rufous Hummingbird
Anna's Hummingbird
Ruby-throated Hummingbird
Black-chinned Hummingbird
Calliope Hummingbird
Costa's Hummingbird
Xantus's Hummingbird
Black Swift
Vaux's Swift
White-throated Swift

Shrikes & Swallows
Northern Shrike
Loggerhead Shrike
Purple Martin
Tree Swallow
Violet-green Swallow
Northern Rough-winged Swallow
Bank Swallow
Cliff Swallow
Barn Swallow

Flycatchers
Western Kingbird
Eastern Kingbird
Tropical Kingbird
Thick-billed Kingbird
Scissor-tailed Flycatcher
Ash-throated Flycatcher
Brown-crested Flycatcher
Olive-sided Flycatcher
Western Wood-Pewee
Black Phoebe
Eastern Phoebe
Say's Phoebe
Western Flycatcher
Cordilleran Flycatcher
Hammond's Flycatcher
Dusky Flycatcher
Willow Flycatcher
Alder Flycatcher
Acadian Flycatcher
Least Flycatcher
Gray Flycatcher
Yellow-bellied Flycatcher

Vireos
Solitary Vireo
Hutton's Vireo
Warbling Vireo
Red-eyed Vireo
Philadelphia Vireo

Crows & Jays
- [ ] Gray Jay (Whisky Jack)
- [ ] Steller's Jay
- [ ] Blue Jay
- [ ] Western Scrub-Jay
- [ ] Clark's Nutcracker
- [ ] American Crow
- [ ] Northwestern Crow
- [ ] Common Raven
- [ ] Black-billed Magpie

Larks
- [ ] Horned Lark
- [ ] Eurasian Skylark

Chickadees & Titmice
- [ ] Black-capped Chickadee
- [ ] Chestnut-backed Chickadee
- [ ] Mountain Chickadee
- [ ] Boreal Chickadee
- [ ] Bushtit

Nuthatches & Creepers
- [ ] Red-breasted Nuthatch
- [ ] White-breasted Nuthatch
- [ ] Pygmy Nuthatch
- [ ] Brown Creeper

Wrens
- [ ] Rock Wren
- [ ] Canyon Wren
- [ ] Bewick's Wren
- [ ] House Wren
- [ ] Winter Wren
- [ ] Marsh Wren

Dippers
- [ ] American Dipper

Gnatcatchers & Kinglets
- [ ] Blue-gray Gnatcatcher
- [ ] Golden-crowned Kinglet
- [ ] Ruby-crowned Kinglet

Bluebirds & Thrush
- [ ] Western Bluebird
- [ ] Mountain Bluebird
- [ ] Townsend's Solitaire
- [ ] Veery
- [ ] Gray-cheeked Thrush
- [ ] Swainson's Thrush
- [ ] Hermit Thrush
- [ ] Eyebrowed Thrush
- [ ] Dusky Thrush
- [ ] American Robin
- [ ] Varied Thrush
- [ ] Northern Wheatear
- [ ] Gray Catbird
- [ ] Northern Mockingbird
- [ ] Sage Thrasher
- [ ] Brown Thrasher
- [ ] European Starling
- [ ] Crested Myna

- [ ] Water Pipit
- [ ] Red-throated Pipit
- [ ] Sprague's Pipit
- [ ] Yellow Wagtail
- [ ] Black-backed Wagtail
- [ ] Bohemian Waxwing
- [ ] Cedar Waxwing

Warbler
- [ ] Tennessee Warbler
- [ ] Orange-crowned Warbler
- [ ] Nashville Warbler
- [ ] Northern Parula
- [ ] Yellow Warbler
- [ ] Chestnut-sided Warbler
- [ ] Magnolia Warbler
- [ ] Cape May Warbler
- [ ] Black-throated Blue Warbler
- [ ] Yellow-rumped Warbler
- [ ] Black-throated Gray Warbler
- [ ] Townsend's Warbler
- [ ] Black-throat Green Warbler
- [ ] Yellow-throated Warbler
- [ ] Blackburnian Warbler
- [ ] Palm Warbler
- [ ] Bay-breasted Warbler
- [ ] Blackpoll Warbler
- [ ] Black-and-white Warbler
- [ ] American Redstart
- [ ] Ovenbird
- [ ] Northern Waterthrush
- [ ] Connecticut Warbler
- [ ] Mourning Warbler
- [ ] MacGillivray's Warbler
- [ ] Common Yellowthroat
- [ ] Hooded Warbler
- [ ] Wilson's Warbler
- [ ] Canada Warbler
- [ ] Painted Redstart
- [ ] Yellow-breasted Chat

Tanagers
- [ ] Western Tanager
- [ ] Scarlet Tanager

Sparrows
- [ ] Brown Towhee
- [ ] Rufous-sided Towhee
- [ ] Green-tailed Towhee
- [ ] House Sparrow
- [ ] Eurasian Tree Sparrow
- [ ] Song Sparrow
- [ ] Fox Sparrow
- [ ] Savannah Sparrow
- [ ] Lincoln's Sparrow
- [ ] American Tree Sparrow
- [ ] Chipping Sparrow
- [ ] Clay-coloured Sparrow
- [ ] Brewer's Sparrow
- [ ] Vesper Sparrow
- [ ] Lark Sparrow
- [ ] Black-throated Sparrow
- [ ] Sage Sparrow

- [ ] Lark Bunting
- [ ] Baird's Sparrow
- [ ] Grasshopper Sparrow
- [ ] Le Conte's Sparrow
- [ ] Nelson's Sharp-tail Sparrow
- [ ] Swamp Sparrow
- [ ] White-throated Sparrow
- [ ] Harris's Sparrow
- [ ] White-crowned Sparrow
- [ ] Golden-crowned Sparrow
- [ ] Dark-eyed Junco

Finches, Grosbeaks & Buntings
- [ ] Lapland Longspur
- [ ] McCown's Longspur
- [ ] Smith's Longspur
- [ ] Chestnut-collared Longspur
- [ ] Rustic Bunting
- [ ] Snow Bunting
- [ ] McKay's Bunting
- [ ] Rose-breasted Grosbeak
- [ ] Black-headed Grosbeak
- [ ] Evening Grosbeak
- [ ] Pine Grosbeak
- [ ] Lazuli Bunting
- [ ] Indig Bunting
- [ ] House Finch
- [ ] Purple Finch
- [ ] Cassin's Finch
- [ ] Gray-crowned Rosy-Finch
- [ ] Brambling
- [ ] Common Redpoll
- [ ] Hoary Redpoll
- [ ] Red Crossbill
- [ ] White-winged Crossbill
- [ ] Dickcissel
- [ ] Pine Siskin
- [ ] American Goldfinch
- [ ] Lesser Goldfinch

Blackbirds & Orioles
- [ ] Bobolink
- [ ] Western Meadowlark
- [ ] Red-winged Blackbird
- [ ] Yellow-headed Blackbird
- [ ] Rusty Blackbird
- [ ] Brewer's Blackbird
- [ ] Common Grackle
- [ ] Great-tailed Grackle
- [ ] Brown-headed Cowbird
- [ ] Baltimore Oriole
- [ ] Bullock's Oriole

Others
- [ ] _____
- [ ] _____
- [ ] _____
- [ ] _____
- [ ] _____
- [ ] _____

Salmon Watching

Adam's River

Some call it 'salmon watching' but watching people watch salmon is more like it. The Adam's River salmon run peaks every four years attracting a quarter million people who line the banks of the crystal clear stream to witness the return of ten times as many sockeye salmon. An elegy of life played out in miniature, the spectacle of the life cycle closing is often described as an emotional experience by onlookers. Many are moved to tears as they watch natural selection in its most perfect expression.

Of the 4000 eggs laid by each female only two will survive to make the return journey four years later to the place of their birth. The others will succumb to natural and human predation, fisheries mismanagement, natural and human-devised ecological disasters and, finally, the rigours of the 490 km journey upstream against the currents of the mighty Fraser and Thompson Rivers. Only the toughest, the canniest survive.

With their reserves of fat entirely depleted the crimson flesh of the weary sockeye can be seen through their skin. In a final heroic act the sockeye pair off, fashion a nest in the river gravel, spawn then guard their precious legacy until exhausted, they die, becoming just food for scavenging eagles and crows and bears and other creatures.

In peak years as many as 2½ million cram the river and spawning channels to overflowing. In off years too however, sockeye, in fewer numbers, return during September and October. The drama is no less inspiring and, since the crush of migrating humans is

Adams River Salmon Watching

Location	Leave Vancouver	Arrive Salmon Arm	Leave Salmon Arm	Arrive Vancouver
Greyhound Canada 1-800 661-8747 (604) 482-8747 in Vancouver www.greyhound.ca Round Trip: $106.89	00:30 06:45 12:15 13:45 18:00 18:45	09:45 13:50 20:50 21:10 00:40 00:40	00:50 05:15 07:50 14:35 20:45 20:55	07:35 13:45 15:00 21:05 05:15 06:00
White Rose Limousine Ltd 1-888-832-4212 (250) 832-4212 Phone/Fax	Taxi and limo service			
Cottonwood Campsite (250) 679-8406	Situated adjacent to Roderick Haig-Brown Provincial Park Cabins, Campsite, Hot showers, Laundry			
Adams River Salmon Society www.salmonsociety.com	Detailed information on upcoming salmon runs and associated events.			
Tourism Shuswap 1-800-661-4800 www.shuswap.bc.ca tourism@shuswap.net	Accommodation, transportation and other local information.			

considerably less, the experience may be all the more satisfying. 1998 was a peak year so, likewise, 2002, 2006 and so on every four years should also mark their triumphant return.

Of course the local Chamber of Commerce, always eager to capitalize on a promising event, has mounted the Sa-

Against All Odds
Salmon are thought to use the earth's magnetic field for navigating on the open ocean. Closer to shore pheromones unique to each river are relied upon to hone in on the waterway of their birth. Salmon are reportedly able to detect the scent of their particular river in concentrations as weak as 1 or 2 parts per million. Upon returning home, a nesting pair typically releases 4000 eggs before dying. Of these 800 will survive to become tiny salmon fry. Predation or mishap in the river means only 200 smolts will ever reach the ocean. Birds of prey, sea mammals or disease take their toll however with just 10 adults setting out to rediscover the river of their birth. Fishermen will snag 8 of those, leaving a single pair to complete the cycle. Such grim calculations leave no margin of error. Unusually virulent disease, overfishing, the tirades of global warming or stream damage through logging, construction or pollution could easily upset such a delicate balance sending the species into a downward spiral.

Nikon F
300 mm Nikkor lens
Kodachrome 200 ISO film

lute to the Sockeye to coincide with the quadrennial return. Typical events include the Squilax Pow Wow, Square Dance Weekends, Family Theatre, North Shuswap Artisans Craft & Pottery Sales, Snowmobile Poker Run and so on. Hokey yes, but then again, 2½ million spawning salmon is a hard act to follow.

Greyhound will take you as far as Salmon Arm, east of Kamloops, six times daily. A 30 minute limo or taxi ride will be enough to complete the journey to the banks of the Adams River. Book accommodation or camping sites well ahead of time to avoid disappointment. If you plan on tenting out make sure your sleeping bag can cut the season. There is no camping allowed at Roderick Haig-Brown Provincial Park where this marvel unfolds but Cottonwood Campsite right next door is ideally situated and features log cabins, showers, even laundry in addition to lakeside campsites.

Capilano Salmon Hatchery

Access: During peak hours Monday through Saturday catch the **#246 Lonsdale Quay via Highland** bus at any of the stops along West Georgia Street in downtown Vancouver. Stay on the bus until the corner of Capilano Road and Woods Drive in North Vancouver. The driver will usually call out the best place to transfer to the **#236 Grouse Mountain** bus. Next, get off at the corner of Capilano Road and Capilano Park Road and walk in to the hatchery. During non-peak hours take the **#240 15th Street** bus to the corner of Marine Drive and Capilano Road where you can catch the **#246 Lonsdale Quay via Highland** bus up Capilano Road. Transfer to the #236 as above. For an alternate route take **SeaBus** to Lonsdale Quay in North Vancouver and board the **#236 Grouse Mountain** bus. No other transfers will be necessary to reach hatchery.

Much closer to home than the Adams River Sockeye run, but also less dramatic, the Capilano River in North Vancouver is home of important coho and chinook salmon runs. The former start heading up the river in July while the latter begin in September. By the middle of November both runs are concluded. Juveniles are released from January to May.

Capilano Canyon [See map page 29] is particularly gorgeous in autumn with fingers of sunlight poking through the thick forest canopy at a low angle. Well-maintained trails along the river's edge allow easy access to the salmon's natural habitat and to "fish ladders" which steer salmon into the Capilano Salmon Hatchery. Glass walls built into ladder of the federal government facility reveal the fascinating underwater world of the Pacific salmon as they queue up for a fate somewhat different from that which nature intended. Rather than dying a noble death after a cosmic struggle these fish receive a bonk on the head and the roe or milt is unceremoniously squeezed from their bellies after which their carcasses are tossed on some dung heap. Isn't science wonderful?

Just a few minutes downstream from the hatchery a more pleasing sight awaits. From a comfortable perch above the canyon walls you'll bear witness to competition in its purest form. Massive chinook vie for control of a tiny patch gravel in which to incubate their eggs. The winner, like the loser, will most surely die but, with a little luck, it's superior genetic material will mature and bolster the overall strength of the species.

While salmon don't generally eat once they enter the river, you may see anglers in the canyon below teasing the aggressive fish into snapping at an obnoxious lure. While catch and release saps the salmon's remaining strength, ripping it away from the nest it so steadfastly defends this is but one of the many perils the salmon faces as it attempts to close the circle of life.

Though virtually all of the forest on the North Shore is recovering second growth, check out the 500 year old giant fir that the loggers missed. At 61 metres tall, this is how much of the province once looked. Be sure to take the 20 minute stroll upstream to Cleveland Dam, construction of which necessitated the building of the province's first fish hatchery.

A network of relatively easy trails makes exploring in the vicinity of the hatchery worthwhile at any time. Following the river downstream you can meet up again with the bus network at Park Royal shopping center. Catch the **#250 Vancouver** bus or indeed any Vancouver-bound bus back downtown from the south side of Marine Drive.

Seymour River Hatchery

Originally built in 1977 by the British Columbia Institute of Technology as a teaching facility, the Seymour River

Dem Bones

Grisly bones are all that remain of another successful salmon run. Yet someting stirs below the frigid waters in the coarse gravel of the river bottom. Life invisibly gathers strength as scavengers and decay erase every vestige of the last generation.

Nikon F
28 mm Nikkor lens
Ektachrome 200 ISO film

Hatchery has since been upgraded and expanded. To date over 5 million salmon fry have been released. The hatchery, which attracts some 10,000 visitors annually, is uniquely situated at the end of an 11 km stretch of paved road which is closed to vehicle traffic. Consequently, a great way to visit the site is on roller blades if you have them, bike, giddy-up or hike in if you don't. To get to the start of the road is somewhat of an ordeal however. Either follow the instructions on page 45 to get to Lynn Headwaters Regional Park and the start of the Rice Lake Hike or take the **#210 Upper Lynn Valley** bus to Phibbs Exchange and transfer to the **#229 West Lynn** bus. Get off at Lynn Canyon Park, cross the suspension bridge and follow the river upstream for a short distance until you find a huge wooden staircase. Climb the stairs and continue uphill for another 20 minutes until you reach the parking lot at Rice Lake where the paved road begins. Alternately take the **#229 West Lynn** bus in reverse from Lonsdale Quay and follow the instructions above. Refer to the Baden-Powell Trail East map on page 59. 🐾

Cave Exploring

Horne Lake Caves

Access: Getting to the Horne Lake caves is not easy but it is most definitely worth it. From Vancouver take the local bus to Horseshoe Bay, details on page 320, and catch a ferry to Nanaimo's Departure Bay. From the ferry you'll want to meet up with the Island Link Shuttle or Island Coach Lines bus headed up Island. Get off at Qualicum Beach and call Parksville Taxi for the final leg of the journey. Horne Lake Caves is situated 14 km from the Island Highway at the end of an active logging road. Camping is available at the entrance to the park. If making a weekend of it try your hand at trout fishing or try tramping some of the local hiking routes in the area. **See Getting "Up Island" on page 331.**

Spelunking, otherwise known as cave exploring, has long had a dedicated core of enthusiasts. And while spelunking will always remain an underground sport, interest has surged in recent years as would-be adventurers thirst for new and exciting kicks.

With over 1000 know caves, Vancouver Island is the locale of choice for coastal cavers. Newcomers to the activity will want to check out the extensive network of caverns at Horne Lake.

The Horne Lake Caves, discovered in 1912 by a local geologist, comprise seven separate caves estimated to be as much as 120 thousand years old.

Vandalism

Amateur explorers rediscovered Main and Lower Caves in 1939 and subsequent vandalism and souvenir collecting damaged or obliterated formations that had taken thousands of years to grow.

Riverbend Cave, a more recent discovery, was sealed in 1971 to protect it from similar idiocy and remains largely unscathed.

Cave Tours

Tours of the caves, now part of the Provincial Parks system, are available but are not recommended for children under 5 or those with frail health. "These are not show caves like you find in the States," notes Richard Varella of Island Pacific Adventures. "The caves are undeveloped and therefore have uneven, rocky floors. A certain amount of agility is required."

The Horne Lake Caves now attract over 50,000 visitors every year. Two different tours of Riverbend Cave are offered. The $13 family-oriented tour lasts 1½ hours and explores the most accessible sections of the caves with an emphasis on geology, conservation and history. Tours start at 10 AM daily and are offered every hour thereafter until 4 PM. Participation is on a first-come first-served basis.

The High Adventure Tour picks up where the first one left off. Participants will crawl, climb and scramble down to the bottom of The Rainbarrel, seven stories high. Basic climbing instruction and all climbing gear is included. Costing $59, the High Adventure Tour last five hours and reservations are required. Participants must be 19

years or older.

Being undeveloped, the caverns have an aura of magic and mystery about them. Calcite formations, built up a molecule at a time over countless aeons, inspire awe at every turn. Spelunkers can expect to find such usual features as stalactites and stalagmites growing from ceiling and floor.

The Ice Cream Waterfall
Calcite formations built up a molecule at a time are a wonder to behold at Vancouver Island's Riverbend Cave.

Nikon F
28 mm Nikkor lens
Kodachrome 64 ISO film

Less pedestrian formations such as the "Howling Wolf," "flow stone," "brainrock," "cave pearls" and, perhaps, pearls of wisdom from the "Smiling Buddha" himself will also be encountered. Those with an appetite for more can feast their eyes on "bacon strips," "moon milk" and the "Ice Cream Waterfall."

Fragile Beauty

Such beauty is fragile, however, and much of every underground tour is devoted to cave ecology in addition to area history and geology. "We feel that only through education can we increase understanding and consequently the preservation of these remarkably fragile underground environments," says Varela who offers tours in the caves on a contract from BC Parks.

Nirvana
The Smiling Buddah eternally ponders his navel and the very essence of existance from his perch across the lotus pond in Riverbend Cave.

Nikon F
28 mm Nikkor lens
Kodachrome 64 ISO film

Bats, creepy crawlies and icky things are notably absent from the caves. "It's just a little bit too cold," Varella explains. One exception can be found in Main Cave where, in certain passages near the entrance, hundreds of daddy long legs spiders crawl in every fall only to die. White mould consumes their bodies leaving behind what looks like, in the light of a head lamp, pearls with legs.

Claustrophobics will be relieved to note that the main tour is limited to exploring relatively open grottos with the only tight squeeze being the iron entrance gate used to keep would-be vandals out. "In all reality most people have some kind of apprehension about going underground. Fully half express some kind of hesitation. But going with a guide, in a group atmosphere makes people feel at ease. It becomes a much more pleasurable experience." Varella adds that very few people ever back out at the door to the cave. "Maybe a dozen out of thousands."

Since the caves maintain a constant cool of five degrees Celsius year round, warm clothes and possibly work gloves are recommended. Footwear should consist of sturdy running shoes at the very least with hiking boots recommended.

Following your cave tour you may wish to explore Main Cave and Lower Main Cave on your own. Helmets and head lamps can be rented from the park office. These two smaller caves offer some tight squeezes, simple climbing, interesting grottos and even a waterfall. Spelunking is a messy business so be sure to pack change of clothes.

A word of warning: Cougars call the park home and may call your poodle supper. Keep pets on a leash at all times and keep a close eye on all children. 🐾

Cave Exploring
Horne Lake Caves, Vancouver Island

Location	Phone	Notes
Parksville Taxi	(250) 248-5741	$35 from Qualicum Beach one way.
Island Pacific Adventures Postal Box 3531 Stn. Main Courtenay, B.C. V9N 6Z8	(250) 248-7829 (250) 757-8687 (250) 339-9150 Fax adventure@hornelake.com	Cave Tours, Helmet and Head Lamp rentals Campsites
Parksville/Qualicum Beach Tourism Association	1-888-799-3222 (250) 752-2388 (250) 752-2392 FAX	
B.C. Speleological Federation	(250) 283-2283	Information for experienced cavers only.
Island Coach Lines	1-800-318 - 0818 (250) 385 - 4411	
Maverick Coach Lines	(604) 662-8051	
Island Link	1-877-954-3556 (250) 954-3556 www.newshuttle.com	Shuttle between Nanaimo & Qualicum Beach Full schedule in Appendix.

River Rafting

River rafting in British Columbia can be a big letdown. Opportunities abound of course. Indeed, with so many mountains and so much rain, the river rafting potential is nearly limitless. Innumerable companies offer a wide variety of rafting experiences for a range of skill levels from easy to challenging. The downside is, without a car, many of these opportunities are not practical even though rafting is the one outdoor activity that truly lends itself to communal modes of transportation. Drawing largely on the Lower Mainland market, commercial rafting companies have tended to proliferate in just a few regions, notably the Thompson-Fraser drainage, the Chilliwack River and Whistler areas. As a consequence a rather silly scenario unfolds daily during prime rafting season. Hundreds of people in dozens of cars set out at approximately the same time each day for approximately the same destinations following the same crowded highways to do exactly the same sort of thing. Yet, thinking only inside the box, no one has come up with a shuttle service to link all these customers with all these rafting companies. The infrequency and logistics of existing public transportation often demand that would-be rafters must turn what should be a day trip into an overnighter or even a weekender in some cases. Fortunately, some exceptions do apply. Those are detailed below. Those companies not listed may come to realize that a certain segment of the recreating public is beginning to demand "ecotourism" that is environmentally friendly from start to finish.

On the matter of safety, all rafting guides must pass a stringent certification procedure before being licensed to operate in the province of British Columbia. All companies include rain gear or wet suits where appropriate as well as life jackets, paddles and usually lunch. Guests are encouraged to bring swimsuits and running shoes for in the raft and should also bring a complete change of clothes for *après*-splash.

There are essentially three kinds of rafting in British Columbia. Power rafting requires at least the fitness ability to hold on and scream. Guests enjoy the ride and take in the scenery while an outboard motor does most of the work. Paddle rafting demands that participants all chip in, paddling frantically to navigate past midstream obstacles at the river guide's command. An oar and paddle combo works similarly with all the frenetic paddling of the above but the guide exercises additional control over the craft using long oars. 🐾

Rafting in Whistler

Rafting from the Whistler area is a happy exception to the inaccessability rule. Numerous companies offer a selection of outings suited to every skill level and all originate from Whistler Village which is well-serviced by public transportation from the Lower Mainland. See **Getting to Whistler** on page 335. The following table lists the offerings by river and season and includes average prices. Prices may vary slightly depending on the services offered by individual companies. For exact prices and details of their shuttle services from Whistler Village contact the companies listed below. 🐾

Whistler Rafting

Season	May	June	July	August	Sept
Green River Class II; 2 hrs	$59 - $61	$59 - $61	$59 - $61	$59 - $61	
Birkenhead River Class III; 3 hrs	$76 - $79	$76 - $79	$76 - $79		
Cheakamus River Class III; 3 hrs	$119	$119	$119	$119	
Elaho-Squamish Rivers Class IV; 8 hrs			$129 - $135	$129 - $135	$129 - $135

Company	Contact & Notes
Canadian Outback Adventure Co.	1-800-565-8735; (604) 921-7250; (604) 921-7860 FAX info@canadianoutback.com; www.canadianoutback.com
Wedge Rafting	1-888-932-5899; (604) 932-7171; (604) 932-1971 FAX wedge@whistlernet.com; www.whistler.net/wedgerafting/
Whistler Outdoor Experience Company	(604) 932-3389; (604) 932-4469 FAX woe@direct.ca; www.whistleroutdoor.com
Whistler River Adventures	1-888-932-3532; (604) 932-3532; (604) 932-3559 Fax info@whistlerriver.com; www.whistler-river-adv.com
Blackcomb Whitewater Adventures	103-4338 Main Street Suite #1031 Whistler, B.C. V0N 1B4 (604) 938-4520; (604) 938-4520 Fax
Rainbow Rafting	6-3102 Panorama Ridge, Whistler, BC V0N 1B3 800-887-7528 or 888-291-3333 (604) 905-7000; 604-932-3840 Fax
Hostelling International - Whistler; (604) 932-5492; (604) 932-4687; whistler@hihostels.bc.ca; 5678 Alta Lake Rd, Whistler, BC PO Box 128, V0N 1B0	
Whistler Backpackers Guest House, (604) 932-1177, 2124 Lake Placid Rd., Whistler, BC V0N 1B0	
Seppo's Log Cabin, (604) 932-8808; 7114 Nesters Rd., Whistler, BC	
UBC Whistler Lodge; (604) 932-6604 2124 Nordic, Whistler; (604) 932-6604	
Fireside Lodge, Whistler; (604) 932-4545; (604) 932-3994 FAX	

Chilliwack River Paddle Rafting

The closest commercial rafting tours can be found on the Chilliwack River just one hour from Vancouver. And while the Chilliwack River suffers from a relatively short season it makes up for it in bumps, grinds and pure white water excitement. Dropping at a rate of 7 metres per kilometre, the Chilliwack is known for seemingly endless stretches of froth and foam. The Tamahi Rapids in particular are home of the annual Canadian Kayaking Championships. The Chilliwack River is rated at between class iii & iv and rocks n' rolls through high water season from May to the end of July. During that time consumer-savvy Hyak Wilderness Adventures operates a daily shuttle service from downtown Vancouver. Pick up at 8 AM can be arranged from any major hotel. Hyak's Chilliwack River paddle-rafting tour lasts 4½ hours and includes a riverside feast. As an added touch participants can warm up at the end of the day with hot showers before returning to the city. 🐾

Chilliwack River Rafting
May - July

Hyak Wilderness Adventures 1-800-663-7238 (604) 734-8622 www.hyak.com	Chilliwack River: One Day Trip May Special $79 June - July $99 Shuttle Service $18 + taxes

This River's Got Class

For recreational purposes rivers and rapids are classified according to a six-category scale encompassing everything from wimpy to deadly.

Class I From flat water to small ripples with clear passages and no obstacles.

Class II Easy. Suited to canoes, these rapids are moderate and all passages are clear.

Class III Medium. Large waves that are numerous and irregular with such obstacles as rocks, back eddies and narrow chutes to be overcome. Suited to kayaks and rafts with pilots adept at reading rivers and expertly maneuvering around hazards.

Class IV Difficult. Stretches of long, powerful rapids with rocks and boiling eddies demanding greater power and precision from pilots.

Class V Very difficult. Extensive, uninterrupted rapids of a wild and violent nature. River course is steep and badly obstructed with major drops.

Class VI Unnavigable. Don't even dream about it.

Thompson & Fraser River Rafting

Though far from British Columbia's population centres, the Thompson River remains the province's rafting mecca.

Leapfrog
Power rafting through the Frog, one of many frothing, foamy terror spots on the Thompson River. Herbie, an old timer among the river rats that ply the Thompson, safely navigates the rapids one more time.

*Nikon F
135 mm Nikkor lens
Kodachrome 64 ISO film*

When setting out to get soaked, many like to hedge their bets by choosing an area with 325 or more days of crystal blue sky each year. And the utterly foreign semi-arid landscape is an added attraction to waterlogged coastal British Columbians. The real reason for the popularity of this waterway, however, is the 25 class iii and iv rapids squeezed into a 40 km stretch of the lower Thompson Canyon. Having an extra long rafting season certainly helps too. Commercial trips on the Thompson River usually start at the beginning of May and continue until the end of September.

While many companies have built respectable rafting operations on the Thompson only two cater specifically to the car-free tourist. After the brief but intense rafting season on the Chilliwack River ends, Hyak Wilderness Adventures starts ferrying participants to the Thompson River. As with their shuttle to the Chilliwack River, this service originates at any major hotel in downtown Vancouver. At present this shuttle is only offered on Tuesdays and Wednesdays starting at the end of July and continuing until the end of September. Pick up is at 6 AM with drop-off scheduled for 9 PM. This is by far the quickest and cheapest way to enjoy a day of rafting on the Thompson. We can only hope that the popularity of this service will push Hyak into extending it to include weekends.

Kumsheen Rafting Adventures offers a "Three Hour Whitewater Quickie" which can be undertaken in a day if travelling by Greyhound. See **Getting to Hope & Lytton**

on page 337. This package is not offered on weekends and does not include lunch but does cram 18 of the Thompson's gnarliest rapids into a compact adrenaline rush for thrill seekers in a hurry. Those recreating at a less frenzied pace may want to consider over-nighting at Kumsheen's riverside resort and undertaking one of their other single or multi-day

Splish-Splash!
...You'll be taking a bath. Plan on getting soaked however you run the Thompson River gorge.

Nikon F
28 mm Nikkor lens
Kodachrome 64 ISO film

rafting packages. Kumsheen is located along the banks of the Thompson River just 5 km east of Lytton. Ask the bus driver to drop you off at the rafting company's doorstep.

Many other companies have developed luxury, full-service camping resorts from which they base their rafting operations. Fraser River Raft Expeditions offers free rustic camping at their home base near Yale. Rent or bring your own tent or use their giant teepee free of charge when signing up for a raft trip. Fraser River Raft Expeditions offers both the usual Thompson River day trip and a power-rafting scream through Hell's Gate on the mighty, muddy Fraser River. Because of scheduling, neither can be undertaken as a simple, car-free day trip from Vancouver.

If a single day of punishment is not nearly enough, the truly jaded might find what they're looking for in a wham-bam two-day package that splices together the Fraser and its biggest tributary, the Thompson River, with a night of riverside camping in between at the mouth of the Nahatlatch River.

Ask the bus driver to drop you off on the highway in front of the rafting company's base of operations just 22 km past Hope. Alternately, since Hope is much more frequently serviced by bus, arrange for staff to pick you up in Hope when you make your rafting reservation. 🐾

Thompson & Fraser River Rafting
June - September

Location	Activity
Hyak Wilderness Adventures 204 - 1975 Maple Street Vancouver, B.C V6J 3S9 1-800-663-7238 (604) 734-8622 (604)734-5718 FAX info@hyak.com www.hyak.com	Thompson River: One Day Trip $99 Shuttle Service $27
Kumsheen Raft Adventures Ltd. P.O. Box 30, Lytton B.C. V0K 1Z0 1 800 663 6667 250 455 2296 250 455 2297 FAX rafting@kumsheen.com www.kumsheen.com	Three Hour Whitewater Quickie: $82 Two Day Heart-Thumper: Thompson & Fraser $265 Luxury Camping Resort $8
Fraser River Raft Expeditions Box 10 Yale, BC V0K 2S0 1 800 363-7238 (604) 863-2336 (604) 863-2355 FAX frre@uniserve.com www.fraserraft.com	Thompson River: One Day Trip $95 Fraser River: One Day Trip $95 Thompson & Fraser Two Day Trip $220 Free Camping at base camp

Sea Kayaking

Kayak camping is the ultimate way to explore the British Columbia coast. Gliding noiselessly along the shore you'll be inspected by curious harbour seals, playful otters and, on rare occasions, even dolphins and orcas may move in close to check you out. Along the beaches you'll encounter foraging bears and wolves and see, close at hand, eagles surveying their domain from craggy snags above.

Originally invented by the Inuit for seal and whale hunting, modern sea kayaks have been lengthened and strengthened, replacing such materials as seal and caribou hides with fibreglass and plastic. Virtually anywhere on the coast of British Columbia is open to these versatile and sturdy craft. There are, however, a number of spots that are particularly suited to bluewater paddling.

Aging backcountry boomers, cursed with hiker's knee may eventually find the demands of backpacking too much. Rather than hanging up the old boots, trading them in for a paddle can be a great way to extend an outback-bent lifestyle.

Pining for the Fjords

The fjords of coastal British Columbia where much of kayaking is undertaken are subject to a predictable weather pattern. Especially during the warm days of summer local winds typically pick up each day during mid-morning. As the land masses warm up the air begins to rise. The resulting vacuum sucks cooler air along the fjord from more open waters such as Georgia Strait. As the day progresses the water and land temperatures equalize and the wind subsides until the advent of evening. The twilight hours bring the rapid cooling of land masses. Water temperatures drop at a much slower rate upsetting the equilibrium once again. Warm air rises off the water throughout the early evening causing cooler air to pour off the mountains and out through the conduit of the inlet. Plying the waters of coastal inlets often demands that kayakers set off at first light planning on a long, seaside siesta at midday, then continuing on throughout the afternoon and early evening.

Back Eddies to the Future

Whenever bucking the tides, particularly in constricted passages where the current is magnified, hug the shoreline where you can often pick up a back eddy or two to propel you on your way. Conversely, to benefit from a following tide move away from the shore to avoid those nasty back eddies.

Stuff It, Buddy

Dry Bags, the plasticized canvas kind favoured by yachters, are ideal for stowing gear in the front and rear compartments of kayaks. They are, however, expensive, Since some water inevitably gets below decks, cutting costs by using just plastic bags can be risky. One solution is to purchase nylon stuff sacks from an outdoor store such as the Mountain Equipment Co-op and line them with heavy-duty, see-through garbage bags. The nylon is enough to protect the plastic from rips and tears which in turn waterproofs all of your camping essentials. Colour code the stuff sacks to help keep things organized.

Bear Proofing

The usual bear proofing precautions, hanging food, making noise and what not, still apply to kayak camping. Though bears can swim well they usually have no need to visit offshore islands. Kayakers can take an extra precaution by camping, whenever feasible, on the abundant islands found along the coast of British Columbia. Incidentally, stowing food in kayak compartments is not bear proof, it's just a great way to get a kayak trashed.

Learning How

Once is certainly not enough for this captivating activity. In order to bring your skills up to the point where you may "do-it-yourself" a certain level of competence must be attained. In fact many kayak rental firms will no longer rent to inexperienced individuals: the liability risks are just too great.

A number of kayak companies offer lessons in the False Creek area adjacent to Granville Island. Though convenient, exceptionally busy sea lanes and a noisy, industrial setting make this a less than satisfactory locale to build the skills necessary to paddle safely. For this reason learning at Granville Island is not recommended and information is not included in this guide book. Far superior alternatives exist.

Check out the excellent video *Sea Kayaking: Getting Started* which is available from the Vancouver Public Library [Call Number 797.1224 S43a.] While a video is a good place to start there is no substitute for competent instruction.

Bowen Island

Bowen Island is an ideal place to dip your first paddle. Though a relative newcomer to the kayaking business, **Bowen Island Sea Kayaking** has put together a top quality program in an equally exceptional location. Getting there is simple. See **Getting to Horseshoe Bay** on page 320. When you reach Horseshoe Bay about 40 minutes later you'll have to rush to catch the Bowen Island Ferry. The ferry terminal is just in front of the last bus stop. This little commuter ferry takes a mere 20 minutes. Once you reach the island Bowen Island Sea Kayaking is easily located in a small hut on the dock just to the right of the ferry loading ramp.

Bowen Island Sea Kayaking has a two courses that should be considered the bare minimum necessary before undertaking any self-guided trips. These full-day modules will take participants from the basics to an intermediate skill level capable of wet exits, assisted and self-rescue. In addition to paddling skills and rescue techniques the basics of marine navigation are covered and practiced with students plotting their routes throughout the islands of Howe Sound with chart and compass. Another course concentrates on perfecting various aspects of the Eskimo roll but should not be considered essential to touring situations unless kayak surfing is involved.

Once you have attained the skills and confidence necessary to paddle unsupervised, Bowen Island makes a great departure point for a number of day or overnight excursions.

Deep Cove

Deep Cove Canoe and Kayak in North Vancouver is equally accessible and has been teaching the fine art of kayaking for over 15 years. Their one day *Trip Preparation Tour* is a fast way to bring your skills up to scratch. Starting at 9:00 am participants are introduced to the basics and then have an opportunity to acquire and polish a number of useful strokes. The rest of the morning is devoted to practice that culminates in a stop for lunch on Racoon Island. In the afternoon expect to really get your feet wet as participants practice the finer points of wet exits, assisted and self-rescues. Before wrapping the day up at 3:30 PM you can wind down by learning such important navigational skills as reading marine charts and tide tables. Lunch and wet suits are included. Take the **#210 Upper Lynn Valley** bus from Dunsmuir Street next to Burrard SkyTrain station to Phibbs Exchange. Change to the **#211, #212 or #290** bus and stay on board to the end of the line at Deep Cove. The kayak company is just downhill along the waterfront.

Deep Cove Canoe and Kayak also has a three hour introductory course for those who simply want to try it out.

On Your Own

While both local operators above have programs designed to teach you the skills required for kayaking on your own, it would be wise to undertake a day trip or two in relatively calm waters to master your skills before attempting any multi-day excursions. The local routes outlined in the next section are perfect for just that. 🐾

Vancouver Area Kayak Training

Activity	Details
Deep Cove Canoe and Kayak Deep Cove, North Vancouver (604) 929-2268	3 Hour beginner course $65 Full day Trip Preparation Tour $95 Rentals $10 Per hour Rentals $60 Overnight
Bowen Island Sea Kayaking Bowen Island, BC 1-800-605-2925 (604) 947-9266	$75 Each 5 Hour lesson $235 Beginner - Intermediate 3 day Sea Kayak Touring course Rentals $11 Per hour Rentals $68 Overnight

Indian Arm

Level: Easy   **Distance:** 36 km

Time: 6 hr   **Tide Table:** Vancouver

Marine Chart: 3495   **Warning:** Heavy Traffic

Weekend Warriors
A quickie lesson in how not to bivouac for the night. Live trees were cut to frame a lean-to and used for firewood. Of course they didn't burn. Garbage was left littering the campsite. Let's hope the mosquitos ate them alive. Indian Arm is in the background.

Nikon F
28 mm Nikkor lens
Ektachrome 100 ISO film

Protected waters and plenty of marine traffic make this local inlet an excellent place from which to embark on your maiden voyage. Indian Arm is the perfect place for a full day of exploring or, better yet, an easy overnighter. Rent your kayaks at **Deep Cove Canoe and Kayak** then, once you've balanced your supplies in the front and rear compartments, head north out of Deep Cove.

While heavy marine traffic is handy in the event of an emergency, recreational boaters are the primary hazard in the inlet. Since no license is required to operate a motor boat in British Columbia the level of care taken by many boaters is appalling indeed. For this reason kayakers must make themselves especially visible by wearing bright clothing. Moreover it is wise to hug the shoreline and avoid allowing your group to become scattered. A tight group is much easier to see and avoid than a succession of single craft spread out all over the sea-lanes. Only cross the sea-lanes when it is absolutely necessary to do so and don't dawdle in the middle. For the sake of this excursion it is advised that you hug the western shore on the outbound leg and the eastern shore on the way back. Descriptions in this book, however, will address main features on either side as they appear.

As you head north you'll soon leave the beachfront

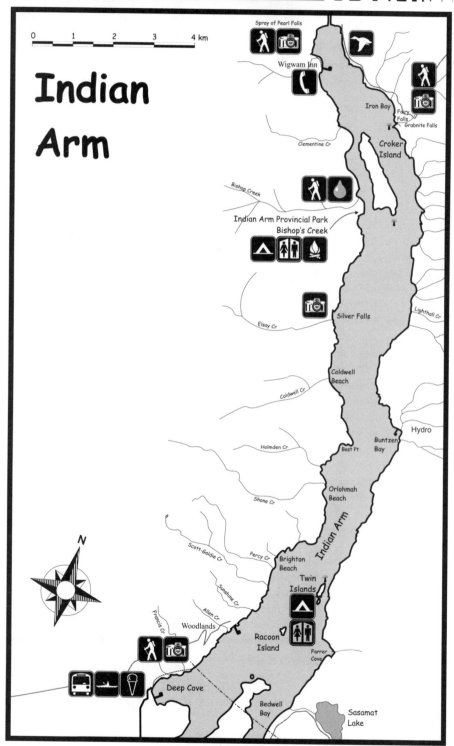

Indian Arm

0   1   2   3   4 km

Spray of Pearl Falls

Wigwam Inn

Iron Bay

Fairy Falls

Grabnite Falls

Clementine Cr

Croker Island

Bishop Creek

Indian Arm Provincial Park

Bishop's Creek

Elsay Cr

Silver Falls

Lighthall Cr

Coldwell Beach

Coldwell Cr.

Hydro

Holmden Cr

Best Pt

Buntzen Bay

Orlohmah Beach

Shone Cr

Indian Arm

Scott-Goldie Cr

Percy Cr

Brighton Beach

Twin Islands

N

Allen Cr

Sunshine Cr

Francis Cr

Woodlands

Racoon Island

Farrer Cove

Deep Cove

Bedwell Bay

Sasamat Lake

homes of Deep Cove and Woodlands behind. On your right you'll notice Racoon Island then Twin Islands, which, taken together, make up the Indian Arm Provincial Marine Park. Camping is permitted on the Twin Islands though only a few rustic sites exist and water is limited to a small spring on the north island.

Continuing northwards you'll pass a number of small recreational communities. Interspersed between these small beaches are stretches of steep, rocky bluffs that dive straight down into the inlet, giving Indian Arm that typical fjord-like appearance found throughout the coast of British Columbia. In fact Indian Arm is the southern-most such inlet on the west coast of North America.

Some 8 km into the paddle you'll notice two old-fashioned looking concrete structures on the eastern shore. Built in 1903 and expanded in 1914 these power generating stations were Vancouver's first hydroelectric facilities. Drawing water from Buntzen Lake [See page 40] high on the bluffs above, these two small power plants still provide significant power to the city, together producing 76,700 kW. A service road from the second power facility to Buntzen Lake itself provides a pleasant half hour stroll and a chance to stretch the kayak cramps out of the legs.

From the power stations on you'll leave civilization largely behind. After 4 more kilometres attractive Silver Falls can be seen pouring off cliffs on the western shore. Watch for large spawning jellyfish in the water in front of the falls.

A further 2½ km will bring you to Bishop's Creek Provincial Marine Park opposite Croker Island whose steep sides forbid landing or camping.

Adjacent to the north end of the island, on the eastern shore is spectacular Granite Falls a popular destination since the last century when the Union Steamship Company began offering weekend excursions for curious Vancouver residents.

North of Granite Falls a short trail leads to a viewpoint with vistas of the head of the inlet and beyond. Note Wigwam Inn to the left of the Indian River estuary. Built in 1910 as a luxury resort for the international rich and spoiled, the Wigwam Inn is now an outport for the Royal Vancouver Yacht Club. Plan to visit the Spray of Pearl Falls a few minutes on foot by trail from the lodge.

Camping sites can be found across the head of Indian Arm at deserted logging or mining sites. Though not the prettiest sites the price is certainly right and exploring the abandoned equipment will prove interesting. A word of warning however: wear thick-soled shoes to avoid cutting your feet on jagged metal and rusted cables left behind once the rape of the land was completed.

The Indian River estuary at high tide makes a great place for further explorations. If you thought to bring a hand line or crab trap you may want to try flounder, cod or crab for dinner. Be sure you have a valid Salt Water Fishing License. Avoid shellfish in Indian Arm as pollution and red tide tends to become concentrated in these filter feeders. 🐾

Indian Arm Kayaking

Deep Cove Canoe and Kayak Deep Cove, North Vancouver (604) 929-2268	Rentals $10 Per hour Rentals $60 Overnight
Red Tide Hotline 666-2828	Area 28

Howe Sound

To keep building your skills locally try taking on the more open waters of Howe Sound. Though less protected than Indian Arm the numerous islands and islets of this nearby waterway offers a degree of shelter during all but

Canadian Original
The stable, seaworthy kayak was originally fashioned out of caribou skin stretched over a wooden frame. Lightweight and silent, northern natives used the craft as a platform for hunting seals and whales. Modern sea kayaks are heavier, deriving additional weight and strength from the fiberglas or other resins typically used in their construction.

Nikon F
135 mm Nikkor lens
Kodachrome 64 ISO film

the worst of conditions. One local anomaly, known as a *squamish*, is a high wind born in the mountains behind the community of Squamish that bears its name. The Coast Salish name means literally "mother of the wind." Though resulting in some of the best wind surfing conditions around, when a *squamish* hits the mouth of the sound it can churn up seas that the inexperienced may find threatening.

The many islands which comprise Howe Sound provide a labyrinth of channels and coves, beaches and banks to explore over many days. Two possible routes are outlined below but bear in mind that detours are possible depending on your schedule and time constraints.

Bowen Island Sea Kayaking has two locations to put

in from. Rent your kayak at their main office on the dock at Snug Cove then, depending on your destination launch there or take advantage of their shuttle to Tunstall Bay to gain immediate access to Howe Sound.

Like Indian Arm, Howe Sound is not wilderness by any means. It is sparsely populated however and the further north you go the less signs of civilization you will encounter. One disappointment is a pulp mill at Port Mellon and another one at Woodfibre at the head of the sound. On windless days, when kayaking is at its best, the whole sound can fill with noxious haze that puts the lie to any notions of untamed wilderness. Yum! 🐾

Bowen Island Circumnavigation

Level: Moderate   **Distance:** 32 km   **Time:** 6 hr

Warning: Marine Traffic   **Marine Chart:** 3526   **Tide Table:** Squamish

Starting from either of **Bowen Island Sea Kayaking's** two locations at Snug Cove or Tunstall Bay will do if you decide to paddle around Bowen Island itself. Let wind and current direction dictate whether you take the Island in a clockwise or counterclockwise direction. Allow plenty of time if you plan to circle the whole island. Two alternate routes are possible. The northern route from Snug Cove to Tunstall Bay is 18 km while the southern route is a mere 14 km. You may wish to spend a few extra hours exploring the group of small islands [Paisley, Hermit, Mickey, etc.] off the southwestern tip of Bowen.

Stay close to shore in the busy Queen Charlotte Channel and be prepared to encounter frequent large wakes from passing BC Ferries south from Snug Cove as far west as Collingwood Channel. Moreover the southern end of Bowen faces on the open Georgia Strait and is sometimes subject to heavy northerly seas. Steep cliffs and a sparsity of beaches further complicate the southern passage during inclement weather.

The northern and western shores are exposed to the aforementioned *squamish* winds as well as the infrequent wakes of ferries plying the Sechelt-Horseshoe Bay route. Luckily numerous small rocky beaches provides a modicum of shelter in the event of heavy swells. There are no beaches suited to camping on Bowen Island.

If lacking confidence at the approach of large boat wakes turn to take the waves head on and you'll easily ride out their passage. As your experience grows you'll discover that sea kayaks are extremely sea worthy craft capable of handling just about anything the sea can throw at them. Technology is not the problem. Paddlers' ability and confidence are more important factors in determining what kind of weather conditions to attempt. The key to safe kayaking is to know your limits and never exceed them. 🐾

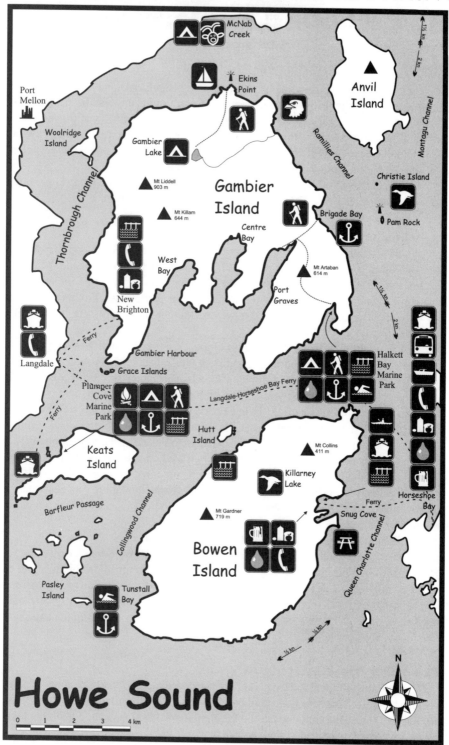

McNab Creek

Ekins Point

Anvil Island

Port Mellon

Woolridge Island

Gambier Lake

Christie Island

Pam Rock

Mt Liddell 903 m

Gambier Island

Ramillies Channel

Montagu Channel

Mt Killam 644 m

Centre Bay

Brigade Bay

West Bay

Mt Artaban 614 m

New Brighton

Port Graves

Thornbrough Channel

Langdale

Gambier Harbour

Grace Islands

Plumper Cove Marine Park

Langdale-Horseshoe Bay Ferry

Halkett Bay Marine Park

Ferry

Ferry

Hutt Island

Mt Collins 411 m

Keats Island

Killarney Lake

Horseshoe Bay

Barfleur Passage

Mt Gardner 719 m

Collingwood Channel

Snug Cove

Bowen Island

Pasley Island

Tunstall Bay

Queen Charlotte Channel

N

Howe Sound

0   1   2   3   4 km

Howe Sound Exploration

Level: Challenging   **Distance:** 49 km   **Time:** 2-3 days

Warning: Marine Traffic   **Marine Chart:** 3526   **Tide Table:** Squamish

While Bowen Island is without suitable camping Gambier Island is well-appointed with beaches and should form a key element to any multi-day paddle in the Howe Sound area. Launch your kayak from Tunstall Bay on the west side of Bowen Island and then head directly west through the Paisley Group of islands towards Plumper Cove on the far side of Keats Island. Since the campground on Keats is relatively close at hand spend some time poking around the Paisley Group.

At Plumper Cove you'll find 20 walk-in campsites, pit toilets and many larger boats moored off shore. See page 212 for a full description of Keats Island

Risky Business

An alternative route takes you directly north from Tunstall Bay along the western shore of Bowen Island towards Hope Point 10 km away on Gambier Island. The final 2 km cuts across open water, use caution and avoid dallying as you cross the ferry lane here. Unlike the busy Horseshoe Bay - Nanaimo route, ferries pass through this waterway only about once an hour. Never, however, attempt such a crossing under foggy conditions or when visibility is limited.

From Hope Point you can explore Port Graves, Centre Bay and West Bay or dash directly across the harbour mouth for the distant Grace Islands 5 km away.

Whichever route you choose follow the Gambier Island coast northwards towards Woolridge Island. To your left you'll notice the communities of Langdale where the ferry docks, Williamsons Landing, Twin Creeks, Port Mellon and Longview stretched out along the shore of the Sechelt Peninsula. With the exception of the small community of New Brighton, the shore of Gambier Island to the east is largely uninhabited.

In spite of the proximity of the pulp mill at Port Mellon, the waters of Thornbrough Channel are reputed to be excellent for salmon fishing. Try trolling at slow speed as you make your way northward. Bottom feeding fish may contain toxins generated at the pulp mills nearby. Pulp manufacturing is a known source of deadly dioxin and furan pollution.

As you round the northern shore of Gambier Island cut across the channel towards the long stretch of beach at McNab Creek. With plenty of potable water, driftwood for fire making, open beach for tenting and few vestiges of civilization this is about as perfect a camping spot as you'll find in the Howe Sound area. An Indian pictograph can even be found on rocks to the east of the creek itself. The future of the McNab Creek area is somewhat uncertain as industrial development in the form of a liquid natural gas plant has been proposed for the area.

Hiking Side Trip

Next morning, invigorated by a good night's sleep, paddle 3 km back across Thornbrough Channel to Ekins Point on Gambier Island and find the hiking route to Gambier Lake behind the yacht club outstation. Taking a mere 1½ hours round trip, this hike, though a bit steep, is most definitely worth it.

From Ekins Point follow the shore east then south and within 4 km you'll note a number of small but suitable camping beaches. Plan to linger here over night at least as this is the closest you'll get to wilderness in Howe Sound.

Rather than set up camp so early you may wish to cut across Ramillies Channel and circumnavigate fortress-like Anvil Island. The steep cliffs of Anvil Island make landing or camping here virtually impossible.

Journey's End

As day three breaks keep in mind that journey's end is still 18 km away. There are, however, a number of worthy points of interest on the way. Christie Island is a rookery for seagulls and cormorants while Pam Rock is a favourite basking place for a colony of harbour seals. Refrain from approaching too closely in both places to avoid startling the wildlife.

From Halkett Bay at the southwestern corner of Gambier Island a six hour return hike to the summit of 614 metre Mount Artaban can be undertaken by the truly adventuresome. The hike is detailed on page 216. Be sure to leave plenty of time to scoot back across the sea lanes to Bowen Island.

Halkett Bay Provincial Marine Park has a few rustic campsites on shore as well as a dock and pit toilets if time is running short and you decide to spend one final night in the out of doors.

The minimum time necessary to circumnavigate Gambier Island is two full days of paddling. 🐾

Sea Asparagus

This salty delicacy will be found wherever sea kayakers lurk. Carpeting the water's edge on mud flats, sheltered coves and estuaries, sea asparagus prefers limited exposure to wave action. Sea asparagus has more aliases than its segmented stems have branches, being known variously as glasswort, pickleweed, samphire and pigeon foot. In the camp kitchen sea asparagus is versatile. Stems can be munched upon as is, used to perk up salads, presented like asparagus or even collected for pickling or freezing. A British Columbia company has developed a market for sea asparagus, shipping the frozen product to upscale restaurants worldwide. Soak sea asparagus in freshwater for several hours before preparing to reduce its salinity.
Illustration by Manami Kimura

Howe Sound Kayaking	
Bowen Island Sea Kayaking Bowen Island, BC 1-800-605-2925 (604) 947-9266 www.bowenislandkayaking.com	Rentals $58/88/33 for first, second and additional days. Kayak rentals 2 for the price of one every Tuesday.
Red Tide Hotline 666-2828	Area 28

Sechelt Inlet

Level: Challenging   **Distance:** 49 km

Time: 2-3 days   **Warning:** High Winds

Chart: 3589/3512   **Tide Table:** Porpoise Bay

Place names of First Nations extraction are common enough hereabouts that localities like Tsawwassen, Nanaimo, Sechelt and Squamish immediately leap to mind. The skunk, raccoon and moose all owe their handles to the original inhabitants of eastern North America. On the west coast of British Columbia sockeye and chinook, delicious smoked, baked or broiled, swam into the lexicon from Chinook Jargon. Sockeye or *suka* meant literally: *the fish of fishes.* Chum salmon -- originally pronounced *tzum samum* -- came from the Sne Nay Muxw language. Salal also arrived via the *lingua franca* called Chinook Jargon. *Bushwacker's bane* might have been a more appropriate name. The geoduck, meaning "neck-attached," is not a *gooey duck*. Gooey yes but the etymology is strictly Chinook Jargon. Neither is that camp robber, the whisky jack, a souse after a hard day of pilfering peanuts. From the original Cree, *wiskatjan* got the misappellation through a case of mispronunciation, Whisky John, with the diminutive being misapplied. Chinook Jargon, incidentally, was a trading language that developed to facilitate communication among the diverse original inhabitants of western Canada and later, those who showed up to barter blankets, bullets and booze. Chinook Jargon was a pidgin comprised mainly of the Chinook language of Oregon, the Nuu-cha-nulth language of Vancouver Island's west coast and French and English. Apart from being a fish name and that of both a language and a pidgin, chinook has the added meaning of a warm winter wind.
Illustration by Manami Kimura

Access: If you aren't hooked on sea kayaking yet, after this trip you will be. The Sechelt Peninsula is just beyond Howe Sound and is easily reached by bus or air from downtown Vancouver. **Malaspina Coach Lines** has twice daily service from Vancouver's Pacific Central Station adjacent to the Main Street Skytrain Station. If you are travelling light you can also catch the bus as it makes its way along West Georgia Street. Wait for the bus at the usual city bus stops near the northwest corner of Granville, Burrard, Thurlow, Bute or Denman Streets and be prepared to flag it down before it passes. The destination written on the front of the bus will be *Powell River.* Carry on baggage only is allowed at these stops.

The bus will board the Horseshoe Bay-Sechelt ferry and, after a brief 55 minute crossing, will continue for another 40 minutes or so to the small community of Sechelt. Grab a cab from the bus depot here and tell the driver you want to go to the Tillicum Bay Marina. Presumably you made reservations and someone from **Peddles & Paddles** will be expecting you. If not, worry not. Use the pay phone at the marina to let them know you have indeed arrived and in a few short minutes someone should show up to outfit you.

If you are carpooling, after disembarking from the ferry follow Highway 101 northward for about 35 km until you hit the first light in Sechelt. Turn right on Wharf Road and follow the blue signs to Porpoise Bay Provincial Park. Continue past the park on East Porpoise Bay Road until you reach Naylor Road. Turn left here and find appropriate parking at the marina mentioned above.

Chances are you took the 8:30 AM bus and arrived in Sechelt at 11:00 AM. By the time you find the launching point, take care of business and load up the boats it will already be nearing 1:00 PM. If you are lucky enough to set off on an ebbing tide you could probably reach Tzoonie Narrows Provincial Marine Park easily during the long evenings of summer but what's the rush?

If you have no need to hurry, head across the inlet for Piper Point, keeping an eye out for a pod of porpoises that make this waterway their home. From Piper Point begin making your way northward, stopping to check out each marine park until reaching the Halfway Provincial Marine Park 7 km away.

Sechelt Inlet and its two arms, Salmon Inlet and Narrows Inlet, are well-protected from the open seas of Georgia Strait. A narrow isthmus at the southern end separates the calm from the chaos while the Sechelt Peninsula itself forms a formidable barrier to the elements beyond. Only at the northern end are the seas connected once again. And what a connection it is! Skookumchuck Narrows is perhaps the most dangerous stretch of water on the entire British Columbia coast. Meaning literally "Big Waters" in Chinook Jargon, Skookumchuck can only be navigated during slack tide, a 20 to 30 minute period that occurs between the tides twice daily and, even then, should never be attempted by any but the most experienced paddlers. Rapids at Skookumchuck can reach beyond 12 knots per hour creating whirlpools capable of sucking a large log underwater and holding it there. You do not want to be here in a kayak. The good news is you have no need to even come close.

The other hazard of Sechelt Inlet, common to most coastal fjords, is high winds. As

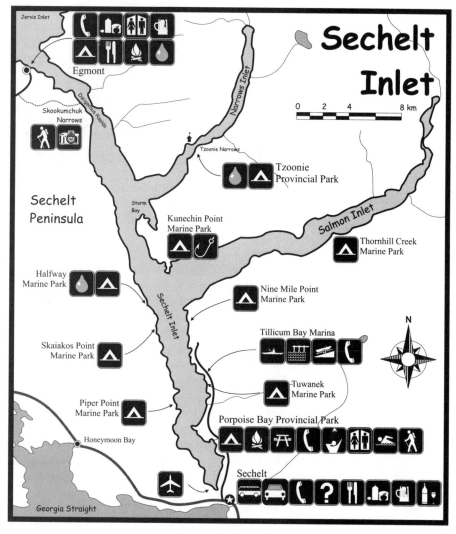

hot air from the adjacent land rises in the summer sun, cooler offshore air rushes in to replace it. The venturi effect of the narrow, steep-sided fjords funnel the wind to high speed. These *squamish* winds typically reach their peak in the late afternoon. 23 km long Salmon Inlet is particularly prone to these winds so paddlers crossing at the mouth can expect to

Roadkill

The author bags another one, posing here with one of Detroit's finest, abandoned on the beach of Sechelt Inlet by oyster farmers gone broke. Seaside ruins and trash are a common sight hereabouts, an ironic memorial to mariculture's early promise.

Nikonos V
35 mm Nikkor lens
Ektachrome 200 ISO film

be buffeted broadside. For this reason following the west side of the inlet to Halfway Provincial Marine Park is recommended. By hugging the shoreline at least some of the wind will be sheared by the landforms up and away from the surface.

Halfway Marine Park is endowed with an excellent water supply. If this is one of the finest campgrounds on the coast it's primarily because of the lovely pea gravel beach that looks directly up the length of Salmon Inlet. I recall fondly sitting around a driftwood fire with friends, sipping Italian red, as an osprey dove into the dusk-lit sea immediately in front of us and emerged victorious, a salmon in its clutches. Within seconds, however, a menacing bald eagle had challenged it. A midair battle ensued before our very eyes. Encumbered with the heavy fish the osprey was hopelessly out manoeuvred by the bullying eagle and, after a courageous effort, dropped the salmon back, plop, into the *salt chuck*. The eagle swooped down and scooped up its prize while the osprey flew off to continue the hunt once more.

Continuing north you'll soon come to a large deserted fish farm, a pioneering aquaculture attempt that faltered. Deserted rearing ponds, docks and shore buildings attest to a fortune lost.

The campsite at Kunechin Point is nicely situated and certainly worth an exploratory visit though a lack of fresh water, exposure to unrelenting sun and frequent high winds makes this a somewhat less than perfect place to pitch a

Car-Free Parking Lot
The rising sun glints off the sterns of kayaks arrayed along the beach at Halfway Provincial Marine Park. Though parked well-above the high tide line, tying the craft to a nearby tree is a precaution that should become habitual.

Nikonos V
35 mm Nikkor lens
Ektachrome 200 ISO film

tent. Be sure to watch for seals around the islands here. They'll certainly be watching for you. The beach immediately to the north is encrusted with oysters but never consume them during the hottest months of summer unless you have first checked with the **Red Tide Alert Hotline**. Red tide can be deadly and the toxins tend to accumulate in many shellfish during June, July, August and September.

Salmon Inlet is, frankly speaking, pretty ugly. Gigantic logging clearcuts and massive power transmission lines mar the landscape for its entire length. Paddle instead towards aptly-named Narrows Inlet which itself has suffered the lack of human foresight but is not nearly so devastated. As you pass under the transmission lines and round the corner into Storm Bay you'll note the current has shifted. If you were following a receding tide you'll suddenly begin bucking it or, vice versa, if you had been fighting the oncoming current you'll now enjoy a reprieve. Either way take some time to enjoy poking around the bay and its tiny islands. There are numerous cabins in the bay dating from the get-away-from-it-all sixties. Please respect this private property.

Continuing up the inlet you'll soon notice the private campsite on the east bank operated by **Tzoonie Outdoor Adventures**. A full service operation that boasts hot showers, a hot tub and fully-equipped kitchen, Tzoonie Outdoor Adventures operates a shuttle service for their customers and their gear including canoes or kayaks. Guests can also borrow crabbing or fishing equipment.

Continue onward to Tzoonie Narrows campsite and onetime logging operation. Rusted, abandoned equipment and apple and cherry trees attest to this bygone era. Stay alert, keeping in mind that bears love fruit. The campsite is top notch with sunny, open grassy lawns for erecting your tent. The water supply too is splendid though a bit far from the main camping area. A collapsible water jug comes in handy here.

Across the inlet a rustic cabin, built for communal use in the spirit of the counter-culture, and much to the chagrin of forest managers in the area, makes interesting exploring. Though some people still put up here it is old, beginning to rot and infested with mice. Just try getting a good night's sleep here. Not recommended.

Further up the inlet you'll encounter the narrows themselves: a mere 25 metres wide. Though not considered dangerous, the waters here can race up to four knots. Sheer, 1000 metre cliffs on the north side yield an awesome sense of nature's power.

If time allows spend an extra night at Tzoonie Narrows and continue exploring at a leisurely pace to the head of the inlet where the Tzoonie River empties. 🐾

Sea Kayaking
Sechelt Inlet

Location	Notes
Peddles & Paddles Tillicum Bay Marina Sechelt, BC (604) 885-6440 (604) 885-8205 Cellular	$70 Two day rental; Fiberglass single $95 Three day rental; Fiberglass single $140 Three day rental; Fiberglass double Lessons available on request. Wet suit rentals not available
Tzoonie Outdoor Adventures Narrows Inlet, BC (604) 885-9802	Camping Resort Boat shuttle from Sechelt Hot showers
Sunshine Coast Taxi 604-885-3666	Taxi Service
Tyee Airways (604) 689-8651 (604) 885-2214	Daily float plane service from Vancouver Harbour to Porpoise Bay (Sechelt)
Sechelt Tourist Information (604) 885-3100 (604) 885-0662 (604) 885-0691 sechelt_chamber@sunshine.net www.thesunshinecoast.com www.bigpacific.com	
Red Tide Alert Hotline (604) 666-2828 (604) 666-0583	A recorded mesasge that gives upto the minute information on paralytic shellfish poisoning. Listen for information for Area 16

Skookumchuck

Access: Take the bus as far as the turn off to Egmont [See **Getting to the Sunshine Coast** on page 333] where you will meet your prearranged pick up for the 8 km ride into Egmont itself. The owner of **Rising Sun Kayak Adventures** will arrange for a pick up as part of multi-day kayak rentals. This is something to add to the negotiations when calling to make your kayak reservations.

The tiny rural backwater of Egmont is an ideally situated jumping off point for a variety of prime kayaking areas including Nelson and Hardy Islands, Hotham Sound, Jervis Inlet in its entirety as well as the jewel at the end, Princess Louisa Inlet. All of Sechelt Inlet is likewise accessible from Egmont though a formidable barrier must first be circumvented. Since the raging rapids of Skookumchuck Narrows stand in the way it is the recommendation of this book that kayakers access Sechelt Inlet from its lower end only. That route is described on page 272.

Skookumchuck Narrows is a must-see phenomenon however and is best viewed from the safety of solid ground. An easy 4 km hike provides access to viewpoints overlooking the Narrows. The trailhead can be reached from Egmont by walking back towards Highway 101 for 20 minutes or so. Time your visit to coincide with a particularly extreme tidal mood swing to see the rapids in all their fury. The worst time to see this natural wonder is of course when the tide is slack. On a typical three-metre tide as much as 9 trillion litres of seawater is flushed through the narrows at speeds up to 26 km/h, spawning cascades as high as 5 metres; giant, basketball court-sized whirlpools; standing waves as big as a bus and a multitude of mixed metaphors.

Many of the place names hereabouts commemorate Commodore Nelson's 1797 victory over the Spanish during the Battle of St. Vincent. Nelson's superior officer was Sir John Jervis while Captain Island takes its name from the *H. M. S. Captain,* Nelson's flagship. Another flagship from Nelson's victory at the Nile has been reincarnated as Vanguard Bay while Nelson's man-of-war, the *H. M. S. Agamemnon* has morphed into the narrow channel separating Nelson's very own island from the mainland. The names date from the 1860s when Captain Richards undertook a detailed survey of the coast from the *H. M. Plumper.* He borrowed names for Hotham Sound, Hardy Island, Cape Cockburn and Fearney Point from captains of other ships which took part in Lord Nelson's celebrated victories. The regal reaches of Jervis Inlet derive their names from fur trading vessels dedicated to royalty which plied the coast hereabouts in the late 1780s.

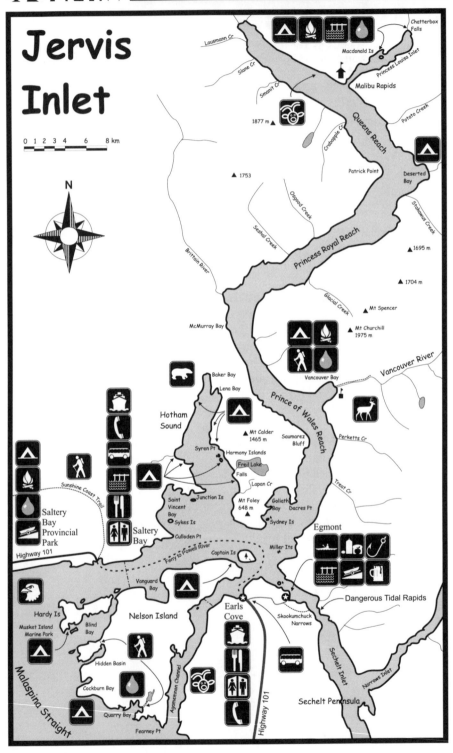

Jervis
Inlet

0 1 2 3 4   6   8 km

N

Lausmann Cr
Slane Cr
Smanit Cr
Chatterbox Falls
Macdonald Is
Princess Louisa Inlet
Malibu Rapids
Queens Reach
Patato Creek
1877 m ▲
Crabapple Cr
Patrick Point
Deserted Bay
1753 ▲
Osgood Creek
Princess Royal Reach
Stakumus Creek
1695 m ▲
Seshal Creek
1704 m ▲
Brittain River
Glacial Creek
Mt Spencer ▲
McMurray Bay
Mt Churchill 1975 m ▲
Vancouver River
Baker Bay
Lena Bay
Vancouver Bay
Hotham Sound
Prince of Wales Reach
Mt Calder 1465 m ▲
Saumarez Bluff
Perketts Cr
Syren Pt
Harmony Islands
Freil Lake
Falls
Lapan Cr
Treat Cr
Sunshine Coast Trail
Saint Vincent Bay
Junction Is
Mt Foley 648 m ▲
Goliath Bay
Dacres Pt
Sykes Is
Sydney Is
Saltery Bay Provincial Park
Egmont
Culloden Pt
Highway 101
Miller Itts
Saltery Bay
Ferry to Powell River
Captain Is
Dangerous Tidal Rapids
Vanguard Bay
Hardy Is
Earls Cove
Skookumchuck Narrows
Musket Island Marine Park
Blind Bay
Nelson Island
Malaspina Straight
Hidden Basin
Agamemnon Channel
Sechelt Inlet
Narrows Inlet
Cockburn Bay
Quarry Bay
Highway 101
Sechelt Peninsula
Fearney Pt

278

Princess Louisa Inlet

Level: Moderate   **Distance:** 14 km r/t

Time: 1 day   **Warning:** Rapids

Marine Chart: Jervis Inlet 3514

Access: Via Egmont as above   **Tide Table:** Egmont

Trickle Treat

Just one of the more than sixty sun-dappled waterfalls gracing the cliffs around Princess Louisa Inlet. Topping up water bottles is a snap hereabouts.

Nikon F
135 mm Nikkor lens
Kodachrome 200 ISO film

Malibu Camp, a nondenominational christian youth centre situated at the mouth of Princess Louisa Inlet, has good news for kayakers. Until recently a visit to this magical little waterway required a boat, an airplane or, for kayakers, a week or more to paddle the full length of Jervis Inlet. Every six days throughout the summer the 38 metre Malibu Princess makes a freight run to Malibu camp and kayakers can piggyback to the head of the inlet, turning a momentous undertaking into a simple day trip. Alternately, more intrepid paddlers can reach deep into the Inlet on the Malibu Princess and paddle back one way. Being on a six-day cycle means the ship leaves on a different day each week. Call to get their schedule of departures or to book passage. Though not explicitly noted in company literature, the captain was adamant about ensuring that we were well-fed on the morning red-eye as well as the return voyage at supper time.

Upon arrival at Malibu Camp the ship will dock at one of two wharves depending on the tides. If water is high and the captain decides to use the inner dock then kayakers can just paddle away once their craft is unloaded. The more likely scenario however is that the Malibu Princess will dock on the outside, presenting kayakers with four choices: shoot the rapids on a flood tide, wait for slack water to navigate Malibu Narrows, portage through the camp and around the whitewater or hitch a ride aboard the smaller vessels which are used to ferry freight around the rapids. In all likelihood kayakers will have to wait until all of the freight is unloaded but this service is included in the price of passage.

If planning to return to Egmont aboard the Malibu Princess on the same day keep an eye on the clock. Be sure to keep the captain apprised of your intentions and find out directly from him exactly what time the ship will be returning in the late afternoon. The Malibu Princess actually makes two return trips along Jervis Inlet on the same day. The first one is the freight run at 6 AM which returns to Egmont with a load of 300 happy campers. On the next run the ship will arrive at Malibu Camp stuffed to the gunwales with a fresh batch of christians teens. If you can return to the camp early enough the arrival ceremony is a spectacle certainly worth watching. On the final run back to Egmont the ship will be virtually empty.

Rising Sun Kayaking will deliver rental kayaks to the Malibu Princess in the morning, picking them up again at the end of the day.

Malibu was originally built for the gliterati of the 1940s. Since wildlife and the wild life are incongruous, the luxury resort failed to attract enough of the spoiled Hollywood crowd to make a profit. Eventually it was sold to the Young Life Foundation which provides christian retreats for hundreds of teens each summer.

From the first dip of the paddle it will become apparent that Princess Louisa Inlet is

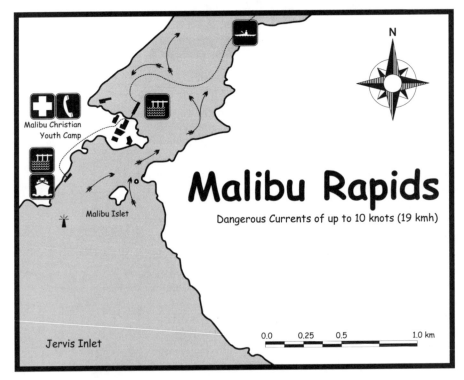

Malibu Christian
Youth Camp

Malibu Islet

Malibu Rapids

Dangerous Currents of up to 10 knots (19 kmh)

N

Jervis Inlet

0.0   0.25   0.5   1.0 km

nothing less than a natural wonder. Surprisingly calm conditions prevail in the narrow waterway which is just 7 km long, sandwiched between towering granite walls laced with countless waterfalls on either side. During spring runoff until late June more than 60 waterfalls can be seen dropping 2000 metres or more into the sea. At the head of the Inlet, Lo-

Yodelaheehoo!
The cliffs at Echo Rock are the perfect place to hone those yodeling skills.

"There is no scenery in the world that can beat it. Not that I've seen the rest of the world. I don't need to, I've seen Princess Louisa Inlet."
by Erle Stanley Gardner
Log of a Landlubber

Nikon F
28 mm Nikkor lens
Kodachrome 200 ISO film

quilts Creek crashes over 37 metre Chatterbox Falls filling the air with thunder and a fine cooling mist. Rustic campsites can be found adjacent to the falls or about halfway along the inlet tucked in behind Macdonald Island.

Though half a day is plenty of time to paddle the length of Princess Louisa Inlet and back it is certainly not enough time to fully appreciate its splendour.

The park at the head of the inlet owes its existence to the generosity of "Mac" Macdonald who purchased the land in 1927. Having struck the motherlode the previous year while prospecting in Nevada, James Macdonald promptly retired, wintering over in Mexico while devoting his summers to Chatterbox Falls. Never the recluse, "Mac" considered himself to be just a custodian of the property which rightfully belonged to the wider society of mariners who frequent the area. As early as 1953 "Mac" transferred title of the property to a perpetual trust which in turn discharged its duty by overseeing the formation of a Provincial Marine Park. "Mac" continued to host all manner of visitor to the park until 1972, when, at the age of 83, he retired for good. He died six years later.

Refer to the map of Malibu Rapids to see the best approach when returning on a flooding tide. The venturi effect of the narrows accelerates the water up to 19 km/h. As it leaves the chute the current bounces off the south wall, cutting across to the other side of the Inlet before straightening out. Kayakers should approach along the southern wall carefully watching the line of foam to discern current patterns. Head into the current at an oblique angle as it cuts across the inlet. Expect your kayak to be jolted hard when it reaches the main stream. Paddle like mad at this point steering with but across the stream towards the cliffs along the opposite bank. Your objective is to catch the back eddies which will sweep you towards the dock. If you miss the back eddies you will be swept back into the inlet from which you must try again. Bucking the tides head on is an exercise in futility.

Unless of course you want to shoot the chute on the ebbing tide hug the cliffs along the north bank to make an end run around the main part of the current. Upon reaching the dock hang on, especially when clambering out, to avoid losing your kayak to the current. Though Malibu rapids is nowhere near as menacing as those at Skookumchuck, better than average kayak competence and the confidence which comes with it are needed to run them. Expect a drop of a third of a metre with the turbulence of a Class III river. Veer to the right of Malibu Islet if possible to reach the outside wharf. 🐾

Vanilla Leaf

While modern adventurers smear their skin with toxic chemicals to keep pesky bugs at bay, natives of the Pacific Northwest took a less carcinogous approach. The fresh-squeezed juice of common Vanilla Leaf was applied to fend off mosquitos and black flies. Dried leaves, smelling faintly of vanilla, were hung in bunches about the longhouse for the same purpose. A potion of boiled Vanilla Leaf was used to wash bedding to eliminate bed bugs and mites and as a hair treatment to fend off lice and fleas. Look for Vanilla Leaf at trailside in heavy forest wherever moisture accumulates.

Illustration by Manami Kimura

Jervis Inlet

Level: Difficult   **Distance:** 77 km o/w

Time: 7 day min   **Warning:** High Winds

Tide Table: Blind Bay   **Chart:** Jervis Inlet 3514

Access: Via Egmont as above

Practice Perfection

When calm, warm conditions prevail set aside time for practicing the techniques which could ensure survival should weather turn gnarly. Wet exits, rolls, self and group rescue drills, once mastered, will enable paddlers to extend their range to any corner of the coast during any season. Practising them with your usual paddling pals can only inspire confidence among the group members.

Nikon F
28 mm Nikkor lens
Ektachrome 200 ISO film

Seasoned kayakers may want to paddle the length of Jervis Inlet in order to reach Princess Louisa Inlet, taking the Malibu Princess or a water taxi out again when time constraints prevent paddling both ways. High winds along Jervis Inlet are common while places to pull kayaks out of the water are not. Unless setting out during slack water expect strong but not perilous currents from the get go at Egmont. Aim for the Sutton Islets in the center of the channel, taking a new bearing on Egmont Point after passing the funky island community. Seals have established their own community on the Miller Islets, 4 km from Egmont. If seas are calm skirt the islands to exchange gawks with the basking brutes. Stay well offshore though to avoid needlessly stressing them.

From the Miller Islets to Vancouver Bay 17 km further on hug the eastern shore of the Inlet. If you happen to see a spot to land and stretch take it, the next one could be hours away. The mouths of rivers and creeks in particular may offer a sliver of gravel on which to pause depending on the tides. The first suitable camping area you are likely to encounter along Prince of Wales Reach will be found at the muddy mouth of the Vancouver River. Though once an important settlement of the Sechelt Indian band, there are at present no full-time residents though land hereabouts is still designated as reserve land. A camp has been set up in the bay however for inculcating native values among band youths. Visitors from outside are discouraged.

A hiking trail follows the Vancouver River inland providing a good opportunity to stretch the cockpit cramps out of leg and back muscles.

Continue hugging the shore of Jervis Inlet as you resume paddling inland. A windless, early morning start on incoming tide would be ideal as you can expect to cover 34 km before reaching Deserted Bay where the next best camping will be found. In a pinch, the Indian reserve at the mouth of the Brittain River should yield a suitable site for camping. Brittain River, formerly a permanent settlement famed for crafting dugout canoes, is 15 km from Vancouver Bay on the opposite side of Princess Royal Reach.

An uncharacteristic lowland stretching from Stakawus Creek to Deserted Bay and beyond suddenly provides numerous opportunities for pitching a tent. Once again the land belongs to the Sechelt Band though no-trace camping is permitted. Deserted Bay, a once thriving community of Tsonai Coast Salish, had been abandonded by the time it got its name.

From Deserted Bay the steep-sided fjord resumes as Queens Reach. Malibu Rapids is a mere 11 km further on. Just 2 km beyond Malibu a pictograph can be seen at cliff side. Another important Coast Salish settlement, that of the Hunaechin, was once situated at the head of Jervis Inlet, 11 km further on in a northwesterly direction.

When Captain Vancouver reached the head of the fjord he was overcome with despondency, tersely noting in the ship's log, "All our hopes vanished." The good captain was of course pursuing that elusive chimera, known as the Northwest Passage. Princess Louisa Inlet evaded him as well. Likely he mistook the Malibu Rapids for the mouth of a river. 🐾

Bull Kelp

Besides being edible, and delicious at that, this gigantic algae had a number of important technological uses for coastal First Nations. The stalks were spliced together to make fishing lines hundreds of metres long. Though brittle when dried the lines could be thus stored indefinitely. Soaking before use would resore pliability and strength suited to hauling halibut from the depths. The hollow stalks could be employed as water conduits as well. Bulb and wide upper stalk were employed in the kitchen as squeeze tubes and storage containers for edible oils. Salves and ointments made of deer fat and other ingredients could be poured in the bulbs as well. Upon hardening the kelp was peeled away leaving a "cake" of skin cream or sun screen

Illustration by Manami Kimura

Nelson Island Circumnavigation

Level: Challenging   **Distance:** 60 km

Time: 2 - 3 days   **Warning:** Winds & Currents

Tide Table: Blind Bay   **Chart:** Jervis Inlet 3514

Access: Via Egmont as above

Topsy-Turvey Tenters
Breaking camp in Agamemnon Channel. An oncoming tide and heavy seas forced us ashore the afternoon before. Though a less than ideal spot to pitch a tent we awoke to placid conditions in which to continue our wanderings. Nelson and Captain Islands in the background.

Nikon F
28 mm Nikkor lens
Ektachrome 200 ISO film

Squeeze three days of freedom from urban reality and you have enough time to explore Nelson Island at a leisurely pace. Those arriving on the last bus of the day can find shelter and sustenance at the Backeddy Pub in Egmont. Be forewarned however that the campsite is a rowdy, noisy fisherman's camp; little more than a parking lot. There will be no guarantee of a good night's sleep in the great outdoors but an early start the next morning is possible. Depending on the drunken cacophony the night before make as much noise is possible when you get up. Keep in mind however that should you get into trouble out on the water these are the guy is who will most likely be in a position to help.

Set off early on a calm, sunny day with a receding tide and life couldn't get better. Let the riffles pull you around the corner to the west where you can anticipate turbulence at the best times. In the waters off Captain Island three separate tidal streams converge with equally fuddled air flows often meeting above the water. Go with the flow and it will suck you 16 km through Agamemnon Channel, the narrow but deep passage between Nelson Island and the Sechelt Peninsula. Did you remember to check the Marine weather forecast before setting out? The currents of Agamemnon Channel will deposit you into the open waters of Malaspina Strait where, on a gusty day, white caps will be waiting to greet you. Whatever the conditions you have little choice but to turn right at Fearney Point and make for Quarry Bay. If tides are incoming, set off around Nelson Island in a counter-clockwise direction instead of bucking the currents in Agamemnon Channel.

Quarry Bay was once the source of the finest masonry granite on the coast. Stone from the abandoned quarry found its way into many of the neoclassical buildings of Vancouver and Victoria. A short trail leads from the bay to Little Quarry Lake, ideal for a dip or drink on a hot summer day.

Let the prevailing southeasterlies push you 6 km further on to Cape Cockburn for prime coastal camping. The sunsets overlooking Texeda Island more than compensate for the sometimes blustery location.

Once around the cape take a moment to explore narrow Cockburn Bay before proceeding on to Hidden Basin. From the head of the lagoon a hiking trail cuts across the narrow isthmus to Blind Bay. During inclement weather portaging across may be preferable to paddling around. The reefs and islets of Blind Bay are sure to offer refuge during even the worst of weather. Camping can be found next to Hardy Island on tiny Musket Island.

An escape hatch, in the form of Telescope Passage, provides a hasty exit from Blind Bay on an incoming tide. On your explorations of the north coast of Nelson Island a wide indentation, Vanguard Bay, has been provided to poke around in. Captain Island will be the last stop before paddling once again across the confused waters at the convergence of Sechelt Inlet, Jervis Inlet and Agamemnon Channel. Camping will be found on Nelson Island just across from the western tip of Captain Island. At the opposite end of the Captain Island a short forest trail leads from the shore to a stand of ancient cedars. Take the opportunity to stretch out here as the next stop is Egmont.

Salal

Though not a popular trail-side snack in modern times, salal berries are not only edible, they are quite tasty. Perhaps the "hairiness" of the berries or the grainy texture imparted by their many, tiny seeds is a turnoff to jaded modern palettes. Being plentiful throughout the coast, salal berries were an important component of pre-European diets hereabouts. Aboriginal groups generally consumed salal berries directly from the bush or processed them into a kind of fruit leather for storage. These cakes were then reconstituted with water and served mixed with the omnipresent oolichan grease. An acquired taste, no doubt. The deep purple colouring of the berries found use in dying bakets. Salal berries are presently used primarily in jams and pies. The bright, leathery foliage is commercially harvested for use in floral displays world-wide.

Illustration by Manami Kimura

Hotham Sound Loop

Level: Challenging   **Distance:** 54 km

Time: 2 - 3 days   **Warning:** Winds, Open Water

Tide Table: Blind Bay   **Chart:** Jervis Inlet 3514

Access: Via Egmont as above

Forked Freil Falls...
...never fails to impress first time visitors to Hotham Sound.

Nikon F
28 mm Nikkor lens
Ektachrome 200 ISO film

No matter how you slice it crossing several kilometres of open water will be necessary in order to reach Hotham Sound. The shortest gap is two kilometres across the ferry lanes from Captain Island to Foley Head. A further sprint of 1.3 km across the ferry lanes through the turbulence at the head of Agamemnon Channel is necessitated by this approach however. Make for Egmont Point after launching your graceful craft instead. Once past the point steer a course for Foley Head 3.4 km away. On this bearing only the currents of Jervis Inlet come into play and marine traffic is far less up-and-down the channel. As a bonus, the seal haul out at the Miller Islets provides a distraction about a quarter of the way across. Powerful winds do emanate from Jervis Inlet so an early morning start is recommended.

At Foley Head zig right for a side excursion to explore

nearby Sydney Island and Goliath Bay or zag left and follow the coastline for another 4 kilometres before rounding into the typically calm waters of Hotham Sound proper. Either way you're bound to encounter a number of active aquaculture operations tucked into the nooks and crannies of the coast hereabouts.

Hotham Sound
An incoming tide threatens to dislodge these Precambrian kayaks from the foreshore at Freil Falls. Fastening the bow line securely, even when leaving kayaks unattended for a few moments only, can save hours of grief not to mention a face omlette. Nelson Island is in the background.

Nikon F
28 mm Nikkor lens
Ektachrome 200 ISO film

Plan to stop at Granville Bay for lunch, a snack or a much-needed stretch at the very least. Paddlers will want to stumble out of their boats again for pictures at the rocky beach in front of 444 m Freil Falls, a spectacular hanging valley visible even from the ferry as it shuttles its way between Earl's Cove and Saltery Bay. The small, oyster-encrusted beach just prior to the falls is an ideal place to pitch up to five tents. A seasonal brook pours fresh water over the rocks at the south end of the beach.

Less than a kilometre further on, Harmony Islands Provincial Marine Park is undeveloped, lacking both water and decent access but the south end could do in a pinch. Being only 12 km from Egmont you may wish to push on however, secure in the knowledge that beaches suited to camping abound in Hotham Sound. The small prominence before Syren Pt, for instance, hides a landing, a dependable source of ice cold water and even a viewpoint from which to toast the sun god's daily demise.

Be sure to include an oyster-shucking knife in your camping kit whenever advisements from the Red Tide Hotline are favourable. Pry open the lid, add a squeeze of lemon and a dash of Worcestershire sauce then tip it back. Yum! There's nothing quite like oysters on the half shell fresh from the source. Return the shells to the water so the microscopic oyster spawn they harbour can mature and so bears with a gourmet flair will not be attracted to your site.

Continue probing the foreshore to the twin bays, Lena and Baker, at the head of the sound before doubling back along the opposite shore to St. Vincent Bay.

A well-developed campsite, established by kayaking outfitters, will be found 3 km from Baker Bay. Several more sites will be found across the sound from the Harmony Islands.

Culloden Point, 18 km from Baker Bay, is the jumping off point for another open water crossing. Currents are not significant here but your group will be crossing the ferry lane. As always cluster together to enhance your visibility as you make the three kilometre sprint to Nelson Island. Numerous spots to pitch a tent will present themselves along the final 10 km of the trip but the best beach by far will be found just before Captain Island. If still uncomfortable with turbulent water choose an early morning or late afternoon slack tide to scoot across the ferry lane of Agamemnon Channel on the final leg of your return to Egmont. Whenever forced to paddle against an outflowing tide in Skookumchuck Narrows hug the shoreline to pick up a boost from the numerous backeddies here.

Jervis Inlet Sea Kayaking

Location	Notes
Malaspina Coach Lines (604) 682-6511 Vancouver (604) 885-2217 Sechelt	See Schedule in Appendix
Rising Sun Kayak Adventures 1-800-632-0722 (604) 929-9230 Vancouver (604) 883-2062 Egmont	Kayak Rentals Kayak Tours Shuttle from Highway 101 with rental
Egmont Marina Resort 1-800-626-0599 (604) 883-2298 info@egmont-marina.com www.egmont-marina.com/	Boat Rentals, Camping, Cabins, Showers, Laundry, Pub, Resturant, Store, Diving Tours, Seaplane Charters
Malibu Princess (604)883-2003 (604) 883-2082 Fax	Return kayak transportation to Princess Louisa Inlet $69 Custom group charters 126 foot luxury cruiser with 3 decks
Egmont Water Taxi (604) 883-2092 taxi@bigpacific.com www.bigpacific.com/egmontwatertaxi	5 Hour Princess Louisa Inlet Tour $75 26 foot aluminum crew boat Local Water Taxi Service
Serve-West Express (604) 883-0262	24 hour Water Taxi Service
Suncoast Charters 1-800-837-2939 Phone 604-740-7413 Fax 604-883-2699 suncoast_charters@sunshine.net www.suncoastcharters.8m.com	Hotham Sound Eco Tours Custom Kayak Transport Fishing Charters
Red Tide Alert Hotline (604) 666-2828 (604) 666-0583	Management Area 16

Clayoquot Sound

Clayoquot Sound was the site of an intense battle in the early 1990s between multinational logging interests and a coalition of environmental and Native Indian groups. Hundreds were arrested for blockading logging roads but ultimately protesters won a number of concessions over big business. Not the least of these was, belatedly, a five year moratorium on all logging in the area with perpetual protection for many major blocks of rain forest.

Kayaking out of Tofino, on the edge of Clayoquot Sound, is logistically very simple. The **Tofino Sea Kayaking Company**, where you pick up your kayak is located next to the Canadian Coast Guard just a few steps away from the bus depot. After you arrive walk down towards the main dock turning right on Main Street. You cannot miss the funky kayak shop and espresso bar.

Getting to Tofino by bus, while pretty simple from Vancouver, is a full day trip. Nonetheless, if you arrive in the mid-afternoon, June to September, there's still plenty of time to get organized, equipped and paddle 4 km over to a gorgeous sandy beach on Vargas Island. Since the beach, which lies south of Rassier Point, is somewhat exposed to the open Pacific you can expect the be kayaking in fairly heavy rollers with surf breaking on the beach making landing troublesome at the very least. There's only one thing to do. Ride the surf in while paddling like mad and then, when the surf recedes leaving you high and dry on the beach, quickly jump out and pull your craft further up the beach before the next breaker rolls in. The southern end of the beach belongs to the Yarkis Indian reserve. Respect this traditional land and refrain from camping here.

If you decide to stay in a hotel with a real bed and a shower check out **Maquinna Lodge**, virtually across the street from the Tofino Sea Kayaking Company. It's nothing special but the rooms are clean and quiet and it's budget-priced. As always reservations are recommended.

From your campsite on the edge of Clayoquot Sound you have choices, many choices. This book will outline two popular routes but the sound is a nearly limitless web of open Pacific and protected inland waterways, islands big and small with channels and inlets and arms and bays reaching in every direction. You could easily spend weeks exploring this part of the coast and still never see it all. A word of warning however. Do not venture beyond land into the open Pacific unless you are a confident kayaker with many nautical kilometres and years of paddling behind you. 🐾

Meares Circumnavigation

Level: Challenging **Distance:** 55 km **Time:** 2-4 days

Warning: Strong Currents **Tide Table:** Tofino **Chart:** 3673

Here's where knowing and understanding your tide chart can be a big bonus. For some reason the tide floods in a huge clockwise circle almost completely around Meares Island. The current ebbs in the other direction. Consulting your tide table, you can decide which direction to tackle the island in, allowing the current to push or pull you around the island. Only for the 10 km stretch along Browning Passage will you likely be fighting the tide. The difference in effort required is quite astounding. We found that tidal actions on the far side of Meares tended to lag about an hour behind times predicted for Tofino in the tide chart.

Assuming you spent the night on the beach at Rassier Point and that you can follow a tidal flow in a clockwise direction, head north into Maurus Channel after launching your craft in the surf. Otherwise follow these instructions in reverse. With a current and the prevailing tailwind you'll make time quickly. At Robert Point 5 km away and again just beyond it are two rough, somewhat inadequate campsites. Continuing on to Sarnac Island and beyond keep in mind that sources of good drinking water can be hard to come by all over the rocky coast of British Columbia. The north side of Meares Island is no exception so stay close to the cliffs and watch for a clean little stream about 3 km past Sarnac Island.

Fourteen kilometres after you started you'll begin to feel the pull of Matlset Narrows. Currents here reach up to 4 knots or 7½ km/h so sit back and enjoy the ride. If you didn't read your tide chart correctly or threw caution to the wind and decided to buck the tide then here you'll regret it. For the next three kilometres you'll be working hard just to maintain. A number of beaches on the north side are good for camping though some are a bit steep. Camping at the little tombolo on the south side is marginal at best. If you continue on into Warn Bay you'll find an excellent site with a good source of water at an unnamed cove just beyond the beaches. Squatters have anchored a float cabin here offshore but will enjoy a friendly hello from their unexpected neighbours. As a bonus this site is well-endowed with large patches of sea asparagus for those craving greens in their diet. For obvious reasons be sure to set your tents well above the most recent high water mark which can be discerned as a thin line of green seaweed and flotsam and jetsam. Beaches are narrow throughout the area but there should be enough space for a tent or two.

On the western side of Warn Bay you may enjoy watching the operation of a salmon farm in full swing. Rearing, feeding, catching and processing these fish is a full time, all-consuming occupation but in the evening hours the workers may find chatting with curious paddlers a pleasant distraction. Who knows, they may be willing to sell you a fish for supper. Try barbequing it the Indian way for a very tasty treat.

Next morning get up with the tides again and catch another subsidized ride, this time heading south along Fortune Channel. As you round Plover Point into Mosquito Harbour keep an eye out for feeding seals. One of the inquisitive sea mammals popped up just 3 metres from my boat for a lengthy peek, so close in fact that his heavy breathing was clearly audible. Moments later, as we sat enjoying our lunch on the largest of the Wood Islets a small pod of Pacific white-sided dolphins cruised by, headed in the direction from which we had just come.

Mosquito Harbour makes a pleasant exploratory side trip and you'll find passable camping at the head of the harbour. Halfway along the deep inlet on the west bank note the pilings and other vestiges of Sutton Cedar Mill, site of a onetime "gypo" lumbering operation. Though few of the forests of Meares Island ever felt the bite of the loggers axe, those hereabouts certainly did. One giant western red cedar, 5 metres in diameter, at the mouth of Sutton Mill Creek was bypassed by fallers of the day and still stands towering 49 metres above the tidal flats.

Continuing south past the Kirshaw Islets we were lucky to encounter a yearling black bear foraging on the beach. As he shared our curiosity we were able to move in close and watch him watching us for several minutes before something deep in his young heart informed him that he was faced with creatures perhaps best avoided and he

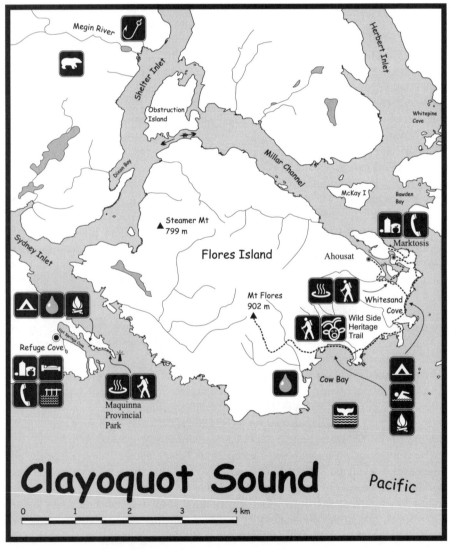

retreated slowly into the gloom of the rain forest understory.

Following that moment of truth we encountered an even stranger phenomenon. Suddenly, maybe half a kilometre in front of us a large ominous-looking standing wave appeared, lasted 10 minutes, then vanished without a trace. Some inexplicable tidal phenomenon? The back of a whale? A hydra-headed sea monster or sun-heated delusion? We'll probably never know.

At Heelboom Bay, otherwise known as C'is-a-qis, you'll find limited if acceptable camping, plenty of water and a dirty, mouse-infested cabin built by The Friends of Clayoquot, an environmental conglomerate designed to eliminate logging. From here, at one time a concerted campaign was mounted to save Meares Island from the loggers' chain saws. Behind the cabin a rough trail leads 4 hours across island to the Great Cedar

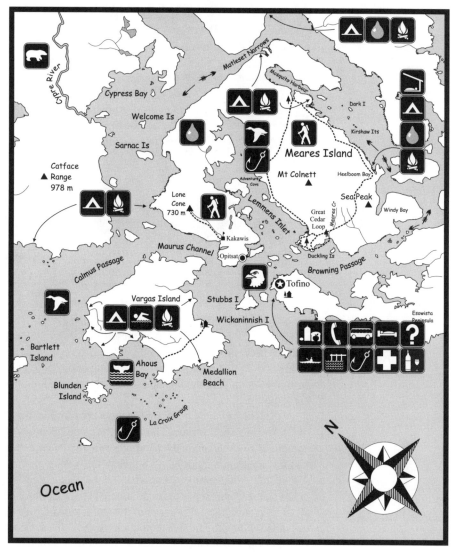

Loop, a grove of giant cedars, once threatened, now protected. If intent on viewing these ancient conifers paddling over to Lemmens Inlet is a perhaps a better choice since you'll be passing it by anyway before the day is out. First however, the confused waters at the southeast corner of Meares Island will have to be overcome.

Beached
A rapidly receding tide leaves this kayaker high and dry on a shell beach. Like the man said: shove off!

Nikon F
135 mm Nikkor lens
Ektachrome 200 ISO film

Strong currents through Dawley Passage will either treat or tease you but here the rip is mercifully short. As you round Auseth Point into Browning Passage the tide abruptly changes direction. With superior planning and a little help from the moon you may be able to ride the last 10 km on a receding tide.

At Duckling Island make for Meares Creek for a glimpse of a towering Sitka spruce. Though the top was sheered off sometime over the ages by wind or snow this spruce still tips the scales at a colossal 48.8 metres tall with a girth of 4.4 metres. Sitka spruce is known to be particularly resistant to salt spray and tends to predominate at the foreshore of BC's wild west coast. For more of the same, paddle over to the other end of the tidal flats to pick up the 2.6 km Great Cedar Loop, a popular ecotourism destination. Alternatively look for a small jetty around the corner adjacent to Morpheus Island. Innumerable venerable old western red cedars and sitka spruce have agglomerated on this lowland peninsula including the world's fourth tallest western red cedar: 42.7 metres tall and 18.3 metres around at the base.

Lemmens Inlet cuts deep into the heart of Meares Island, revealing an environment rich in mud flats and eel grass, the cradle of life for so many species from lowly molluscs and crustaceans to apex species like dolphins and bald eagles and black bears. Herring seek the eel grass for spawning while young salmon smolts use it as a hideout in which to mature. In addition, fishermen will find bottom feeders such as rock cod or flounder in abundance. Lemmens Inlet is also an important stopover on the flyways of many migratory birds and should be particularly animated in spring and fall.

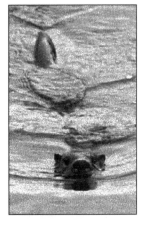

Adventure Cove is site of Fort Defiance, built in 1791 by American entrepreneur Robert Gray. Though the centuries have erased the trading post completely, the site is now classified as a BC Heritage Site.

When you head back to Tofino swing by Beck Island for a good look at a low level eagle's eyrie. Boat and seaplane traffic can be heavy in Tofino Harbour so stay together and be aware of activity around you. In the event of fog stay close to channel markers, something other navigators will be intent on avoiding.. 🐾

You Otter Know

Many confuse ocean-going river otters with sea otters. The latter are rare though were once common enough to have played a significant role in the exploration of the province. Europeans, mad as hatters, scoured coastal British Columbia in their quest after sea otter pelts, hunting the mammals nearly to extinction. They have staged somewhat of a comeback in places like Nootka Sound and the Queen Charlotte Islands.

River otters on the other hand are a common sight to coastal kayakers, often allowing the silent craft to approach within a few metres.

Nikon F
300 mm Nikkor lens
Ektachrome 200 ISO film

Hot Springs Cove

Level: Difficult   **Distance:** 114 km

Time: 2-3 days   **Tide Table:** Tofino

Warning: Open Ocean   **Marine Chart:** 3673 & 3674

Shower Power
Getting into hot water is fine when it is the sulpher-scented kind. Ramsay Hot Spring at Maquinna Provincial Park gushes over a cliff at a temperature of 51° C, tumbling down through a succession of pools, each one cooler than the last.

Nikon F
28 mm Nikkor lens
Kodachrome 64 ISO film

This extremely popular route begins much the same as the previous Meares Island circumnavigation. From Maurus Channel however, veer west into Calmus Passage under the stern gaze of the Catface Range. After some 4½ km of protected paddling you'll break into the relatively open waters between Flores and Vargas Island. Granted, a wide array of small islands, rocks and reefs break up the breakers somewhat as they roll in off the Pacific but, on a stormy day, that protection is spurious at best. The most direct route across the gap is still 5½ km ending at Gibson Marine Park on the southeastern tip of Flores Island. Hugging the coast of Vancouver Island, though longer, provides access to many beaches for camping, exploring or just stretching the cramps out of legs and shoulders.

Though very likely crowded, Whitesand Cove at Gibson Marine Park is well worth a visit. The park, 17 km from Tofino, is comprised of two sandy crescents that make great camping and a somewhat coolish hot springs located at the southern end of Matilda Inlet and accessible by trail from Whitesand Cove. The clear, odourless spring water gurgles out at 25°C into a cement pool measuring 6 x 2.4 metres and 1.2 metres deep.

In addition, the Ahousaht Wild Side Heritage Trail cuts across Whitesand Cove, stretching from the community of

Marktosis to Cow Bay 11 km away and beyond, for the truly energetic, to the peak of Mount Flores. The interpretive trail was established by Ahousaht women to build pride and develop employment locally. Guides are available to share native history and culture with the many visitors who pass through each year. Guided tours can be prearranged by calling 1-888-670-9586. Ancient forests, middens, culturally modified trees and a dozen secluded beaches are just some of the highlights of the tour.

The route along the lee side of Flores Island is generally protected and as such is the waterway of choice for local fishermen, forest workers, tour boats and water taxis. Being protected from the breakers of the open Pacific, the foreshore of Millar Channel [16 km] and Shelter Inlet [8 km] are steep and fjord-like with suitable places to pitch a tent less common than on the weather ravaged windward side of Flores Island.

As the name suggests Obstruction Island creates a venturi effect, magnifying tidal currents throughout the 2.4 km length of Hayden Passage. Plan to reach the narrow waterway at slack or, better yet, on an ebbing tide and let the man in the moon do the driving.

After rounding the north west corner of Flores Island at Starling Point expect wind and wave to pick up. Depending on the conditions, scoot across the Sydney Inlet to enjoy the refuge provided by Openit Peninsula. Though camping is prohibited anywhere in the park, pull out at the tiny sandy cove just 2½ km further on, just prior to Sharp Point at the very tip of Maquinna Provincial Park. Those dying for a soak will be heartened to know that Ramsay Hot Spring, as the geothermal vent is called, is just a few steps away. Otherwise continue paddling for another couple kilometres into Hot Springs Cove , landing at the busy government wharf. Camping can be found, for a fee, on adjacent private property. Drinking water, available from a hand pump just above the dock, is foul-tasting though potable in a pinch. Avoid it altogether by topping up well-before reaching the cove.

From the wharf the hot spring is a pleasant 1½ km jog along a split cedar boardwalk. Many mariners have replaced boards with name plates from their ships making for interesting reading along the way.

The hot spring is one of the province's finest, clear, slightly sulphurous, gurgling out of a crack in the rocks at 51° C, far too hot for immediate use. Thankfully the water tumbles over a short cliff, cascading down through a succession of soaking pools, each one slightly cooler than the one above it. Soaking in the bottom pool is a delight. Hot

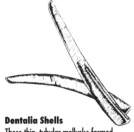

Dentalia Shells
These thin, tubular mollusks formed the currency of commerce throughout the Pacific Northwest as long as 3000 years ago. Pre-European civilization is often considered a barter economy, with, for instance, coastal tribes swapping oolichan grease directly for prized Oregon obsidian. Commodity traders, however, could rely on this *wampum* to close a transaction when interest in the goods was decidedly one-sided. Dentalia shells possessed all the necessary attributes of money being portable, recognizable and durable but rare and desirable enough to foster trade. Being available in a variety of sizes, the tusk-like shells were even divisible into small change. Professional traders are known to have tattooed measuring lines on their forearms as a handy calculator of individual shell values. Only a handful of groups, including the Nuu-chah-nulth in the vicinity of Tofino, possessed dentalia in quantities sufficient enough to make them wealthy. Harvesting the deep water mollusks was no easy undertaking however. From a dugout canoe a long, broom-like apparatus was thrust straight down into the muddy sea bottom then retrieved. With any luck a shell or two would be trapped amongst the stiff twigs at the end of the handle.
Dentalia were also ostentatiously displayed as symbols of wealth and power in the form of body adornments. Perhaps most recognizable are the breast plates invariably worn by cheesy Hollywood Indians.
Illustration by Manami Kimura

water pours in from above while chilling saltwater slops in from the ever-active sea. The whole scene occurs in a cleft in the rocks facing the setting sun and, if that were not enough, the whole cleft is usually lit by candlelight as the sky darkens to a deep purple. Clothing is optional but footwear is not. The rocks are jagged enough but usually some dope has just dropped a wine glass, scattering glass about in the pools. Do watch where you sit. If you must drink, use plastic.

When you've had enough soaks to make your fingers look like those movie theatre hot dogs then it may be time to make a decision on how to return whence you came. Only advanced kayakers should consider taking the open ocean route around Flores and Vargas Islands. The weather along the West Coast can change literally minute by minute. Gentle Pacific rollers can become furious breakers whipped to a frenzy by gale-force winds in an instant. Fog can quickly roll in, obscuring all landmarks and the myriad of treacherous reefs and rocks that line the route. On the other hand, if your paddling skills are up to it the rewards of this route are many. Uncountable sandy beaches, a rugged, wind-torn landscape, seclusion and a sense of being on the very edge of the world can all be expected. The choice is yours but err on the side of caution.

Landing in the surf can be especially problematic. In many cases there may be rocks off either end of a beach that can serve as a breakwater. Scoot in behind them to make your landing. Alternatively, surf the waves in as hard and as fast as you can manage then scramble out and up the beach before the next wave fills your cockpit with sand and seaweed. Be sure to decide upon your plan of action well before reaching the line of breakers. Once committed there is no way out. Never allow your kayak to go broadside to the breakers or indeed you will flip.

Beaver Fever

Beavers have gotten a bad rap, taking most of the blame for spreading a disease that can just as easily be passed into the water system by deer, muskrats, raccoons, coyotes and squirrels. Indeed any mammal including domestic pets, livestock and humans are guilty of carrying the protozoan parasite into the back-country. Giardia lambia, as the microbe is called, enters the environment in hardy cyst form where it can survive for weeks at a time. Giardia cysts can exist under the most pristine, wilderness conditions. Clear running water is not a sure sign that it is drinkable. Ingestion of a single cyst is enough to cause infection in humans. The hard, capsule-like shell dissolves, releasing the infectious form of the parasite which multiplies exponentially.

Full-blown giardiasis may take from 5 to 25 days to manifest itself though symptoms typically appear within 10 days. The giardia protozoa latch themselves on to the intestinal tract, severely impairing the body's ability to absorb nutrients and water. Food and water pass straight through the digestive system instead, appearing as the principal symptom of giardiasis, diarrhea. Infection usually lasts for around two weeks and is usually treated with antibiotics though some individuals may never show symptoms at all and others recover without treatment.

The many clusters of offshore rocks and small islets are ideal for harvesting mussels, keeping in mind the usual caveats about red tide. Bottom feeders can be taken just about anywhere but for a challenge try trolling for salmon through the rocky shoals. The La Croix Group, well off the tip of Vargas Island, is a particularly good place to hook dinner.

Dependable freshwater can be found at Cow Bay on the south west coast of Flores Island. On a fine day enjoy poking around the many islets clustered around Bartlett Island in the gap between Flores and Vargas. The collection of fine camping beaches at the northwest corner of Vargas Island are a popular destination for guided kayaking tour groups and can be crowded during the summer.

Orcas prowl the coast with residents feasting on fish and transients filling up on fellow sea mammals like seals and sea lions. During spring and fall keep an eye open for migrating Gray whales while paddling. At any time while relaxing on the beach, resident Grays may pop into your particular cove to sluice up a snack from the crustacean-rich foreshore. Ahous Bay on Vargas Island in particular is popular with these baleen whales. Around the corner at Medallion Beach expect to find a proliferation of sand dollars from which the beach was named.

On the final approach to Tofino stay together and stay alert for boat and sea plane traffic. You may find the sights and sounds of civilization, even Tofino's, surprisingly jarring after an extended wilderness excursion. 🐾

Giardiasis has been known to persist for months on end in those with weakened immune systems.

The best treatment of course is prevention and prevention typically means water purification. The surest method of water treatment is boiling. Five minutes at a steady boil will destroy every living organism in the water. Additional time is needed at higher elevations. Boiled water can be bland and dull tasting. Shaking oxygen back into it will help improve the taste.

Expensive, heavy filters are available which claim to strain out giardia lambia. Studies have shown however that not all filters are effective. In order to effectively purify water the filter porousness must be no bigger than 0.2 microns. Such fine filters are hard to pump but produce great tasting water. Chlorine-based water treatments are not effective against giardia cysts. Iodine treatments fare better but studies have shown that a typical 20 minute treatment is not enough to eliminate all cysts. Eight hours is the minimum required for effective iodine treatment. Iodized water taste horrible however and in rare cases may cause thyroid problems. 🐾

Illustration by Manami Kimura

Clayoquot Sound Sea Kayaking

Location	Notes
Tofino Sea Kayaking Company 320 Main Street, Tofino 1-800-863-4664; paddlers@island.net (250) 725-4222; (250)725-2070 FAX www.tofino-kayaking.com	Fiberglass Single: $35/day rental for multiple days; 1 day/$45 Lessons & Guided tours available
Remote Passages Kayaking 71 Wharf St, Tofino 1-800-666-9833; (250)725-3330; (250)725-3380 Fax webmaster@remotepassages.com www.remotepassages.com	Rentals, Lessons & Guided tours available
Maverick Coach Lines Vancouver Bus Terminal (604) 662-8051 (604) 255-1171	Bus Transportation: $88.45 Round Trip Leave Vancouver: 8:00 AM Daily Arrive Tofino 3:30 PM Leave Tofino: 10:00 AM Daily; Arrive Vancouver 5:20 PM Leave Tofino: 4:00 PM Daily; Arrive Vancouver 11:20 PM
Maquinna Lodge 1-800-665-3199 (250) 725-3261	Hotel, Pub, Beer & Wine Store Inexpensive ; Great location Restaurant not recommended
Paddler's Inn 320 Main Street, Tofino (250) 725-4222	Bed & Breakfast Shares premises with Tofino Sea Kayaking Kitchenettes & pay showers available
Tofino Backpackers Hostel 2431 Campbell Street Tofino, BC V0R 2Z0 (250) 726-2288	
Whalers on the Point Guesthouse 81 West Street Tofino, BC (250) 725-3443; (250) 725-3463 FAX info@tofinohostel.com; www.tofinohostel.com	Hostelling International Members $22/night Guests enjoy substantial discounts with select local merchants and outfitters.
Hummingbird International Hostel Ahousaht, B.C. (250)670-9679 ; (250)670-9697 FAX blaze@island.net	Twice daily shuttle from Tofino to Vargas Island. Departs 10:30 am & 4:00 pm $12 each way
Vargas Island Inn and Hostel Box 267, Tofino, BC V0R 2Z0 (250) 725-3309	Accessible only by boat. Phone ahead for boat transport. 1910 Tudor-style Heritage House Gorgeous Beach; Wilderness Hiking
Matt & Benz Indian Island, Grice Bay (250) 726-8578 or (250) 726-5055	Camping $20/night Cabins $50/night Customized whale watching tours available
Wild Side Hiking Trail; Ahousaht, BC 1-888-679-9586 (250) 670-9586; (250) 670-9696 FAX	Guided hiking tour of Flores Island 8AM - 1PM $40 Boat transportation: $55 return Emphasis on native history and culture.
Dave's Excellent Adventures (250) 725-2268	Water Taxi
Rainforest Boat Shuttle (250) 726-8631	Specializing in trips to Meares Island
Pacific Rim National Park 1-800-689-9025	Camping at Green Point; 94 drive-in sites, 54 walk-in sites
Island Link 1-877-954-3556; (250) 726-7779 www.newshuttle.com	Shuttle between Tofino & Ucluelet to Long Beach and the Airport. Full schedule in Appendix.
Tofino Taxi (250) 725-3333	Taxi Service, Shuttle to Park, Airport & Ferries
North Vancouver Air 1-800-228-6608	Vancouver - Tofino Full schedule in Appendix.
Tofino Airlines (250) 725-4454	Local area seaplane charters
Red Tide Hotline 666-2828	Area 24
Tofino Travel Info Centre (250) 725-3414; (250) 725-3296 FAX tofino@island.net; www.island.net/~tofino	Information Services

Trincomali Channel

Level: Challenging **Distance:** 82 km

Time: 2-3 days **Tide Table:** Dionisio Pt

Warning: Strong Winds **Marine Chart:** 3313

Note: For a map of Galiano Island refer to page 158.

Native Bar-B-Q

Heat radiating from a cedar driftwood fire sears fresh-caught coho. To prepare salmon for the barbie slit along the back instead of the belly. Remove the spine, ribs and entrails then spread it flat with a lattice of green alder or maple saplings. Thread the whole thing onto a hefty green stick and and plunge it into the ground at the edge of your fire. Pour water on the sticks from time to time to prevent them from burning up.

Nikon F
28 mm Nikkor lens
Kodachrome 64 ISO film

    The Gulf Islands is the name commonly associated with a group of more than 200 rocks, islets, and islands sprinkled all along the southeastern shore of Vancouver Island. And while just about any place among the islands is interesting enough for day or overnight paddling, the following route ties a number of features together including exquisite geology, limited human habitation, bountiful nature, convenient access, two kayak rental companies and excellent camping in a route rarely travelled by commercial water craft. There are a few drawbacks to this otherwise perfect location. Water is scarce so bring plenty, four or five litres per day at least. The sea is polluted from sewage making any kind of shellfish consumption out of the question. Crabs or fish are fine however and swimming is not a problem.

You may reach Trincomali Channel via Tsawwassen Ferry terminal [See Appendix **Getting to Tsawwassen** Page 321.] Ferry service is very limited to Galiano Island so give yourself plenty of time to board the ferry. Debark at Sturdies Bay and call a taxi to take you to either one of two kayaking outfitters at Montague Harbour. If you decide not to begin paddling in earnest right away Montague Harbour Provincial Park is an excellent place to camp while preparing for an early morning start. Reservations are recommended but be sure to specify the more scenic walk-in campsites when you call. Even without reservations there should be plenty of space in the grassy overflow camping area.

An added bonus to spending a night on Galiano is the shuttle bus that arrives at the park gate every hour on the hour to whisk thirsty campers away to the renowned Hummingbird Pub for exceptional micro-brewery beer and the finest fish and chips in the

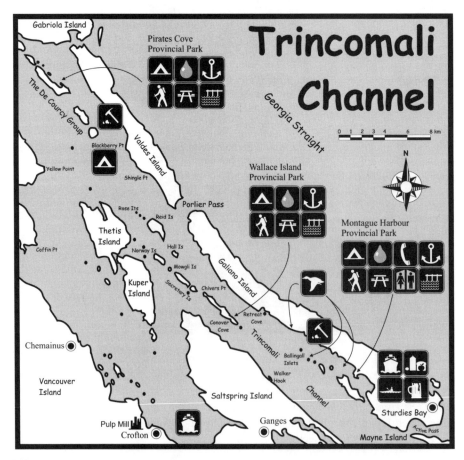

Gulf Islands. The bus returns to the campground on the half hour all evening long. The bus service, which costs $2 round trip, is seasonal, beginning on the May 24th long weekend and wrapping up on the Labour Day weekend in September. Service commences at 6 PM and continues on until last call at 11:30 PM.

Don't drink too much, however, as an early morning start is recommended to take advantage of the typically calmer conditions that dawn brings. With luck and planning you'll be able to catch an incoming tide to help propel you along to your destination.

Choose your route depending on wind and weather conditions. If calm you may want to explore the group of islands just off Montague Harbour including the bird sanctuary at the Ballingall Islets. From here you'll have to make a dash across the open waters of Trincomali Channel. It is recommended that you head straight across the Channel to Saltspring Island in order to limit your exposure to wind, wave and marine traffic. Out of harm's way, you'll want to check out Walker Hook before continuing on to Wallace Island.

Alternately hug the coastline of Galiano as you paddle northward. Even though you can expect to repeat this section on the return voyage it is certainly worth repeating.

Just 2 km beyond the white shell beach of Montague Harbour Marine Park you will encounter a large low-lying rock that serves as a harbour seal nursery. Remain well offshore to avoid stressing these sea mammals. Likely, the younger seals will plop into the security of the sea at your approach, popping up in your wake to check out the curious creatures called kayakers.

Moving along the high sandstone cliffs of Galiano keep an eye peeled for eagles surveying their fishing turf or turf-grazing deer on the bluffs above. At the 5½ km mark you'll encounter a large cliff-side cormorant rookery.

At kilometre nine, the beach at the north end of Retreat Cove makes an ideal spot to stop for lunch and stretch cramped leg muscles before darting across the open waters of Trincomali Channel. Since you will, in all likelihood, be exposed to broadside wave and wind action some members of your group may feel uncomfortable during the half hour crossing to Wallace Island. To provide support and increase the visibility of your group remain clumped together while crossing the two kilometres to Panther Point where, incidentally, the *HMS Panther* ran aground in 1874. No need to repeat the performance.

Flawless Wet Exit
"Hey, these things *are* stable!" he said, rocking his craft back and forth. Then a winter white cap caught him leaning the wrong way. "Hey, this water is cold!"

Nikon F; 135 mm Nikkor lens
Ektachrome 100 ISO film

A Provincial Marine Park, Wallace Island offers excellent camping, hiking and the best drinking water you'll encounter in the area. The main camping area at Conover Cove is the site of a once thriving vacation resort operated by David Conover from 1946 to 1966. Numerous historic buildings, an orchard and bountiful herb gardens have been preserved by BC Parks. You may want to plan a recipe that calls for fresh mint, chives or oregano during your stay on the island. A hand pump 400 metres north of the dock supplies deliciously cool water, perfect for replenishing supplies or a refreshing scrub down. You'll find a photogenic old truck and tractor in the same meadow.

The popularity of Conover Cove among the yachting set and the difficulty of landing or launching a kayak at low tide makes this a less than ideal place for over-nighting. Cabin Bay and Chivers Point, 3.3 km further along, both offer more seclusion though their growing popularity with kayakers means you'll likely still be sharing with others, particularly on weekends. The campfire ban is strictly enforced on Wallace Island by parks staff patrolling in motorized zodiacs. Even after dark Big Sister will be watching from her beach front home on Galiano. Violators will be fined.

Continuing northward, you'll want to explore the Secretary Islands, Mowgli and Norway Islands, Reid Island and the Rose Islets before zipping back across Trincomali Channel towards the Indian reserve at Shingle Point. Follow the Valdes Island shore for another 1.7 km to Blackberry Point for ideally-situated camping. As yet unembraced by the BC Parks system, beach fires are permitted here but you will find no toilets or potable water. Be sure to secure kayaks well and pitch your tents in the bush above the beach as it all but disappears during the highest tides of the year. Competition for suitable sites is fierce so arrive early.

The coast north of Blackberry Point is, reminiscent of Galiano Island, comprised largely of eroded sandstone galleries of every imaginable abstraction. At some point you may want to pay a visit to the De Courcy Group of Islands.

De Courcy Island was once the home of a secretive cult known as the Aquarian Foundation. After bilking and boinking his way to infamy, the charismatic leader, Brother XII, vanished in 1933 amidst charges of fraud and rumours of hidden treasure. Besides the allure of buried gold, all that remains of the lascivious cult is Brother XII Trail, a short footpath along the sandstone bluffs of Pirates Cove Provincial Marine Park.

Today the park offers camping, drinking water, toilets, the yachting crowd and mosquitoes in abundance. If possible camp along the western shore well away from the main campsite to avoid the latter two. Better yet, establish Blackberry Point as a base camp and investigate this area as an excursion.

All good things must end and exploring Trincomali Channel is no exception. To save time you may want to make a beeline following the coast of Valdes and Galiano directly back to Montague Harbour. Plan your crossing of the gap between the two islands to coincide with slack tide. Savvy paddlers will choose the lull after high water in order to catch the ebbing current homeward. A word of warning: DO NOT attempt to navigate any of the major narrows, Porlier Pass, Gabriola Passage or Active Pass at any time except slack tide and you had better be equipped with accurate tide information. Misjudgement could cost dearly. It is best to avoid these areas altogether as heavy commercial marine traffic compounds the problems of racing currents, rapids, standing waves, back eddies and whirlpools. 🐾

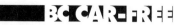
Trincomali Channel

Contact	Notes
Discover Camping (604) 689-9025 1-800-689-9025 http://www.discovercamping.ca	Campground Reservation Service $15 per night at Montague Harbour plus $6.42 per night [to a maximum of $19.26] reservation fee. Changes or cancellations will cost another $6.42. Recommended during high season. Make reservations up to three months in advance. Specify the more scenic walk-in campsites if available.
Go Galiano Island Shuttle (250) 539-0202	Public transportation
Gulf Islands Kayaking (250) 539-2442 kayak@gulfislands.com http://www.sea kayak.bc.ca/tour	Kayak rentals , lessons & tours Located at the dock in Montague Harbour. In operation since 1985.
Galiano Island Sea Kayaking 1-888-539-2930 (250) 539-2930	Kayak & Canoe rentals; Kayak & Catamaran tours B & B; Located at the foot of Southwind Road. Free pickup from the ferry.
Cliffhouse Oceansports (250) 539-5239	Kayak rentals , lessons & tours Sailing charters
Red Tide Hotline (604) 666-2828	Paralytic Shellfish Poisoning Information Information on the Gulf Islands will be found under Red Tide Area 17-2.
Canadian Gulf Islands Reservations 1-888-539-2930 (250) 539-2930 reservations@gulfislands.com	Free booking service for B&Bs, resorts, lodges, and cabins throughout the Gulf Islands.
Galiano Getaways (250) 539-5551	Free booking service for B&Bs, inns, cabins and adventure packages.

Desolation Sound

Level: Moderate   **Tide Table:** Prideaux Haven   **Time:** 1-7 days

Marine Chart: 3312 Desolation Sound   **Warning:** Water Scarce

Distances Below:

Lund - Copeland Islands 3 km   Lund - Tenedos Bay 25 km

Tenedos Bay - Prideaux Haven 9 km

Prideaux Haven - Refuge Cove 15 km   Prideaux Haven - Grace Harbour 19 km

Okeover Arm - Grace Harbour 9 km

Okeover Arm - Wootton Bay 11 km   Okeover Arm - Prideaux Haven 25 km

Desolation Sound is one of the crown jewels of kayaking in British Columbia. A week most certainly will not be enough to explore all the nooks and crannies of this vast Provincial Marine Park. The park itself encompasses more than 60 km of shoreline. Arrange for pick up with your kayaking outfitter upon arrival at the Powell River bus depot or take a thirty-dollar taxi ride to either Okeover Arm or Lund 23 km north of town. If arriving on the second bus of the day you'll find camping at both departure points. The cramped conditions at **Okeover Arm Provincial Park** are somewhat less than what one has come to expect from BC Parks. Private camping and showers can be found at nearby **Y-Knot Camping & Charters**.

Though catering to the RV crowd, the private walk-in campsites at Lund are well-situated, overlooking picturesque Lund Harbour. Expect to find showers, laundry facilities and plenty of mosquitoes at **Lund RV and Trailer Park**. If looking for something to do while swatting the bugs away head for the patio at adjacent Lundlubber's BBQ where you can find a mean burger and frosty brew. Lund, with a population of just 800, has more than its share of funky cafes, coffee shops and gift boutiques. Keep in mind of though that the sidewalks vanish rather early hereabouts. The general store doubles as a licensed liquor outlet for those who forgot to pack "provisions." With luck you can even catch some culture before dipping your paddle as an active theatre group regularly mounts amateur productions in the local community center.

Upon awakening in the morning, coffee hounds will want to head directly for Cinnamamma's Bakery in front of the Lund Hotel and Pub. The boat launching ramp behind the hotel is as good a place as any to meet up with your kayak outfitter if you went the taxi route. One of the four outfitters which service the Powell River area calls Lund Hotel home. Ironically-named **Good Diving & Kayaking,** though ideally situated, offers the worst, surliest service on the coast. Only clunky plastic kayaks are offered for rent here though it is doubtful you will be told of that prior to renting. If you ask however, the owner will assure you that nobody uses fibreglass any more. Having rented kayaks at nearly every outfitter in British Columbia I can assure you that once again the exact opposite is true. Good is not equipped to transport kayaks back across Malaspina Peninsula so a circuit starting in Lund and ending in Okeover Arm is out of the question. Y-Knot Camping & Charters, situated at Okeover Arm, offers a good selection of fibreglass boats but lack of a shuttle service also precludes the circuit as described below. Only **Powell River Sea Kayak** and **Wolfson Creek Ventures** will

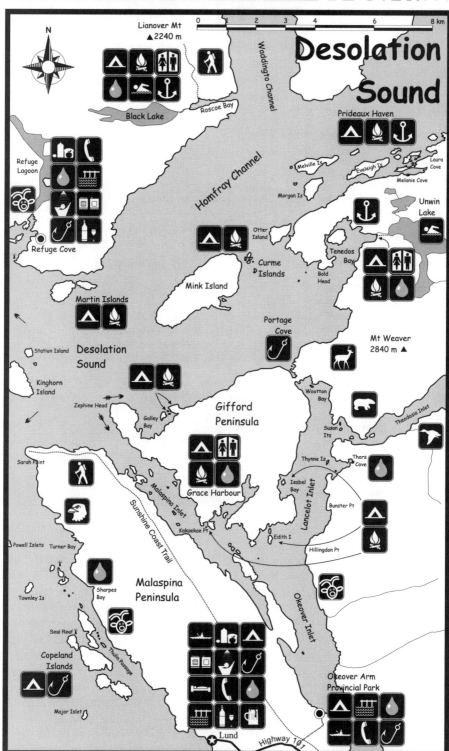

Desolation Sound

0 2 3 4 6 8 km

Lianover Mt
▲2240 m

Waddingto Channel

Roscoe Bay

Black Lake

Refuge Lagoon

Refuge Cove

Homfray Channel

Prideaux Haven

Melville Is
Eveleigh Is
Laura Cove
Melanie Cove

Morgan Is

Unwin Lake

Otter Island

Curme Islands

Tenedos Bay

Bold Head

Mink Island

Martin Islands

Station Island

Desolation Sound

Kinghorn Island

Zephine Head

Galley Bay

Portage Cove

Mt Weaver
2840 m ▲

Wootton Bay

Gifford Peninsula

Susan Its

Thynne Is

Thors Cove

Sarah Point

Malaspina Inlet

Grace Harbour

Isabel Bay

Lancelot Inlet

Bunster Pt

Sunshine Coast Trail

Kakaekae Pt

Edith I

Hillingdon Pt

Powell Islets

Turner Bay

Sharpes Bay

Malaspina Peninsula

Townley Is

Seal Reef

Thulin Passage

Copeland Islands

Major Islet

Okeover Inlet

Okeover Arm Provincial Park

Lund

Highway 101

307

transport boats to your destination of choice. Both of these latter outfitters will also pick customers up at either the bus depot or airport in Powell River for a modest fee. No matter which outfitter you choose be sure to arrange to leave your backpacks with them before booking your boats.

Catching the first bus out of Vancouver will enable pad-

Pearly Stowaway

Can you spot the Japanese import in this photo? Actually it's a trick question as both the woman and her giant oyster came from Japan. The introduction of oysters however predates the Sony Walkman by more than a century. Sailing ships carrying lumber to Japan had to fill up with ballast for the return voyage. Crews scooped up sand and rocks and everything else including oyster spawn from Japanese beaches, carried it across the ocean then dumped it overboard before loading up with BC forest products again. The oyster obviously liked what it saw, proliferating rapidly along the coast and supplanting the indigenous *Olympia oyster* as it did so. *Screw shells* and *oyster drills* likewise stowed away then multiplied, with the latter predator becoming somewhat of a pest. As their name suggests these sea snails bore through the protective shells of their prey, slurping up the delicacies inside. Oyster drills can wreck havouc on mariculture.

Nikon F
28 mm Nikkor lens
Ektachrome 100 ISO film

dlers to be on the water by late afternoon if everything goes according to plan. From Lund Harbour turn north and if the prevailing winds are blowing, ride the breeze to the Copeland Islands just half an hour away. Some may be tempted to skip this 437-hectare Provincial Marine Park, taking advantage of the long evenings of summer to reach deep into Desolation Sound itself. Missing this charming archipelago would be aesthetic folly however. Set up camp early instead and use the extra daylight to explore the many rocks and islets in and out of the park known collectively as the Ragged Group. A word of warning: one of the islands we camped on had an inordinate number of wood ticks. Be sure to keep the mosquito netting on your tent closed all times.

Look for a small collection of pictographs on the cliffs of Thulin Passage including one of a clearly discernable dolphin or orca-like creature. The prehistoric rock paintings are easy to find, just look for graffiti on top of them. That's right, some moron splashed the word **ACTIVE** in bold, black letters across this priceless, irretrievable rock art. How someone could commit such an atrocity may be beyond comprehension but, if in your travels around the coast you ever happen upon a boat called *Active*, feel free to drill a few holes in the hull below the waterline.

Awaken refreshed and continue exploring northwards past Townley Island and the Powell Islets before rounding Sarah Point into Desolation Sound itself. If running short of water the Ragged Island Marina in Sharpes Bay is a dependable source. Sarah Point, named after one of Captain Vancouver's sisters, is the northern terminus of the recently completed Sunshine Coast Trail [See page 87] stretching 180 km south to Saltery Bay ferry terminal. During inclement weather it is possible to haul kayaks out and even camp here though the location is somewhat exposed.

Nearby Kinghorn Island is the tidal midpoint of Georgia Strait. Water to the north of the island flows northwards rounding Vancouver Island at Cape Scott while that on the south shore is sucked by the moon past Victoria and out into the open Pacific. Being the last part of the inland waterway to feel the influence of the tides, the waters of Desola-

Wood Ticks

Coastal British Columbia has no poisonous snakes, deadly spiders or scorpions and plants like poison ivy or poison oak are rare. We do however have ticks. These blood-sucking arachnids are a carrier of a multitude of deadly diseases including Rocky Mounted Spotted Fever and Lyme's Disease.

At the end of each day pause for a moment to check your body, particularly the hairy bits, for any unusual protrusions. Get a buddy to survey your back. Ticks may vary from pin head size to the size of a huckleberry when engorged with blood.

Spring and early summer see the greatest numbers of ticks but their presence is certainly not limited to this time of year.

The best way to remove a tick is with a pair of inexpensive tick pliers. Outdoor stores carry them. Tweezers will work as well. Do not squeeze the body of the tick, you will only inject more deadly microbes into the wound. Cradle the tick lightly at the neck, below the body and pry up gently, levering against your skin. Doing so may take some time but the tick finds this mild pressure unpleasant and will eventually unclench its mouth parts. Save the tick in a film container for medical analysis upon returning to civilization.

Not all ticks carry contagion but the severity of associated diseases make precaution worthwhile. The same kind of preventative measures that work against mosquitos will also limit your exposure to tick bites. Insect repellent and long pants and sleeves will all help keep the critters away. 🐾

Illustration by Manami Kimura

tion Sound are not so thoroughly flushed and mixed by the tides as the waters on other parts of the coast. As oysters and swimmers alike can attest, the waters of Desolation Sound are considerably warmer than elsewhere.

Next scamper past Malaspina Inlet and the sometimes turbulent water off Zephine Head, making for a small islet

Snapshot
Plying the sun-dappled waters of Desolation Sound near Galley Bay. Salt water is anathema to the fine micro-electronics of a camera. Keep it well-wrapped in multiple layers of plastic. A large tupperware container securely bungeed to the deck will keep photo tools handy while paddling.

Nikon F
28 mm Nikkor lens
Ektachrome 200 ISO film

at the far end of Galley Bay. This is one of the few spots beyond the Ragged Islands where kayakers can step out and stretch the kayak kinks out of their legs. Though a delightful place to camp, many will want to push on to Tenedos Bay.

From the Copelands to Galley Bay should take three to four hours depending on tides, winds and paddling ability. Continuing on to Tenedos Bay requires an additional two to three hours. Halfway there, the oyster-encrusted beaches of Portage Cove are a good place to stretch once again. Don't be bullied by the "No Trespassing" signs here. While the land above the high tide mark may well be private property, the foreshore belongs to you and me. At some point in your explorations of Desolation Sound you may be tempted to sprint across the narrow isthmus at the head of enticingly named Portage Cove. Don't even dream of it. Once a convenient short cut for native Indian paddlers, hence the name, Portage Cove is now a dead end. In spite of the best efforts of BC Parks negotiators, the owner has an unwavering faith in the supremacy of private property. Fortunately for him the law is on his side. You, however, have to paddle around Gifford Peninsula. Kayakers have no other option but to respect that privacy. There is however, no better place -- *perhaps in the world* -- to collect oysters, keeping collection limits and red tide warnings in mind. Let's hope someone remembered to pack the soy sauce and wasabi.

At Tenedos Bay, also known as Deep Bay, you'll find a number of rustic campsites, fire pits, outhouses and all the water you could ever want to drink. Unwin Lake, just a short, 5-minute hike away, is a great place to swim and wash the salt scum away. Though lacking similar amenities, the nearby Curme Islands are an exceedingly popular place to pitch tents as well. The northern grouping of islets offers the most accessible camping.

Further on, Prideaux Haven is paddlers' heaven. This intricate maze of islands, rocks and deep narrow coves is just the sort of place the yachting set have in mind when they talk about "gunkholing." Sadly, because of sewage from the many yachts and kayakers alike, the waters of Melanie Cove and Laura Cove are closed to the harvesting of bivalve molluscs.

Those who want to stretch their legs a bit can walk between the two coves along an old logging road. Look also for the remains of Old Phil's homestead at the head of Laura Cove. Melanie Cove had its hermit hand logger too but time and forest have reclaimed the last vestiges of Philosopher Mike's cabin. The shallows of Prideaux Haven reach bathtub temperatures on a hot summer day, perfect for practising group and self-rescue techniques.

Places to camp abound throughout Prideaux Haven though drinking water can be difficult to find. A small, seasonal stream near the tiny island at the head of Melanie Cove may yield potable water. Numerous creeks beyond Prideaux Haven trickle into the salt chuck but the nearest dependable source is a brisk 1½ hour paddle up Homfray Channel at Lloyd Creek. Don't drink it all on the way back.

Across the channel from Prideaux Haven water can also be found at Black Lake at the head of the Roscoe Bay on West Redonda Island. The warm waters of Black Lake attract an inordinate number of swimmers so you are advised to top drinking water up at the little spring that dribbles into the lake some 100 metres along the northern shore. There is also a waterfall on the northern shore at Roscoe Bay's widest point. Hereabouts you'll find plenty of evidence of bygone logging operations as well as remnants of an unsuccessful homestead.

After topping up some paddlers may enjoy a hike up to Lianover Mountain [2240 metres.] Allow two hours round trip. At 5215 metres, Mt. Addenbroke, on adjacent East Redonda Island is the tallest point on any of the islands of BC's tattered coast.

Whether hiking, camping or paddling you may want to pause for a moment to wonder what it was that inspired Captain George Vancouver in 1792 to label this area "desolate." Was it a simple case of the blues or did Desolation Sound's peculiar doldrums oppress him somehow? Certainly calm would have been of great concern to a sailor dependent on the wind for locomotion. He complained about the fishing as well as the stillness of the air. Of course oysters could not have been on the menu but mussels and clams should have been a complement to the then abundant salmon, cod, snapper and other fish. Maybe he forgot to pack the "buzzbombs."

Naturally, at that time, Cap'n George couldn't just scoot over to Refuge Cove, civilization's nearest outpost in Desolation Sound. Present day explorers can find a range of services including telephone, water, groceries, liquor store, laundry and shower facilities, a restaurant, gift shop, post office and even "buzz bombs" and other fishing tackle.

Those not craving a black cherry ice cream cone may want to explore the shores of Mink Island before setting a course for the protected waters of Malaspina Inlet. Be sure to keep together when crossing the open sound in order to heighten the visibility of your group.

Arbutus Arcania
Seen here clutching the rocky foreshore overlooking Lund Harbour, arbutus is a coastal oddity. Arbutus thrives in the arid micro-climes scoffed at by other local species. Known as madrona south of the border, arbutus is the only deciduous species hereabouts which does not drop its leaves every autumn. Instead, its terracotta-coloured bark peels off seasonally to allow for expansion underneath. Though its technological uses were limited, the Coast Salish were known to employ a decoction of arbutus bark in the tanning of hides. The bark contains high levels of tannic acid. A poultice of leaves was used as a burn treatment while groups on Vancouver Island fashioned jewelry out of the bright red berries.

Mamiya DTL 1000
50 mm Mamiya lens
Kodachrome 64 ISO film

The nest of fjords hidden behind Malaspina and Gifford Peninsulas is home to extensive aquaculture operations. The first suitable beach camping will be found near Kakaekae Point. Delightful Grace Harbour beyond offers more developed facilities including water, pit toilets and a number of onshore campsites. A third alternative will be found at Edith Island overlooking the junction of Malaspina, Okeover and Lancelot Inlets. Allow four to five hours to cover the distance between Prideaux Haven and Grace Harbour.

Set aside at least a day for exploring Lancelot and Theodosia Inlets. The best water in the area will be found at Thors Cove so top up before heading deeper into the fjord. Thynne Island is one of just two spots that are ideal for camping in the area. Captain Vancouver is known to have breakfasted on the island more than 200 years ago following the disappointing revelation that Theodosia Inlet was not the beginning of the mythical Northwest Passage after all. You too can discover the massive tidal flats that broke his heart at the head of the inlet. Theodosia Inlet was home to a bustling logging community of 5000 in the early 1900s. The logging railway which eventually reached 50 km inland closed down during the Dirty Thirties though active logging continues to the present day.

Good camping can also be found on Madge Island in

Isabel Bay. Expect to find artifacts dating to the days of hand logging on the island while on shore, at the north end of the bay, the remains of a number old cabins and a seasonal creek that in a pinch may provide water will be found.

The route as described should take from five days to a week though exploration could easily be broken down into a series of weekenders as well. Exploration of the Ragged Islands could be accomplished as an overnighter. Likewise a two or three-day weekend would be plenty of time to poke around in the various fjords adjacent to Okeover Arm. A similar amount of time would be needed to reach Tenedos Bay and Prideaux Haven though the pace would be far from leisurely. ☙

Kayaking Desolation Sound

Location	Services	Notes
Powell River Sea Kayak Phone: (604) 485-2144 6812E Alberni Street Powell River, BC V8A 2B4 kayak@prcn.org	Single/Double 1 day $38/$60 2 days $65/$100 3 days $90/$138 4 days $115/$175 extra days $23/$35	Kayak pickup and drop off: $15 for first 2 kayaks; $5 for each additional kayak. Passenger pickup and drop off $15 per group when renting.
Wolfson Creek Ventures RR#3 Nassichuk Rd Powell River BC V8A 5C1 (604) 487-1699 (604) 487-4445FAX canoe@prcn.org	Single/Double 1 day $30/$50 2 days $58/$98 3 days $84/$144 4 days $108/$188 5 days $130/$230 6 days $156/$276 7 days $182/$322	Kayak and passenger pickup and drop off typically costs $60 per group but depends on the number of customers.
Y-Knot Campground Okeover Arm, BC (604) 483-3243	Single/Double 1 day $40/$60 2+ days $35/$55	Camping $10 per group
Good Diving & Kayaking Box 47 Lund, BC V0N 2G0 (604) 483-3223		Poor service. Should be seen as a last resort. Plastic kayaks only
Powell River Chamber of Commerce (604) 485-4701 (604) 485-2822 FAX prvb@prcn.org	Travel Information	
Pacific Coastal Airlines (604) 273-8666 1-800-663-2872	M-Fr 6 flights daily Sat 3 flights daily Su 5 flights daily	$182 return taxes included
Powell River Taxi Company (604)483-3666	Approximately $30 to Lund or Okeover Arm	
Red Tide Alert Hotline (604) 666-2828 (604) 666-0583		Desolation Sound Area 15

Canoeing

The Powell Forest

Morning Mist
The sun peeks weakly through the early morning mists of Dodd Lake.

Nikon F
28 mm Nikkor lens
Ektachrome 100 ISO film

Level: Flatwater Paddling Distance: 63 km
Time: 5 days   Season: June till October

Access: See **Getting to the Sunshine Coast**, pg 333.

A paddler's paradise on the Sunshine Coast.

When the going got tough for the one company town of Powell River the town got thinking. With the forest industry on a decline locals took a new look at the bountiful forest that had so long buttered their bread.

At the behest of people like Powell River map maker Gerhard Tollas, with the co-operation of the local Chamber of Commerce and the B.C. Forest Service and with the financial support of a federal make-work scheme the project took off. Unemployed loggers were hired and the rest is history.

Just half a day from the Lower Mainland, the Powell Forest Canoe Route now rivals even its more famous cousin the Bowron Lakes Canoe Route in the central interior of the province.

Unlike the Bowron route, Powell Forest is not a truly circular route. And while some will denigrate the experience because of active logging in the area the same can be said of the Bowron Lakes since, in recent years, massive clearcuts, just outside the park boundaries, have marred the landscape forever.

The Powell Forest route does not even pretend to be wilderness. Indeed part of the canoeing experience is complimented by the historical aspect of logging throughout the area.

Lois Lake, the first of the eight lakes embraced by the route, owes its eerie quality to the flood first and ask questions later approach to damming that was prevalent in the frontier days of coastal industry.

Throughout the Powell Forest Canoe Route notched cedar stumps, now moss-covered and topped with shocks of salal, attest to the bygone era of springboard and hand-saw logging.

When developing the route, work crews uncovered a corduroy logging road built by Japanese immigrants to retrieve cedar shake bolts. The technology of the day dictated the use of horse pulled sleds with greased wooden runners to drag the valuable cargo over the wood-plank road. And while the road remains as a portage between Dodd and Windsor lakes, the loggers themselves were infamously rounded up and sent to de facto concentration camps more than half a century ago.

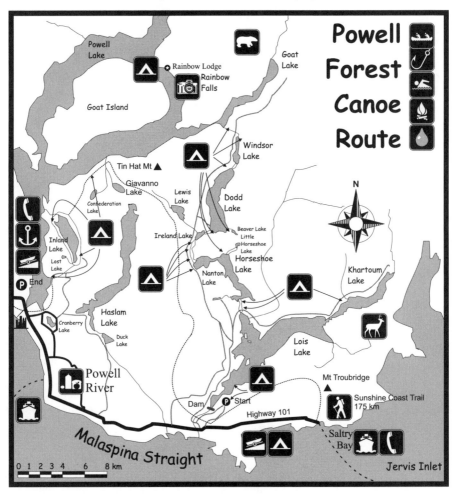

Starting at Lois Lake, the main route connects with Horseshoe, Nanton, Ireland, Dodd, Windsor, Goat and finally Powell Lake.

And while the main route comprises eight lakes and 55 km of paddling with 8 km of portaging, a less direct approach offers four further lakes and as much as 160 km of

You Old Goat
Look for billys, nannys and their kids on the slopes above Goat Lake and on those of Goat Island in Powell Lake. This little kid sports a fine new coat but his mom looks the worse for wear and tear. Gradually she will rub her winter coat off on the rocks. Collecting the wool and weaving it into clothing or blankets was traditionally the responsibility of First Nations women.

Nikon F
135 mm Nikkor lens
Ektachrome 200 ISO film

paddling with only one added portage.

All portages are wide-laned avenues with canoe rests spaced every 300 metres. The shortest is 0.7 km while the most taxing of these portages links Windsor and Goat lakes. The 2.4 km long trail is further complicated by a steep grade. For this reason, starting the journey at the Powell Lake Marina instead of Lois Lake is not recommended.

Powell Lake itself, a giant fjord long since cut off from the sea, can be subject to afternoon squalls that at best will impede your progress. At worst these unexpected winds could capsize a canoe paddled by novices. Powell Lake is best tackled in the calmer morning hours.

Ancient cedar snags and submerged deadheads, especially in Lois and Goat Lakes present considerable hazard to the inexperienced as well.

Yet one canoeist's hazard is another osprey's habitat. The abundance of ancient dead wood has allowed these fish-hunting birds of prey to proliferate.

Osprey breakfast tastes mighty fine to canoeists too. Rainbow and cutthroat trout and a tiny landlocked salmon called kokanee are found in abundance throughout the Powell Forest Canoe Route.

These fish are not so readily caught however, especially in the dead of summer when it takes a pretty convincing lure to tempt them away from their ample food supply.

With sharp eyes the chance of spotting a family of mountain goats on the cliffs of aptly named Goat Island or those above Goat Lake is good.

Black bears abound throughout the canoe route environs so be especially vigilant in hanging food high and away from sleeping areas.

Trout Time

Though fished-out when compared with its early years, fine trout can still be pulled from the depths of Powell Lake. And deep it is, measuring 347 metres at its deepest point. Down there we find a layer of seawater dating from the days when Powell Lake was not a lake at all but rather an inlet of the sea. In addition to rainbow and cutthroat trout, Powell Lake is home to kokanee, a small, land-locked variety of salmon.

Mamiya DTL 1000
50 mm Mamiya lens
Kodachrome 64 ISO film

The best place in the area to catch a glimpse of bears is in the vicinity of Rainbow Lodge, a fishing resort operated since the 1930s for newsprint clients of, first the Powell River Company, then later MacMillian Blodel.

Staff at the lodge dump all edible garbage on a point across the bay to keep bears away from the buildings. Early morning feedings invariably attract several of the hungry creatures.

Powell Forest Canoe Route

Location	Services	Notes
Wolfson Creek Ventures RR#3 Nassichuk Rd Powell River BC V8A 5C1 (604) 487-1699 (604) 487-4445FAX canoe@prcn.org www.canoeingbc.com	Canoe Rental 16/17 foot 1 day $27/$30 2 days $52/$58 3 days $75/$84 4 days $96/$108 5 days $115/$130 6 days $138/$156 7 days $161/$182	Transportation to and from the canoe route available on request.
Pacific Coastal Airlines (604) 273-8666 1-800-663-2872	M-Fr 6 flights daily Sat 3 flights daily Su 5 flights daily	$182 return taxes included
Powell River Taxi Company (604) 483-3666		
Fiddlehead Farm Box 421 Powell River, B.C. (604) 483-3018 (604) 485-3832 FAX retreat@fiddleheadfarm.org	Wilderness Retreat located on the Powell Forest Canoe Route	
Powell River Chamber of Commerce (604) 485-4701 (604) 485-2822 FAX prvb@prcn.org	Travel Information	

Appendix: Getting There

Transit

Faced with the challenges of being caught greeting the new millenium wearing old garb, the appellation BC Transit, was hastily dumped. A new Greater Vancouver Transit Authority or GVTA was created. Admittedly a bit of a mouthful either way, the monicker TransLink was then bestowed on the GVTA. Then the bus service was dubbed Coast Mountain BusLink presumably to distinguish it from the West Coast Express, SeaBus, SkyTrain, HandyDart and so on. While the old name persists this newspeak is gradually taking hold. Official documents, tourism pamphlets and so on will use the GVTA, Coast Mountain BusLink and TransLink to mean essentially the same thing. For the purposes of this book I will use TransLink to mean what BC Transit has meant since the days BC Hydro ceased to provide public transportation services in the lower mainland. What's in a name? Going for complexity when simplicity would do is more than just a trademark with these guys.

The TransLink dudes have created an excellent online schedule but those unfamiliar with local bus numbers or names will be lost at *www.gvta.bc.ca*. Or contact Translink the old fashioned way at **(604) 521-0400** for start to finish directions from a real human being. While stuck in the interminable messaging queue think of it as practice for the real thing, waiting for buses that may never come. For West Vancouver bus information call (604) 985-7777.

During Peak Hours the Translink Zone System is in effect, meaning the fare increases depending on the number of zones crossed during the voyage. Translink defines Peak Hours as weekdays before 6:30 PM. After rush hour and all day during weekends and holidays the regular single zone fare ($1.75) applies throughout the Translink system in the Lower Mainland. Transfers are valid for 90 minutes in any direction, on any route. From downtown Vancouver, North and West Vancouver, Horseshoe Bay, Bowen Island, New Westminster and Richmond are all two zones ($2.50) while Delta, Tsawwassen and Surrey are three zones ($3.50.)

A DayPass, valid for unlimited travel for a full day costs $7 while discount books of 10 FareSaver ticketss are available for all three zones.

Ferries

The schedules in this appendix were up-to-date for a millisecond just prior to publication. The BC Ferry Corporation, however, maintains a cadre of full-time schedule tinkerers who no doubt rendered all of the below obselete moments later. Log in to the fleet's website, *www.bcferries.bc.ca*, for the latest tweaks. At this award-winning site you'll find detailed information on ferry traffic patterns, delays, even parking lot capacity and usage in addition to more mundane information like when your ship was actually supposed to have come in and how much it would have cost if you could have gotten on. Walk on, it's cheaper and certainly more certain. 🐾

Getting to Horseshoe Bay

From any bus stop on the north side of Georgia Street in downtown Vancouver catch the **#257 Horseshoe Bay Express**. The express bus takes just thirty minutes but only runs once an hour. The express bus is usually packed too so carrying bulky back-packs can be a nightmare. More frequently, the **#250 Horseshoe Bay** bus runs every half hour but takes nearly an hour to reach the same place. Both buses stop on the north side of the road in front of Park Royal Shopping Centre for the convenience of those on the North Shore. For up-to-date information on West Vancouver Blue Buses, call (604) 985-7777, weekdays 6:30 AM to 8:00 PM, weekends & holidays 9:30 AM to 6:30 PM.

Ferry to Nanaimo

Leave Horseshoe Bay	Leave Departure Bay
6:30 am	6:30 am
8:30 am	7:30 am*
9:30 am*	8:30 am
10:30 am	10:30 am
12:30 pm	11:30 am*
1:30 pm*	12:30 pm
3:00 pm	3:00 pm
5:00 pm	4:00 pm*
6:00 pm*	5:00 pm
7:00 pm	7:00 pm
9:00 pm	9:00 pm

* Summer only

Getting to Tsawwassen

Getting to the Tsawwassen ferry terminal from downtown Vancouver is a relatively simple matter. Getting there in time to board the ferry is a completely different story however. The **#601 South Delta** bus leaves from outside of the Burrard SkyTrain station on half-hour intervals everyday of the week starting before 7 AM. The only exception is on Sunday when the same bus operates on hourly intervals until 9:30 AM. Boarding is also possible at any of the bus stops along Howe Street as well as at important cross streets such as Granville and Broadway or Granville and 41st Avenue. The whole trip takes approximately an hour and one transfer is necessary at Ladner Exchange about 40 minutes from downtown. At any time of the year the **#640 Tsawwassen Ferry** bus will complete the journey. Unhappily the **#640** bus only operates on an hourly schedule. That inadequate service is supplemented in the *summertime only* by an extension to the **#404** bus which originates at the Vancouver International Airport. So from April to September look for either the **#640** or **#404 Tsawwassen Ferry** bus at Ladner Exchange to provide connecting service with the **#601 South Delta** bus from downtown Vancouver every 30 minutes. At other times of the year expect to arrive at Tsawwassen hourly on the half hour, which should leave plenty of time to board a ferry bound for Swartz Bay near Victoria. These Ferries always leave on the hour, hourly in the summer and less frequently through much of the winter.

The majority of recreational ferry users are more likely to be bound for the Gulf Islands instead of Swartz Bay near Victoria or Duke Point near Nanaimo however. The following section, **Getting to the Gulf Islands**, provides desination-specific details on reaching the poorly-serviced archipeligo. More often than not those planning a recreational trip to the Gulf Islands will want to bring along bicycles. What may have previously sounded like a logistical nightmare is about to turn into a living horror show.

There are three ways to reach Tsawwassen by bicycle and by bicycle isn't really one of them. The George Massey Tunnel is a formidable barrier that cannot be overcome by bicycle alone. A shuttle service has been set up by the Ministry of Transport to move bicycles through the Tunnel but it is more of a public relations patch implemented to cover up the incompetent engineering that went into the tunnel than a reliable alternative. Some Translink buses are equipped with bike racks but demand for this fine service far outpaces supply. The only other option is to catch an expensive lift to the ferry on Pacific Coach Lines subject to limited availability.

The reason getting to and from Tsawwassen with a bike is so difficult is poor planning associated with Highway 99 south and especially the ill-thought out design of George Massey Tunnel which slides under the south fork of the Fraser River. Not only is it illegal, it is also extremely dangerous to attempt to pedal through the tunnel. For this reason, the **BC Ministry of Transport** operates a bicycle shuttle in both directions through the tunnel at the times listed below. The highway leading up to the tunnel is fast, busy and perilous, especially when crossing exit and entrance ramps.

To avoid cycling along the highway as much as possible follow these instructions. From downtown Vancouver take either Granville or Cambie Streets south across False Creek. Take a left from the former or a right from the latter on any of the main drags you encounter from Broadway on. Turn south on to Oak Street and continue puffing and huffing up and over the hump, crossing the Oak Street Bridge upon reaching the Fraser River. Take the first exit off the Oak Street Bridge in Richmond and follow Sea Island

Way to Garden City Rd. Take a left here and continue south past Cambie Rd. then Alderbridge Way, finally following Westminster Highway to the left. Sprint down to No. 5 Rd. where a right turn will be required to continue southwards. Stay with No. 5 Rd. past Steveston Highway to Rice Mill Rd. Take a left here and one further left on to an access road to the freeway where you will meet up with the shuttle which will take you under the George Massey Tunnel. On the opposite side access Highway 17 and follow it south to its end at the ferry terminal. Northbound cyclists will find the shuttle operating from the Town and Country Inn on the corner of Highway 17 and Highway 99.

The George Massey Tunnel Bike Shuttle operates according to the following infrequent schedule daily throughout the summer until Labour Day in September, continuing on weekends until early October. Plan to arrive early as missing the shuttle could result in a wait of up to two hours.

Southbound
——   8:00 AM   9:00 AM   11:00 AM   1:00 PM   3:00 PM   5:00 PM   6:00 PM   7:00 PM

Northbound
7:15 AM   08:30 AM   09:30 AM   11:30 AM   1:30 PM   3:30 PM   5:30 PM   6:30 PM   7:30 PM
The bike shuttle is operated by Mainroad Contracting Ltd. (604) 574-3164; FAX: (604) 574-4399

Why such a poorly-conceived work-around? The shuttle service was never actually intended to be used by cyclists. The ad hoc bandage was put in place to show the cycling constituency that they too have friends in high places. A real shuttle would be a co-ordinated effort between the Ministry of Transport, BC Ferries and TransLink to connect cyclists with ferries in both Horseshoe Bay and Tsawwaasen. The two terminals, Lions Gate Bridge and the George Massey Tunnel were all built with automobiles soley in mind. The thorny issues of ferry and byway traffic will not be tackled by paving over Stanley Park or squandering billions on FastCat Ferries. Bigger, faster ferries, wider bridge lanes and better tunnels only conspire to encourage more auto traffic. 23,000 additional cars take to Lower Mainland streets each year. Encouraging alternatives that are palatable to mom, pop and the kids will reduce the number of cars burdening existing infrastructure. How many new bus riders can be directly attributed to the preening of BC Transit? The dollars wasted on TransLink's name change and facelift could have been more wisely spent on bike racks or indeed, bike buses.

As mentioned previously, select **Translink** buses are equipped with bike racks to assist long distance commuters. There is no additional charge for your bike. Be forewarned that this excellent service, while growing, is still very limited. Only two bikes can be carried at a time and the competition is fierce. Even if you arrive one hour in advance of the bus departure be prepared to be disappointed.

Drivers will not help you put bikes on the rack as this is a self-service operation. Instructions are simple and obvious. You must however remove all equipment from the bike and drag it aboard the bus with you. If touring, that means juggling a sleeping bag, sleeping pad, a tent, a couple of panniers and a handle bar bag while spilling coins and trying to squeeze in amongst the morning commuters.

In a pinch it is possible to place a third bike between the two bikes already on the rack and bungee the whole bunch together but you will need the driver's permission to do this. Usually drivers will disavow any responsibility in the event of an accident but

let you do it.

In downtown Vancouver take bus **#601 South Delta** from the north side of Dunsmuir Street between Burrard and Thurlow. Be prepared to transfer to the **#640** or **#404 Tsawwassen Ferry** bus at Ladner Exchange. These operate on an alternating schedule and one or the other should be waiting for connecting passengers from downtown. If the bike rack on the **Tsawwassen Ferry** bus is already in use stay on the **#601 South Delta** bus until the corner of Route 17 and 56th Street [Ask the driver] then pedal like mad along the causeway to the ferry terminal. Pedalling from Ladner Exchange is also possible and should take about 30 minutes by bike, compared to 15 minutes by bus.

An alternative to Translink is to load your bike on a **Pacific Coach Lines** bus at Vancouver's Pacific Central Station. In the summer high season buses leave every hour starting at 5:45 AM until 7:45 PM while in the low season they only operate every other hour. You must be at the bus station at least 30 minutes prior to departure and there is the possibility that your bike will be bumped if cargo loads are unusually heavy. One final drawback is that it is impossible to catch the bus back from Tsawwassen to Vancouver. This is clearly an inferior service that may do in a pinch but cannot be relied upon with any degree of certainty. The cost of $26.95 includes taxes as well as passenger fare for the ferry. Since the bus is going to Victoria, those hoping to connect with the direct ferry to the Gulf Islands have to disembark at Tsawwassen. While your ferry fare is included in the price of your bus ticket it may be necessary to pay an additional $5 for your bicycle once you board the ferry. Fortunately the staff are usually too busy loading cars and carbos to bother to collect it.

Bike BC Hotline (604) 737-3165

Shuttle through George Massey Tunnel (604) 737-3034

Translink Passenger and Bike Transit Information (604) 521-0400

Ferry to Victoria

Leave Tsawwassen Bay	Leave Swartz
7:00 am	7:00 am
8:00 am*	8:00 am*
9:00 am	9:00 am
10:00 am	10:00 am
11:00 am	11:00 am
12:00 noon *	12:00 noon*
1:00 pm	1:00 pm
2:00 pm	2:00 pm
3:00 pm	3:00 pm
4:00 pm	4:00 pm
5:00 pm	5:00 pm
6:00 pm	6:00 pm
7:00 pm	7:00 pm
8:00 pm F/Su*	8:00 pm F/Su*
9:00 pm	9:00 pm
10:00 pm F/Su*	10:00 pm F/Su*
* Summer Only	

Ferry to Nanaimo

Leave Tsawwassen	Leave Duke Point
5:15 am*	5:15 am*
7:45 am*	7:45 am*
10:15 am	10:15 am
12:45 pm	12:45 pm
3:15 pm	3:15 pm
5:45 pm	5:45 pm
8:15 pm	8:15 pm
10:45 pm	10:45 pm
*No Sunday Sailing , Winter Only	

Getting to the Gulf Islands

The previous section, *Getting to Tsawwaasen*, details how to reach the ferry with or without a bike.

The infrequency of ferry service to the Gulf Islands means special attention must be paid to logistics. The following schedule will get you aboard the Gulf Island ferry if strictly adhered to. The tweak-meisters at both the ferry corporation and Translink are notorious for making bizarre, ill-thought out changes to scheduling so verify the schedule wherever possible before setting out. As you will note it may take over two hours from the time you get on the bus to the time you board the ferry. The bus schedule is optimized for reaching Swartz Bay efficiently and the Gulf Islands routing suffers as a consequence. In many cases one bus later would arrive just minutes before the ferry was due to depart. BC Ferries has instituted a policy of closing the ticket gate 10 minutes prior to sailing time making an assured departure impossible. Moreover this is a worse case scenario based on infrequent off-season schedules. Times can be often shaved by 30 minutes when the supplemental **#404 Tsawwassen Ferry** bus service is in operation.

Day	Burrard Station	Ladner Exchange	Tsawwassen	Ferry Departs
M-Th	8:28 AM	9:21 AM	9:33 AM	10:15 AM
M-Th	5:34 PM	6:24 PM	6:36 PM	7:35 PM
F	9:36 AM	10:21 AM	10:33 AM	10:50 AM
F	4:33 PM	5:28 PM	5:40 PM	6:30 PM
Sa	6:36 AM	7:22 AM	7:37 AM	8:45 AM
Sa	7:43 PM	8:25 PM	8:40 PM	9:10 PM
Su & Hol	9:38 AM	10:25 AM	10:37 AM	11:10 AM
Su & Hol	5:36 PM	6:25 PM	6:37 PM	7:15 PM

A simple if somewhat time consuming work-around exists, however. Instead of taking the direct ferry to the Gulf Islands it is possible to take the much more frequent Swartz Bay-bound ferry and, after arriving, turn right around and hop on a ferry to the Gulf Island of your choice. Tsawwassen to Swartz Bay ferries run hourly in the summer high season and every other hour on the odd hour in the low season starting at 7:00 AM with the final sailing each day at 9:00 PM.

For each of the five islands described in detail below information on both approaches will be provided.

One other approach requires ample time to cycle first to Nanaimo on Mid-Vancouver Island then south to Crofton where a small ferry service frequently connects with Saltspring Island. This route is best done over a period of several days.

Gulf Island Ferry Schedules

Inter-island ferries not included. Pick up a schedule as soon as you board one of the ferries below if undertaking a multi-island tour.

Galiano Island

To Galiano Island from Vancouver (Tsawwassen)

Days	Leave	Stops/Transfers	Arrive
M-Th	10:15 am	non-stop	11:10 am
M-Th	7:35 pm	non-stop	8:30 pm
F	10:50 am	non-stop	11:45 am
F	6:30 pm	non-stop	7:25 pm
Sa	8:45 am	non-stop	9:40 am
Sa	9:10 pm	non-stop	10:05 pm
Su/Hol M	11:10 am	non-stop	12:05 pm
Su/Hol M	7:15 pm	1 stop Mayne	9:00 pm

To Vancouver (Tsawwassen) from Galiano Island

Days	Leave	Stops/Transfers	Arrive
M-F	8:40 am	non-stop	9:35 am
M-Th	6:10 pm	non-stop	7:05 pm
F	7:35 pm	2 stops Mayne, Penders	10:00 pm
Sa	9:55 am	1 stop Mayne	11:45 am
Sa	6:05 pm	non-stop	6:55 pm
Su/Hol M	9:50 am	non-stop	10:40 am
Su/Hol M	5:45 pm	non-stop	6:45 pm

To Galiano Island from Victoria (Swartz Bay)

Days	Leave	Stops/Transfers	Arrive
M-F	5:35 am	non-stop	6:45 am
M-F	10:25 am	non-stop	11:35 am
M-Th	4:00 pm	transfer at Mayne	6:05 pm
M-Th	6:10 pm	2 stops Penders, Mayne	7:50 pm
F	4:00 pm	1 stop Mayne	5:30 pm
F	7:00 pm	1 stop Penders	8:20 pm
Sa	6:00 am	non-stop	6:55 am
Sa	9:10 am	2 stops Penders, Mayne	11:05 am
Sa	3:15 pm	2 stops Penders, Mayne	5:00 pm
Sa	6:45 pm	2 stops Penders, Mayne	8:30 pm
Su/Hol M	6:55 am	1 stop Mayne	8:35 am
Su/Hol M	10:20 am	non-stop	11:30 am
Su/Hol M	3:15 pm	2 stops Penders, Mayne	4:55 pm
Su/Hol M	6:50 pm	2 stops Penders, Mayne	9:00 pm

To Victoria (Swartz Bay) from Galiano Island

Days	Leave	Stops/Transfers	Arrive
M- F	6:50 am	2 stops Mayne, Penders	8:25 am
M-F	11:45 am	1 stop Mayne	1:05 pm
M-Th	8:00 pm	1 stop Penders	9:20 pm
F	5:35 pm	non-stop	6:45 pm
F	8:30 pm	2 stops Mayne, Penders	10:10 pm
Sa	7:00 am	2 stops Mayne, Penders	8:55 am
Sa	11:15 am	2 stops Mayne, Penders	1:10 pm
Sa	5:10 pm	1 stop Penders	6:30 pm
Sa	8:40 pm	non-stop	9:50 pm
Su/Hol M	8:15 am	2 stops Mayne, Penders	10:10 am
Su/Hol M	11:40 am	2 stops Mayne, Penders	1:25 pm
Su/Hol M	5:05 pm	1 stop Penders	6:30 pm
Su/Hol M	9:05 pm	1 stop Penders	10:30 pm

Mayne Island

To Mayne Island from Vancouver (Tsawwassen)

Days	Leave	Stops/Transfers	Arrive
M-Th	10:15 am	1 stop Galiano	11:50 am
M-Th	7:35 pm	1 stop Galiano	9:00 pm
F	10:50 am	1 stop Galiano	12:25 pm
F	6:30 pm	1 stop Galiano	8:00 pm
Sa	8:45 am	1 stop Galiano	10:25 am
Sa	9:10 pm	1 stop Galiano	10:35 pm
Su/Hol M	11:10 am	1 stop Galiano	12:40 pm
Su/Hol M	7:15 pm	non-stop	8:15 pm

To Vancouver (Tsawwassen) from Mayne Island

Days	Leave	Stops/Transfers	Arrive
M-F	8:00 am	1 stop Galiano	9:35 am
M-Th	5:35 pm	1 stop Galiano	7:05 pm
F	8:10 pm	1 stop Penders	10:00 pm
Sa	10:40 am	non-stop	11:45 am
Sa	5:30 pm	1 stop Galiano	6:55 pm
Su/Hol M	9:15 am	1 stop Galiano	10:40 am
Su/Hol M	5:05 pm	1 stop Galiano	6:45 pm
Su/Hol M	8:30 pm	non-stop	9:30 pm

To Mayne Island from Victoria (Swartz Bay)

Days	Leave	Stops/Transfers	Arrive
M-F	5:35 am	1 stop Galiano	7:10 am
M-F	10:25 am	1 stop Galiano	12:05 pm
M-Th	4:00 pm	non-stop	4:50 pm
M-Th	6:10 pm	1 stop Penders	7:25 pm
M-Th	7:40 pm	1 stop Penders	8:55 pm
F	4:00 pm	non-stop	4:40 pm
F	6:40 pm	1 stop Penders	8:00 pm
F	7:00 pm	2 stops Penders, Galiano	8:55 pm
Sa	6:00 am	1 stop Galiano	7:30 am
Sa	9:10 am	1 stop Penders	10:25 am
Sa	9:50 am	1 stop Penders	11:00 am
Sa	3:15 pm	1 stop Penders	4:30 pm
Sa	3:15 pm	1 stop Saturna	5:10 pm
Sa	6:45 pm	1 stop Penders	7:55 pm
Su/Hol M	6:55 am	non-stop	7:55 am
Su/Hol M	10:20 am	1 stop Galiano	12:05 pm
Su/Hol M	2:45 pm	1 stop Saturna	4:40 pm
Su/Hol M	3:15 pm	1 stop Penders	4:20 pm
Su/Hol M	6:50 pm	1 stop Penders	8:25 pm
Su/Hol M	6:10 pm	1 stop Saturna	8:00 pm

To Victoria (Swartz Bay) from Mayne Island

Days	Leave	Stops/Transfers	Arrive
M-F	7:20 am	1 stop Penders	8:25 am
M-F	7:50 am	1 stop Penders	9:10 am
M-F	12:15 pm	non-stop	1:05 pm
M-Th	5:05 pm	non-stop	5:55 pm
M-Th	7:35 pm	2 stops Galiano, Penders	9:20 pm
M-Th	9:20 pm	1 stop Saturna	11:25 pm
F	5:05 pm	1 stop Galiano	6:45 pm
F	8:20 pm	1 stop Saturna	10:30 pm
F	9:00 pm	1 stop Penders	10:10 pm
Sa	7:35 am	1 stop Penders	8:55 am
Sa	11:55 am	1 stop Penders	1:10 pm
Sa	4:35 pm	2 stops Galiano, Penders	6:30 pm
Sa	5:20 pm	1 stop Penders	6:50 pm
Sa	8:00 pm	1 stop Galiano	9:50 pm
Su/Hol M	9:00 am	1 stop Penders	10:10 am
Su/Hol M	12:15 pm	1 stop Penders	1:25 pm
Su/Hol M	4:50 pm	non-stop	5:50 pm
Su/Hol M	8:25 pm	1 stop Saturna	10:30 pm
Su/Hol M	8:35 pm	2 stops Galiano, Penders	10:30 pm

Pender Islands

To the Pender Islands from Vancouver (Tsawwassen)

Days	Leave	Stops/Transfers	Arrive
M -Th	10:15 am	2 stops Galiano, Mayne	12:30 pm
M-Th	7:35 pm	2 stops Galiano, Mayne	9:40 pm
F	10:50 am	2 stops Galiano, Mayne	1:05 pm
F	6:30 pm	2 stops Galiano, Mayne	8:35 pm
Sa	8:45 am	1 stop Galiano, transfer at Mayne	12:15 pm
Su/Hol M	11:10 am	2 stops Galiano, Mayne	1:10 pm
Su/Hol M	7:15 pm	transfer at Mayne, 1 stop Galiano	9:45 pm

To Vancouver (Tsawwassen) from the Pender Islands

Days	Leave	Stops/Transfers	Arrive
M-F	7:20 am	2 stops Mayne, Galiano	9:35 am
M-Th	4:55 pm	2 stops Mayne, Galiano	7:05 pm
F	8:45 pm	non-stop	10:00 pm
Sa	10:00 am	transfer at Mayne	11:45 am
Sa	4:50 pm	2 stops Mayne, Galiano	6:55 pm
Su/Hol M	7:50 pm	transfer at Mayne	9:30 pm

To the Pender Islands from Victoria (Swartz Bay)

Days	Leave	Stops/Transfers	Arrive
M-F	5:35 am	2 stops, Galiano, Mayne	7:45 am
M-F	8:40 am	non-stop	9:20 am
M- F	9:25 am	1 stop Saturna	11:50 am
M - Th	2:05 pm	non-stop	2:45 pm
M -Th	4:25 pm	1 stop Saturna	6:25 pm
M -Th	6:10 pm	non-stop	6:50 pm
M-Th	7:40 pm	non-stop	8:20 pm
F	2:05 pm	non-stop	2:45 pm
F	3:20 pm	1 stop Saturna	5:20 pm
F	6:40 pm	non-stop	7:20 pm
F	7:00 pm	non-stop	7:40 pm
Sa	6:15 am	non-stop	6:55 am
Sa	9:10 am	non-stop	9:50 am
Sa	9:50 am	non-stop	10:30 am
Sa	3:15 pm	non-stop	3:55 pm
Sa	6:45 pm	non-stop	7:20 pm
Sa	7:05 pm	1 stop Saturna	9:05 pm
Su/Hol M	6:55 am	transfer at Mayne	9:25 am
Su/Hol M	10:20 am	2 stops Galiano, Mayne	12:35 pm
Su/Hol M	3:15 pm	non-stop	3:55 pm
Su/Hol M	6:50 pm	non-stop	7:30 pm

To Victoria (Swartz Bay) from the Pender Islands

Days	Leave	Stops/Transfers	Arrive
M-F	7:50 am	non-stop	8:25 am
M-F	8:20 am	non-stop	9:10 am
M-F	9:30 am	non-stop	10:10 am
M-F	11:55 am	non-stop	12:45 pm
M-Th	3:00 pm	non-stop	3:40 pm
M-Th	6:35 pm	non-stop	7:25 pm
M-Th	8:40 pm	non-stop	9:20 pm
F	3:00 pm	non-stop	3:40 pm
F	5:30 pm	non-stop	6:20 pm
F	9:30 pm	non-stop	10:10 pm
Sa	8:10 am	non-stop	8:55 am
Sa	8:45 am	non-stop	9:35 am
Sa	12:25 pm	non-stop	1:10 pm
Sa	12:55 pm	non-stop	1:40 pm
Sa	5:45 pm	non-stop	6:30 pm
Sa	6:00 pm	non-stop	6:50 pm
Sa	7:25 pm	2 stops Mayne, Galiano	9:50 pm
Sa	9:15 pm	non-stop	10:05 pm
Su/Hol M	9:30 am	non-stop	10:10 am
Su/Hol M	12:45 pm	non-stop	1:25 pm
Su/Hol M	5:50 pm	non-stop	6:30 pm
Su/Hol M	9:50 pm	non-stop	10:30 pm

Saturna Island

To Saturna Island from Vancouver (Tsawwassen)

Days	Leave	Stops/Transfers	Arrive
M - F	7:00 am	transfer at Swartz, 1 stop Penders	10:50 am
M-Th	7:35 pm	1 stop Galiano, transfer at Mayne	9:55 pm
F	6:30 pm	1 stop Galiano, transfer at Mayne	9:05 pm
Sa	8:45 am	1 stop Galiano, transfer at Mayne	11:55 am
Su/Hol M	7:15 pm	transfer at Mayne	9:05 pm

To Vancouver (Tsawwassen) from Saturna Island

Days	Leave	Stops/Transfers	Arrive
M-F	7:05 am	transfer at Mayne, 1 stop Galiano	9:35 am
Sa	4:40 pm	transfer at Mayne, 1 stop Galiano	6:55 pm
Su/Hol M	4:05 pm	transfer at Mayne, 1 stop Galiano	6:45 pm

To Saturna Island from Victoria (Swartz Bay)

Days	Leave	Stops/Transfers	Arrive
M-F	5:25 am	non-stop	7:00 am
M-F	9:25 am	non-stop	10:50 am
M-Th	4:25 pm	non-stop	5:35 pm
M-Th	7:40 pm	2 stops Penders, Mayne	9:55 pm
F	3:20 pm	non-stop	4:35 pm
F	6:40 pm	2 stops Penders, Mayne	9:05 pm
Sa	6:15 am	1 stop Penders	7:50 am
Sa	9:50 am	2 stops Penders, Mayne	11:55 am
Sa	3:15 pm	non-stop	4:35 pm
Sa	7:05 pm	non-stop	8:20 pm
Su/Hol M	6:55 am	1 stop Galiano, transer at Mayne	9:35 am
Su/Hol M	2:45 pm	non-stop	4:00 pm
Su/Hol M	6:10 pm	non-stop	7:05 pm

To Victoria (Swartz Bay) from Saturna Island

Days	Leave	Stops/Transfers	Arrive
M-F	7:05 am	2 stops Mayne, Penders	9:10 am
M -F	11:05 am	1 stop Penders	12:45 pm
M -Th	5:45 pm	1 stop Penders	7:25 pm
M -Th	10:05 pm	non-stop	11:25 pm
F	4:40 pm	1 stop Penders	6:20 pm
F	9:10 pm	non-stop	10:30 pm
Sa	7:55 am	1 stop Penders	9:35 am
Sa	12:00 noon		1 stop
Penders	1:40 pm		
Sa	4:40 pm	2 stops Mayne, Penders	6:50 pm
Sa	8:25 pm	1 stop Penders	10:05 pm
Su/Hol M	9:40 am	transfer Mayne, 1 stop Pender	1:25 pm
Su/Hol M	4:05 pm	1 stop Mayne	5:50 pm
Su/Hol M	9:10 pm	non-stop	10:30 pm

Saltspring Island

To Saltspring (Long Harbour) from Vancouver (Tsawwassen)

Days	Leave	Stops/Transfers	Arrive
M-Th	10:15 am	3 stops Galiano, Mayne, Penders	1:15 pm
M-Th	7:35 pm	3 stops Galiano, Mayne, Penders	10:30 pm
F	10:50 am	3 stops Galiano, Mayne, Penders	1:50 pm
F	10:25 pm	non-stop	11:50 pm
Sa	12:50 pm	non-stop	2:15 pm
Sa	9:10 pm	2 stops Galiano, Mayne	11:20 pm
Su/Hol M	11:10 am	3 stops Galiano, Mayne, Penders	2:00 pm
Su/Hol M	10:00 pm	non-stop	11:30 pm

To Saltspring (Long Harbour) from Vancouver (Tsawwassen)

Days	Leave	Stops/Transfers	Arrive
M-Th	10:15 am	3 stops Galiano, Mayne, Penders	1:15 pm
M-Th	7:35 pm	3 stops Galiano, Mayne, Penders	10:30 pm
F	10:50 am	3 stops Galiano, Mayne, Penders	1:50 pm
F	10:25 pm	non-stop	11:50 pm
Sa	12:50 pm	non-stop	2:15 pm
Sa	9:10 pm	2 stops Galiano, Mayne	11:20 pm
Su/Hol M	11:10 am	3 stops Galiano, Mayne, Penders	2:00 pm
Su/Hol M	10:00 pm	non-stop	11:30 pm

To Vancouver (Tsawwassen) from Saltspring (Long Harbour)

Days	Leave	Stops/Transfers	Arrive
M-F	6:30 am	3 stops Penders, Mayne, Galiano	9:35 am
M-Th	4:05 pm	3 stops Penders, Mayne, Galiano	7:05 pm
F	4:25 pm	non-stop	5:50 pm
Sa	6:50 am	non-stop	8:15 am
Sa	4:00 pm	3 stops Penders, Mayne, Galiano	6:55 pm
Su/Hol M	8:30 am	2 stops Mayne, Galiano	10:40 am
Su/Hol M	4:15 pm	2 stops Mayne, Galiano	6:45 pm

Salt Spring Island (Fulford Harbour) - Victoria (Swartz Bay)

Leave Fulford Harbour	Leave Swartz Bay
6:15 am	6:55 am
7:35 am	8:20 am
9:15 am	10:00 am
11:00 am	11:15 am
12:30 pm	11:45 am
2:15 pm	1:10 pm
3:45 pm	3:00 pm
5:15 pm	4:30 pm
6:45 pm	5:15 pm
8:15 pm	6:00 pm
————	7:30 pm
————	9:05 pm

Salt Spring Island (Vesuvius Bay) - Crofton

Leave Vesuvius Bay	Leave Crofton
7:00 am except Saturdays	7:30 am except Saturdays and Sundays
8:00 am except Sundays	8:30 am
9:00 am	9:30 am
10:00 am	11:00 am
11:30 am	12:00 noon
12:30 pm	1:00 pm
1:30 pm	2:15 pm
3:00 pm	3:30 pm
4:00 pm	4:30 pm
5:00 pm	5:30 pm
6:00 pm	6:30 pm
7:00 pm	8:00 pm
8:30 pm	9:00 pm
9:30 pm	10:00 pm
10:30 pm Saturdays only	11:00 pm Saturdays only

Gulf Islands Water Taxi

(250) 537-2510; Fax: (250) 537-9202
watertaxi@saltspring.com
$15 per person, Bikes free, Kayaks $5 extra
Located below the Kanaka Restaurant at the Kanaka Visitors' Dock in central Ganges on Salt Spring.

Summer Schedule: Sailings on Saturdays and Wednesdays only from June - August

Departs	Departs	Arriving at	Arrives
Ganges, Salt Spring	9:00 AM	Sturdies Bay, Galiano Isl.	9:45 AM
Sturdies Bay, Galiano Isl.	9:50 AM	Miners Bay, Mayne Isl.	10:00 AM
Miners Bay, Mayne Isl.	10:00 AM	Ganges, Salt Spring	10:45 AM
Ganges, Salt Spring	3:00 PM	Miners Bay, Mayne Isl.	3:40 PM
Miners Bay, Mayne Isl.	3:40 PM	Sturdies Bay, Galiano Isl.	3:50 PM
Sturdies Bay, Galiano Isl.	3:50 PM	Ganges, Salt Spring	4:30 PM

Winter Schedule I: Regular school days from September to June

Departs from	Departs	Arriving at	Arrives
Ganges, Salt Spring	6:45 AM	Sturdies Bay, Galiano	7:43 AM
Sturdies Bay, Galiano	7:45 AM	Miners Bay, Mayne Isl.	7:53 AM
Miners Bay, Mayne Isl.	7:55 AM	Ganges, Salt Spring	8:45 AM
Ganges, Salt Spring	3:45 PM	Miners Bay, Mayne Isl.	4:33 PM
Miners Bay, Mayne Isl.	4:35 PM	Sturdies Bay, Galiano Isl.	4:48 PM
Sturdies Bay, Galiano Isl.	4:50 PM	Ganges, Salt Spring	5:45 PM

Winter Schedule II: Regular school days from September to June

Departs from	Departs	Arriving at	Arrives
Ganges, Salt Spring	6:45 AM	Lyall Harbour, Saturna Isl.	7:43 AM
Lyall Harbour, Saturna Isl.	7:45 AM	Horton Bay	7:58 AM
Horton Bay	8:00 AM	Port Washington, Pender	8:23 AM
Port Washington, Pender	8:25 AM	Ganges, Salt Spring	9:00 AM
Ganges, Salt Spring	3:45 PM	Port Washington, Pender	4:18 PM
Port Washington, Pender	4:20 PM	Horton Bay	4:43 PM
Horton Bay	4:45 PM	Lyall Harbour, Saturna	4:58 PM
Lyall Harbour, Saturna	5:00 PM	Ganges Harbour, Salt	6:00 PM

Getting to Tofino

Just an hour flight separates Vancouver from the rugged west coast of British Columbia. By contrast the bus is a full-day ordeal but costs just a third of what air fare does. Maverick Coach Lines provides twice-daily service between the lower mainland and Tofino as below. Catch the bus at Pacific Central Station, 1150 Station Street, or from any stop along the north side of West Georgia Street from Granville to Denman Streets.

There is now a public transportation link between the communities of Ucluelet, Tofino and the National Park at Long Beach. The IslandLink Shuttle, which operates from May - September, also services the airport.

Maverick Coach Lines

$49.80 one way; $88.45 round trip

Leave Vancouver	Transfer Nanaimo	Arrive Tofino
5:45 AM	8:30 AM	12:40 PM
9:30 AM	12:30 PM	4:15 PM

Leave Tofino	Transfer Nanaimo	Arrive Vancouver
10:00 AM	2:30 PM	5:15 PM
4:30 PM	830 PM	11:15 PM

(604) 940-2332; (604) 255-5770 FAX; info@maverickcoachlines.bc.ca
www.maverickcoachlines.bc.ca

IslandLink Shuttle

Tofino	Airport	Long Beach	Ucluelet
8:00 AM	--	8:15 AM	8:50 AM
11:30 AM	11:50 AM	11:45 AM	12:40 PM
2:45 PM	3:00 PM	3:05 PM	3:45 PM
4:35 PM	--	5:10 PM	--
6:30 PM	--	6:50 PM	7:30 PM
9:00 PM	--	9:15 PM	9:50 PM

Ucluelet	Long Beach	Airport	Tofino
7:15 AM	7:40 AM	--	7:55 AM
9:30 AM	9:55 AM	10:00 AM	10:30 AM
11:15 PM	--	--	12:05 PM
1:45 PM	2:15 PM	2:20 PM	2:45 PM
5:15 PM	5:50 PM	5:55 PM	6:15 PM
8:00 PM	8:30 PM	--	8:50 PM

1-877-954-3556 or 726-7779 (in Ucluelet & Tofino;) www.newshuttle.com

North Vancouver Air

$165 one way; $325 round trip; Stand by $120 one way

Leave Vancouver   **Arrive Tofino**
1:30 PM   2:30 PM

Leave Tofino   **Arrive Vancouver**
3:00 PM   4:00 PM

5360 Airport Road South
1-800-228-6608; (604) 278-1608; (604) 278-2608 FAX
travelinfo@northvanair.com

Tofino Air Charters

Box 99, Tofino , BC
(250) 725-4454; (250) 725-4421 FAX; tofinoair@tofino-bc.com

Getting "Up Island"

Together Greyhound and Island Coach Lines provide seamless service from downtown Vancouver to Nanaimo on Vancouver Island and then up island through Parksville/Qualicum Beach to Port McNeill. The new kid on the block, Island Link can save you money by shuttling passengers up island from Nanaimo to Parksville/Qualicum Beach. See **Getting to Horseshoe Bay** on page 320 for details on reaching Vancouver Island using transit and the BC Ferry Corporation. Though my first dealings with Island Link did not inspire confidence, let's hope those were just growing pains. Competetion to these and other routes is most welcomed and should be applauded.

Bus Information

Island Coach Lines: 1-800-318 - 0818; (250) 385 - 4411; www.victoriatours.com
Greyhound Canada: 1-800-661-8747; (604) 482-8747; www.greyhound.ca

Departing from Pacific Central station in Vancouver. Pickup possible from bus stops on the north side of West Georgia Street at Homer, Burrard, Bute and Denman Streets. Be prepared to flag the bus down. One way: $27.30; Round trip: $53.25

Vancouver	Nanaimo	Parksville	Qualicum	Pt McNeill
5:45 AM	8:30 AM	9:10 AM	9:26 AM	3:00 PM
9:30 AM	12:25 PM	1:05 PM	1:21 PM	
11:30 AM	2:45 PM	3:25 PM	3:41 PM	
2:00 PM	5:00 PM*	5:40 PM*	5:56 PM*	
6:00 PM	9:15 PM	9:50 PM	10:00 PM	

*Saturday Only
Vancouver to Nanaimo via Maverick Coach Lines
Nanaimo to Parksville/Qualicum Beach via Island Coach Lines

Pt McNeill	Qualicum	Parksville	Nanaimo	Vancouver
	8:51 AM	9:05 AM	9:50 AM	12:45 PM
	12:50 PM	1:06 PM	1:50 PM	5:15 PM
10:35 PM	3:02 PM	3:20 PM	4:05 PM	7:15 PM
	7:16 PM	7:30 PM	8:15 PM	11:15 PM

Parksville/Qualicum Beach to Nanaimo via Island Coach Lines
Nanaimo to Vancouver via Maverick Coach Lines

BC CAR-FREE

Island Link Shuttle Service

1-877-954-3556; (250) 954-3556; www.newshuttle.com

Nanaimo (Departure Bay)	Parksville	Qualicum Beach
8:15 AM	8:45 AM	9:10 AM
10:15 AM	10:45 AM	11:10 AM
12:15 PM	12:45 PM	1:10 PM
2:15 PM	2:45 PM	3:10 PM
4:45 PM	5:15 PM	5:40 PM
6:45 PM	7:15 PM	7:40 PM
8:45 PM	9:15 PM	9:40 PM

Qualicum Beach	Parksville	Nanaimo (Departure Bay)
7:00 AM	7:25 AM	8:00 AM
9:00 AM	9:25 AM	10:00 AM
11:00 AM	11:25 AM	12 noon
1:00 PM	1:25 PM	2:00 PM
3:30 PM	3:55 PM	4:30 PM
5:30 PM	5:55 PM	6:30 PM
7:30 PM	7:55 PM	8:30 PM

Getting to the Sunshine Coast

Malaspina Coach Lines offers twice daily service to the Sunshine Coast. Start off from Pacific Central Station or flag down the bus at any stop along West Georgia Street between Granville and Denman. Be sure you are waiting at a bus stop on the *north* side of Georgia.

Northbound	Departure Times	
Vancouver	8:30 am	6:30 pm
Sechelt	10:45 am	8:50 pm
Earl's Cove	11:55 am	10 pm
Powell River	1:50 pm	11:50 pm

Activity

Kayaking Sechelt Inlet; p 272
Kayaking Skookumchuck; p 277
Kayaking Desolation Sound; p 306
Canoeing Powell Forest; p 314
Backpacking Sunshine Coast Trail p87

Southbound		
Powell River	8:30 am	2:30 pm
Earls' Cove	10:20 am	4:20 pm
Sechelt	11:20 am	5:20 pm
Vancouver	1:45 pm	7:45 pm

Take shower, guzzle beer

Powell River: (604) 485-5030
Gibsons: (604) 886-7742

Sechelt: (604) 885-2217
Vancouver: (604) 682-6511

Ferry to Sechelt Peninsula

Leave Horseshoe Bay	Leave Langdale
	6:20 am
7:20 am	8:20 am
9:20 am	10:20 am
11:20 am	12:20 pm
1:20 pm	2:30 pm
	3:00 pm*
3:30 pm	4:30 pm
5:30 pm	6:30 pm
7:25 pm	8:20 pm
9:15 pm	10:10 pm
11:00 pm	
*Summer Only	

Ferry to Powell River

Leave Earls Cove	Leave Saltery Bay
6:30 am*	5:40 am*
8:25 am	7:30 am
10:20 am	9:25 am
12:20 pm	11:20 am
2:25 pm	1:25 pm
4:25 pm	3:30 pm
6:25 pm	5:25 pm
8:20 pm	7:25 pm
10:10 pm	9:15 pm
*Sundays and Holidays Only	

Getting to Buntzen Lake

Getting to Buntzen Lake from downtown Vancouver would be a breeze if it were not for the infrequency of the service. Take **Skytrain** to New Westminster Station then catch the **IOCO Bus #148** to end of the line. The last stop is in Anmore just in front of Alpine Riding Academy and the entrance to Buntzen Lake Reservoir Recreation Area. South Beach is a further two-kilometre walk from there. From downtown give yourself at least an hour and a half. If you happen to miss the bus don't despair, Bus **#148** itself runs every 30 minutes. Unfortunately it's final destination alternates between Anmore where you want to be and Belcarra Village where you don't. Every bus goes at least as far as 1st Avenue. From this point it is possible to walk to Anmore. The pleasant stroll, via 1st Avenue then along Sunnyside Road to the park, takes an additional 30 minutes through rural landscape.

Catch the return bus from Anmore across the street from where it dropped you off. Use the following as a guide only since Translink schedules are constantly being tweaked to provide more confusing service. If possible, call Translink [(604) 521-0400 from 6:30 am - 11:30 pm] or check their excellent website [www.gvta.bc.ca] to be certain.

Regrettably the buses servicing Buntzen Lake are not equipped with bicycle racks at this time.

IOCO Bus #148
New Westminster SkyTrain Station to Anmore General Store

Monday to Friday	Saturday	Sunday
6:50 am - 7:43 am		
7:19 am - 8:16 am	7:08 am - 8:08 am	8:35 am - 9:35 am
10:26 am - 11:23 am	10:56 am - 11:55 am	10:35 am - 11:35 am
3:28 pm - 4:34 pm	2:56 pm - 3:56 pm	2:35 pm - 3:35 pm
4:27 pm - 5:33 pm	4:25 pm - 5:26 pm	4:35 pm - 5:35 pm
4:58 pm - 6:12 pm		
10:36 pm - 11:36 pm	10:36 pm - 11:35 pm	10:36 pm - 11:35 pm

Anmore General Store to New Westminster SkyTrain Station

Monday to Friday	Saturday	Sunday
6:21 am - 7:24 am		
7:47 am - 9:00 am	8:09 am - 9:20 am	9:38 am - 10:50 am
8:36 am - 9:31 am	11:59 am - 1:05 pm	11:38 am - 12:50 pm
4:42 pm - 5:36 pm	3:59 pm - 5:05 pm	3:38 pm - 4:50 pm
5:44 pm - 6:38 pm	5:29 pm - 6:35 pm	5:38 pm - 6:50 pm
11:36 pm - 12:37 pm	11:36 pm - 12:37 pm	

Getting to Whistler

Recreational activities abound in the Sea to Sky corridor which extends from Horseshoe Bay to the Pemberton Valley. The cities of Squamish, Whistler and Pemberton are the best sources of services. At one end peaks rise straight out of the waters of Howe Sound. At the other end the fertile soil of the expansive, glacial Pemberton Valley is North America's most important source of seed potatoes. In between the jagged, glacial-covered peaks of the Coast Range provide a nearly limitless range of recreational opportunities extending literally from sea to sky.

Bus and train are the most common alternative forms of transportation into the Sea to Sky country.

Bus

Pick up the Maverick Coach Lines bus to Whistler at Pacific Central Station near the Main Street SkyTrain station or at any bus stop on the north side of West Georgia Street including Granville, Burrard, Thurlow, Bute and Denman streets. Be prepared to flag down the bus when you see it approaching. Keep your cash handy in order to purchase your ticket from the driver on the spot. You will not be able to stow your backpack under the bus if you're planning to get off between scheduled stops. Be sure to tell the driver exactly where you will be getting off to allow plenty of time to plan the unscheduled stop along the treacherous Sea to Sky Highway. The driver will not pull over unless it is safe to do so and many drivers will not let women off in remote locations if they are travelling on their own. Since hiking or backpacking alone is foolhardy at any rate this may not be such a bad policy. On the return, when catching the bus in the opposite direction, be sure to wait for the bus in a place with plenty of visibility and shoulders wide enough to safely pull over. Otherwise, the bus will breeze on by.

Vancouver	Squamish	Whistler	Pemberton $21.75
8:00 AM	9:10 AM	10:30 AM	11:10 AM
11:00 AM	12:15 PM	1:30 PM	---
1:00 PM	2:00 PM	3:30 PM	4:10 PM
3:00 PM	4:00 PM	5:15 PM	6:00 PM
5:00 PM	6:15 PM	7:30 PM	---
7:00 PM	8:15 PM	9:30 PM	10:10

Pemberton	Whistler	Squamish	Vancouver $21.75
4:15 AM	5:00 AM	6:16 AM	7:45 AM
7:30 AM	8:30 AM	9:45 AM	11:15 AM
---	10:30 AM	11:45 AM	1:15 PM
12:35 PM	1:30 PM	2:45 PM	4:15 PM
---	4:45 PM	5:55 PM	7:20 PM
6:20 PM	7:15 PM	8:30 PM	9:45 PM

Train

For an attractive alternative to the Sea to Sky Highway try B.C. Rail's "Cariboo Prospector." Though the stations are sometimes inconveniently located, fares higher and schedule less frequent than the purely utilitarian bus service to Whistler and beyond, there's something romantic and decidedly civilized about riding the rails in this era of congested highways and raging road warriors. BC Rail's daily passenger service follows a route that encompasses scenic seashore and rugged canyon as well as a 1300-metre tunnel past the Horseshoe Bay ferry terminal. Be sure to sit on the left side when leaving Vancouver and the right side on your return journey to get the most out of the scenery. To make things easier, from June 1 to October 30 each year TransLink provides a special bus to connect with the "Cariboo Prospector." Pick up the **#274 BC Rail** bus daily at 6:17 AM from any bus stop on the north side of West Georgia Street including at the corner of Granville, Burrard, Thurlow, Bute and Denman streets. Expect to arrive at the sation in North Vancouver at 6:35 AM. Incoming trains, due to arrive at 9:15 PM are met by a Vancouver-bound bus. Both of these special buses have a special price of two dollars.

Station	Time	Activity	$ One Way	Return time (in reverse)
North Vancouver	**07:00**			**21:05**
Lions Bay	07:32			20:06
Porteau Crossing	07:55	*Deeks Lake p 62; Furry Creek Hikes p 64*		20:12
Britania	08:05	*Britania Mines*		20:02
Squamish	**08:22**	*Eagle Watching; p 238* **The Chief; p 67**	**$16**	**19:46**
Cheakamus	08:41			19:29
Water Tank	09:08	*Black Tusk; p 76*		19:00
Whistler	**09:35**	*Singing Pass; p 80* **Rafting; p 256**	**$31**	**18:35**
Canadian Hostel	09:46			18:25
Nicklaus North	09:53			
Pemberton	10:18		$39	17:49
Birken	11:03			17:18
Shalath	12:03			16:10
Lillooet	**12:35**		**$66**	**15:45**

Scheduled stops in **bold***; Flag stops in* regular *type.*

BC Rail, 1311 W. First St., North Vancouver, B.C.
Mailing Address: P.O. Box 8770, Vancouver, BC V6B 4X6
(604) 986 2012; (604) 984 5201 FAX
1-800-339-8752 Within BC; 1-800-663-8238 Outside BC and USA
passinfo@bcrail.com; www.bcrail.com

Getting to Hope & Lytton

Greyhound [1-800-661-8747] offers twice daily service to Lytton and beyond. A round trip ticket to Hope costs $37 while those continuing on to Lytton must pay $70 return. If expecting to board on the return journey at other than the scheduled stops be prepared to flag the bus down. Greyhound Canada has a great website, *www.greyhound.ca*, that makes getting updated schedule information simple indeed. In Vancouver call Greyhound at (604) 482-8747.

Vancouver	Hope	Lytton
7:00 AM	9:15 AM	--
7:30 AM	10:10 AM	11:55 AM
1:45 PM	4:20 PM	--
5:45 PM	--	10:15 PM
6:00 PM	8:30 PM	--

Lytton	Hope	Vancouver
6:30 AM	8:30 AM	11:00 AM
--	9:35 AM	12:40 PM
--	10:55 AM	1:45 PM
--	12:40 PM	3:00 PM
--	12:40 PM	3:35 PM
4:30 PM	6:20 PM	9:15 PM
--	18:25	21:30*
--	19:20	22:00

*Except Saturday

Getting to Manning Park

Greyhound [1-800-661-8747] services the Manning Park area with buses scheduled daily as follows. A one-way ticket is $30.12 including applicable taxes. If you can accurately anticipate what time and place along the highway you expect to be picked up at inform information staff of your special requirements in advance to assist drivers in picking you up. In Vancouver contact Greyhound at (604) 482-8747 or check out the website *www.greyhound.ca*.

Vancouver	Manning Park Lodge
12:30 AM	3:10 AM
6:15 AM	10: 15 AM
7:00 AM	10:15 AM
5:00 PM	9:45 PM*
6:00 PM	9:45 PM*

Manning Park Lodge	Vancouver
11:10 AM	3:00 PM
5:15 PM	9:30 PM*

*Except Saturday

Seasons

Day Hiking	Pg	Jan	Feb	Mar	Apr	May	Jun	Jul	Aug	Sep	Oct	Nov	Dec
Lighthouse Park	26												
Capilano Canyon	29												
Dorman Point Trail	32												
Killarney Lake	33												
Mount Gardner Trail	34												
Gambier Lake	36												
West Bay Amble	39												
Buntzen Lake	40												
Energy Trail	42												
Buntzen Lake Trail	42												
Diez Vistas Trail	42												
Lindsay Lake Loop	42												
Swan Falls Loop	43												
Dilly Dally Loop	43												
Rice Lake	45												
Lynn Loop	45												
Norvan Falls	46												
Grouse Mountain	48												
Lynn Peak	49												
Mosquito Creek	50												
Mount Fromme	41												
Baden-Powell Centennial Trail	53												
Deeks Bluffs Trail	62												
Deeks Lake Trail	63												
Phyllis Creek	64												
Mount Capilano	64												
Petgill Lake	66												
The Chief & Squaw	67												
Shannon Falls	69												
Cal-Cheak Trail	70												
Brew Lake	72												
Wedgemount Lake	73												

Backpacking	Pg	Jan	Feb	Mar	Apr	May	Jun	Jul	Aug	Sep	Oct	Nov	Dec
Garibaldi Lake	76												
Black Tusk	78												
Panorama Ridge	79												
Singing Pass Loop	80												
Henrietta Lake & Mount Roderick	84												
Sunshine Coast Trail	87												
Stein Lower Canyon to Mid-Valley	101												
Stein Valley Mini-Traverse	107												
Nicomen Lake	109												
Juan De Fuca Marine Trail	114												
The West Coast Trail	123												
The Mid-Coast Trail	139												

Cycle Touring	Pg	Jan	Feb	Mar	Apr	May	Jun	Jul	Aug	Sep	Oct	Nov	Dec
Gabriola Island	146												
Galiano Island	158												
Mayne Island	163												
Pender Island	170												
Saltspring Island	178												
Saturna Island	185												
Lopez Island	192												
Shaw Island	195												
Orcas Island	197												
San Juan Island	201												

In The Sun

Weekend Getaways	Pg	Jan	Feb	Mar	Apr	May	Jun	Jul	Aug	Sep	Oct	Nov	Dec
Newcastle Island	209					▓	▓	▓	▓	▓			
Keats Island	212					▓	▓	▓	▓	▓			
Gambier Island (Halkett Bay)	216					▓	▓	▓	▓	▓			
Mount Artaban	217					▓	▓	▓	▓	▓			
Horseback Riding	218												
Whale Watching	Pg	Jan	Feb	Mar	Apr	May	Jun	Jul	Aug	Sep	Oct	Nov	Dec
Orca Watching: Northern Vancouv	223						▓	▓	▓	▓	▓		
Orca Watching: Victoria	228					▓	▓	▓	▓	▓			
Gray Whale Tours	229			▓	▓								
Bird Watching	Pg	Jan	Feb	Mar	Apr	May	Jun	Jul	Aug	Sep	Oct	Nov	Dec
Snow Geese	234	▓	▓								▓	▓	▓
Snowy Owls	236	▓	▓									▓	▓
Sandpipers	237				▓	▓							
Bald Eagles	238	▓	▓									▓	▓
Brant Festival	243			▓	▓								
Salmon Watching	Pg	Jan	Feb	Mar	Apr	May	Jun	Jul	Aug	Sep	Oct	Nov	Dec
Adam's River	247										▓		
Capilano Salmon Hatchery	249							▓	▓	▓			
Seymour River Hatchery	250										▓		
Cave Exploring													
Horne Lake Caves	251												
River Rafting	Pg	Jan	Feb	Mar	Apr	May	Jun	Jul	Aug	Sep	Oct	Nov	Dec
Rafting in Whistler	256					▓	▓	▓	▓	▓			
Chilliwack River Rafting	257				▓	▓	▓						
Thompson & Fraser River Rafting	258					▓	▓	▓	▓	▓			
Sea Kayaking	Pg	Jan	Feb	Mar	Apr	May	Jun	Jul	Aug	Sep	Oct	Nov	Dec
Indian Arm	264			▓	▓	▓	▓	▓	▓	▓	▓		
Bowen Island Circumnavigation	268					▓	▓	▓	▓	▓			
Howe Sound Exploration	270					▓	▓	▓	▓	▓			
Sechelt Inlet	272					▓	▓	▓	▓	▓			
Princess Louisa Inlet	279					▓	▓	▓	▓	▓			
Jervis Inlet	283					▓	▓	▓	▓	▓			
Nelson Island Circumnavigation	285					▓	▓	▓	▓	▓			
Hotham Sound Loop	287					▓	▓	▓	▓	▓			
Meares Island Circumnavigation	291				▓	▓	▓	▓	▓	▓			
Hot Springs Cove	296					▓	▓	▓	▓	▓			
Trincomali Channel	301				▓	▓	▓	▓	▓	▓	▓		
Desolation Sound	306					▓	▓	▓	▓	▓			
Canoeing	Pg	Jan	Feb	Mar	Apr	May	Jun	Jul	Aug	Sep	Oct	Nov	Dec
Powell Forest Canoe Route	314					▓	▓	▓	▓	▓			

Playing around is always risky business but in the outback it is necessarily a seasonal affair. The above grid highlights in grey the seasons when activities in this book can be flirted with. Common sense would dictate that the duration of a season will vary year-to-year depending on about a gazillion factors like climate, snow pack, greenhouse gases, participants' abilities and conditioning. Whenever planning an excursion factor in current conditions rather than just blindly following the guidebook. Afterall, there is a big difference between visiting a mountain top in July and October. Plan for the worst-case scenario every time and you should be able to avoid serious trouble.

Brian Grover

Born in the Maine backwoods and raised on both sides of the border in Oregon and British Columbia, the author kicked around the B.C. coast for a number of years after fleeing high school. Doing time in forestry, warehouses, saw-

The author peers through a sandstone portal on Gabriola Island, visualizing a brave, new world of people-friendly transportation alternatives for the outback-bent. Or, who knows, maybe it was just the Gabriola Red Hair.

Manami Kimura Photo
Canon AE-1
50 mm Canon lens
Kodacolor 200 ISO film

mills, plywood mills and Canada Post convinced the youth that perhaps education was indeed all they said it was. While attending Malaspina College a quirk of fate landed the aspiring writer in the editor's chair of the student newspaper. Between bouts of higher education Grover worked variously as a fishing guide, a cycling guide, a newspaper reporter and a graphic artist, training which eventually landed him a job handling communications for the Outdoor Recreation Council of British Columbia. A degree in English literature and a qualification in language teaching led the author away from his beloved West Coast to four years of teaching in Japanese universities. A further year of bohemian Parisian lifestyle left him pining for the fjords of British Columbia. Upon returning Grover founded Explore Canada Outdoor Adventures, an adventure in itself aimed at marketing British Columbia's renewable recreation resources to overseas, principally Japanese and American, visitors. Teaching, freelance writing, photography, web design and mucking about in the British Columbia outback all figure prominently in Grover's present way of life. 🐾

Notes....

Notes....

BC CAR-FREE
Notes....